Who Does What? On the allocation of regulatory competences in European Private Law

Bram Akkermans
Jaap Hage
Nicole Kornet
Jan Smits

Who Does What? On the allocation of regulatory competences in European Private Law

intersentia

METRO

Ius Commune Europaeum

Editors:
Bram Akkermans
Jaap Hage
Nicole Kornet
Jan Smits

Who Does What? On the allocation of regulatory competences in European Private Law

Intersentia Ltd
Sheraton House | Castle Park
Cambridge | CB3 0AX | United Kingdom
Tel.: +44 1223 370 172 | Email: mail@intersentia.co.uk

ISBN 978-17-8068-325-6
D/2015/7849/62
NUR 822

Cambridge - Antwerp - Portland
www.intersentia.com | www.intersentia.co.uk

British Library Cataloguing in Publication Data. A catalogue record for this book is available from the British Library.

TABLE OF CONTENTS

LIST OF AUTHORS

Bram Akkermans is assistant professor in European Private Law and associate director of the Maastricht European Private Law Institute (*M*-EPLI).

Anna Beckers is assistant professor of Private Law and Legal Methodology and fellow of the Maastricht European Private Law Institute (*M*-EPLI).

Anna Berlee is a PhD candidate of Comparative Property Law, specializing in Access to Property Registration and Privacy, and a member of the Maastricht European Private Law Institute (*M*-EPLI).

William Bull is a PhD candidate of European Private Law and a member of the Maastricht European Private Law Institute (*M*-EPLI).

Caroline Cauffman is associate professor at Maastricht University, associate director of the Maastricht European Private Law Institute (*M*-EPLI) and an assessor to the Belgian competition authority.

Kristel De Smedt is assistant professor of Foundations and Methods of Law and a member of the Maastricht European Private Law Institute (*M*-EPLI).

Michael Faure is professor of International and Comparative Environmental Law, at the Faculty of Law at Maastricht University, and professor of Comparative Private Law and Economics, at the Erasmus School of Law Rotterdam, and fellow of the Maastricht European Private Law Institute (*M*-EPLI).

Jiangqiu Ge is a PhD candidate of Comparative Consumer Contract Law and a member of the Maastricht European Private Law Institute (*M*-EPLI).

Catalina Goanţă is a PhD candidate of European Private Law and a member of the Maastricht European Private Law Institute (*M*-EPLI).

Jaap Hage is professor in Jurisprudence and fellow of the Maastricht European Private Law Institute (*M*-EPLI).

Mark Kawakami is a PhD candidate researching the role of private actors in reducing instances of labour exploitation in the global supply chain. He is a member of the Maastricht European Private Law Institute (*M*-EPLI).

Nicole Kornet is associate professor in Commercial law and associate director of the Maastricht Private Law Institute (*M*-EPLI).

Willem Loof is a PhD candidate of Comparative Property Law, specializing in Comparative Trust Law, and a member of the Maastricht European Private Law Institute (*M*-EPLI).

Janwillem Oosterhuis is assistant professor of Foundations and Methods of Law and a member of the Maastricht European Private Law Institute (*M*-EPLI).

Niels Philipsen is associate professor in Law and Economics and Vice-Director of the Maastricht European Institute for Transnational Legal Research (METRO), and a resident fellow at (*M*-EPLI).

Jan M. Smits is professor of European Private Law and director of the Maastricht European Private Law Institute (*M*-EPLI).

Bram Akkermans
Jaap Hage
Nicole Kornet
Jan Smits

WHO DOES WHAT IN EUROPEAN PRIVATE LAW? AN INTRODUCTION

1. Introduction

As the European Union (EU) matures, there is an increasing debate, partly fuelled by fierce national criticism offered by Eurosceptic politicians such as the UK Prime Minister David Cameron, partly initiated by the EU institutions themselves, on the way in which the EU has developed and what the EU must look like in the future. This debate includes a discussion on one of the core aspects of European integration: at which level should the rules be set and who decides where the authority to do so should lie.

Private law has an important role to play in this discussion. Many private law rules touch on the core of the internal market as they serve to foster trade or to offer protection to market participants, such as consumers. Moreover, the rich field of European private law, which builds on decades of comparative and European scholarship, is well-equipped to take a central role in this discussion.

In 2011, we founded the Maastricht European Private Law Institute (M-EPLI) in which we combine European private law scholarship in the fields of contract, property, commercial and procedural law as well as legal theory. A group of enthusiastic scholars meets on a bi-weekly basis to discuss research and work on common projects. This book, which seeks to take the central stage in the debate on the allocation of regulatory powers in European private law, is a result of our joined efforts.

In 2013, we started a series of seminars with the objective to develop and collect our criteria for deciding who should do what in the EU internal market. Each of the contributors to the book then presented his or her research ideas, on which the others commented, leading to first drafts that were discussed again within the research group. Although the four authors of this introduction took responsibility for the overall editing process, we see this book as a joint effort of all researchers involved. It testifies of the way in which we see legal research evolve in the future: the product of a collective effort of specialists in various fields, all contributing from their own perspective to one or more common research questions. In this respect, this volume is also an exercise in much-needed *intra*disciplinary legal research: it seeks to find similarities and differences between various fields *within* the law.

2. The Structure of this Book

In this book we offer perspectives on the allocation of regulatory competences by not only looking at the EU internal market, but also beyond that as some fields, such as commercial law, lend themselves to a global, rather than European perspective. For other fields that are traditionally considered more national in nature, such as property law, advancing a European perspective is already viewed as progressive by some.

The book starts off with a part offering general perspectives in which Jan Smits and Jaap Hage offer their views on the central theme. The second part of the book is devoted to branch-specific contributions in which criteria for the allocation of regulatory competences are developed from the perspective of a specific field of European Private Law. William Bull, Jiangqiu Ge, Catalina Goanță, Mark Kawakami and Jan Smits deal with consumer law, Bram Akkermans with property law from a constitutional perspective, Willem Loof and Anna Berlee with property law from a security rights perspective, Anna Beckers, Nicole Kornet and Jan-Willem Oosterhuis offer their views on commercial law, Caroline Cauffman and Niels Philipsen on competition law, and Kristel De Smedt and Michael Faure on environmental liability.

All contributions share a common approach in which each author or team of authors addresses the same two questions: (i) What are the *criteria* to decide upon the ideal design of their field of law for the EU? The starting point thus is that private law consists of a multilevel system, i.e. it is produced by different law-makers at different levels of governance; (ii) *Who* should set the rules: what is in the author(s) view the optimal mix of national and European producers of legal norms?

3. Towards Criteria

On the basis of discussions within M-EPLI we were able to agree on five common assumptions on which the authors based their contributions:

1. Presently we lack the knowledge that is needed to determine what is the optimal level of regulation for each specific field.
2. Ultimately it makes little sense to discuss the best level of regulation without the benefit of a clear normative theory. Such a theory consists of one, or a few, values which are considered to be intrinsic and – if more than one value is involved – a view on how to balance the colliding reasons based on these values.
3. Autonomy in the sense that everybody decides for himself which rules he is to follow is *not* a good standard to determine the optimal level of regulation. This is not even the case if – rather arbitrarily – States are seen as the bearers of autonomy (sovereignty).
4. Neither pluriformity nor uniformity is an intrinsic value.
5. The mere fact that a particular standard is so abstract that it cannot be applied easily in a concrete case is not a reason against the use of this standard, but

rather a reason to investigate (empirically) what the standard requires in such a concrete case.

Based on these assumptions, the contributions in this collection provide an argued answer to the question what is the best level to regulate private law in Europe. A conclusion concerning the best level of regulating a particular branch of law will be based on two kinds of premises. One kind consists of criteria or standards on the basis of which a comparative value judgment will be made. These criteria often consist of goals that are pursued by the law, such as the satisfaction of the preferences of legal subjects, the coherence of the law concerning a particular subject, the avoidance of externalities, or bringing about economies of scale. The other kind of premises concern facts that relate to the used criteria. Is regulation at a local level better able to satisfy the preferences of legal subjects than regulation at the EU level, or even at the global level? Which level of regulation is better able to avoid externalities?

Obviously the factual premises will depend strongly on the branch of private law that is concerned. For example, the contribution by Bull *et al.* argues on the basis of one and the same set of standards that doorstep selling should be regulated at a national level, while internet shopping should be regulated by the EU. If we want to find commonalities in the arguments of the different contributions, we will have to look for them not in the facts that are adduced to support conclusions, but in the standards and in the reasoning strategies that they employ. In the following brief discussion of the contributions the emphasis will therefore be on the criteria or standards that the authors use to justify their conclusions, ignoring other interesting aspects of the contributions. Moreover, the different arguments in the contributions are related to the general account of the justification of value judgments as described in another contribution to this volume, Hage's paper 'The Justification of Value Judgments' (*Justification*).

Jan Smits - Who does What? On the Distribution of Competences among the European Union and the Member States

Which facts are relevant for the determination of the best level of regulation depends on the standards that have been adopted. Two contributions provide more general insights on which these standards should be selected. The first is Jan Smits' paper 'Who Does What? On the Distribution of Competences among the European Union and the Member States'. Smits discusses, amongst others, the development of normative criteria for the optimal assignment of competences *for various policy fields*. This last addition is important, because Smits does not believe that the criteria are the same for all fields. Moreover, they may vary with changing economic and social circumstances and changing visions of Europe. Still it should be possible to develop parameters and factors that can be used in all fields, be it that their relative weight may vary from one field to another. Smits mentions ten criteria ('parameters') that are relevant in this context:

1. Local preferences. In case these are too divergent, there is less room for European intervention.

2. Responsiveness. If it is difficult for the EU to obtain the necessary information, regulation at a lower level is called for.
3. The desire to internalize externalities: a level of regulation is presumed better if it leads to fewer externalities.
4. The capacity to set rules.
5. The achievement of economies of scale.
6. The desire to experiment with different solutions: the 'higher' the level of regulation, the less diversity and the less opportunities to learn from experiments.
7. The risk of a race to the bottom. The desire to avoid such a race calls for central regulation.
8. Legitimacy. Citizen participation is explicitly mentioned in this connection.
9. Coherence of the resulting legislation.
10. The extent to which the existing division of competences stands in the way of achieving an optimal distribution. If the costs of change in the level of regulation are too high, change should not take place.

The ten criteria mentioned function as premises in Smits' argument, in the sense that Smits does not adduce further reasons why these criteria should be used. This does not mean that Smits does not provide any support for the criteria. In his contributions, he explains the nature of the parameters and in that way tries to convince his readership. This strategy, which aims at conviction rather than proof, is described in *Justification*, section 10.3.

It deserves special mention that Smits considers none of the factors as decisive in and of itself; they need to be balanced. Smits apparently also adopts the balancing model of justification as described in *Justification*, section 8. Smits does not indicate how the relative weight of the factors is to be determined and writes that this judgment depends on normative ideas and more in particular on the view one has of the goals of European integration. In doing so, He also uses an argumentative strategy that was not discussed in *Justification*: for some factors, such as the desire to experiment with different solutions, and the view one has of the goals of European integration, he presents his conclusions as offering argumentative material in a dialogue about the optimal level of regulation.

Jaap Hage - On Which Level Should Private Law In Europe Be Created?

Like Smits, Hage also deals with the question concerning the best level of regulation in a general way, and does not focus on a particular field of law. The emphasis in this contribution is on the adoption of an ultimate standard for the justification of the value judgement concerning what is the best level for regulation. Hage proposes utilitarianism (maximization of average happiness) as the ultimate standard, but emphasizes, as Smits did, that for practical purposes more concrete standards are required. The role of utilitarianism is to provide the justification for these 'intermediate' standards. Hage then continues by distinguishing two categories of reasons calling for a particular level of regulation. The first category has to do with the substantive quality of the resulting rules, the second with autonomy as the right to regulate. Concerning the question which level of regulation leads to the best rules, Hage falls back on the happiness criterion to establish what are the best rules.

One reason to assign the competence to regulate to a particular level is that the agent(s) on this level have the best knowledge as to what the best rules are. In this context, Hage discusses the view that the decentralized level has the greater expertise. This reason returns in many other contributions to this volume under the heading 'economics of federalism'. Hage dismisses this argument for decentralized regulation as not (necessarily) correct, and adduces a reason why the centralized rule-maker might be more knowledgeable.

A second reason to assign legislative competence to a centralized level is that this may avoid the externalities consisting of legislators who promote local happiness above happiness elsewhere. Hage does not elaborate why externalities would be bad from the perspective of maximizing average happiness.

A third reason mentioned by Hage why centralized legislation would lead to better rules is that rules are related to each other and that centralized regulation would promote coherence between the rules of different national legal systems. The same point returns also in the contribution of Bull *et al.* about consumer protection law.

Strongly related to the previous reason is a fourth that Hage adduces for centralized regulation, namely that centralized regulation tends to lead to rules with a broader scope of application. That would be an advantage, because a broader scope strengthens the coordination function of rules.

The second category of reasons concerning the best level of regulation concerns the right to create rules. Basically, reasons from this category tend to favour decentralized regulation, because agents should be autonomous, and the best way to promote autonomy is to have every agent make his own rules, to the extent that this is viable. However, Hage emphasizes that there is no reason to assume that more autonomy leads to greater happiness, unless via the already discussed greater expertise of the legislator. Therefore, from a utilitarian perspective, the autonomy argument has no independent force.

The overall picture of Hage's argumentation is that it is foundationalist (*Justification,* section 6), with utilitarianism as the unfounded basic premise. The logical structure of Hage's contribution is rather straightforward, but the contribution differs from other papers in the present volume in its emphasis on the need to find the foundation for the intermediate criteria such as the avoidance of externalities in an ultimate standard.

William Bull, Jiangqiu Ge, Catalina Goanță, Mark Kawakami, Jan Smits - Who does What in Consumer Law? A Search for Criteria for Centralized Lawmaking

The authors of this contribution (Bull *et al.*) address whether the law concerning consumer protection is best created on the central level of the EU, or whether decentralized regulation by the Member States is a better option. By framing their research question in this way, they treat their topic as concerning a comparative value judgment (*Justification,* section 9). Moreover, they translate the research question of the present volume – what is the best level of regulation – into the more specific question: which of two designated levels (EU or Member States) is the better one. This is a viable argumentation step if it may be assumed that these alternatives are the only ones, or at least the best two possibilities. The possibility that this might not be the case and that an even more decentralized level of regulation might be preferable is briefly mentioned but immediately discarded because of an economies of scale argument.

The overall argumentation structure of the contribution is the following: First, three reasons are offered why decentralized regulation is the best alternative. These three reasons are that decentralized regulation is better suited to satisfy local preferences, that decentralization will constrain monopolist behaviour by the central government, and that decentralized regulation offers more opportunities for experimentation with different regulations.

It is then pointed out that whether these three reasons are convincing depends on the circumstances. Therefore, Bull *et al.* continue their argument by addressing how convincing the three reasons against centralization are and by considering whether there may be grounds why in particular the first reason (satisfying local preferences) might not hold in the particular circumstances of consumer law. Such grounds would be exclusionary reasons as mentioned in *Justification*, section 8.1. However, the authors argue that such exclusionary reasons are not present in the case of consumer law. Therefore, the three mentioned reasons for decentralized regulation are real reasons, also in the case of consumer law.

The next step in the argument is to investigate whether there are reasons that plead for central regulation and therefore against decentralized regulation. Bull *et al.* find two factors which, if they both hold, together favour centralized regulation. The first factor is that without central regulation, the law would be fragmented throughout the EU, which would lead to diminished consumer confidence. The second factor is what the authors refer to as 'permeability', which stands for the extent to which the regulation of one country has effects in other countries. The combination of fragmentation and permeability may lead to externalities, and also to coordination issues as discussed in the contribution by Hage.

The combination of fragmentation and permeability is a reason against decentralized regulation, which at least in theory should be balanced against the three reasons for decentralization (*Justification*, section 8.2). Bull *et al.* assume that if fragmentation and permeability are present, this reason outweighs the three reasons calling for decentralization. However, they point out that this combination of factors is not always present in consumer law. In doorstep selling, for instance, permeability would be lacking, and then the reasons for decentralization are present. By way of contrast, in the case of the virtual internal market (e-commerce), fragmentation and permeability would be present in combination, and then the reason for centralization outweighs the reasons against it.

Anna Beckers, Nicole Kornet and Janwillem Oosterhuis - Who does What in Commercial Law? The Case for a Multi-level & Multi-Actor Approach to Regulating Commercial Transactions

The authors of this contribution (Beckers *et al.*) aim to answer two questions. The first question is what the normative criteria are to decide upon the appropriate design of commercial contract law. The second question is which regulatory actors, i.e. private or public actors, and where, at what regulatory level, i.e. local, national, regional or global, the rules of commercial law should be set.

At the outset of their argument, Beckers *et al.* adopt two premises. The first one is that commercial law exists to facilitate the exchange of goods and services between commercial parties in a free market economy. The second one reads that facilitating such exchange of goods and services can best be achieved by means of exercising party autonomy. Given these premises, it is obvious to look for a level of regulation that is best suited to promote party autonomy. This includes regulation to safeguard party autonomy, which may be needed for cases such as fraud.

However, Beckers *et al.* immediately add two other purposes for regulation in commercial law, namely to avoid that party autonomy has negative effects on the market and on society. They claim that regulation may be needed if the result of the exercise of party autonomy interferes with the proper functioning of the market, or results in non-compliance with fundamental societal values.

The structure of the argument in this contribution is therefore essentially consequentialist. The regulation of commercial law (or the lack thereof) should serve three purposes, being the exchange of goods and services between commercial parties in a free market economy (the commercial interest), the functioning of the commercial market (the market interest), and the protection of societal values (societal interest). This will require them to balance these interests in one way or another.

The next step in the argument is to identify for each of the purposes of commercial law the agent who can best serve this purpose. The authors argue that there is no single agent who is best suited to serve all three interests.

With respect to the commercial interest, Beckers *et al.* argue that the rules should preferably be set by the commercial parties themselves, because they have the best knowledge of the relevant interests and surrounding circumstances. They also mention autonomy as a value to be served, but on closer inspection autonomy seems to be valued because of the greater knowledge of the autonomous parties. This line of argumentation is comparable with Hage's argument according to which the level of regulation should be determined by the agent who will make the best rules, and where available knowledge is an important factor in determining which agent will make the best rules. Also in Hage's argument, the value of autonomy is reduced to that of being more knowledgeable.

When it comes to protecting the market interest and the societal interests, Beckers *et al.* see a role for both the commercial parties in the form of self-regulation because of their greater knowledge, and for public bodies in case self-regulation turns out to be biased. In the case of regulation by public bodies, the authors connect the appropriate level of regulation to the interest holder: global regulation for global interests, national regulation for the interests of national society, and local regulation for interests of local communities. The reason for this approach lies again in the local preferences idea: agents on a particular level would be the most knowledgeable about the interests on that level.

Summing up, in regulating commercial law Beckers e.a. see a major role for the commercial parties themselves, because they know their preferences in relation to the commercial transaction best, and the primary purpose of commercial law is to further those transactions. In case the commercial parties are too focused on their own interests and neglect market and societal interests, there is a supplementary role for public authorities, preferably at the level corresponding to the nature of the interests.

Bram Akkermans - European Union Constitutional Property Law: Searching for Foundations for the Allocation of Regulatory Competences

In his contribution, Akkermans places property law in the perspective of constitutional law and discusses the implications of this perspective for the relation between the EU level and the national level of making property law. In this context, he focuses on two needs: the need to adapt rules to local circumstances and/or preferences and the need to keep property law in Europe coherent.

With respect to the first need, Akkermans refers to the 'decentralization theorem' as developed and used by law and economic scholars in the context of the economics of federalism. According to this theorem, 'local provision of public goods will be Pareto superior to centralized provision of public goods, given that centralized provision is presumed to be synonymous to a uniform level of output across jurisdictions'. In other words, if centralized regulation leads to uniform regulation, then, barring exceptional circumstances, it is better to have decentralized regulation.

With respect to the second need, Akkermans points to an 'algorithm' which 'derives criteria from existing EU principles and EU law (in that order) to provide arguments when property law should be regulated at the EU level'. This algorithm is based on an understanding of the EU legal order and the EU internal market as a uniform order, respectively market. This is essentially a plea for centralized regulation where the basic structure of EU law and the internal market is at stake. Where these are not at stake, the decentralization theorem still applies. Akkermans also mentions that regulation should take place on the EU level if the EU can offer additional value by reducing transaction costs and other externalities by providing uniform transactional rules.

From a logical point of view, Akkermans adopts a balancing of reasons model (*Justification*, section 8), and in balancing coherence against the decentralization theorem, he assigns greater weight to coherence.

Willem Loof & Anna Berlee - Case Study: Harmonizing Security Rights

The coherence theme that takes a central role in Akkermans' contribution is also prominent in the contribution by Loof and Berlee. They point out that a regulation of security rights for undertakings usually involves a balance between the interests of financiers, usually banks, and the suppliers of the undertaking. National legal systems are characterized both by the balance they strike between these competing interests and by the technical rules through which they regulate security rights. The authors claim that harmonization of regulations is desirable if national regulations only differ in their technical rules, but not in their policies concerning the balance of interests. In that case harmonization leads to a decrease in transaction costs (lower costs of legal advice, contractual costs, risk assessments etc.). However, if harmonization would also require that national legal systems adapt their policy choices concerning the balance of interests, it would not be desirable.

In this argument, it is possible to identify two values that need to be promoted. One is the coherence of national legal systems, where a balanced interplay of rules that impact security and trade interests may be disturbed by transborder harmonization of the law on security rights. The other is the avoidance of transaction costs, which result from regulations that differ between national legal systems. If harmonization only involves the technical rules, there is only the gain of diminished transaction costs, while there is no loss in coherence. However, if harmonization threatens coherence, this disadvantage apparently outweighs the gain concerning transaction costs.

Although Loof and Berlee write about harmonization, rather than the level of regulation, their argument translates into an argument on the who-does-what-question if it is assumed that harmonization will be brought about on the level of the EU, while otherwise national legislators will remain in charge.

From a logical point of view, Loof and Berlee also adopt a balancing of reasons model (*Justification,* section 8). If harmonization does not involve changes in the balance of interests, there is no need to weigh the advantage in transaction costs against anything, and then this advantage decides the harmonization issue. If harmonization does involve changes in the balance of interests, the advantage in transaction costs needs to be weighed against the loss of coherence. On that issue, the authors implicitly assign greater weight to coherence than to transaction costs. In this respect, their approach strongly resembles the approach adopted by Akkermans.

Caroline Cauffman and Niels Philipsen - Harmonizing the Rules on Damages for Infringements of the EU Competition Rules?

Cauffman and Philipsen use the proposal for a Directive on antitrust damages actions as one of the reasons to raise, amongst others, the question whether the law on antitrust damages actions in the EU Member States should be harmonized, or - which in the view of the authors apparently boils down to the same thing - whether the law on antitrust damages actions should be made at the level of the EU, rather than that of the Member States.

The authors discuss in this context both arguments from a law and economics perspective and non-economic arguments, but they primarily focus on the economic arguments. They distinguish two potential arguments against harmonization:

1. The already familiar argument from the economics of federalism that, barring exceptional circumstances, national legislators should be allowed to offer their citizens rules that best fit their preferences. Cauffman and Philipsen briefly indicate what the exceptional circumstances might be, but do not discuss whether they are present in the case of the Directive.
2. The argument, also mentioned by Smits and by Bull *et al.*, that non-harmonized rules allow for experimentation. The authors point out that, although the opportunity for experimentation was present, in many Member States little was done in this regard. Presumably they mention this fact to indicate that

they do not consider this second reason very strong in the case of the Directive.

Cauffman and Philipsen also mention four economic arguments in favour of harmonization:

1. Harmonization may prevent a race to the bottom. Such a race to the bottom might lead to a reduction of social welfare, and in that case 'there is an economic justification for moving legislation (e.g. on workplace safety, consumer protection or environmental standards) to the EU level rather than leaving it at Member State level'. Apparently, the authors see the promotion of social welfare as an economic reason for harmonization. However, the authors consider the possibility that a race to the bottom would occur in relation to antitrust damages actions as possible, but unlikely.
2. A second potential justification for moving legislation to a higher (than the national) level is, according to Cauffman and Philipsen, the presence of transboundary externalities. The existence of such externalities, such as transboundary pollution, might lead to a reduction in social welfare. However, the authors doubt whether harmonization of procedural rules would in itself be effective as a means to avoid transboundary externalities in the field of the Directive.
3. A third potential reason for harmonizing the law on antitrust damages actions is that it would produce economies of scale. According to Cauffman and Philipsen, this argument makes sense in the case of antitrust damages actions to the extent that infringements of competition law have cross-border effects, and because the European Commission is already responsible for enforcing the substantive rules on cartels, abuse of dominance, and mergers.
4. The reduction of transaction costs constitutes the fourth potential reason for harmonization. As costs that might be reduced, the authors point to the costs for business to find out which rules (on private enforcement; or competition law more broadly) apply in which Member State and how to adapt their behaviour in order to comply with the rules that are in force in each Member State. However, they also point out that harmonization also brings costs, such as the costs for individuals, businesses, legal practitioners, courts and legal education to adapt to the new rules and the costs of the application of harmonized rules in the future. In any case, the authors claim that the argument that harmonization can be justified if it reduces transaction costs, is valid only when the marginal benefits of harmonizing law outweigh the marginal costs thereof.

Since all the six reasons mentioned are economic, they have an underlying value in common, namely the promotion of efficiency. The authors apparently view social welfare as an aspect of efficiency, and therefore their notion of efficiency might not deviate very much from the notion of happiness that is propagated by Hage.

Kristel De Smedt and Michael Faure - Who does What? Environmental Liability in the EU

De Smedt and Faure address the question 'Who does what?' in the second section of their paper. More specifically, they deal with the justification of regulation of environmental tort liability on the level of the EU by means of the Environmental Liability Directive.

However, rather than formulating their own standards to determine whether centralized regulation is justified, they analyse the reasons adduced by the European Commission for European action in the field of environmental liability. Such a centralized regulation would lead to, or promote (i) a solution for trans-boundary environmental damage, (ii) a solution against the race-to-the-bottom, (iii) equal marketing conditions in the EU, (iv) the realization of the precautionary, polluter-pays and preventive principles, (v) decontamination and restoration of the environment, and (vi) it would guarantee a minimum level of protection. The authors argue that none of these reasons justifies regulation by the EU, because the adduced objectives are not, or insufficiently realized by centralizing the regulation of environmental liability. They then continue to explain, rather than justify, the existence of the Directive.

4. Conclusions

Can any general conclusions be drawn from these seven contributions on the 'who does what'-question? Apart from the five common assumptions set out above, it seems that two general points can be made.

First, the authors do not have significantly different views of what the main factors for decentralized lawmaking should be. However, the difficult question is how to balance these factors against each other. It seems that this is highly dependent upon the exact sub-field that we deal with and the aim one wants to achieve within this field. In addition, one must distinguish between norm-setting, enforcement and dispute resolution. The more precise one is able to define the topic at hand, the more likely it is that anything sensible can be said about the level at which it should be dealt with.

Second, this book demonstrates that it is possible to have an academically informed discussion about the appropriate level of governance. The 'who does what'-question is thus not only a political question, but also one that legal academics can fruitfully take up. Perhaps this is even the most important conclusion from this book.

PART I

GENERAL PERSPECTIVES

Jaap Hage

THE JUSTIFICATION OF VALUE JUDGMENTS. THEORETICAL FOUNDATIONS FOR ARGUMENTS ABOUT THE BEST LEVEL TO REGULATE EUROPEAN PRIVATE LAW

1. The Role of Value Judgments in Law

Value judgments abound in law and legal science. Many legal rules explicitly mention values in their conditions of applicability. For instance, Article III-I: 103 Section 1 of the Draft Common Frame of Reference states that 'a person has the duty to act in accordance with *good faith and fair dealing* in performing an obligation ...'. Article 4:101 of the Principles of European Tort Law reads that 'A person is liable on the basis of *fault* for intentional or negligent violation of the required standard of conduct'. Moreover, according to Article 3:201 of the same Principles, the attribution of damages to the tort-feasor depends on '... the nature and the *value* of the protected interest; ...'.[1]

Even where legal rules do not explicitly invoke valuation, legal decision makers attempt to give decisions which are not only in accordance with the (positive) law, but which are also *equitable*.[2] Therefore legal decision making also requires value judgments.

It has been argued that legal science should concern itself with the normative question what the law ought to be[3] or with which norms ought to be enforced by collective means.[4] Strictly speaking these ought questions do not require value judgments for their answers because ought judgments are not value judgments, but in practice ought judgments are often based on value judgments, and therefore these two views on the (main) purpose of legal science assign a central role to value judgments.

In this book one particular evaluative question takes a central place. It is the question on which level the private law in Europe is best created. Many different agents present themselves as potential creators of law, both private and public

1 Italics added in all three examples.
2 See Wiarda 1988, p. 23, Alexy 1983, p. 23, and MacCormick 2005, p. 73-74.
3 Smits 2012, p. 35 and 41.
4 Hage 2011.

agents, on levels varying from municipalities through countries and the European Union (EU) to the whole world. In particular within the EU the issue whether regulation should take place on the national or on the EU level is hotly debated.[5]

This assigns the question how value judgments can be justified a high ranking on the list of questions that need to be addressed by legal theory in general and by theoretical reflection on the foundations of European private law in particular. And yet the question has not received a lot of attention. There are many books on legal decision making, interpretation in law, and legal justification[6] but they seldom address the question how value judgments, rather than legal judgments in general, are to be justified.

It is the purpose of the present chapter to remedy this shortcoming of legal theory, at least to some extent. A full discussion of the justification of value judgments requires lengthy excursions into the fields of ontology, epistemology, practical reason, and ethical theory. Here I will try to sidestep these complications as much as possible, while recognizing that this leaves important issues unexplored.[7]

2. Outline of the Argument

The argument of this article is divided into two main parts. The first part deals with justification as if it were an argument that leads from a set of premises to the value judgment as its conclusion. Within it, a subdivision is made between approaches to justification that take deductively valid arguments as their model (the 'deductive' approach), and approaches that are based on the balancing of reasons for and against the value judgment (or any other conclusion). The deductive approach (sections 3-7) will be used to discuss the main issues, and the reason-based approach (section 8) is sketched as a refinement of the deductive approach.

In the context of the deductive approach to justification, three issues that are of general relevance for the justification of value judgments receive special attention. One of these issues concerns the supervenient nature of value judgements, and the related topics that value judgments can be universalized and that they presuppose standards which are not true or false. These basic topics are discussed in the sections 4.4 and 4.5.

A second issue is whether an attempt is made to find a foundation for value judgments in premises which are beyond dispute, or whether such an attempt is not made. The former approach to justification is called 'foundationalist', while the latter approach is called 'coherentist'. The foundationalist approach is discussed in section 6, while coherentism is discussed in section 7.

A third issue concerns the distinction between 'ordinary' value judgments, such as the judgment that a particular law is just, or that an agent acted unlawfully, and comparative judgments, such as the judgment that contract law is *better*

5 For references, see the other contributions to this volume.

6 For instance, Aarnio 1987; Alexy 1983; Canaris & Larenz 2014; Dworkin 1986; MacCormick 1978; Peczenik 2008.

7 This deficit is remedied to some extent in Hage 2011, 2013a and 2013b.

regulated on the level of the EU than on state level. Comparative judgements are discussed in section 9, after the reason-based approach.

The second part of the article (section 10) deals with justification as a kind of dialogue between the person who pleads for the value judgment, and an audience that is opposed to it, or at least needs to be convinced of it. This distinction between these two approaches is basically one between a static timeless approach to justification and a dynamic or procedural one, according to which justification is a process that stretches out in time.

The article is summarized and some conclusions are drawn in section 11. In section 12 an attempt is made to translate the findings of the previous sections into a method for justifying value judgments in general, and value judgments about the best level of regulation for European private law in particular.

3. Syllogistic Justification

Justification can very well be seen as a kind of argument, with the judgement that is to be justified as its conclusion. It is often assumed that such justificatory arguments are deductive ones, and more in particular syllogisms.[8] The idea of syllogistic justification is quite simple: a judgment is justified by a syllogistic argument with two premises. The one premise formulates a kind of law, rule or standard. It has the form of a conditional sentence: 'If…. Then …'. The other premise contains facts about a particular case, situation, or kind of action, facts that match the condition (if-part) of the first premise. This syllogistic model of justification can be used for analysing the justification of value judgments, but also for the justification of purely factual judgments, predictions and normative (must, should, ought) judgments.

Let us have a look at some examples. The first one concerns the justification of an ordinary 'factual' judgment:

Conditional:	If two witnesses testified that Jerry murdered his mother in law, then Jerry did commit that murder.
Facts	Both Jerry's wife and his father in law testified that they saw Jerry murder his mother in law.
Judgment that is being justified:	Jerry murdered his mother in law.

The second concerns the justification of a prediction:

Conditional:	If the interest rates rise, the stock market will go down.
Facts	The interest rates are climbing.
Judgment that is being justified:	The prices of stocks will decrease.

The third is the justification of a should-judgment.

8 For examples from several fields, see Hempel 1966, p. 49-54; Hare 1952; p. 32-55; Alexy 1983, p. 273-283; MacCormick 1978, p. 19-52.

Conditional:	If somebody promised to do something, then she should do it.
Facts	Jane promised to buy an ice cream for Peter.
Judgment that is being justified:	Jane should buy an ice cream for Peter.

And finally an example about a value judgment:

Conditional:	If an audio set satisfies the DIN 45500 standard, it is good.
Facts	Jan's audio set satisfies the DIN 45500 standard.
Judgment that is being justified:	Jan's audio set is good.

This syllogistic model of justification has several attractions, not the least of which is that there is one uniform model that covers very heterogeneous kinds of justification. However, it is not without complications, and these complications become very visible if the syllogistic model is applied to the justification of value judgments. Issues that arise have to do with the correctness ('truth') of both the standard that is being applied and of the value judgment that is being justified. For a proper understanding of these complications, it is necessary to take a closer look at the nature of value judgments.

4. Valuation

The justification of value judgments, such as 'This is a good soccer match' is different from the justification of other judgments, such as the judgment 'There is a horse right in front of me.' To understand properly why this is the case, it is useful to have a closer look at the nature of valuation. This section addresses some of the relevant issues, in particular the naturalistic fallacy, evaluative non-cognitivism and constructivism as views of what is involved in giving and justifying value judgments, and the supervenience and universalizability of value judgments as essential preconditions for the justification of value judgments.

4.1. The Naturalist Fallacy

Originally the naturalist fallacy had to do with attempts to *define* evaluative terms, and in particular evaluative terms as used in moral judgments. For a proper understanding of what the naturalistic fallacy amounts to, this connection to morality is not crucial, however. In the following discussion, the examples will be taken from law and sport.

A bachelor is an unmarried man of marriageable age. This is not an empirical finding; it is a matter of definition. The word 'bachelor' just means 'unmarried man of marriageable age'. This definition of 'bachelor' specifies both a necessary and sufficient condition for the applicability of the word 'bachelor' and in that way gives the meaning of the word.

Suppose that we have a similar necessary and sufficient condition for the applicability of the expression 'good faith' in contract law, would we then also have the meaning of this expression? Lawyers sometimes create the impression that they believe so, when they write that they want to know what 'good faith' means in connection with this or that statutory provision. But are they right when they formulate their interest in when a contract party acts in good faith in this way?

At the beginning of the 20th century, the Cambridge philosopher Moore offered a very influential argument why this would not be the case.[9] He considered the possibility that we had a satisfactory set of conditions for the applicability of the word 'good'. Let us assume for the sake of argument that this set contains the characteristics A, B and not-C. Does 'good' then mean 'A, B and not-C'? If it did, the question 'This television set has the characteristics A, B and not-C, but is it also good?' would not make any sense. It would be comparable to 'Henry is an unmarried man of marriageable age, but is he also a bachelor?' Asking the latter question merely illustrates that the questioner does not know what 'bachelor' means. But does the person who asks 'This television set has the characteristics A, B and not-C, but is it also good?' similarly demonstrate that she does not know what 'good' means?

Moore famously claimed it did not. It is an 'open question' whether something that has the characteristics A, B and not-C is also good. And because it is an open question, 'good' does not mean 'A, B and not-C'. And – this is Moore's main point – this open question argument can be applied to any substitution for A, B and not-C, with only one exception, namely the characteristic 'good' itself. Goodness cannot be defined in terms of 'natural' characteristics and any attempt to do so would amount to committing the 'naturalistic fallacy'.

Originally the term 'naturalistic fallacy' was only used to denote the attempt to define evaluative terms in non-evaluative ('naturalistic') ones, but in the course of time it has also be used for any attempt to derive normative or evaluative judgments from purely non-normative and non-evaluative premises. An example would be the argument 'Everybody approves of this article, so it must be good.' That everybody approves of this article is a matter of fact, and the sentence that expresses it is purely descriptive and non-evaluative. Since being good is an evaluative characteristic, it would then be a naturalistic fallacy to derive from only the sentence that everybody approves of this article that the article is good.

There is a lot to be said about – and against - Moore's argument[10] but it is a fact that it has been quite influential during the 20th century and that many a derivation of normative or evaluative conclusions has been accused of committing the naturalistic fallacy and therefore being inconclusive. As we will see, the desire to avoid the naturalistic fallacy strongly influences the way in which value judgments are to be justified.

9 This argument can be found in Moore 1903, chapter I.

10 Baldwin 2010.

4.2. *Non-Cognitivism*

According to a popular view, the universe exists in a way which is independent of human beings, the human mind, and human knowledge. Of course, human beings and human minds are part of the universe and in that sense the universe is not independent of human beings etc. But it does not depend for its existence on our knowledge of it, on the minds that produce this knowledge, or on the humans whose minds are at stake.[11] This view is so widely shared that only philosophers dare to cast doubt on it.[12]

The universe is filled with things which exhibit characteristics and mutual relations. For instance, the universe contains mountains which are high, and human beings, the one taller than the other. That these things exist, have characteristics and stand in relations towards each other can be described by means of declarative sentences such as 'The mountain is high' and 'Joan is taller than Geraldine'. If these sentences describe the universe as it actually is, if the description 'corresponds to the facts', the sentences are true; and otherwise they are false. Because the facts are assumed to be mind-independent, the truth and falsity of declarative sentences are also assumed to be mind-independent.

All of this seems so obvious that one easily overlooks some complications. Value judgments constitute one of these complications. The sentence 'Joan is prettier than Geraldine' looks very much like 'Joan is bigger than Geraldine'. At first sight it seems to describe a fact. But is there a fact of the matter concerning the relative beauty of persons? Is there beauty to be found in the universe in the same manner in which length is to be found? Is it possible to measure beauty, more or less in the same way as we can measure length? Many have thought that these questions should be answered negatively. The fact that beauty resembles length in the sense that they are both characteristics which somebody or something can have, is merely a trick that language plays upon us. Grammatically, 'beauty' and 'length' function in similar ways, but if we look at the underlying reality, they are very different. Length is to be found in the mind-independent universe, beauty is not.

So what do we state if we say that a soccer match or a television set is good, or that Joan is prettier than Geraldine? One set of ethical theorists held that such 'statements' are not really statements at all, but merely ways to express our feeling or attitudes about things. These theorists have become known as 'non-cognitivists',[13] because they held that evaluative judgments have no cognitive content. These judgments would not give us any information about the universe; in fact they would not aim to inform at all, but merely to recommend, or to express a positive or negative attitude or feeling.

11 An example of something that does depend for its existence on minds is a sound. Sound is the way in which longitudinal vibrations in the air are experienced. If there were no minds, there would not be experiences of sound either, but only vibrations,

12 Philosophers who dare to do so used to be called 'idealists' or 'non-realists', although the term 'constructivists' becomes popular too. See Haslett 1995; Bagnoli 2011.

13 Representatives of this view in meta-ethics are Ayer 1936; Stevenson 1944; Hare 1952; Blackburn 1993.

The view that evaluative judgments are little else than expressions of feelings, or recommendations and that a sentence such as 'This is a good television set' is 'really' a kind of recommendation, rather than the description of a fact has been attacked by Geach and Searle.[14] Basically, their criticism boils down to it that the speech act which can be performed with a sentence does not determine the meaning of the sentence. That a sentence can be used to recommend does not mean that its meaning is 'recommending'. The sentence 'This is a good television set' means the same if it stands on its own as when it is used the conditional sentence 'If this is a good television set, I should buy it'.

More in general, the meanings of sentences should not be looked for in the speech acts that are typically performed by the use of these sentences. The version of non-cognitivism that attempts to do so, is for this reason misguided.

It is, however, possible to give non-cognitivism a twist and to interpret it as the view that evaluative judgments do aim to give us information, but not to inform us about the mind-independent universe. Evaluative judgments would be true or false, not depending on a mind-independent reality, but on the outcome of rational argumentation.[15] This view has become well-known under the heading of 'constructivism'.[16] In legal theory, constructivism can be found in, amongst others, the work of Dworkin[17] and Smits.[18] [19]

4.3. *Supervenience*

Support for the constructivist view can be found in the phenomenon of supervenience. If a value judgment is to be correct, there must be reasons for it. Take, for instance, a good soccer match, or a beautiful piece of music. It is impossible that a soccer match is good, or a piece of music beautiful, just for no reason. There must be something that makes the match good, and the music beautiful. It may be hard to indicate and there may be disagreement amongst people about what these good, respectively beautiful making characteristics precisely are, but despite this possible disagreement and lack of clarity, there *must* be reasons that make a good soccer match good and a beautiful piece of music beautiful. This 'must' is a logical must, and it has to do with what philosophers call the 'supervenience' of valuation.[20]

14 Geach 1956; Searle 1969.

15 Because value judgments are on this view true or false, it can be argued that the view is cognitivist, be it that the cognition concerns facts that depend on argument and therefore on the mind.

16 According to Bagnoli 2011, 'constructivism in ethics is the view that insofar as there are normative truths, ..., they are in some sense determined by an idealized process of rational deliberation, choice or agreement'.

17 Dworkin 1986, p. 225.

18 Smits 2012, p. 76.

19 Extensive discussions of constructivism in law can be found in Hage 2012a and 2012b.

20 The point that value judgments are supervenient has been emphasized in Hare 1963, chapter 2, be it that Hare used the expression 'descriptive meaning' for what is presently called 'supervenience'.

A characteristic or phenomenon is supervenient if it depends completely on one or more other characteristics or phenomena (which are then 'subvening' characteristics or properties), but if it does not coincide with them.[21] An ordinary object has several characteristics which are independent of each other. For instance, the monitor before me is more or less rectangular, has a black border with white letters on it, and was made by a Korean firm. Each of these characteristics might have been different without any change in the other characteristics. This means that none of the mentioned characteristics supervenes on any of the other, or on a combination thereof. Suppose now that this monitor is suitable for my purposes. It is not possible to take the suitability of the monitor away, while leaving all its other characteristics as they were.[22] Taking away the suitability must take the shape of modifying one or more other characteristics. That makes suitability a supervenient characteristic.

A legal competence is also an example of such a supervenient phenomenon. Legal competences are often attached to, supervene upon, a particular status. The competence to dispose over a good is attached to the ownership of this good (and to a few other phenomena), but does not coincide with the ownership. The competence to create emergency regulations is attached to being a mayor, but does not coincide with it. The competence to pass legal verdicts is attached to being a judge, without coinciding with it. For the presence of all these competences there must be a reason lying in the status of the person possessing the competence in question and if this reason (the status) is lacking, the competence does not exist.

What holds for most competences also holds for goodness, beauty and the presence of any other value: there must be a reason for their existence and this reason is to be found in the characteristics that subvene the value, and upon which the value supervenes.

4.4. *Universalizability*

That value characteristics supervene on other characteristics makes judgments about them 'universalizable'. *Every* soccer match that has exactly the same characteristics as a particular good match must be a good one too. The same holds for identical pieces of music: if one of them is beautiful, all the others must be beautiful too. There can be no difference in valuation without an underlying difference in non-evaluative characteristics.

So if a particular soccer match is good because both teams play in an offensive style, all soccer matches where both teams play in an offensive style will be good too. One may argue that things are not that easy. It is well possible that the players in the good match were technically gifted, while the players in a second match were not, and that therefore the second match was not as good as the first, or even bad.

21 Jones 1995, defines 'supervenience' as a dependency relation according to which one set of properties (the supervening properties) is so related to a second set (the subvening properties) that there could be no difference in the first without there being a difference in the second, although there could be a difference in the subvening properties without a difference in the supervening properties.

22 It is assumed that the author's needs concerning monitors did not change.

That may be a good argument, but this does not show that value judgments are not universalisable, but only that they should be universalized in the correct way: all soccer matches in which both teams play offensively and where all the players are technically gifted are good soccer matches. Obviously it is still possible to think of other characteristics of soccer matches which might make a difference. But the reaction would invariably be to include those characteristics, whether they be positive or negative (no foul play, for instance), in the set of relevant subvening characteristics. And when that has been done, the value judgment can be universalized.

This process of amending the set of relevant subvening characteristics may be difficult and time consuming, and every stage in it is then merely an approximation of the final result in which all aspects that are relevant for a supervenient characteristic are given. The development of case law on a particular legal question, for instance, whether there is liability for defects in a product,[23] illustrates this well.[24] The first case mentions some characteristics which support the supervenient legal judgment about the case. Subsequent cases can serve to broaden the set of cases for which this judgment applies, or to distinguish cases. At every stage in this development one or more sets of characteristics are available which are, according to the then accepted view, sufficient to support the legal judgment in question. The theoretical end point of this development, which may never be reached in practice, is a set of one or more rules *without exceptions*, each of which specifies by means of its conditions a sufficient condition for a particular legal judgment, e.g. whether the producer of a good is liable for damage caused by a shortcoming of this good. This sufficient condition is the subvening characteristic that underlies the legal liability.

That value judgments are universalizable means that for every value judgment it should be possible to identify a set of characteristics, positive and/or negative, on which the valuation supervenes, and which is such that all cases in which this set of characteristics is present, the same value judgment is correct. For instance, if a particular soccer match is good because both teams play offensively, the players are technically gifted and there is hardly any foul play, then all soccer matches with these characteristics are good too. It may be hard to formulate the set of conditions which provides sufficient support for a value judgment, but the supervenient nature of valuation makes that for every value judgment there must be such a set.

The result of universalizing a value judgment is a kind of 'rule', called a 'standard'.[25] One such standard might be that soccer matches in which both teams play offensively, the players are technically gifted and in which there is hardly any foul play are good ones. Another, fictitious, example would be that a contract party acts in good faith if, in deciding how to perform the contract, he assigns the same weight to the interests of his contract party as to his own.

23 The development of case law for this particular subject is nicely discussed from a logical point of view in Golding 2001.

24 The presence of liability supervenes on characteristics of a case, but this does not imply that being liable is a value judgment. Value judgments are supervenient, but so are many other judgments.

25 The word 'rule' is between quotes, because the rule is the outcome of universalization, and not - as is customary in a legal setting - the product of rule creation.

Notice that the standards formulated by universalizing a value judgment provide sufficient conditions for a particular valuation, but not always a necessary condition. There may be more than one way in which a soccer match is good, and more than one way to perform a contract in good faith. For each of these ways there will be a standard ('rule'), and the conditions in these standards are individually necessary and unitedly sufficient for the valuation *on the basis of this standard.*

5. The Justification of Standards

After the digression on the nature of valuation, it is time to return to syllogistic justification. For a while we will focus on the justification of value judgments only. A syllogistic justification of value judgments is an argument with as conditional sentence a standard and as facts the characteristics of what is to be evaluated.[26] If these characteristics satisfy the standard, the evaluative judgment logically follows and is justified. This simple seeming picture of syllogistic evaluation hides some complications, however.

5.1. *Deductive Validity?*

In a good argument, the conclusion 'follows' from the premises. But what does that mean? In logic there is one standard for when a conclusion follows from the premises that is above all discussion, and that is the standard of deductive validity. Deductive validity of an argument is defined in terms of the truth of the premises and the conclusion of the argument. An argument is deductively valid if and only if it is (logically) impossible that all the premises of the argument are true, while the argument's conclusion is false.[27] This means that this standard can only be applied to arguments in which all the premises and the conclusion have a 'truth value', meaning that they are either true or false. If the conditional premise is not a statement with a truth value, but a standard, the argument cannot be deductively valid. Not because it is deductively invalid, but because the very notion of deductive validity is not defined for arguments that have premises without a truth value.

Even though the standard of deductive validity is usually not applicable, we seem to be capable to evaluate arguments as good ones, if the conclusion somehow follows from the premises, and bad ones, if the conclusion does not follow. Apparently we apply different standards for validity next to the one of deductive validity. What these standards are, seems to vary with the field of the argument.[28] Standards for medical diagnosis differ from the standards that engineers use to calculate how strong the foundations of a building should be, which in turn differ from the standards applied by lawyers to determine whether the defendant is guilty, or whether the debtor acted in good faith.

26 For some value judgments other facts than about these characteristics may be relevant too. To simplify the argument, this complication will be ignored.

27 See, for instance, Haack 1978, p. 13-15.

28 The field dependence of standards ('warrants') is one of the main points of Toulmin 1958.

In all these fields it is possible to distinguish between good and bad evaluative arguments, but the standards used to distinguish good arguments from bad ones differ. Only by abstracting from all the differences it is possible to formulate a universal standard: an argument is good if, in the light of the premises, it is rational to accept the conclusion of the argument, rather than to reject the conclusion or to suspend judgment. That leaves the question open what counts as rational, which again would depend on standards that are field-dependent.

This leads us back to the universalizability of value judgments. If a value judgment is universalized, the result is a standard that specifies what are the good or bad making characteristics of, say, a soccer match, an audio set, or a legal rule. This standard is needed to support the value judgment and can at the same time be used to distinguish between good and bad evaluative arguments.[29] Universalization of value judgments is a kind of inductive reasoning, meant to establish the standard underlying the value judgment. Evaluative reasoning is to apply an evaluative standard in order to support a value judgment. Although such an argument cannot be deductively valid, because a standard is not true or false, the style of reasoning involved in the application of an evaluative standard has much in common with a traditional syllogism.

Schematically the relation between universalization and the application of a standard can be represented as follows:

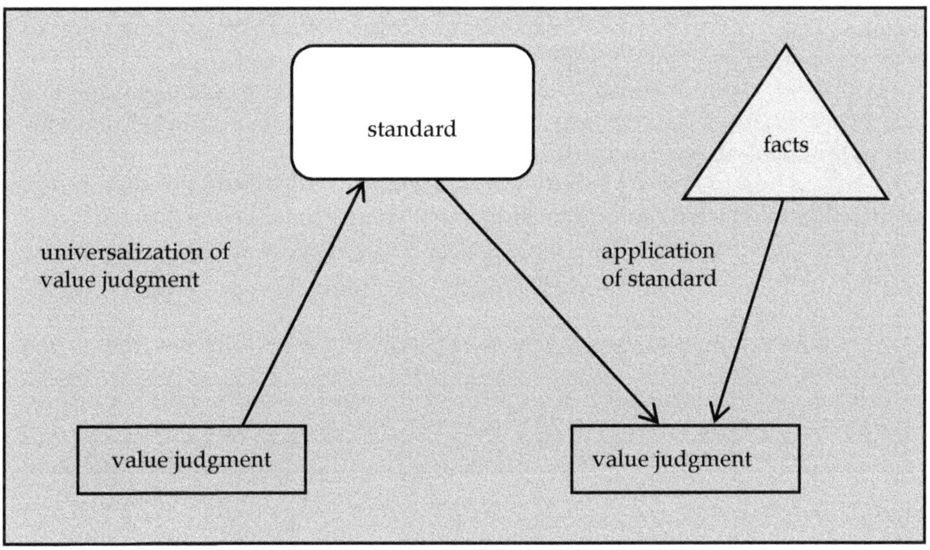

29 Logicians should notice that this gives the standard two roles which are traditionally considered to be distinct. In the first place the standard provides the 'major premise' needed for the justificatory argument. In the second place it provides the inference rule that guarantees that the result of applying the standard to a true description of the facts leads to a justified judgment. In terminology that used to be fashionable, the standard is a 'material inference rule' as opposed to the formal inference rules that are used in traditional logics. Reiter's (1980) 'defaults' are another example of such material inference rules.

An example of universalization was given in section 4.4. Let us suppose that soccer match A was evaluated as good because both teams played offensively, the players were technically gifted and there was hardly any foul play. From this evaluation, based on these reasons, we can by means of universalization 'derive' the standard that a particular soccer match is good (sufficient condition) if both teams play offensively, the players are technically gifted and there is hardly any foul play. This same standard can then be applied to match B which has the same relevant factual characteristics and then the argument in which this standard is applied counts as justification for the value judgment that match B is good too.

Notice that this line of argumentation has many similarities to an argument by analogy, but that it is not such an argument. It is not argued that soccer match B is similar to match A and that therefore match B must be good since match A was good. That would be reasoning by analogy, based on the comparison of soccer matches. The line of argumentation presented here is more explicit and makes the standard which is applied explicit.[30]

5.2. *Justification and Truth*

Although the formulation of a standard that supports value judgements can be found by universalizing an existing value judgement, this procedure does not guarantee that the thus found standard is 'correct'. The 'correctness' of the standard depends both on whether the value judgment that formed the starting point of the universalization was correct itself, and on whether the proper good and bad making characteristics were identified by means of the universalization. We will soon return to the correctness of the standard, but first it must be pointed out what precisely the role of the standard's correctness is.

To see this role in perspective, it is useful to return to the original model of justification in which a descriptive judgement was justified on the basis of a descriptive major premise and a true description of the facts of a case or an object. As example of this kind of justification we used the argument

If two witnesses testified that Jerry murdered his mother in law, then Jerry did commit that murder.
Both Jerry's wife and his father in law testified that they saw Jerry murder his mother in law.
Jerry murdered his mother in law.

The point of justifying the conclusion is to show that the conclusion is correct, and correctness in connection with descriptive sentences is truth. This conclusion can

30 Some might argue that in the common law legal reasoning by analogy is based on identifying the *ratio decidendi* of a precedent, which is quite similar to identifying a standard by means of universalization. That there exists a similarity is correct, but that is a reason to interpret 'analogizing' on the basis of a *ratio decidendi* as a kind of rule-based reasoning, where the rule is derived from a precedent (rather than a statute or other regulation), and not as reasoning by analogy properly speaking.

therefore be justified by showing that it is true. And that can in turn be shown by means of a deductively valid argument that has two true premises. The minor premise is a description of the case facts and for the sake of argument we can assume that this description is true and that Jerry's wife and his father in law actually testified that they saw Jerry murder his mother in law.

If the argument is to be a successful justificatory argument, its major premise must be true too. This is somewhat harder to establish, because the major premise is a conditional sentence and the truth of conditional sentences cannot be established by means of sensory perception alone. We will return to this complication later (section 6.4) but apart from that we can establish that the major premise is a sentence with a truth value. If the major premise is true, the argument, which is deductively valid, proves the truth of the conclusion and in that strong sense justifies the conclusion.

If we move from the justification of a descriptive conclusion to the justification of a value judgement, two things change. First the major premise becomes a standard, and standards are not true or false. And second, it may at least be doubted whether a value judgment can be true or false. If a value judgment has a truth value, it is in the eyes of most people not because it corresponds to an objective, mind-independent fact. These two differences make that the simple picture of justification as a deductively valid argument with two true premises cannot apply to the justification of value judgments.

It is possible, however, to save much of this simple picture by broadening the notion of justification. A conclusion counts as justified if it follows from a major and a minor premise which are both justified themselves. There may be several ways in which a premise can be justified, but one of them is being true: a premise counts as justified if it is true.[31] If this step is taken, the notion 'being justified' takes the place that was held by 'being true' in the more simple picture. And yet the role of truth is maintained by counting any premise that is true as being justified. This adapted version of the deductive picture of justification underlies explicitly or implicitly many discussions about the justification of legal judgments.[32] [33]

6. Foundationalism and its Pitfalls

A standard cannot be justified in the sense that it is true, since standards have no truth values. On the assumption, which will be challenged later (section 7), that a premise of a justificatory argument can only be justified by being true or by being the conclusion of another justificatory argument, it follows that if a standard is to be justified, it must be as the conclusion of a justificatory argument. This opens the question which kinds of arguments can justify a standard.

31 In section 6.4 it will be argued that this move, which seems to solve the problems, is in the end not satisfactory.

32 Cases in point are the views of Alexy 1983, p. 273-283 and of MacCormick 1978, chapter II.

33 We ignore here the complication that reasoning on the basis of premises that lack a truth value cannot be deductively valid, and that some other standard for the quality of arguments needs to be applied.

A standard is not correct in the sense of being true, but rather in the sense of being a good standard. That a standard is good is a value judgement itself, and can only be justified by means of an argument that applies a standard. In general, an argument that justifies a standard must itself have a different standard as its major premise. For instance, the standard that good laws must be understandable can be justified by the argument that good laws must be capable of guiding conduct and that only rules which are understandable can guide conduct.[34]

The insight that an argument that justifies a standard must itself have standard as its major premise immediately leads to a complication. The standard which is used to justify another standard must itself be justified too. And this justification apparently must consist in another justificatory argument with a standard as its premise, and this standard must itself be justified by means of still another argument which ...; and so on. It seems that the justification of a value judgement leads to an infinite chain of standards that justify standards.

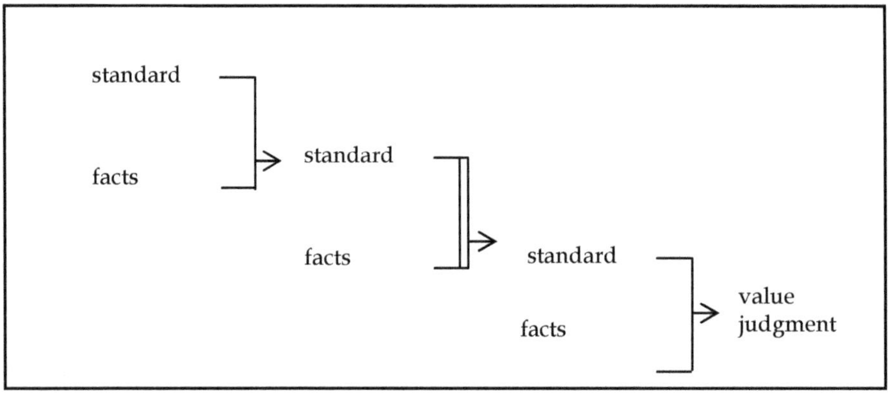

Can such an infinite chain be avoided? That is possible, but only at some costs. In the following subsections a number of possibilities will be discussed. None of them is fully satisfactory, and therefore section 7 discusses an alternative for the foundationalist approach to justification.

6.1. *Use of Existing Standards*

One solution for the problem of a threatening endless regress is not to use 'good' standards but existing standards. In fact, this is a solution which will appeal to many lawyers, because it is used in law to determine what people should do. Instead of requiring from people that they do what is morally required or what is the best possible act, it 'only' requires that people comply with the rules that actually exist as part of the law. This not only avoids the endless regress that may be involved in the justification of value judgments, it also prevents continuing discus-

[34] This argument is based on Fuller's (1963) account of the internal morality of law.

sions about what is morally right or what is the best thing to do. Avoiding such discussions is valuable in itself.

Analogous to the application of positive law as standard for behaviour, one can appeal to positive standards as the basis for value judgments. The DIN standard that was mentioned in an earlier example illustrates this possibility. It has actually been adopted as standard that must be satisfied by hifi-sets in order to qualify as good ones. Similar standards exist in sports such as gymnastics where they are used to evaluate the quality of, for instance, free exercises. These standards exist in the sense that they are actually accepted within a social practice: they are being used, they can be cited as reasons for value judgments, and if they are not used, this is a reason for criticism. The existence of such standards can be established as a matter of social fact, and the empirical social sciences are in principle able to give 'hard' outcomes as to the existence of a particular standard.[35] The judgement that a particular standard exists is true or false, which means that the justificatory chain can end with a standard that is considered to be 'justified' in the sense that it actually exists.

Related to the use of standards that actually exist is the use of standards that are 'presupposed' by an existing social practice. Law provides a good example again. There are legal rules which exist as a matter of fact, for instance, because they were created by means of legislation or were adopted by the judiciary as case law. These rules apply only to the cases that satisfy the rule conditions, the cases to which the rules are applicable. However, it is possible that some legal principle underlies a set of these rules. Examples would be the principle that third parties in good faith deserve protection, or the principle that nobody should profit from his own wrongs. These principles do not exist in the sense that they are normally used when the opportunity presents itself. In ordinary cases the rules in which the principles are incorporated are used, not the principles themselves. However, the use of rules based on principles illustrates that in some sense these principles do 'exist'. And if a case arises to which no rule applies but which nevertheless falls under such a presupposed principle, it may be possible to justify the judgment about this case by invoking the principle.[36] This holds for legal judgments, but also for evaluative social practices. The existence of 'presupposed standards' is something that can in principle also be established by means of social science, be it that it not only requires the establishment of which rules belong to a social practice, but also the additional interpretational step of finding the principles (rationales) behind the rules.

Somewhat related to standards that are actually being used or which are presupposed by an existing social practice are policies that have been adopted by a person who, or a body that, is competent to set standards. For instance, a legislative body may formulate a policy to determine under which circumstances new legisla-

35 This is compatible with the phenomenon that the application of such standards still requires the exercise of judgment, which may lead to differences between evaluators.

36 This possibility, in combination with the view that legal principles are not identified on the basis of their pedigree, underlies Dworkin's famous argument in Dworkin 1978, p. 14-45.

tion is desirable. The existence of such policy standards can also be established as a matter of social fact.

6.2. *Naturalistic Fallacy*

The invocation of existing rules and standards, explicit or presupposed, or of policies, has the clear advantages of increased objectivity and cutting off potentially endless lines of regress of standards underlying standards. There are also disadvantages, however. Actually existing standards may be bad ones, as is sadly illustrated by the actual use of standards according to which coloured people are 'worse' than non-coloured ones, or women inferior to men. Is a value judgment based on such a bad standard really justified?

The same question may also be approached from the perspective of the naturalistic fallacy. Is the argument from 'This standard is actually used' to 'This standard justifies the value judgments based upon it' not a clear instance of the naturalistic fallacy? We encounter this discussion in the law too, when the question is raised whether bad 'laws' are really law, or whether they 'really' deserve compliance.

This complication can be solved by means of a definition. It is possible to define a social practice in terms of the standards that are actually being used within this practice. For instance, one may define the moral point of view in terms of the standards that are in a particular society actually used for moral evaluation (positive morality), or the legal point of view in terms of the legal sources that are recognized in a particular legal system (positive law). Then it can be established 'objectively' what is morally right or wrong, and what legally is the case. This definitional approach has the disadvantage, though, that the question may pop up whether one should 'really' evaluate acts and situations morally, or whether one should 'really' live in accordance with the law. The more objective standards become, the more easily the question will arise whether these standards should 'really' be used.

6.3. *Appeal to Self-evidence*

The use of actually existing standards, whatever shape they may take, gives rise to the question why these positive standards should be used. If that happens we are back at the phenomenon that the use of a standard only justifies a value judgment if the standard is itself justified by means of a standard applying argument. How to avoid the infinite regress of standards underlying standards to which this phenomenon threatens to lead?

An alternative for the invocation of 'positive' rules and standards seems to be an appeal to self-evidence. Such an appeal is not often made explicitly, but some arguments seem to presuppose it. An example of such an implicit appeal to self-evidence as a means to stop a chain of infinite regress is the 'defence' by John Stuart Mill of the Greatest Happiness Principle, the principle that those acts are best that maximize the total amount of happiness.[37] Mill starts in the introductory chapter of his booklet Utilitarianism to claim that ultimate ends, such as happiness, cannot be proven in the ordinary sense, because such an ordinary proof would require the availability of an even more ultimate end which by definition is lacking in the case of ultimate ends. Mill gives, amongst others, the example of the medical art which is proved to be good with an appeal to health, but that it is not obvious how to prove that health is good. In the fourth chapter of utilitarianism, Mill 'proves' the utilitarian doctrine that happiness is desirable from the fact that each person actually desires to be happy. Being aware that this does not sound very convincing, Mill adds that this is '... not only all the proof which the case admits of, but all which it is possible to require, ...'.

The problem with such appeals to self-evidence, as Mill apparently makes in this very brief argument why happiness is desirable, is that it only convinces those who were already convinced. Those who were not convinced already will not consider such an argument a real justification.

6.4. *The 'Myth of the Given'*

In general, the attempt to find a firm foundation for standards fails because the search ends in an infinite regress, or in some way of dogmatizing one or more particular standards.[38] At first sight this problem seems peculiar to the justification of value judgments, because the justification of a value judgment needs a 'good' standard as a premise. On closer inspection, the problem is not confined to value judgments, however. We have already encountered an 'ordinary' justificatory argument with two true premises, the first of which was a conditional sentence. It was then remarked that it is not so easy to *show* the truth of a conditional sentence. We lack the senses to perceive conditional facts. The same counts for universal statements such as the statement that metal bars expand when heated. We assume that such law-expressing statements are true or false, but it is far from obvious how this truth or falsity can be established.

This problem of establishing truth does not only play a role in connection with conditional and law-expressing sentences, but also in the case of 'ordinary' descriptive sentences, such as 'This is a metal bar'. It is one question whether this sentence is true, and another how it can be shown to be true. In a number of cases this may seem simple: the truth of a sentence is 'given' to our senses. We can see a horse before our eyes, and we can hear the music play. But even in these simple cases there are grounds for doubt. Does the fact that we see a horse prove that there is a horse? In a sense, it does, because if there were no horse we could not have seen a horse. However, this observation immediately backfires: did we really see a horse, or did we only believe to see one? Does the experience of seeing a horse provide one with sufficient evidence to be *justified* in believing what is apparently experienced? And the justificatory issue is back: even on the truth of the sentences that are

37 Mill 1861.

38 Albert 1980, p. 13.

obviously true because their truth is 'given' to our senses doubts may be cast. Is our sensory evidence really sufficient evidence? In case somebody is tempted to point out that if anything is obvious, this is, the equally 'obvious' reply is that this is a typical example of an appeal to self-evidence, an appeal that was found to be unattractive in case of other standards. Why would such an appeal suddenly be attractive if the standard is that beliefs are justified if they are based on sensory perception? This point can be made in a more general way: there is no information that is 'given' to us, either through our senses, or to some other faculty that may provide us with knowledge. The idea that there would be such information has become known as the 'Myth of the Given'.[39]

If the hope is abandoned that true descriptive sentences are in a privileged position with regard to justification, because sensory perception provides us with the necessary justification for our beliefs in them, it turns out that it does not matter whether a premise is true. What counts is whether the acceptance of the premise was justified. This holds for standards just as well as for descriptive premises. Being true cannot take the place of being justified, as was suggested earlier (section 5.2). All premises of a justificatory argument must themselves be justified, and this recursion – the definition of 'being justified' in terms of being justified - cannot bottom out on premises that are justified because they are true. The problem with a foundationalist approach to justification is even worse than it seemed at first. It does not only relate to standards which lack a truth value; it relates to *all* premises of justificatory arguments. Apparently these premises either must be assumed dogmatically, or the justification of any judgment, including any value judgment, turns into an infinite regress.

The enterprise to justify value judgements seems to be hopeless, but happily it is possible to challenge the syllogistic model of justification from which the foundationalist problems result. The traditional alternative for the foundationalist approach to justification is to look at justification in a coherentist fashion.

7. Justification through Coherence

The difference between the syllogistic/deductive model of justification and the coherentist one can well be represented by means of a metaphor. According to the syllogistic/deductive model, justification is like a pyramid, with at the top the position that is being justified, in the present context a value judgment. At the bottom of the pyramid are the ultimate premises of the justificatory argument, and in between are the intermediate conclusions that function as premises for the arguments built on top of them. The problem of the syllogistic/deductive model is that the foundation of the pyramid seems to float in the air.

The most appropriate metaphor for the coherentist approach to justification is that of a bundle of standing sticks that remains in balance because the sticks support each other. No stick remains unsupported, but in a sense the chain of support is circular because the one stick is supported by another stick which is supported by

39 Sellars 1956.

still another stick .... etc. until the first stick reappears again as support for a stick that through a series of other sticks indirectly supports the first stick.

The intuition behind a coherentist view of justification is that something cannot be justified in isolation, but only as an element of a larger set. This set is to be coherent, and all the elements of the coherent set are justified for the reason that they belong to a coherent set. There are some obvious objections against this view, and they will be mentioned and briefly discussed in section 7.2. However, first the idea of justification through coherence needs to be elaborated.

7.1. *Consistency, Comprehensiveness and Completeness*

Before continuing the discussion, it is useful to introduce some technical terms. The elements that belong to a coherent set can be very diverse. They include not only descriptive sentences that are true or false, but also value judgments of which some people doubt whether they are true or false, and standards that support value judgments and which are certainly not true or false. They may also include rules, both mandatory rules as they abound in the law, but also rules of inference such as the ones used in logic, which allow one to draw conclusions from sets of premises. Rights and interests can also be elements of a coherent set, just as values and policies. Some of these entities, in particular descriptive sentences, and maybe also value judgments, can be believed. Others, such as rules may exist in the sense that they are valid. Again others, such as policies, can be adopted or accepted. It is useful to have one term that can be used for all elements of a coherent – or not yet coherent – set, and I propose to use the term 'position' for this purpose. Positions can then be said to be 'accepted' by the person who believes them (in case of descriptive sentences), considers them to be valid (in case of rules), or to exist (values, rights). So a set that aspires to be coherent consists of positions that are accepted by the agent (person, or organization) holding this 'position set'. The opposite of being accepted is being rejected. A rejected element is not an element (anymore) of the position set held by an agent.

The metaphor of sticks supporting each other that underlies coherentism may have its attractions, but it is far from easy to substantiate the idea of coherence. What makes a position set coherent? A first demand is that the elements of the set do not 'contradict' each other; a coherent position set must be 'consistent'. The words 'contradict' and 'consistent' are within quotes, because their meanings must be stretched somewhat if they are not only to be applied to descriptive sentences, which are true or false, but also to other positions such as values, standards and rules. This is not the place to elaborate how different kinds of positions can be (in)consistent. Suffice it to claim that a position set is not consistent (inconsistent) in the sense used here, if and only if at least one of its elements should rationally be rejected in the light of (the acceptance of) its other elements.

An inconsistent position set is not coherent, but does consistency suffice to make a set coherent? Many have thought that mere consistency is too weak a demand to make for coherence. It should not only be required that the elements of a coherent set do not contradict each other; they should also *support* each other. However, it turned out to be quite difficult to define what this 'support' might amount to.[40] Again, this is not the place to elaborate that theme, and I will confine myself to proposing a possible solution to the problem of defining support. This solution is to drop the demand that the elements of a coherent position set should support each other and replace it by the even more challenging demand that a coherent position set be 'comprehensive'.

To see what this demand implies, and why it is so demanding, we must return to consistency again. The requirement that a set be consistent becomes more demanding, the larger the set is. A single elementary sentence, such as 'This is a good rule' cannot even be inconsistent. To make the set inconsistent, it is at least necessary to introduce a second sentence; 'This is not a good rule.' The more sentences are added to a set, the more opportunities arise for the occurrence of contradictions. Where a small set can hardly be inconsistent, a very large set easily becomes inconsistent. Therefore, the requirement that a set be consistent is more demanding if the set is very big than if the set is only small.

Here is where the requirement of comprehensiveness enters the picture. A comprehensive set of beliefs consists of everything that an agent believes. A comprehensive position set is even bigger, since it does not only contain beliefs, but also all the values, rules etc. which the agent accepts. The requirement that such a set be consistent is very demanding, because it amounts to the demand that the agent is completely rational and does not accept anything that rationally should not be accepted in the light of everything else that the agent (rationally) accepts. In fact, this requirement is so demanding that no human agent will ever be able to fully meet it.[41]

If a comprehensive position set is consistent, this means that no decisive criticism of any element in it is possible on the basis of the other elements of the set. An agent holding such a set would seem to be fully justified in doing so, and what more could be asked? 'Truth', some may be tempted to answer, but as was argued above (section 6.4), what counts for justification is not whether a belief is true, but whether it is justified. Therefore it seems that an agent who holds a consistent comprehensive position set is justified in doing so, and this justification not only applies to the set as a whole, but to every position in it. So an agent would be justified in accepting a value judgment if this value judgment is an element in the comprehensive position set held by this person, and if this position set is consistent.

This is not the whole story, however. It may be the case that an agent's position set is consistent, but that it lacks some elements which rationally should be included. Suppose, for instance, that an agent both accepts the standard that soccer matches in which both teams play offensively, the players are technically gifted and in which there is hardly any foul play are good ones, and that in the match between Liverpool United and Schalke 04 both teams played offensively, the players were technically gifted and there was hardly any foul play. Then this agent rationally should also accept the value judgment that this match between Liverpool United and Schalke 04 was a good one. If this judgment is not yet part of the agent's positions set, the agent is not fully rational, and the set is not coherent. A coherent

40 An example of an attempt can be found in Peczenik 2008, p. 132-140.

41 I will return to this impossibility in section 7.3.

set should be consistent, but it should also include everything that rationally should be included given (the rest of) the set. So if, for instance, a particular value judgment follows from a position set, this value judgment should also be in the set. This will be called the requirement that the position set is 'complete'. Completeness is a requirement on coherent position sets.

Sometimes an agent deliberately refuses to include a position is her position set, even it should rationally be included given the rest of what she accepts. Then the set can also be made coherent by dropping an element. In the above example, the agent may drop one of the beliefs that both teams played offensively, that the players were technically gifted or that there was hardly any foul play. The agent may also stop accepting the standard that soccer matches in which both teams play offensively, the players are technically gifted and in which there is hardly any foul play are good ones. So coherence can not only be restored by adding elements that are lacking, but also by giving up elements which require that some undesirable element should be added to the set.[42]

7.2. *Agent-Relativity of Justification*

The attentive reader may have noticed that in the exposition of justification by means of coherence, a change of formulation occurred. The phrase was not anymore whether a belief or standard, or - in general - a position was justified, but whether an agent was justified in accepting this belief, standard or position. This change in formulation reflects a fundamental change in the question that is being answered. When we talk about a belief or standard being justified, it seems that we presuppose that 'being justified' is a characteristic that beliefs and standards can possess. We encountered this presupposition in section 5.2 in discussing the replacement of truth by justification for positions like standards which are not true or false. In section 6.4 it was pointed out that even when a position can be true or false, in particular when it is a belief, it is not the truth that counts, but being justified. However, it remained unclear what kind of characteristic 'being justified' is. Truth can be defined in terms of correspondence to the facts, but how should we define 'being justified'? Is it a way of being right, just like truth, but then more abstract to make it potentially applicable to entities that have no truth values, such as standards or rights? If so, it remains unclear in what way entities without a truth value can be right. What does a justified standard have that a non-justified standard lacks?

If it is not the position that is, or is not, justified, but rather the agent in accepting a particular position or position set, it becomes easier to see what justification amounts to. An agent can be said to be justified in accepting a position if accepting this position is the rational thing to do. That would, on a coherence theory of justification, be the case if this position is an element of a coherent position

42 There are even more possibilities, such as making an exception to a standard which is maintained for other cases. Discussion of these possibilities is outside the scope of this article, however.

set held by this agent. The agent is then also justified in holding this position set, for the reason that the set is coherent (comprehensive, consistent and complete).

The view that it is the agent who is justified, and not the positions accepted by the agent, fits a coherentist approach to justification, since coherentism tends to make justification agent-relative. This has to do with the requirement that a coherent position set be comprehensive, since a comprehensive position set consists of every position *accepted by an agent*. This definition makes comprehensiveness and therewith coherence agent-relative. This relativity is in the eyes of many a disadvantage of coherentism. If two agents disagree about a value judgment, what does it help if the one agent is justified in holding this value judgment, if at the same time the other agent can be justified in rejecting it?

Often the focus of the criticism is not so much on the agent-relativity, but rather on the isolation of the positions in a coherent theory from the facts in the world. A positive metaphor for coherentism is that of a bundle of sticks which can all stand because of the support they receive from the other sticks. However, Haack borrows from C.I. Lewis the more negative metaphor of a bunch of drunken sailors who can only remain upright because they hang together.[43] The problem is that according to coherentism, the justification of any position, inclusive beliefs about the external world, only depends on other positions held by the agent. This not only makes coherence and justification agent-relative, but there also seems to be no guarantee that the positions in the set are in any way related to the facts. Sosa describes in this connection a thought experiment.[44] Suppose than an agent holds a particular coherent position set, created under the influence of the facts in the world. All beliefs in the set are true. Through a miracle all the facts in the world change, and all beliefs in the position set have become false. But allegedly, the position set itself would still be coherent. Can this coherence still justify the beliefs and other positions in the set?

Apparently the correct answer to this question is negative. However, the question should not be whether the positions are justified. We still lack an adequate theory of what being justified means in relation to positions. The proper question is whether the agent is justified in accepting the positions in her position set. If the agent in the thought experiment is not aware of any change in the facts – which is highly unlikely, because some of the facts concern his own mental states – the agent would still be justified in holding the belief set. Why should she modify any positions if the set satisfied the highest demands of rationality and nothing came up to create the impression that this is not the case anymore? Much more likely is the situation that the agent is aware of at least some of the changes in the world. That would mean that some positions in her set have changed spontaneously, that is because of factors outside the position set itself. Most likely the set is not coherent anymore and the agent would not be fully rational in returning to the set as it originally was.

The conclusion from this all is that if we take the agent as the entity that is to be justified, justified in accepting positions, the fact – if it is one – that a position set

43 Haack 2009, p. 65-66.

44 Sosa 1980.

can be completely disconnected from the world is no decisive objection against coherentism. It may make coherentism less attractive for some, because the claim that an agent is justified in subscribing to a particular value judgment may be considered as less ambitious than the claim that the value judgment itself is justified. Those who want justified value judgments may not be satisfied with agents being justified in accepting these value judgments. However, since it is not clear at all what a justified value judgment would be, it is questionable whether those who strive for justified value judgments make any sense.

That does not end the discussion. What if two agents are both justified in accepting conflicting value judgments? Would they both be 'right' then? It depends. For some value judgments this might be the appropriate solution, for instance, for value judgments like 'Apple-sauce tastes better than broccoli', if both agents agree that this is merely a matter of taste. But then the value judgment 'Apple-sauce tastes better than broccoli' is being considered as shorthand for 'I prefer apple-sauce above broccoli'. If two agents disagree about the truth of this sentence as applied to themselves, they do not disagree after all.

If the agents do not believe that a particular value judgment, for example that one rule is better than another, is merely a matter of taste, they will probably assume that they have good reasons for sticking to their own value judgments. Then, most likely, the rational thing to do is to listen to the reasons of the other agent. This may change one's position set, and possibly also one's value judgment. And if not, there may be reason to continue the search for what is the best value judgment. Although there is no guarantee that this process makes that any of the agents *rationally should* (rather than 'will') change his mind, most likely it will make it rational for an agent, or for both, to change their minds.

7.3. *Defeasible Coherentism*

A coherent position set is a complete, consistent and comprehensive - that also means actually held - position set. In reality such things do not exist. The idea of a coherent position set is a theoretical construct, useful for defining what it means for an agent to be justified in accepting a particular position, such as a value judgment. If coherentism is to be used as a real test on the justification of positions, a less demanding version should be devised.

One such less demanding version is *defeasible coherentism*.[45] The starting point is again the idea that justification should be based on coherence and that a coherent set is to be consistent and complete. However, the requirement that this set is comprehensive must be dropped, because a comprehensive set would be unmanageable. Therefore the position the acceptance of which is to be justified does not have

45 A position is defeasible if it is possible that it needs to be modified in the light of additional information. A legal example would be that the conclusion that a buyer of a car needs to pay the price of the car is liable to be defeated in the light of the information that the sales contract came about under undue influence. More on defeasibility in connection with law in Hage 2005, p. 7-32.

to be an element of the full comprehensive set, but merely of a 'representative' subset thereof. This subset should be consistent.

The crucial extra demand on the subset is that it is 'representative'. A representative subset is a subset which does not give a wrong picture of the full set where the position that is to be justified is concerned. Ideally, the subset should only contain this position if the full set would also contain it. Obviously this cannot be established without having disposal over the full set, and that is precisely what will not be available. The solution to this problem can be found in the use of meta-knowledge. Somebody can hold a belief which, *as far as she can see*, fits in the set of all her positions. This means that she believes that her belief fits in her actual comprehensive position set. She does not know whether this meta-belief about the adequacy of her subset is true, but she nevertheless has it. Moreover, as long as she does not have counter-evidence, she is defeasibly justified in sticking to it. Not having counter-evidence means in this connection: not being aware of counter-evidence and not having counter-evidence in the same defeasible sense that the subset of her positions of which she is aware contains reasons not to trust it.

An example may make this clearer. A public prosecutor believes that John is a thief and that the rule exists that thieves are punishable. Given this limited position set, she should adopt the belief that John is punishable. Actually she also believes that minors are not punishable, but she has no reason to assume that John is a minor. Therefore she actually believes that her small position set is representative for her actual comprehensive set where the belief that John is punishable is concerned. Moreover, as long as she is not aware of counter-evidence (there is no counter-evidence in her subset) she is justified in sticking to this meta-belief. The subset is defeasibly coherent and therefore this public prosecutor is defeasibly justified in believing that John is punishable. That would become different if somebody informs the prosecutor that John is a minor. Maybe the prosecutor does not immediately believe that, but now she has reason to conduct additional research to rebut what was told her, or – if the information turns out to be correct – to modify her limited position set to make it include the beliefs that John is a minor and that he is not punishable. The belief that John is not punishable should at the same time be removed from the position set then.

This version of defeasible coherentism is an example of a procedural approach to justification, since it makes use of the set of positions that are actually being held by an agent and its transformations in time, and not of an ideal set such as a coherent one. In section 10 we will encounter other procedural approaches to justification.

8. Justification on the Balance of Reasons

Often value judgments are the outcome of balancing reasons. Take the value judgment that contract law is better regulated on the level of the EU than on the national levels of the EU Member States. One reason why this value judgment might be correct is that there are many contracts between businesses in different EU countries. There is also a reason against this value judgement, however, and that is that regulation on the EU level is an infringement on the national autonomy of the EU Member States. To determine the correctness of the value judgement, these reasons need to be balanced. It is not so easy to account for the balancing of reasons in a syllogistic model of justification, however. Therefore, the account of syllogistic justification as given above will here be supplemented by a brief description of how justification on the balance of reasons works.[46]

8.1. *Reasons*

The word 'reason' is not always used in the same way by everyone, and neither does it have a single meaning.[47] The following is therefore to some extent stipulative.

Reasons are facts, which can be described by true descriptive sentences. For instance, the fact that it is raining is a reason to carry an umbrella, the fact that the metal bar is heated is the reason why it will expand, the fact that the polygon has four straight corners is the reason why it is a rectangle and the fact that John was treated with disdain is the reason why he started to cry.

As these examples illustrate, there are different kinds of reasons. Some guide behaviour, such as the fact that it is raining. Others cause events, such as the fact that the metal bar was heated. Again others make that something is the case, such as the fact that a polygon has four straight corners. And still others explain events that took place, such as the fact that John was treated with disdain.

All reasons have in common that they are facts that are somehow relevant for other facts. Since relevancy if not a one-time affair, reasons can be universalized. If fact F is a reason for fact P, then normally facts like F will be reasons for facts like P. We have already encountered this phenomenon in section 4.3 when supervenience was discussed. A fact P is supervenient on another fact F if F is (part of) the reason why P obtains. Being good is an example of a supervenient fact, just like the presence of any other value characteristic. This means that if a particular soccer match is good for the reason that it has characteristic C, then if some other soccer match also has characteristic C that is a reason why this other match is also good.

A kind of fact F that is normally a reason for another kind of fact P, does not have to be a reason under all circumstances. There may be exceptional circumstances. For instance, the fact that I promised to give you €50 is normally a reason why I should give you €50. But if I was forced to make this promise, that is a reason why my promise does not constitute a reason in this particular case. Reasons which make that facts which are normally reasons are exceptionally not reasons, are called 'exclusionary reasons'.[48]

Contributory reasons are reasons that plead into a particular direction, but which may have to be balanced against other reasons pleading in the opposite direction. For instance, the fact that it is raining is a contributory reason to carry an

46 More extensive accounts can be found in Hage 1997, chapter IV, and in Hage 2005, p. 69-99.

47 A good general account of reasons that guide behaviour is Alvarez 2010. An account that focuses on *legal* reasons for action is Redondo 1999.

48 The notion of an exclusionary reason was popularized in a legal context by Raz. See, for instance, Raz 1975, p. 40-48. In epistemology, the same phenomenon has become known as an 'undercutter' or an 'undercutting defeater'. See Pollock & Cruz 1999, p. 196.

umbrella, which may have to be balanced against the reason that there are more important things to carry.

Decisive reasons decide the issue for which they are a reason, without any need for balancing. For instance, the fact that there are three male elephants and four female ones are together a decisive reason why there are seven elephants. There is no room for balancing here. It is well possible to treat the combination of a standard and the facts that match the standard together as a decisive reason for the value judgment based on this standard. For instance, the standard that soccer matches in which both teams play offensively, the players are technically gifted and in which there is hardly any foul play are good ones, in combination with the facts that in the match between Liverpool United and Schalke 04 both teams played offensively, the players were technically gifted and there was hardly any foul play together might be seen as a decisive reason for adopting the value judgment that this match between Liverpool United and Schalke 04 was a good soccer match.

Notice that if a contributory reason decides an issue after balancing, this does not make it into a decisive reason. It remains a contributory reason, be it a contributory reason that has decided the issue.

Sometimes an event occurs which makes that something that was a reason is not a reason anymore. If John promised Jane to give her €50 this is a reason why John should give Jane €50. However, as soon as Jane released John from his promise, the reason does not exist anymore. It is still the case that John made the promise, but this fact has lost its relevance for what John should do. Such events which make that facts that were reasons lose their status as reasons, are called 'cancelling conditions'. Cancelling conditions should be distinguished from exclusionary reasons, because exclusionary reasons makes that some other facts are not reasons at all, while cancelling conditions make that some facts that were reasons lose their force as reasons, are not reasons *anymore*.[49]

8.2. *Balancing*

Any judgment, including a value judgment, counts as justified if there exists a decisive reason for it.

In the case of value judgments there will often be no decisive reasons, and in that case the justification of the judgment must be based on the balancing of contributory reasons.

In this connection a misunderstanding lurks. The term 'balancing' may be used for the mental process of making up a decision, but that kind of balancing does not lead to the justification of a value judgment. At best it can *explain* why a person adopted a particular value judgment, and explanation is not justification.

For the present purposes, 'balancing' stands for a logical step in which a conclusion is derived on the basis of three premises. One premise states the contributory reasons that plead for the conclusion. Another premise states the contributory

49 The distinction has a legal counterpart in the distinction between void and a rescinded contract.

reasons that plead against the conclusion. And a third premise, the 'weight-premise', states which of these two sets outweighs the other set. For instance:

The fact that there are many contracts between businesses in different EU countries is the only contributory why contract law should be created on the level of the EU.
There are two contributory reasons why contract law should NOT be created on the level of the EU: 1. that regulation on the EU level is an infringement on the national autonomy of the EU Member States; 2. that national states know better than the EU which contract law is good for them.
The set consisting of the single reason why contract law should be created on the level of the EU outweighs the set consisting of the two reasons why contract law should NOT be created on the level of the EU.
Therefore: It would be good if contract law were created on the level of the EU

It is important to notice that the weight-premise, indicating the relative weight of the two sets of reasons, is a *premise* of the balancing step, *not the result* of it. Given this premise the logical step to the conclusion is 'logical', as it should be in logic. Often the most difficult step in the reasoning *process* that leads to a decision is to establish which set of reasons is the stronger one. The weight-premise of the argument only gives the result of this decision making process.

Notice, by the way, that it is not automatically the case that the set with the larger number of reasons outweighs the other set. In the present example, a set containing only a single reason is taken to outweigh a set containing two reasons.

The balancing of contributory reasons takes place between two sets of reasons, the reasons pleading for the conclusion, and the reasons pleading against. This is also the case if a set contains only one reason, or even no reasons at all (the 'empty set'). The reasons in these two sets consist of all the facts that plead for, respectively against the conclusion. They must be facts, so the sentences expressing them must be true. They must also be relevant, so the relevancy of the facts should not be excluded by an exclusionary reason, or taken away by a cancelling condition.

8.3. *Reasoning about Relative Weight*

The determination of which set of reasons outweighs which other set is often a matter of decision making for which no additional reasons can be adduced. In that case the weight premise is a premise of the full argument indeed, and not an intermediate conclusion. However, it is sometimes possible to argue why one set of reasons outweighs the other, and then the weight premise is an intermediate conclusion in the full argument.

The simplest case is when there are only two reasons, the one for a conclusion, the other against it, where these two reasons somehow fit on a single scale. The attractiveness of the law and economics approach is that it provides a scale, that of efficiency, on which many legal reasons fit. The same counts for utilitarianism, which measures everything on the single scale of the maximization of happiness. It may be a reason pleading for the creation of contract law on the level of the EU that there are many contacts between agents in different EU countries. Uniform contract law then leads to less transaction costs and that leads in turn to larger efficiency; at least that is arguable. That would, on the assumption that efficiency is desirable, be a contributory reason for regulation of contract law on the EU level. However, uniform contract law may force many companies to adapt their standard contracts to the new EU law. That is costly and less efficient and therefore a reason against regulation on the EU level. In this example, efficiency constitutes a common scale on which both reasons can be positioned. Moreover, it can, at least in theory, be computed whether the gain in efficiency of the decreasing transaction costs is bigger than the loss in efficiency caused by the necessary modifications of the standard contracts. The outcome of this computation then decides which reason outweighs the other.

Very often, however, such a common scale is lacking, and then the question arises how at first sight very different reasons can be balanced against each other. In this connection the term 'incommensurability' has become popular:[50] reasons that do not fall on a single scale would be incommensurable. In the present author's opinion, incommensurability is not very problematic. Some facts exist without there being any reason for their existence. Why would not the fact that one set of reasons outweighs some other set belong to this category of facts that can exist without a reason?

Interestingly, it is sometimes possible to argue about the relative weight of sets of reasons even if initially there were no reasons why one set of reasons would outweigh another. Precedent plays a role in this connection. If one set was once taken to outweigh another set, this may count as a reason why the 'same' reason also outweighs the 'same' other reason the next time too.[51] In this connection different kinds of a fortiori arguments are possible too.[52] For example, if in the first case there was only one reason why some reason set outweighs another reasons set, in a next case there may even be an additional reason why this is so. Then there are good grounds to assume that also in the next case the first set of reasons outweighs the second set.[53]

9. Comparative Value Judgments

Value judgments do not only deal with the question whether something is good, beautiful, or polite, but also with issues such as which act is better than which other act, or what is the best level to regulate criminal procedure. Such judgments are comparative value judgments and their justification (or the justification of the agent in accepting them) is somewhat more complicated than the justification of 'ordinary' value judgments. As a matter of fact, we already dealt to some extent with comparative value judgments, since the balancing of sets of reasons is an example of something that at least strongly resembles comparative valuation, since the judg-

50 See Chang 1997.

51 'same' is between quotes because reasons are facts and two cases will seldom consist of the same facts. The facts may be of the same kind. For details see Hage 2005, p. 101-134.

52 Details in Hage 2005, p. 101-134.

53 A different example of an *a fortiori* argument will be given in section 9.

ment that one reason set outweighs another set is comparable to the judgment that the former reason set is 'better' than the latter.

Just like with the comparison of reason sets, the easy case for comparative value judgments is when the items which must be compared derive their values from the same scale. One level of regulation is better than another level if the only relevant aspect is the efficiency of the regulations and if the one level is more efficient than the other. If two rules must be compared and they both have only one good making characteristic, namely that they increase the level of employment, the rule that increases the level of employment more is the better rule.

As these two examples illustrate, comparative value judgments can sometimes be based on characteristics which obtain to a larger or lesser degree. The promotion of employment is bigger or smaller; the efficiency of a level of regulation is bigger or smaller; one picture was painted craftier than another and is for that reason better.

However, this easy mode of comparison is often not available because the one item has a different good or bad making characteristic than the other. Incommensurability lurks again. The 'solution' is the same as with balancing reason sets: the determination that one alternative is better than another may merely be a matter of decision making. Once such a decision exists, it functions as a precedent for future comparative value judgments. For instance, if it is was once decided that the efficiency of regulating contract law of the EU level is more important than the autonomy that is promoted by regulating contract law on the level of national states, efficiency will normally be more important than autonomy in a next case too. And, again, a fortiori arguments are possible here too. If one alternative has been found better than another in the past, a similar new alternative that has the good making characteristic to an even bigger degree while its competitor is the same as its predecessor, the new alternative will almost certainly be better than its competitor. For instance, if in a new case the gain in efficiency is even bigger than in the old case in which the efficiency was already decided to be more important than the autonomy, efficiency will a fortiori win out in the new case.[54]

Some value judgments are not concerned with the question what is the better item, but what is the best item. For instance, what is the best level to regulate contract law? These absolute comparative value judgments can be justified by identifying a number of alternatives and by showing that the allegedly best item is better than all of the alternatives in the set. In this connection the argument can be made easier by assuming that the better-than relation is transitive: if item A is better than B and B is better than C, then A is also better than C. There may be exceptions to transitivity, but then the burden of proof is on who wants to make the exception.

The topic 'burden of proof' leads us to the final approach to the justification of value judgments, the procedural one.

54 Details and more examples can be found in Hage 2005, p. 101-134.

10. Procedural Approaches to Justification

The word 'justified' suffers from the process/product ambiguity. It may stand for the 'rightness' of a judgment such as a value judgment or of an agent accepting a judgment or other position. It may also stand for a finished process of justification. If a judge argues in court why she will condemn a suspect to three months imprisonment, she is involved in the procedure of justifying this verdict. After she has successfully finished this procedure, the verdict has been justified. That the verdict was justified in this procedural sense does not tell us anything about the substantial quality of the judgment, about its correctness or legal or moral qualities. It only tells us that the procedure of justification has successfully been brought to an end. However, if this procedure can only be completed successfully if the verdict satisfies certain substantial conditions, there is a connection between the verdict having been procedurally justified and its content being substantially justified (correct).

In this section we will have a closer look at the justification of value judgments by means of a procedure. To have a better understanding of procedural justification in general, we will start with a distinction between three kinds of procedures aimed at gathering 'information' in a very broad sense, including information about what is good, better, or best.

10.1. Pure, Perfect and Imperfect Procedures

To acquire information it is always necessary to follow some procedure. This procedure may involve sensory perception, such as when we look to see something, or listen to hear something. It may also involve reasoning, such as when we multiply 3 and 5 to know the value of the product of these two numbers, or when we hypothetically fill in numbers in order to solve a Sudoku puzzle. More serious examples are the reasoning performed by a judge in order to 'find' the correct outcome of a case, or of a legal scientist who tries to figure out whether contract law is better regulated at the level of national states or at the EU level.

Because the acquisition of information always requires the application of some procedure, it is important to know how the outcome of a procedure relates to the correctness of the information provided by the procedure. In this connection Rawls has made a useful threefold distinction, on the basis of two questions.[55] The first question is whether the correctness of the information provided by the procedure depends on the procedure. A lottery is an example where this is the case. What the winning ticket is depends only on the correct application of the rules of the lottery; there is no independent standard to determine which ticket has won. It will, for instance, not do to argue that the wrong person was pointed out by the drawing, because somebody else needed the money more. Moreover, there is no reason to assume that repeated application of the procedure should lead to the same outcome. Procedures like this, where the proper outcome is defined in terms of a correctly executed procedure, are called 'pure procedures'.

55 Rawls 1972, p. 84-86.

The proper amount of income tax that a citizen should pay is also determined by means of a procedure. In the Netherlands, for instance, the amount of tax to be paid is decided by the tax inspector. However, there are tax rules that determine, at least for standard cases, which amount of tax the inspector should come up with. The procedure of having the tax inspector establish the tax assessment leads, if it is executed perfectly, to the proper amount of taxes. Procedures like this, where the proper outcome is defined independent of any procedure, but where some procedure, if executed well, is guaranteed to lead to the correct outcome, are called 'perfect procedures'. If a perfect procedure is correctly executed more than once, it will always produce the same correct outcome.[56]

There are also procedures that aim to reach an independently existing proper outcome, but where there is no guarantee that the procedure, even if executed perfectly, leads to the correct outcome. A jury trial aimed at determining whether the defendant did what he was accused of is an example of such a procedure. The proper outcome, conviction if and only if the defendant did what he was accused of, is determined independent from the procedure, and the procedure is designed to reach the proper outcome as often as possible, but there is no guarantee that a properly executed criminal trial always leads to the correct outcome. Such procedures, where the proper outcome is defined independent of any procedure, but where the procedure is not guaranteed to lead to the correct outcome, are called 'imperfect procedures'. There is no guarantee that repeated execution of an imperfect procedure leads to the same outcome every time.

10.2. *Single Agent Justification of Value Judgments*

In our discussion of coherentism we have seen that the theoretical ideal of constructing a coherent position set is unrealistic. Human beings are unable to turn their initial incoherent position set into a coherent one. As a potential remedy we considered defeasible coherentism, according to which an agent tries to construct a coherent representative subset of its full position set and determines on the basis of this subset whether a particular value judgment is justified. The feasibility of this approach depends on the possibility to construct a representative subset and the problem in this connection is that it will not be possible to compare the subset with the full set for which it should be representative. A perfect substantive test whether the subset is representative is therefore not possible.

However, it is possible to work with an imperfect procedure. If an agent has sufficient reason[57] to assume that a consistent subset of his full position set leads to a different outcome concerning a particular value judgment than the coherent reconstruction of his full position set, then the agent should not go by the subset in its present state, but revise it until he has no sufficient reason anymore to assume that

56 An exception would be that relevant facts have changed in between the execution of the procedures.

57 The expression 'sufficient reason' is used for the situation that either there is a decisive reason, or that one set of reasons outweighs another set.

the subset is not representative.[58] Then the agent is justified in believing that the subset is representative and in accepting the value judgment on the basis of this subset.

The procedure in this connection is to keep modifying the position subset until it is consistent and the agent has no reason anymore to believe that the subset is not representative. This procedure is imperfect because there is no guarantee that repeated execution of this revision procedure all times leads to the same outcome.[59]

10.3. *Two-Agent Justification of Value Judgments*

An altogether different procedural approach to the justification of value judgments takes dialogs as its starting point. The basic idea is that justification is justification for a particular audience. A value judgment counts as justified if ..., and then there are two possibilities:

- the audience has actually accepted the value judgment as result of the procedure;
- the value judgment logically follows from what the audience has accepted in the course of the procedure.

In the discussion of syllogistic/deductive justification we have seen that the main problem lies in the justification of the premises of a justificatory argument. As soon as the premises are given, the remainder is a matter of logic: does the value judgment logically follow from the accepted premises or not? In first instance (section 5.2) in particular the choice of a standard as starting point for the evaluation appeared to be problematic, since standards are not true or false. However, it turned out that judgments of fact fare little better than standards, since it is not truth or falsity that counts, but acceptance being justified. Acceptance of facts is in this connection not really different from acceptance of standards (section 6.4).

How can procedural justification help to overcome the above foundational problem? By replacing justified premises by premises that were actually accepted in a dialog between the proponent of the value judgment and her audience. Instead of an extensive specification of how that works, the following example may for the present purposes give sufficient insight.

58 Notice that this demand is weaker than the demand that the agent has reason to assume that the subset is representative.

59 That there is no such guarantee has to do with the fact that there is a test to recognize a coherent set, but no procedure for arriving at such a set. This means that it is at least theoretically possible to follow different routes to a coherent position set, and also that these different routes lead to different outcomes, all coherent. That would be problematic if the function of a coherent position set were to represent an independently existing reality. However, that is not its function. Its function is to indicate when an agent is justified in holding the position set he actually holds, and it is very well possible that an agent might be justified in holding different position sets, although not at the same time.

Proponent	Audience	Comments
This was a good soccer match!	Do you think so?	The audience does not accept the value judgment without justification.
Yes, the play was offensive, the players are technically gifted and there was hardly any foul play.	That is all correct, but does it make the match into a good one?	The proponent mentions the facts on which his value judgment is based. The audience accepts these facts, and these are now settled for the dialog. However, the audience has still doubts about the standard that was (implicitly) used.
What more should we expect from a good soccer match?	Well, that Liverpool wins … ;-)	The proponent attempts a shift in the burden of proof: if the audience does not agree with the standard, it should provide (and if necessary justify) a better standard itself. Apparently the audience accepts this shift in the burden of proof, by 'proposing' an alternative standard.
You cannot be serious …	No you are right. Actually your standard is okay.	The proponent casts doubt on the standard proposed by the audience. The audience does not even attempt a justification and accepts the standard originally proposed by the proponent.
So you agree that the match was a good one.	Well, if you insist: yes.	In the end the audience accepts the value judgment which has now been justified. Obviously, the audience could have made the proponent's job much harder by not accepting the shift in the burden of proof and by asking for justifications for everything the proponent claims. If the audience clings to that strategy, the proponent will ultimately loose the dialog because he has the burden of proof.

This is an example of a dialog with rules that give the participants plenty of room. They can, for instance, make fake claims, or they can try to change the dialog rules in the course of the game (shift the burden of proof). The example dialog is purely procedural. Any judgment proposed by the proponent and accepted by the audience counts as justified, no matter whether it is 'really' true. It is also possible to have dialogs which are imperfect procedures that aim to lead only to conclusions that are actually true or justified. That can, for instance, be promoted by disallowing participants in a dialog to accept conclusions that do not follow logically from what has previously been established, or by committing the participants to a set of rules, standards and factual beliefs about which they have no choice (e.g. the rules of positive law and facts that are generally known). As a matter of fact, there are many variants possible.[60]

10.4. *Concluding on Procedural Justification*

It is possible to define many different kinds of procedures and depending on their definitions, these procedures will be pure, perfect, or imperfect. However, they have in common that their outcomes count as justified because they are the outcomes of the procedures. In a sense, judicial procedures as they are used in law are an example of procedural justification. That holds even for value judgments given by judges. If judges are bound by legal rules or standards, judicial procedures are examples of perfect or imperfect procedures. If judges exercise a discretionary power, they are examples of pure procedures.

11. Summary and Conclusions

In the previous sections several variants and aspects of the justification of value judgments have been discussed. Perhaps the main conclusion was that there is nothing special about the justification of value judgments. The fact that their justification will be based on standards which lack a truth value does not raise the complications that are traditionally connected to this use of standards. Not that the complications do not arise; they do. The reason why the justification of value judgments does not differ fundamentally from the justification of other judgments is that the complications arise with all judgments, and not in particular in connection with value judgments. The complications are the result from the impossibility to find an unshakeable foundation on which value or other judgments can be built. There is no such a foundation and the foundationalist approach to justification is doomed to fail.

There exists an alternative for foundationalism, however, and that is coherentism. A judgment is justified, or – better - an agent is justified in accepting a judgment, if this judgment is an element of a coherent position set held by this agent. What coherence amounts to is a topic that deserves an extensive discussion. Above it was only very briefly argued that a position set is coherent if and only if it is comprehensive, consistent and complete. There is no procedure that guarantees to lead to such a coherent position set, and neither is there a guarantee that an agent can only arrive at one coherent position set. This is less problematic than might seem at first sight, since the issue at stake is not any more whether a value judgment is justified, but whether an agent is justified in accepting a value judgment.

Because a coherent position set will normally be infinitely large, there is a guarantee that no human agent will ever arrive at a coherent position set. The alternative for full-blown coherentism is to be satisfied with defeasible coherentism: an agent is justified in accepting a judgment if and only if this judgment is an

60 Examples of elaborated sets of dialogue rules can be found in Gordon 1995 and in Lodder 1999. A general discussion of different kinds of procedural justification is Hage 2005, p. 227-264.

element of a consistent position set of which the agent is justified in believing that it is with regard to this judgment representative for the full coherent position set at which the agent would ideally arrive.

In this connection the development in time of an actually held position set into a coherent position set is an example of a procedure in which the agent is both the proponent and the opponent of all the positions in his position set. The rules in his position set determine how this procedure of updating his position set can correctly take place in time.

Similar rules can guide procedures in which two or more agents develop their ideas about a particular judgment. If such a procedure leads to agreement on a particular judgment, the proponents of this judgment have justified the judgment for the audience consisting of the opponents of this judgment. Noteworthy in this connection is that a third notion of 'being justified' is at stake. It is not anymore the value judgment as such that is justified, nor the agent who is justified in accepting the value judgment. In the procedural approach, the value judgment has been (rather than *is*) justified before a particular audience.

12. Recommendations

In this last section, an attempt will be made to translate the findings of the previous sections into a brief method for setting up an argument that leads to a value judgment about the best level of regulation for European private law. In this connection it is most fruitful to treat the justification of judgments, including all value judgments and all legal judgments, as a procedure in which the proponent of the judgment tries to make his audience accept the judgment that he wants to justify.[61] If this procedure is conducted in a rational fashion, the proponent adduces reasons to convince the audience. The audience counts as being convinced if either it actually accepts the judgment, or is rationally committed to accepting it, e.g. because it follows logically from what the audience has in fact accepted.

The simplest argument is to give a decisive reason for the judgment. Such a reason is a fact that is relevant for accepting the judgment and which makes all counterarguments superfluous. A deductively valid argument would provide such a decisive reason, on the assumption that all the premises are true. The demand that all the premises are true can be weakened to the demand that the audience accepts all the premises. Given that the argument is deductively valid, an audience that accepts al the premises is rationally committed to accepting the conclusion. For example, if the audience agrees that European private law should be created as close to the people as possible and that regulation by national governments is as close to the people as possible, then the conclusion must be that European private law should be created by national governments.

If an audience does not accept one or more of the premises of an argument, these premises can be treated as judgments standing in need of justification, and

61 This is more or less the starting point of the 'pragma-dialectical' approach to argumentation. See Van Eemeren & Grootendorst 2000, p. 57-61.

what is recommended here as general procedure to justify judgments can be applied to these premises too. So, if the audience does not believe that regulation by national governments is as close to the people as possible, then an additional argument should be presented that has this thesis as its conclusion.

Most often a judgment cannot be justified by means of a decisive reason, and then the best possible rational approach is to justify it by means of contributory reasons. The proponent of a judgment has the burden to adduce one or more contributory reasons for the judgment. Any such reason has two components *which need to be made explicit*: an alleged fact, and a standard that declares the fact to be supportive for the judgment. Both the fact and the standard need to be accepted by the audience, and if that is not immediately the case, the proponent has the burden of proof for both the fact and the standard. The same procedure that applies to all judgments also applies for this justification.

For instance, one might argue that European private law should where possible be created by private agents, and present as a reason for this conclusion that the preferences of agents are best satisfied by regulations made by the agents themselves (alleged fact), a reason that is made relevant by the standard that it is the purpose of regulations to satisfy the preferences of the persons to whom these standards apply.

If the audience has accepted one or more contributory reasons for the judgment, it is rationally committed to accepting this judgment, unless it produces counter-reasons. The audience has then the burden of proof for these counter-reasons. Assume for example that an audience accepts that the fact that the preferences of agents are best satisfied by regulations made by the agents themselves is a reason for letting the agents make the regulations themselves. If this audience is not convinced, it has the burden to prove a counter reason. Such a counter reason might, for instance, be that regulation by the national government prevents a race to the bottom.

The same procedure that holds for pro-reasons also holds for counter-reasons. If the audience succeeded in making the proponent accept one or more counter-reasons, the proponent has the burden to convince the audience that the contributory reasons that plead for the judgment outweigh the contributory reasons that plead against it. In this connection the proponent must *explicitly indicate* what the pro- and con-reasons are, and consequently what the required 'weight-premise' involves. Only if the proponent succeeds in making the audience accept this 'weight premise', the audience is rationally committed to accepting the judgment.

For instance, the proponent of regulation by the agents must convince the audience that the reason based on the satisfaction of personal preferences outweighs the reason of the race to the bottom.

If an argument is presented on paper, for instance, in order to convince the readership of a scientific journal, the author takes both the roles of the proponent and of the audience. The author must therefore not only offer reasons of which he assumes that they will convince the readership, but must also critically ask whether these reasons are really convincing, and whether there are (in the eyes of the readership) no reasons pleading against his conclusion. The quality of such an argument depends on how good the author judges his actual readership, and on how serious she takes her task to represent a critical audience in justifying the judgment that she defends.

Bibliography

Aarnio 1987
Aarnio, A., *The Rational as Reasonable. A Treatise on Legal Justification*, Dordrecht: Reidel 1987.

Albert 1980
Albert, H., *Traktat über kritische Vernunft*, Tübingen: Mohr 1980.

Alexy 1983
Alexy, R., *Theorie der juristischen Argumentation* (7e Auflage), Frankfurt a/M: Suhrkamp 1983.

Alvarez 2010
Alvarez, M., *Kinds of Reasons. An Essay in the Philosophy of Action*, Oxford: Oxford University Press 2010.

Araszkiewicz & Šavelka 2013
Araszkiewicz, M. & Šavelka, J. (eds.), *Coherence: Insights from Philosophy, Jurisprudence and Artificial Intelligence*, Dordrecht: Springer 2013.

Ayer 1936
Ayer, A.J., *Language, Truth and Logic*, Harmondsworth: Penguin 1971 (2nd edition; 1st edition 1936).

Bagnoli 2011
Bagnoli, C., 'Constructivism in Metaethics', in: E.N. Zalta (ed.), *The Stanford Encyclopedia of Philosophy* (Winter 2011 edition). URL = <http://plato.stanford.edu/archives/win2011/entries/constructivism-metaethics/>.

Baldwin 2010
Baldwin, T., 'The Open Question Argument', in: J. Skorupski (ed.), *The Routledge Companion to Ethics*, Abingdon: Routledge 2010, p. 286-296.

Blackburn 1993
Blackburn, S., *Essays in Quasi-Realism*, Oxford: Oxford University Press 1993.

Canaris & Larenz 2014
Canaris, C-W. & Larenz, K., *Methodenlehre der Rechtswissenschaft* (4e Auflage), Berlin: Springer 2014.

Chang 1997
Chang, R. (ed.), *Incommensurability, Imcomparability, and Practical Reason*, Cambridge: Harvard University Press 1997.

Dahlman & Feteris 2012
Dahlman, C. & Feteris, E. (eds.), *Legal Argumentation Theory: Cross-Disciplinary Perspectives*, Dordrecht: Springer 2012.

Dworkin 1978
Dworkin, R., *Taking Rights Seriously* (2nd edition), London: Duckworth 1978.

Dworkin 1986
Dworkin, R., *Law's Empire*, London: Fontana 1986.

Feigl & Scriven 1956
Feigl, H. & Scriven, M. (eds.), *Minnesota Studies in the Philosophy of Science* (volume I), Minneapolis: University Of Minnesota Press 1956.

Fuller 1963
Fuller, L.L., *The Morality of Law* (revised edition), New Haven: Yale University Press 1963.

Geach 1956
Geach, P.T., 'Good and Evil', 17 *Analysis*, 1956, p. 33-42.

Ginsberg 1980
Ginsberg, M.L. (ed.), *Readings in Nonmonotonic Logic*, Los Altos: Morgan Kaufmann Publishers 1980.

Golding 2001
Golding, M.P., *Legal Reasoning*, Petersborough: Broadview 2001.

Gordon 1995
Gordon, Th.F., *The Pleadings Game. An Artificial Intelligence Model of procedural Justice*, Dordrecht: Kluwer 1995.

Haack 1978
Haack, S., *Philosophy of Logics*, Cambridge: Cambridge University Press 1978.

Haack 2009
Haack, S., *Evidence and Inquiry. A Pragmatist Reconstruction of Epistemology* (2nd edition), Amherst: Prometheus Books 2009.

Hage 1997
Hage, J.C., *Reasoning with Rules*, Dordrecht: Kluwer 1997.

Hage 2005
Hage, J.C., *Studies in Legal Logic*, Dordrecht: Springer 2005.

Hage 2011
Hage, J.C., 'The Method of a Truly Normative Legal Science', in: M. van Hoecke (ed.), *Methodologies of Legal Research*, Oxford: Hart Publishing 2011, p. 19-44.

Hage 2012a
Hage, J.C., 'Construction or Reconstruction? On the Function of Argumentation in the Law', in: C. Dahlman & E. Feteris (eds.), *Legal Argumentation Theory: Cross-Disciplinary Perspectives*, Dordrecht: Springer 2012, p. 125-144.

Hage 2012b
Hage, J.C., 'Legal Reasoning and the Construction of Law'. 7(16) *i-Lex*, 2012, p. 81-105 (<http://www.i-lex.it/us/previous-issues/volume-7/issue-16/103-legal-reasoning-and-the-construction-of-law.html>.

Hage 2013a
Hage, J.C., 'Three Kinds of Coherentism', in: M. Araszkiewicz & J. Šavelka (eds.), *Coherence: Insights from Philosophy, Jurisprudence and Artificial Intelligence*, Dordrecht: Springer 2013, p. 1-32.

Hage 2013b
Hage, J.C., 'The Deontic Furniture of the World', in: J. Stelmach, B. Brożek & M. Hohol (eds.), *The Normativity of Law*, Kraków: Copernicus Press 2011, p. 73-114.

Hare 1952
Hare, R.M., *The Language of Morals*, Oxford: Oxford University Press 1952.

Hare 1963
Hare, R.M., *Freedom and Reason*, Oxford: Oxford University Press 1963.

Haslett 1995
Haslett, D.W., 'Idealism, philosophical', in: T. Honderich (ed.), *The Oxford Companion to Philosophy*, Oxford: Oxford University Press 1995, p. 860.

Hempel 1966
Hempel, C.G., *Philosophy of Natural Science*, Englewood Cliffs: Prentice Hall 1966.

Honderich 1995
Honderich, T. (ed.), *The Oxford Companion to Philosophy*, Oxford: Oxford University Press 1995.

Jones 1995
Jones, O.R., 'Supervenience', in: T. Honderich (ed.), *The Oxford Companion to Philosophy*, Oxford: Oxford University Press 1995.

Lodder 1999
Lodder, A., *Dialaw. On Legal Justification and Dialogical Models of Argumentation*, Dordrecht: Kluwer 1999.

MacCormick 1978
MaCormick, N., *Legal Reasoning and Legal Theory*, Oxford: University Press 1978.

MacCormick 2005
MacCormick, N., *Rhetoric and the Rule of Law*, Oxford: University Press 2005.

Mill 1861
Mill, J.S., 'Utilitarianism', in: M. Warnock (ed.), *Utilitarianism*, London: Collins 1962, p. 251-321.

Moore 1903
Moore, G.E., *Principia Ethica*, Cambridge: Cambridge University Press 1903.

Peczenik 2008
Peczenik, A., *On Law and Reason* (2nd edition), Dordrecht: Springer 2008.

Pollock & Cruz 1999
Pollock, J.L. & Cruz, J., *Contemporary Theories of Knowledge* (2nd edition), Lanham: Rowman and Littlefield 1999.

Rawls 1972
Rawls, J., *A Theory of Justice*, Oxford: Oxford University Press 1972.

Raz 1975
Raz, J., *Practical Reason and Norms*, London: Hutchinson 1975.

Redondo 1999
Redondo, C., *Reasons for Action and the Law*, Dordrecht: Kluwer 1999.

Reiter 1980
Reiter, R., 'A Logic for Default Reasoning', in: M.L. Ginsberg (ed.), *Readings in Nonmonotonic Logic*, Los Altos: Morgan Kaufmann Publishers 1980, p. 68-93.

Searle 1969
Searle, J., *Speech Acts*, Cambridge: Cambridge University Press 1969.

Sellars 1956
Sellars, W., 'Empiricism and the Philosophy of Mind', in: H. Feigl & M. Scriven (eds.), *Minnesota Studies in the Philosophy of Science* (volume I), Minneapolis: University Of Minnesota Press 1956, p. 253-329.

Skorupski 2010
Skorupski, J. (ed.), *The Routledge Companion to Ethics*, Abingdon: Routledge 2010.

Smits 2012
Smits, J.M., *The Mind and Method of the Legal Academic*, Cheltenham, Edward Elgar 2012.

Sosa 1980
Sosa, E., 'The Raft and the Pyramid: Coherence versus Foundations in the Theory of Knowledge', 5 *Midwest Studies in Philosophy*, 1980, p. 3-25.

Stelmach, Brożek & Hohol 2013
Stelmach, J., Brożek, B. & Hohol, M. (eds.), *The Normativity of Law*, Kraków: Copernicus Press 2011.

Stevenson 1944
Stevenson, C., *Ethics and Language*, New Haven: Yale University Press 1944.

Toulmin 1958
Toulmin, S., *The Uses of Argument*, Cambridge: Cambridge University Press 1958.

Van Eemeren & Grootendorst 2000
Van Eemeren, F.H. & Grootendorst, R., *Kritische discussie*, Amsterdam: Boom 2000.

Warnock 1962
Warnock, M. (ed.), *Utilitarianism*, London: Collins 1962.

Wiarda 1988
Wiarda, G.J., *Drie typen van rechtsvinding* (3rd edition), Zwolle: Tjeenk Willink 1988.

Jan M. Smits

WHO DOES WHAT? ON THE DISTRIBUTION OF COMPETENCES AMONG THE EUROPEAN UNION AND THE MEMBER STATES*

1. Introduction

On 23 January 2013 the British Prime Minister David Cameron gave his much publicized speech on the future of the European Union.[1] Next to the announcement that the United Kingdom will hold a referendum on its membership of the EU,[2] Cameron pleaded for a fundamental debate on the distribution of competences among the European Union and the Member States. The goal of this debate would be 'to examine thoroughly what the EU as a whole should do and should stop doing'. This message did not come as a surprise. Already in September 2012 the UK Foreign and Commonwealth Office had launched a so-called 'review of the balance of competences' on the question to what extent membership of the European Union is beneficial or not to the British national interest.[3] This audit should be completed at the end of 2014.[4]

The United Kingdom does not stand alone in its desire to consider which competences belong where (the 'who does what'-question). In June 2013 the Dutch government headed by Prime Minister Mark Rutte published an 'inventory' of 54 topics that should preferably be dealt with at either the national or the European level, inspired by the motto that things should be dealt with 'European if necessary,

* An amended version of this paper was published in Dutch in (2013) 19 *Nederlands Tijdschrift voor Europees Recht* 213 and in English in Kai Purnhagen & Peter Rott (eds.), *Varieties of European Economic Law and Regulation: Liber Amicorum Hans Micklitz*, Springer 2014, p. 343-358.

1 Cameron 2013. A transcript of the speech is available at <www.gov.uk/government/speeches/eu-speech-at-bloomberg>.

2 A referendum on the question 'Do you think that the United Kingdom should remain a member of the European Union?' should be held after the elections for the House of Commons in 2015 and before 2018. See draft European Union (Referendum) Act 2013 of 14 May 2013.

3 See Secretary of State for Foreign and Commonwealth Affairs 2012. The Review claims: 'Now is the right time to take a critical and constructive look at exactly which competences lie with the EU, which lie with the UK, and whether it works in our national interest.'

4 The 32 reports will become gradually available at <www.gov.uk/review-of-the-balance-of-competences>.

national if possible'.[5] This 'subsidiarity exercise' had been announced as a precursor to a 'common debate in the European Union on the extent to which the current distribution of competences among the EU and national governments is fit for the future'.[6] The leader of one of the main parties in Dutch Parliament had in a previous stage even proposed his own list of competences belonging to The Hague and not to Brussels, including topics as diverse as pregnancy leave, cookie-legislation, procurement of smaller projects and various aspects of environmental law.[7] The list of the Dutch government itself includes, among many other things, insurance of natural and man-made disasters, harmonization of criminal procedure and substantive criminal law, a ban on refillable olive oil jugs in restaurants, school milk and fruit programmes, freedom and pluralism of the media, tunnel safety and gender balance of non-executive directors of companies.

The question of 'who does what' belongs to the most important questions one can ask in multilevel legal orders such as the European Union. It is a question that goes to the root of thinking about not only the foundations of European private law, but also of law in general in a globalizing society. This makes it an excellent topic to be discussed in a *Festschrift* for someone whose work always aims to take up fundamental issues of the transforming European legal order.[8] My starting point in discussing the issue is that the debate on distribution of competences in the EU should not be seen as merely a sign of Euro-scepticism. It would be wrong if the British and Dutch governments have the preconceived view that certain competences surely do not belong at the European level. But this is, unlike the reading of the German and French governments,[9] not my interpretation of these initiatives. Cameron and Rutte seem to aim for an objective assessment of the question at which level a competence belongs. This is confirmed by the first six reports published as part of the British review of competences. These reports are rather positive and generally highlight the benefits of European integration for the UK.[10]

The aim of this contribution is to investigate how viable criteria can be found for the optimal distribution of competences among the EU and the Member States. There is every reason for taking up this question. When the Eurozone crisis was at its peak, both German Chancellor Merkel[11] and President of the European Commis-

5 Letter of Dutch Minister of Foreign Affairs, 21 June 2013, MIN-BUZA-2013.184321; Inventory EU-legislation for subsidiarity and proportionality – Dutch list points of action.

6 Letter of Dutch Prime Minister Rutte and Minister of Foreign Affairs Timmermans of 29 January 2013, DIE-2013.5904.

7 List of Sybrand Buma, MP. See Visser 2013.

8 See e.g. Brownsword, Micklitz *et al.* 2011.

9 German Chancellor Angela Merkel and French President Francois Hollande rejected Cameron's request to participate in the study. See Parker 2013.

10 Review of the Balance of Competences between the United Kingdom and the European Union: report on The Single Market, 2013 ('That integration has brought to the EU, and hence to the UK, in most if not all observers' opinions, appreciable economic benefits'); report on Health, 2013 ('Overall, based on the evidence submitted, stakeholders felt that the current balance of competence between the EU and the UK was considered to be broadly appropriate.'), available at <www.gov.uk/review-of-the-balance-of-competences>.

11 See e.g. 'Germany's Chancellor Merkel urges EU political union,' *BBC News Europe* 7 June 2012.

sion Barroso[12] pleaded, against Cameron, for far-going European integration in the form of a political Union. With so much political dispute on the desired level of integration, it seems highly useful to establish what it is that academia can contribute. This was rightly seen by the Royal Netherlands Academy of Arts and Sciences that, in 2011, published a list of 49 questions that should in the coming years be given priority when doing research. Only two questions were of direct relevance for legal scholars, including the question formulated as 'Will we soon live in the United States of Europe?'[13] The 'who does what'-question seems to come close to this one.

2. State-of-the-Art: Focus on Subsidiarity and Federalism

2.1. *Introduction*

It is generally assumed that the European Union can be best described as a multilevel legal system.[14] With increasing European integration the creation of rules has to a large extent become a shared competence of both national legislatures and the European Union. The national competence to be active in a certain field often overlaps to such an extent with the European competence that only qualifications such as 'fusion' of regulatory levels[15] or 'network governance'[16] still do justice to reality. This is not only caused by a greater significance of 'Europe', but also by increasing assignment of competences to the sub-national, supranational and functional level.

The existing literature concentrates on two main aspects of Europe as a multilevel polity. First, political scientists aim to *describe* the emergence of authority beyond the State and to *explain* it in terms of political theories.[17] Second, legal scholars seek to *classify* the competences as laid down in the European treaties.[18] In addition, they work on how *conflicts* between the different levels of government should be solved in the absence of an overarching institution responsible for ensuring coherence and unity of law – the EU Court of Justice having only limited ability to fulfil this role.[19] The *normative* question of which competences belong at which level of government has thus remained largely uncharted territory. The state-of-the-art on this question can be best described by reference to what legal academics (2.2), economists (2.3) and political scientists (2.4) have to say on this.

12 Barroso 2011.
13 KNAW 2011.
14 See e.g. Hooghe & Marks 2001; Enderlein, Wälti & Zürn 2011; Van Gerven & Lierman 2010.
15 See e.g. Wessels 2005, p. 11.
16 See e.g. De Visser 2009.
17 For an overview: Benz & Zimmer 2010.
18 See De Witte & De Burca 2002, p. 201.
19 Cf., for example, Joerges 2000; Smits 2011, p. 323.

2.2. *The Legal Approach: Distribution of Competences and Subsidiarity*

The 'who does what'-question does not emerge in a traditional view of law, in which the nation-state is the natural *locus* to create rules. The traces of this approach are still visible in European law. Despite the ever-increasing influence of European law on national legal orders, the treaties do not give criteria for the attribution of competences to the European Union. On the one hand, the Treaty on the Functioning of the European Union (TFEU) lists three types of competences: next to exclusive competences (as in the field of customs union and competition: Art. 3), the Treaty mentions shared competences (as in internal market, environment and consumer protection: Art. 4) and supporting competences (such as protection of human health, culture and education: Art. 6). On the other hand, Article 5 of the Treaty on European Union codifies three classic principles of European law. The principle of conferral makes explicit that the EU only has the competences attributed to it by the treaties and that any other competences remain with the Member States. In addition, the exercise of these competences by the Union is governed by the principle of proportionality and, in so far as shared competences are concerned, the principle of subsidiarity.[20] Nothing can be concluded from this about the optimal distribution of competences.

This justifies the conclusion that the underlying reasons for attributing a competence to the European level are highly political.[21] However, the decision of the EU on *how* it decides to exercise its non-exclusive competences is clearly governed by law and in particular by the principles of subsidiarity and proportionality. Under the principle of subsidiarity, the EU shall act only if and in so far as the objectives of the proposed action cannot be sufficiently achieved by the Member States (Art. 5(3) TEU). Yet, in the twenty years since this principle was codified - it was inserted into the Treaty of Maastricht (1992) in order to ease concerns of the Member States about increased powers of the EU - it did not develop into a useful criterion for the vertical distribution of competences. Subsidiarity suggests that decisions are to be taken at the lowest appropriate level of government, but it remains unclear what is 'appropriate'. The EU Protocol on the application of the principles of subsidiarity and proportionality (1997) indicates that subsidiarity is a dynamic concept that should be applied in the light of the objectives set out in the Treaty and that legislation should be enacted 'as closely as possible to the citizens of the Union', but this does not offer much guidance either. Subsidiarity was therefore criticized for not providing an 'effective limit',[22] being 'empty',[23] leading to an 'exercise in speculation',[24] and was even referred to as a 'weasel word'.[25]

The present lack of clarity about the meaning of subsidiarity is also not solved by the Court of Justice of the European Union, which has exercised self-restraint in

20 On all this: Craig & De Búrca 2011, p. 73 *et seq*.
21 In this sense also Bermann 1994; Noam 1982, p. 278.
22 Craig 2011, p. 41.
23 Estella de Noriega 2002.
24 Bermann 1994, p. 335.
25 Easterbrook 1994, p. 125 and 126.

developing practical criteria for the appropriate degree of centralization: although it does exercise a procedural review of the grounds brought forward by the European legislature to justify the proposed measure, it does not see itself as suited to develop substantive criteria.[26] This 'light touch review'[27] by the Court makes it relatively easy for the European Commission to take the initiative for legislative action. It remains to be seen to what extent this will change as a result of the European Commission's Impact Assessment Guidelines,[28] asking to examine for each measure whether European action is justified.[29] With this, the importance of subsidiarity lies primarily in the fact that it forces the European legislature to give reasons for its intended actions and to consider whether other norm-givers would not be better suited to deal with a given problem.

In the context of the so-called 'European Convention' (2002-2003), an extensive debate took place regarding competences in the failed draft European Constitution (2003). The approach was to first identify categories of competences (legislative and non-legislative) and then to assign policy areas to each of these. However, also in the context of this well-documented[30] process, there was no real discussion about the substantive reasons for assigning a certain competence to one of the relevant levels of government. The same can be said of subsequent treaty revisions, including the latest major reforms brought about by the Lisbon Treaty (2009).

The preliminary conclusion is therefore that it is fair to say that at the moment there are no viable substantive legal criteria for the allocation of competences within the European polity. Although the TEU and TFEU succinctly indicate what are the competences of the EU, it remains unclear what are the exact criteria for conferring exclusive competences to the EU and how the subsidiarity principle is to serve as an effective mechanism to allocate concurrent and supporting competences. This raises the question whether these criteria can be derived from other disciplines than the law.

2.3. *The Economic Approach: the 'Economics of Federalism'*

Unlike legal scholars, economists have extensively dealt with the 'who does what'-question. The theory of (fiscal) federalism provides a general normative framework for the assignment of functions to different levels of government. According to this theory, things must be dealt with at a higher level if they create cross-border effects (as with certain types of environmental pollution) or if economies of scale can be achieved.[31] This means, for example, that the central government must take the responsibility for macroeconomic stability and income redistribution through taxes

26 Cf. Case C-84/94 *UK* v *Council* [1996] ECR 1-5755 and Portuese 2011, p. 231.
27 Craig 2011, p. 41.
28 European Commission 2009.
29 The ever-increasing use of impact assessments will surely contribute to a better application of subsidiarity. Cf. Meuwese 2008.
30 Available through <www.european-convention.eu.int/EN/bienvenue/bienvenue2352.html?lang=EN>.
31 Benz & Zimmer 2010.

and for public goods like defence. Lower levels of government must provide goods and services of which the consumption is limited to the own jurisdiction because the efficient level of output of a local public good will vary across jurisdictions.

Several arguments plead in favour of this allocation at the lowest possible level of government.[32] The first is that local governments are closer to their constituency and have therefore better knowledge of the preferences of local people and of other local conditions. Decentralized regulation will thus also allow for better citizen involvement in the democratic process. The second argument is that the central government cannot vary levels of public output across jurisdictions because it is expected to treat everyone as equal, an argument already made by De Tocqueville:[33] the national legislator has to uniformly apply laws, which does not suit the diversity of customs and districts. A third argument is that decentralization provides an effective mechanism for constraining government: competition among decentralized governments can limit monopolist behaviour by the central government and make government more responsive.[34] The legal diversity resulting from this will usually also better facilitate experimentation with innovative solutions.[35]

Despite the importance of these general insights, they do not offer much guidance as to which level of regulation is best for dealing with a certain topic. The conclusion that Kerber[36] reaches on basis of a survey of economic criteria similar to those just discussed, is that the optimal solution depends completely on the specific circumstances: we lack easy and clear answers. In addition, it has always remained controversial whether theories of federalism can be applied to the European context: the European Union is not a federal state and this calls for cautiousness in relying on federalist theories of competence assignment.

2.4. *The Contribution of Political Science*

In so far as the political science literature deals with the assignment of competences, it bases itself on the economics of federalism or on theories of multilevel governance. However, the normative question of the optimal distribution of competences is not a particularly thriving part of academic political science. Taking this scarcity in to account, Scharpf notes that the conceptual tools of political science are ill suited to deal with multilevel interactions.[37] Political scientists working on the European Union usually find the main reason for decentralization in the democratic deficit at the European level, pointing in the direction of making use of national democratic procedures.[38] This is in line with the thesis of Schumacher that 'Small is Beautiful', pointing out that, when designing institutions, it is better to have many small autonomous units combined with a large-scale coordination, than one supra-

32 Oates 2005, p. 349.
33 De Tocqueville 1961.
34 Brennan & Buchanan 1980.
35 Hayek 1968.
36 Kerber 2008, p. 64. See also Van den Bergh 2010, p. 57.
37 Cf. Scharpf 2001, p. 1.
38 See e.g. Salmon 2003, p. 197.

national regulator.[39] However, political science also recognizes that the coordinating and regulatory functions are the most effective if taken up at the EU-level. This inherent tension is difficult to solve in general terms. Benz and Zimmer therefore rightly claim that 'the recommendations for the allocation of competences between nation states and the EU remain rather abstract and rarely refer to particular policies'.[40]

Frey and Eichenberger have sought to replace the territorial allocation of competences by a functional one.[41] In their model of functionally overlapping competing jurisdictions (FOCJ), they assume that the need and demand for public services do not run parallel to the organization of nation-states. They therefore argue that overlapping functional jurisdictions should not only exist, but also ought to compete for the support of citizens. But trading in territorial for functional governance does not necessarily solve the question of how to distribute the relevant competences. Treisman (2007) was therefore able to conclude that political scientists find it 'hard to reach any general conclusion whether (...) decentralization will improve or impair the quality of government or economic performance'.[42]

3. Gaps in Present-Day Scholarship and a Search for Criteria

3.1. *Introduction: Problems of the Present Approach*

The above overview shows that the disciplines of law, economics and political science provide only little information on the optimal distribution of competences within the European polity. The academic focus is on classification of existing (politically established) competences and on explaining shifts from the national to the European level rather than on finding an answer to the assignment question. And in so far as the literature does deal with optimal allocation of competences, it suffers from three major deficiencies.

First, it provides only very general criteria that, if being applied to concrete policy fields, give little guidance or point at best in different directions. The way in which the subsidiarity principle is applied, namely to a large extent as an empty concept only lightly reviewed by the EU Court of Justice, is exemplary. This gives the entire debate about the optimal distribution of competences a highly abstract character. No doubt there are advantages of decentralized law making and a case for central regulation can be made if a measure is to be sufficiently effective or is to address external effects or economies of scale, but this does not tell us much about *when exactly* this is the case. Clearer guidelines are needed to transform the abstract into practical terms.

Second, the available literature does not sufficiently distinguish between different policy fields. It is not likely that the optimal level of decentralization should be the same in fields as divergent as, e.g., consumer protection, financial regulation,

39 Schumacher 1973.
40 Benz & Zimmer 2010, p. 8.
41 Frey & Eichenberger 1999.
42 Treisman 2007, p. 274.

environmental policy and labour law. Each of these fields aims to pursue different goals and it is likely that these goals will shape the optimal distribution of authority. There is therefore little hope of finding new ex ante (top-down) criteria *of a general nature* to delineate European from national competences. This calls for a thorough discussion of assignment in specific fields.[43]

Third, the available theories largely leave open what is to be understood under 'competences', 'government,' 'governance' or 'regulation'. Yet, it is clear that a discussion of which level of decentralization is appropriate for each kind of activity requires a clear view of what the government intervention exactly consists of.[44] This, again, differs from one field to another. While the debate in European consumer law is mainly about methods to achieve a more coherent and more uniform European *acquis* (e.g. by aiming for more maximum harmonization or by creating optional instruments), the discussion in criminal justice focuses on institutions (such as the establishment of a European Public Prosecutor's Office) and in financial services on supervisory mechanisms and the tightening of rules on risky financial transactions. This prompts the need for identifying different dimensions of competence.

3.2. *How to make Progress?*

The above raises the question how to make progress in the search for criteria on an optimal distribution of competences. This is also the question that prime ministers Cameron and Rutte – in my perhaps naïve reading of their plans – will have to ask themselves if they are after an objective assessment of who should do what in the European polity. In this section I will sketch the framework that forms in my view the way forward and that consists of two separate elements.

First, the *existing* distribution of authority among the European Union and the Member States must be mapped in a better way. At present, authority is usually described in terms of the EU-competences as laid down in the European treaties. This may lead to an adequate description in the rare situation in which the EU has exclusive powers (although also in that case the Member States still have a role to play), but reliance on formal texts is certainly not an effective means to describe shared and supporting competences. In these two situations, the treaties do not provide guidance on who does what. This calls for an alternative method to describe the existing distribution of authority, preferably by way of objective indicators that inform us about the extent to which a certain policy field is shaped by European and national sources. A quantitative description could be based on the work of Osterkamp and Eller,[45] who measure the degree of decentralization in a certain field on basis of the sub-national actors' share of total public expenditures in a certain field. This description can be supplemented with a qualitative analysis of the de facto use of authority by the European Union and the Member States. This is not only useful to compare the present situation with the normative findings. It also has

43 Wildason 1996, p. 323; Estella de Noriega 2002.

44 Cf. Van Zeben 2012, p. 22 *et seq.*

45 Osterkamp & Eller 2003, p. 32 *et seq.*

self-standing importance as giving more insight into the actual European influence in some important policy fields.

Second, *normative* criteria for the optimal assignment of competences must be developed for various policy fields. There are two methodological challenges in doing so. The first is that what is 'optimal' always depends on a valuation of the relevant policy goals that one aims to achieve in a certain field. There will always be a tension between, e.g., internalizing externalities or achieving economies of scale on the one hand, and the realization of local preferences or legitimacy through citizen participation on the other. One can reasonably argue about which of these goals is more important in the circumstances of the case. Second, particular objectives may rise and fall in prominence over time, changing economic and social circumstances and changing visions of Europe. Hence, it is far from it that an optimal distribution of competences can be codified for once and for all. However, I do believe that it is possible to develop parameters with which one can work in any field, but that have to be weighed differently in the various policy fields.

These parameters can be found in (i) the *dimensions* of competence, (ii) the *factors* relevant to the assignment of a competence, (iii) the *techniques* to balance these factors against each other and (iv) the *goals* of European integration in the policy field in question. Finally (v), it is important to involve the extent to which it is burdensome to change the existing division of competences (*path dependence*). The interaction between these five parameters provides a flexible framework for optimal distribution. Each of these parameters will now be briefly discussed.

The first parameter consists of the various dimensions of competence. These can be found in rule setting, implementation and enforcement (including supervision). It was already made clear in the above that a clear view of what the government intervention exactly consists of must be an essential element of the discussion on competences.

The second parameter consists of the factors relevant to the assignment of the competences. These 'assignment indicators' are local preferences (in case these are too divergent, there is less room for European intervention), responsiveness (including the extent to which information can be made available to different regulators: if it is difficult for the EU to obtain the necessary information, this calls for regulation at a lower level), the desire to internalize externalities, the capacity of governments at different levels to effectively set, implement and enforce rules, achieving economies of scale, the desire to experiment with different solutions, the risk of a race to the bottom, legitimacy (including citizen participation) and legal-systematic arguments. This last factor is particularly interesting in the field of private law: European influence in this field is often regarded as having adverse effects on the informative value and transparency of the law, prompting the need to avoid fragmentation by a greater role of either the national or the European legislatures and courts.

Third, special attention must be paid to the question of how to balance the various assignment indicators. In traditional views of balancing, it is impossible to do so without a common metric. For example, if the value of experimentation with diverse solutions is to be weighed against the benefits of centralized law making, one would need a common standard that may be difficult to find. However, this does not mean that rational reasoning is impossible. Even if criteria providing a definitive method for resolving conflicts between competing values cannot be found, it is still possible to define the steps that are necessary to reach the optimal outcome.[46] This is likely to lead to a greater coherence of the decision to assign a task to a given level of government.

The fourth parameter concerns the goals of European integration that are to be achieved in the specific policy field. The question of how to balance the assignment indicators ultimately depends on alternative views of the European polity as a whole. It is obvious that a Europe primarily driven by market integration and economic efficiency will weigh the assignment indicators in a different way than a Europe driven by concerns of social justice. Put differently: normative ideas about a legitimate political order will influence the outcome. This calls for relating the question of optimal allocation to different models of the (future development of the) European polity.[47]

The fifth and final parameter concerns the extent to which the existing division of competences stands in the way of achieving an optimal distribution. Even if balancing of the first four factors would lead to the result that existing European competences – after treaty change or renegotiation of regulations and directives – must be 'repatriated', this is not always desirable. Rules of European origin have often become so much part of the national legal order that they are difficult to separate there from. In addition, the mere fact that the European Union would 'give back' a competence does of course not mean that the existing law changes automatically. European legislation, the national implementations thereof and the case law of the EU Court of Justice and national courts remain intact and will have to be amended by legislatures and possibly the courts. This can be expensive[48] and, more importantly, it can be questioned whether the new rules will substantively differ very much from the present law. For example, in the Dutch discussion an oft-mentioned example of a topic that should not be dealt with by the EU is maternity leave. However, Dutch law protects women better than the fourteen weeks that European law offers them.[49] This makes the discussion about competences in this field largely obsolete.

4. Finally: the Academic Challenge

Robust criteria for the distribution of competences in the European Union are needed in order to investigate for different policy fields whether more or less European integration is needed. A lack of criteria tends to lead to unrealistic expectations on what the European Union can achieve. The typical reaction in times of economic crisis is for example to plea for more and deeper integration. Barroso

46 Bengoetxea, Moral Soriano & MacCormick 2001.

47 Jachtenfuchs, Diez & Jung 1998, p. 409.

48 See on this 'path dependence' also De Witte & Thies 2013, p. 23.

49 Directive 92/85 on the introduction of measures to encourage improvements in the safety and health at work of pregnant workers and workers who have recently given birth or are breastfeeding, OJ L 348, 1.

spoke of 'either unite or face irrelevance',[50] while Habermas claimed that 'more Europe' is the only right answer to the Eurocrisis.[51] However, these are highly debatable theses. Transfer of more competences to the EU is not only politically difficult (as the recent example of the Banking Union proves), it is probably also not required. It is not the size of the political community that is decisive for effectively solving a problem, but the extent to which a goal can be achieved in the most effective way.[52] In this respect Cameron is right: in the last few decades, too little thinking was put into the optimal assignment of competences.[53] This contribution is a plea to take this view seriously. The proposed framework for assignment of competences would allow to apply a uniform set of parameters to different policy fields in order to answer the 'who does what'-question. The further elaboration of such a framework should rank high on the academic agenda.

50 Barroso 2011.

51 Habermas 2012, p. 485.

52 Cf. Majone 2012, who mentions 'social and cultural cohesion, clear objectives, and great flexibility'.

53 Cameron 2013: 'Let us not be misled by the fallacy that a deep and workable single market requires everything to be harmonized, to hanker after some unattainable and infinitely level playing field.'

Bibliography

Barroso 2011
Barroso, J.M., 'The Speed of the European Union can no Longer be the Speed of the Most Reluctant Member,' *The Observer*, 13 November 2011.

Bengoetxea, Moral Soriano, & MacCormick 2001
Bengoetxea, J., Moral Soriano, L. & MacCormick, N., 'Integration and Integrity in the Legal Reasoning of the European Court of Justice', in: G. De Búrca & J. Weiler (eds.), *The European Court of Justice*, Oxford: Oxford University Press 2001.

Benz & Zimmer 2010
Benz, A. & Zimmer, C., 'The EU's Competences: the "Vertical" Perspective on the Multilevel System', *Living Reviews in European Governance*, 2010 (5, No. 1), <www.livingreviews.org/lreg-2010-1>.

Bermann 1994
Bermann, G.A., 'Taking Subsidiarity Seriously: Federalism in the European Community and the United States', 94(331) *Columbia Law Review*, 1994, p. 339-343.

Brennan & Buchanan 1980
Brennan, G. & Buchanan, J.M., *The Power to Tax: Analytical Foundations of a Fiscal Constitution*, Cambridge: Cambridge University Press 1980.

Brownsword, Micklitz et al. 2011
Brownsword, R., Micklitz, H. *et al.*, *The Foundations of European Private Law*, Oxford: Hart Publishing 2011.

Cameron 2013
Cameron, D., *EU Speech at Bloomberg*, 2013, available at <www.gov.uk/govern ment/speeches/eu-speech-at-bloomberg>.

Craig 2011
Craig, P., 'Institutions, Power, and Institutional Balance', in: P. Craig & G. De Búrca (eds.), *The Evolution of EU Law* (2nd edition), Oxford: Oxford University Press 2011.

Craig & De Búrca
Craig, P.P. & De Búrca, G., *EU Law: Text, Cases, and Materials* (5th edition), Oxford: Oxford University Press 2011.

De Tocqueville 1961
De Tocqueville, A., *De la démocratie en Amérique* (1835 edition), Paris: Gallimard 1961.

De Visser 2009
De Visser, M., *Network-Based Governance in EC Law*, Oxford: Hart Publishing 2009.

De Witte & De Burca 2002
De Witte, B. & De Burca, G., 'The Delimitation of Powers between the EU and its Member States', in: A. Arnull & D. Wincott (eds.), *Accountability and Legitimacy in the European Union*, Oxford: Oxford University Press 2002, p. 201-222.

De Witte & Thies 2013
De Witte, B. & Thies, A., 'Why choose Europe? The Place of the European Union in the Architecture of International Legal Cooperation', in: S. Blockmans *et al.* (eds.), *The Legal Dimension of Global Governance: What Role for the EU?*, Oxford: Oxford University Press 2013, p. 23-38.

Easterbrook 1994
Easterbrook, F., 'Federalism and European Business Law', 14(2) *International Review of Law and Economics*, 1994, p. 125-132.

Enderlein, Wälti & Zürn 2011
Enderlein, H., Wälti, S. & Zürn, M. (eds.), *Handbook on Multi-level Governance*, Cheltenham: Edward Elgar 2011.

Estella de Noriega 2002
Estella de Noriega, A., *The EU Principle of Subsidiarity and its Critique*, Oxford: Oxford University Press 2002.

European Commission 2009
European Commission, *Impact Assesment Guidelines*, 15 January 2009, SEC, Brussels 2009, 92.

Frey & Eichenberger 1999
Frey, B. & Eichenberger, R., *The New Democratic Federalism for Europe: Functional, Overlapping and Competing Jurisdictions*, Cheltenham: Edward Elgar 1999.

Habermas 2012
Habermas, J., 'Bringing the Integration of Citizens into Line with the Integration of States', 18(4) *European Law Journal*, 2012, p. 485-488.

Hayek 1968
Hayek, F.A., *Der Wettbewerb als Entdeckungsverfahren* (Kieler Vorträge N.S. 56), Kiel: Universität Kiel 1968.

Hooghe & Marks 2001
Hooghe, L. & Marks, G., *Multi-Level Governance and European Integration*, Lanham: Rowman & Littlefield 2001.

Jachtenfuchs, Diez & Jung 1998
Jachtenfuchs, M., Diez, T. & Jung, S., 'Which Europe? Conflicting Models of a Legitimate European Political Order', 4(4) *European Journal of International Relations*, 1998, p. 409-445.

Joerges 2000
Joerges, C., 'Interactive Adjudication in the Europeanisation Process? A Demanding Perspective and a Modest Example', 8(1) *European Review of Private Law*, 2000, p. 1-16.

Kerber 2008
Kerber, W., 'European System of Private Laws: an Economic Perspective', in: F. Cafaggi & H. Muir-Watt (eds.), *Making European Private Law*, Cheltenham: Edward Elgar 2008, p. 64-97.

KNAW 2011
Koninklijke Nederlandse Akademie van Wetenschappen, *Nederlandse wetenschaps-agenda*, Amsterdam: KNAW 2011.

Majone 2012
Majone, G., *Patters of Post-national Europe: the Future of Integration after the Crisis of Monetary Union*, unpublished paper presented at the conference Democracy and Law in Europe, University of Helsinki 27-28 September 2012.

Meuwese 2008
Meuwese, A., *Impact Assessment in European Union Lawmaking*, Alphen aan den Rijn: Kluwer Law International 2008.

Noam 1982
Noam, E., 'The Choice of Governmental Level in Regulation', 35(2) *Kyklos*, 1982, p. 278-291.

Oates 2005
Oates, W.E., 'Toward a Second-Generation Theory of Fiscal Federalism', 12 *International Tax and Public Finance*, 2005, p. 349-374.

Osterkamp & Eller 2003
Osterkamp, R. & Eller, M., 'How Decentralised is Government Activity?', 1 *Journal for Institutional Comparisons*, 2003, p. 32-35.

Parker 2013
Parker, G., 'Cameron Snubbed over Brussels Review', *Financial Times*, 1 April 2013.

Portuese 2011
Portuese, A., 'The Principle of Subsidiarity as a Principle of Economic Efficiency', 17(2) *Columbia Journal of European Law*, 2011, p. 231-262.

Salmon 2003
Salmon, P, 'Assigning Powers in the European Union in the Light of Yardstick Competition among Governments', in: M.J. Holler *et al.* (eds.), *Jahrbuch für Neue Politische Ökonomie*, Tübingen: Mohr Siebeck 2003, p. 197-216.

Scharpf 2001
Scharpf, F.W., 'Notes Towards a Theory of Multilevel Governing in Europe', 24(1), *Scandinavian Political Studies*, 2001, p. 1-26.

Schumacher 1973
Schumacher, E.F., *Small is Beautiful: a Study of Economics as if People Mattered*, London: Blond & Briggs 1973.

Secretary of State for Foreign and Commonwealth Affairs 2012
Secretary of State for Foreign and Commonwealth Affairs, *Review of the Balance of Competences between the United Kingdom and the European Union*, presented to Parliament, July 2012, Cm 8415.

Smits 2011
Smits, J.M., 'Plurality of Sources in European Private Law, or: How to Live with Legal Diversity?, in: R. Brownsword *et al.* (eds.), *The Foundations of European Private Law*, Oxford: Hart Publishing 2011, p. 323-335.

Treisman 2007
Treisman, D., *The Architecture of Government: Rethinking Political Decentralization*, Cambridge: Cambridge University Press 2007.

Van den Bergh 2010
Van den Bergh, R, 'Private Law in a Globalising World: Economic Criteria for Choosing the Optimal Regulatory Level in a Multilevel Government System', in: M. Faure & A. van der Walt (eds.), *Globalization and Private Law*, Cheltenham: Edward Elgar 2010, p. 57-97.

Van Gerven & Lierman 2010
Van Gerven, W. & Lierman, S., *Algemeen deel 40 jaar later*, Antwerpen: Kluwer 2010.

Van Zeben 2012
Van Zeben, J.A.W., *Competence Allocation and Regulatory Functioning: a Study of the European Union Emissions Trading Scheme*, PhD-thesis University of Amsterdam 2012.

Visser 2013
Visser, J., 'Buma: een sterk en zelfbewust Europa weet ook wat het niet moet doen' ('a strong and self-conscious Europe also knows what it must not do'), *De Volkskrant*, 5 February 2013.

Wessels 2005
Wessels, W., 'The Constitutional Treaty: Three Readings from a Fusion Perspective', 43 *Journal of Common Market Studies*, 2005, p. 11-36.

Wildason 1996
Wildason, D., 'Comment on "Fiscal Federalism and Decentralization: A Review of Some Efficiency and Macroeconomic Aspects" by Vito Tanzi', in: M. Bruno & B. Peskovic (eds.), *Annual World Bank Conference on Development Economics*, Washington D.C.: World Bank 1996, p. 323-330.

Jaap Hage

ON WHICH LEVEL SHOULD PRIVATE LAW IN EUROPE BE CREATED?

1. Introduction

One night a man was walking around, stooping and intensively looking at the pavement under his feet. He moved in small circles in the close neighbourhood of the single street lamp that illuminated the otherwise dark alley. A passer-by greeted the man and asked what he was doing 'I am looking for my car keys' the man explained, somewhat to the surprise of the passer-by since the alley was closed for cars. 'Did you lose the keys here?' the passer-by inquired cautiously. 'Oh no', the man replied, 'Not here. In the street over there where cars are allowed.' 'But why are you looking here then?' the passer-by asked, now obviously amazed. 'Because there is no street lamp where I lost my keys' was the reply.

Sometimes it seems as if legal researchers are like the man who looked for his car keys under the street lamp, rather than at the place where he could expect them to be. They search for answers where they are not to be found, because it is too difficult to search where the answer is to be expected. Or, possibly even worse, they look for what they do not need, because what they need is hard to find.

One example is the question what is the best level to create law. Most law is explicitly created, in the shape of statutes, by-laws, treaties, regulations, directives, contracts, last wills etc. This raises the question what the optimal level of regulation for particular topics is. For instance, should the EU determine which taxes are to be raised, or should this decision be taken by national states or by subnational levels such as the Länder of Germany, or even by municipalities? Should the rules that govern business to consumer contracts be established in the contracts themselves, by national legislators, or by the EU? Should traffic rules be given by municipal legislators, or by national legislators? Or should the traffic rules even be determined on a worldwide scale by a specialized body that only deals with traffic matters?

These are evaluative or normative questions, and to answer them it is necessary to apply a relevant standard to facts. Such a standard might, for instance, be that law should be created on the most efficient level, and the relevant facts then concern the efficiency attached to every possible level of regulation. However, efficiency is only one of the many possible standards. A serious discussion about the best level of regulation should also deal with the appropriate standard.[1] If we look at legal research about the proper level of regulation within the European Union, we do not find discussions about the appropriate standards, but an appeal to standards which have as a matter of fact been adopted in the founding treaties, such as proportionality and subsidiarity. Moreover, these standards are not standards for the proper level of regulation, but for the factual question who is competent to make law.[2] This recourse to standards which exist as a matter of legal fact and which do not even address the relevant question can well be explained from the situation that the search for standards that ought to be applied can be very hard, as hard as finding one's car keys at night in a street without lighting. Explainable as it may be, this appeal to existing legal standards is not the right way to go about. Just as it is better to look for one's car keys at the place where they can be expected rather than at the place where the search is easy, it is better to apply the standard that really answers the question what is the best level of regulation, rather than use the standards that happen to be the ones adopted by the positive law. We will find that the lack of relevant information is a serious limitation on our possibilities to answer the question on which level law should be regulated, but the discovery which knowledge we are lacking can at least suggest a research agenda for the future.

2. Methodic Preliminaries

The question what is the best level for creating law asks for a comparison of alternative levels. Since it is not feasible to consider all possible levels of law-making (e.g. an individual person, the head of a family, the main inhabitant of a house, a delegation of inhabitants of a street, a neighbourhood, the city, a province, a state, or a federation, some functional organization such as the Red Cross or the WTO, etc.) it is necessary to single out a limited set of possible levels, and to determine which of these levels is the best one. The difficult question after the best possible level is then replaced by the easier question which level from a limited set is better than the others.[3] This can only work under the presumption that the selected subset includes the best possible level, an assumption that may be false. How should this possibility be dealt with?

2.1. *Default Reasoning and Shifts in the Burden of Proof*

Often it is impossible to prove the correctness of some thesis, while it is still possible to adduce sufficient reasons to make it plausible that the thesis is correct. If one's audience is not prepared to accept the thesis on the basis of the adduced reasons, the burden of proof shifts from the proponent of the thesis to the audience: the audience must produce convincing reasons why the thesis is incorrect despite the reasons that plead for it. If the audience does not succeed in producing these

1 Hage 2015, section 6.1.
2 For example, see Smits 2015.
3 Hage 2015, section 9.

counter-reasons, the thesis counts as justified by default of sufficient counter-reasons.[4]

This style of reasoning in which some thesis is adopted on the basis of convincing, but nevertheless inconclusive evidence is called 'default reasoning', because it is assumed by default that there are no exceptional circumstances which make that the thesis is wrong despite the convincing reasons pleading for it. In actual reasoning situations, default reasoning often goes hand in hand with shifts in the burden of proof. To justify a thesis, the proponent of the thesis has to a produce reasons which are convincing as long as no exceptional circumstances have been proven. The opponent of the thesis, including an audience that is not convinced yet, then has the burden of proof for the exceptional circumstances which would make the thesis incorrect.

If we apply this style of default reasoning to the selection of possible levels of regulation, and focus on the regulation of private law within Europe, it might be assumed that, in the absence of counterevidence, the best level of regulation is one of the following three: the level of the EU, of national states, or of private legal agents. That this might be assumed has more to do with the actual practice than with deep reasons. This reliance on actual practice may be justified by pointing out that the existing practice is the result of a kind of evolutionary process in which worse alternatives have been weeded out. Obviously this is not a decisive argument, but it may be strong enough to shift the burden of proof to those who want to introduce other potential legislators. Notice, moreover, that the likelihood of these three alternatives was brought about by narrowing down the research question to the regulation of private law within Europe. Other ways of narrowing the question down might have led to a different selection of alternatives, for instance, by leaving out private agents.

2.2. *Comparing the Alternatives*

On the presumption that private law in Europe should be regulated on one of the three selected levels, the issue at stake is which of these three levels is the best, that is: better than the other two. Notice that making a preliminary selection has changed the research question from an absolute one ('What is the best level?') to a comparative one ('Which level is better than the two other levels?').

If it is possible, the easiest way to compare alternatives is to measure them on a single scale. If the three alternatives can be positioned on a single scale, running from worst to best, the best alternative can be identified by looking at its position on the scale. Whether this method is available depends on the standard(s) that are used to evaluate the alternatives.[5] In section 3 the utilitarian standard of the maximization of happiness will be defended, and this standard allows, at least in theory, the comparison of the three levels of regulation on a single scale: which level of regulation produces the maximum amount of happiness?

[4] Hage 2015, sections 10.3 and 12.

[5] See Hage 2015, sections 4 and 5.

2.3. *The Relevant Data*

When the relevant standards have been adopted (and justified), these standards determine which data are relevant for the evaluation of the alternatives. Assuming that the utilitarian standard of maximizing happiness is appropriate, the relevant data are easy to point out: for each level of regulation of private law in Europe it should be computed to how much happiness it leads. The level that produces the most happiness is the best one.

As can be seen immediately, it is practically impossible to ascertain which level of regulation produces the highest amount of happiness. There are several reasons for this. It is not easy to measure the happiness of a single person, let alone to quantify this happiness as is required by the demand for the highest total amount of happiness.[6] Moreover, the happiness that will result from regulating law on a particular level may vary from one topic to another topic, depending on a broad and as yet unknown range of different circumstances. One part of these circumstances deserves separate mentioning, namely the development of the world in time. Measuring the happiness that results from a particular level of regulation involves prediction of the future, which is not easy.

In the light of these unsurmountable seeming difficulties, it is tempting to abandon the utilitarian standard and try to determine the best level of regulation in a different way. This temptation should be ignored. There may be reasons to replace the utilitarian standard by one or more different ones, but the difficulty of collecting the relevant data does not belong to these reasons. Remember the story of the man looking for his car keys under the street lamp. That it is difficult to gather the data required for taking a particular kind of decision does not make other kinds of data relevant.

The problem of collecting the relevant data for the application of the utilitarian standard may be huge, but it can be made manageable. One important tool to do so is default reasoning. The standard that happiness should be maximized is too abstract to be applied directly to concrete issues. It must be replaced by more concrete standards that are adapted to specific questions, such as the question on which level to regulate private law in Europe, or even more specific ones. Moreover, these more specific standards should require data that can effectively be collected. And, last but not least, the use of these more specific standards should contribute to the maximization of happiness.

The happiness standard is best seen as a standard to evaluate more concrete standards which are used to evaluate even more concrete standards, and so on until we have arrived at a standard which is sufficiently concrete to be practically applicable. An example of such a chain of ever more concrete standards would be:

- maximize happiness;
- maximize welfare;
- create a really free market;

6 However, see Layard 2003, chapter 2; Dolan & Peasgood 2010, p. 5-31.

- eliminate transaction costs;
- harmonize legal rules.

This chain of more and more concrete standards is only valid if all of the following claims are true:

i. the maximization of welfare leads to the maximization of happiness;
ii. a truly free market leads to (is necessary for) the maximization of welfare;
iii. the elimination of transaction costs leads to (is necessary for) a truly free market;
iv. harmonization of legal rules leads to (is necessary for) the elimination of transaction costs.

Whether these claims are actually true should be determined by means of economic (iii), empirical psychological (i) and sociological (ii, iv) research. In this connection, default reasoning plays a crucial rule, because the findings of these sciences will seldom be definitive. However, that does not exclude that it is possible to reach results on which one can with justification rely to develop a policy. These results are justified as long as counterevidence is lacking.

A large part of the discussion about the proper concrete standards on which value judgements should be based concerns issues that are amenable to, and should therefore be established by means of, empirical research. Such empirical research concerning the standard for the best level of regulation is to the present author's knowledge almost completely lacking.[7] It cannot be replaced by desktop research, unless this desktop research is meta-research about relevant empirical investigations. That does not exclude, however, that the study of literature and other desktop research are relevant for the formulation of hypotheses that can be tested empirically. The sections 4 and 5 deal with such heuristic considerations that can lead to the formulation of hypotheses which ultimately must be tested by empirical research. First, section 3 will explain the ultimate standard that is presupposed in this article, the utilitarian standard that the best act is the one which maximizes happiness.

3. Utilitarianism

Utilitarianism is an ethical theory which has become quite popular since the works of Jeremy Bentham (1748-1832) and John Stuart Mill (1806-1873). Many variants of Utilitarianism are in circulation, and there is no room here to discuss even an important subset of them. Therefore, inevitably, the following account of Utilitarianism is highly eclectic. According to the version of Utilitarianism that is presented here, the best act is the one which maximizes mean happiness.

[7] See also the negative findings of Smits 2015.

3.1. *Consequentialism*

Perhaps the most noteworthy characteristic of Utilitarianism is that it is a consequentialist theory. Acts are evaluated on the basis of their consequences only. The type of the act is in first instance not relevant. For example, an act is not good for the reason that it is polite, but it may be good because it makes some people a little bit more happy. An act is not bad because it is an instance of adultery, but because, and to the extent that, it makes some people less happy.

This does not mean that the kind of act is completely irrelevant. Polite acts tend to make people more happy and therefore politeness is relevant. By default it may be assumed that polite acts lead to more happiness than impolite ones. However, if some polite act under exceptional circumstances decreases the total amount of happiness, this act is wrong. Moreover, there is no reason to balance the politeness against the unhappy consequences, because politeness is only relevant to the extent that it causes happiness.

That Utilitarianism in last instance only has eye for the consequences of acts, and not for the action type under which the act falls is an advantage. It is unclear why the single fact that an act belongs to an action type, independent of the act's consequences, might make the act good or bad.

3.2. *One Intrinsic Value*

Going by its name only, Utilitarianism is in favour of maximizing utility. However, the variant proposed here (and defended by Bentham) recognizes only one kind of utility, namely happiness. Other things such as liberty, equality, wealth, friendship, and all human rights may be useful and valuable too, but they are only useful to the extent that they produce happiness. Happiness is the only intrinsic value; all other values are instrumental. Therefore Utilitarianism aims at the maximization of happiness.

Whether happiness is the only intrinsic value can be tested by means of a thought experiment. Suppose that apart from happiness some other intrinsic value exists, freedom for instance. Then there should be circumstances, at least in theory, where one should sacrifice some happiness in order to gain more freedom. Because then it would be clear that freedom is wanted for its own sake, and not to become happier. It seems likely that those who say that they would sometimes prefer freedom above happiness still expect to be more happy with the freedom than with the 'happiness' that they sacrificed.[8]

Not only human beings can be happy or unhappy; higher animals are, in varying degrees, also amenable to being more or less happy. Therefore the variant of Utilitarianism proposed here does not distinguish between human and non-human bearers of happiness.

[8] This likelihood was not established by me in any scientific fashion, but it is the repeated finding of informally querying students who follow a course on ethics, including Utilitarianism, both in Hasselt (Belgium) and in Maastricht (Netherlands).

In theory it is possible that the maximization of happiness requires a growth in the population which leads to less mean happiness. Then a choice needs to be made between maximum total happiness and maximum mean happiness. The variant of Utilitarianism proposed here opts for maximum mean happiness.

Another choice that needs to be made concerns the time span for which happiness is to be maximized. Given that Utilitarianism only has eye for consequences this time span must start in the present, but the question is how far it continues. The answer is: for eternity. The happiness of future generations should therefore also be taken into account. However, since the effects of acts in the far future are uncertain, their impact on the evaluation of acts in the present is less than the impact of immediate and highly certain consequences. The farther in the future, the more uncertain the effects and the less impact they have on the evaluation of present acts. Possible effects in the very far future, which are therefore highly uncertain, are to be discounted so strongly that they can be ignored for practical purposes.

3.3. *Aggregation*

Possibly the most controversial aspect of Utilitarianism is that it aims at the maximization of happiness as aggregated over all bearers of happiness. This means that less happiness in one individual can be 'compensated' by more happiness in another individual. In this connection each individual counts equally. Nobody's happiness is more important than the happiness of somebody else.

Many object against this characteristic of Utilitarianism, stating that it is wrong to sacrifice (the interests, or rights of) one individual to (the interests of) another individual.[9] The obvious reply asks whether the latter individual should then be sacrificed to the former. For instance, should the social security of the poor and disadvantaged be sacrificed to the property rights of the rich? Should the properties of innocent citizens be sacrificed to the liberty of the thieves? Obviously, these rhetoric questions cannot decide the issue about the desirability of Utilitarianism, but neither can the rhetoric questions whether we should allow torturing possible terrorists to increase society's security, or whether (almost) everybody in a rich society should give more than half of his money to poor people in as yet underdeveloped countries. These are complicated issues, but if Utilitarianism is correct, the ultimate standard for answering them is the maximization of average happiness on the long run.

3.4. *Practical Implications*

Utilitarianism is much too abstract to function as a standard by means of which actual acts can be evaluated. As pointed out above, we need concrete standards that are pinpointed to specific domains, which require data that can be obtained without too much trouble. The point of Utilitarianism is that *in the end* all these more con-

9 A prominent example is Rawls 1972 that can be read as an extended argument why Utilitarianism is wrong for this very reason.

crete standards should be valuable in the sense that their application leads to more happiness. The value of Utilitarianism does not lie in its immediate practical applicability but in its function as basis for all concrete standards and as a pointer to the kind of data that we need to assess these more practical standards.

An important advantage of Utilitarianism that was not mentioned before is that it provides a common yardstick against which all standards, but in theory also all acts can be measured. Moreover, it allows comparison of alternatives, because Utilitarianism recognizes only one intrinsic value. There are no trade-offs to be made. In last instance only one question needs to be answered: what maximizes average happiness in the long run? Incommensurability does not play any role, because all concrete standards and all acts are commensurable.[10] Of course, the lack of relevant data is an important problem in this connection, but that is a problem which can at least in theory be solved by means of empirical research.

Utilitarianism and concrete standards that are based upon it apply to all acts, including legislative acts. A legislative act is good if it increases the average amount of happiness, and the best legislative act is the one which produces most happiness. Three things should be noted in this connection. First, the legislative act that produces most happiness may still be suboptimal, because abstaining from legislation, perhaps in combination with alternative measures, may be still better.

Second, a legislative act should not be identified with the rules that are produced by means of it. An act of legislation may be good even it produces a bad rule, for instance, because the legislation proves to the public at large that the legislator is concerned with a particular problem. ('The government is doing something about this problem.')

Third, there are good and bad making characteristics of a legislative act which are not necessarily connected to the rules that are produced by means of it. The central topic of this article illustrates this point, because it concerns the *level* of legislation, not the content. Level and content may be connected, but they are different issues. It may, for example, be argued that contract law should as much as possible be regulated by the contract parties, because this allows for maximum autonomy in a field (contracts) in which autonomy is very valuable (leads to more happiness). This autonomy-based argument does not necessarily have anything to do with the quality of the contractual rules made by the parties.

4. The Best Rules

After having adopted, at least for the purpose of this article, Utilitarianism as the ultimate standard at the hand of which more concrete standards must be evaluated, it is time to take a look at the reasons why private law in Europe should be created at the level of the EU, at the level of national states, or at the level of private legal subjects. There are at least two kind of reasons that are relevant for determining the best level of regulation. One kind has to do with the content of the rules that are being created. The assumption here is that if some level produces better rules than

10 Cf. Hage 2015, section 8.3.

some other level, this is a reason why the former level should make the rules. The reasons based on the quality of the produced rules are discussed in the present section.

The other kind of reasons has to do with the authority, or - maybe better - autonomy, of the rule producing agent. The assumption underlying this kind of reasons is that some agents are somehow entitled to make rules, by and large independent of the quality of the rules they produce. The most familiar candidate in this connection is nowadays that agents should legislate for themselves (autonomy), and that nobody should be subjected to somebody else's rules. These reasons are the subject of section 5.

4.1. *What are the Best Rules?*

If we only want to consider the possibility that rules should be created by the agent who produces the best rules, we should have some clarity about what the best rules are. Does the question what the best rules are have an objective answer, if only objective in the sense that it reflects the will or the interests (not necessarily the same!) of the people who are affected by the rules? Or is it merely a matter of taste what the best rules are, and even whether some particular rule is better than another rule? If it is merely a matter of taste, it makes little sense to point out a rule-making agent for the reason that this agent would make the best rules.

Having adopted the happiness criterion as the ultimate standard for evaluating acts, including decisions with which rules to organize society, the answer to the question what the best rules are is objective. It is not merely a matter of taste which rules create most happiness, although the objective answer to the question what these rules are may depend, amongst others, on the tastes or preferences of people.

Even if the question after the best rules has an objective answer, this answer is hard to establish. Therefore an important factor in determining what the right level of regulation is, is which agent has the best knowledge. This factor will be discussed in section 4.2. Even if an agent knows what the best rules are, it may be unwilling to create those rules, for instance, because it has an interest in creating other rules. Here the phenomenon of 'externalities' plays a role. Externalities and the way to deal with them are discussed briefly in section 4.3. A third important factor has to do with the phenomenon that rules are not individually good or bad, but as a set. A rule is a good rule if it belongs to a set of rules which as a whole is good. The implications of this phenomenon are the subject of section 4.4. The final factor that will be discussed (in section 4.5) is that the quality of rules may depend on the scope of their application. Some issues should be regulated for large territories; for other issues this is not necessary or even desirable.

4.2. *Expertise*

In order to make the best possible rules, it is important to know what the best possible rules are. Given the standard of happiness, a rule is the better, the more happiness it produces. The quality of a rule depends therefore on its effects. These effects are not only determined by the content of the rule, but also by the circumstances under which the rule must function. Part of these circumstances are factual ones, such as demographic, geographical and economic circumstances. It is well imaginable that if these circumstances are different in different regions, the best rules for one region, the rules which maximize happiness there, may differ from the best rules for another region.

At first sight the phenomenon that the best rules for one region may differ from the best rules for another region suggests that the rules for which this holds should be made regionally, with as extreme case rules that only apply to contract partners and which should therefore be made by the partners themselves. However, it would be too hasty to draw this conclusion in general, because there is no reason why the relevant knowledge should only be available to local law-makers. Take, for instance, rules about marriage. Perhaps the Italian culture differs sufficiently from the Swedish culture to justify different rules for Italy and Sweden. Does this mean that the rules for Italy should be made in Italy and those for Sweden in Sweden because the relevant information about a country is only available in that country? Not at all![11] There is no reason why the reports that are used for the preparation of legislation in some European country should not be made available to, for instance, the European Commission. There may be some lower boundaries on the available legislative staff to allow for the necessary diffusion of knowledge, but as long as those are respected,[12] the availability of knowledge is no reason to regulate a subject on one level, rather than another level.

On the contrary, from the perspective of available expertise there are good reasons to regulate many subjects as central as possible because the prediction of the effects of regulation requires highly specialized knowledge. The more and the better the staff that is available to collect this knowledge, the better the prospects for good rules. If the EU is sufficiently funded, it seems more likely that the required expertise can be developed on a central level, eventually assisted by local representatives, than on the level of national states.

The above plea for centralized legislation does not apply to rules which only affect a few agents, such as rules in many contracts. For most individually negotiated contracts it holds that the rules affect mostly or even only the contract partners and that these partners have better knowledge of the involved interests than anybody else. From the perspective of expertise, this pleads for leaving the determination of the consequences of contracts to the contract partners. However, if contracts are not individually negotiated, there may be reason to have their content – or relevant mandatory law – determined on a more central level.

11 Remember that we are considering only one reason (expertise) to legislate locally, rather than globally. There may be other reasons, for instance, based on autonomy. These reasons will be discussed in section 5.

12 These boundaries would not be respected if private persons would be the law-makers, as they are in contracts.

4.3. *Externalities*

Even if an agent knows what the best rules are, there is no guarantee that it will create these rules. If we ignore the possibility of malevolence, the creation of 'wrong' rules may be the result of externalities. Externalities are effects of acts on interests which are not the interests of the agent, and which therefore run the risk of not being taken into account by the agent. The best rules promote overall happiness, but not necessarily the maximum amount of happiness for the law-creating agent or the persons it feels responsible for. Even if a national legislator promotes the happiness of the inhabitants of the state, it may ignore the from an utilitarian point of view equally important happiness of non-inhabitants. Contract partners are prone to ignore other interests than their own. Functional legislators, such as, for instance, water boards, may not take other interests than those connected to their functions sufficiently into account.

One solution to this problem of externalities is to make sure that they are 'internalized', that they also become interests of the agent and are consequently being taken into account in deciding which acts to perform. The fact that an agent has internalized possible externalities may be a reason, not necessarily a conclusive one, to point out this agent as the proper level of legislation.

Another solution is to make sure that there are as few externalities as possible by having a rule-making agent who feels responsible for as many as possible potential bearers of happiness. Although it is theoretically possible that national legislators or even private persons take everybody's happiness into account, it is more likely that central legislators, such as the EU, have eye for everybody's happiness. The desire to limit the amount of externalities provides a contributory (prima facie) reason why the creation of law should be centralized.

4.4. *Coherence*

Legal rules do not operate in a vacuum. They are part of a system of rules and the effects of individual rules combine with the effects of other rules, and it is this combined effect that affects the happiness of persons. Therefore it is undesirable to study the effects of isolated rules, unless there are good reasons to assume that these effects are not influenced by the effects of other rules. Legal rules should cohere, work together, and the best rules are those which are elements of the best sets of rules.

The desirability of coherent rules impacts the best level of regulation, at least if it is assumed that rules created by a single legislator are prone to be more coherent than rules stemming from different legislators. An example is the regulation of security property rights. These rules function within a setting of other rules on legal procedure, obligations, and redress. If these other rules are created on the national level and the rules about security property rights were to be created on the European level, the chances are real that at least in some national states the total set of rules becomes incoherent.

The desirability of coherent law may therefore provide us with a reason for having related rules made on the same level. In the case of property security rights that might be the national level, but it might also be the level of the EU.

4.5. *Scope of Rules*

Rules have scopes that determine, in combination with the rule conditions, on which territory, to which persons, and during which time frame the rules can be applied. International private law determines the scope of rules of private law. The different national systems of criminal law determine to which crimes and to which suspects the rules of these systems apply. Most rules of constitutional law apply to the governmental agencies of a particular country only, but the human rights provisions of constitutional law tend to have a wider scope of application. Laws that are connected to a religion, such as Talmudic law and the Shari'a apply normally to adherents of these religions, while canon law applies to cases which somehow concern the Roman Catholic church.

For our present purposes, the territorial scope of a rule is the most relevant type of scope. It is usually, but not necessarily, determined by the body that created the rule. A national legislator makes rules that can apply to cases within the territory of the national state; rules created by provinces and municipalities can apply to cases within the provinces, respectively the municipalities. Regulations created by the EU apply within the EU Member States (Art. 288 TFEU) and there is little reason to assume that this is different for directives which are applied directly to citizens and non-state organizations within the EU. In general, rules with a wider territorial scope prevail in case of a conflict over rules with a smaller scope. EU-law prevails over the law of the EU Member States (CJEU C-6/64; *Costa* v *Enel*), national law normally prevails over the law of subnational government agencies such as provinces and municipalities, and the mandatory rules of state law normally prevail over law made by private law makers such as contracts and by-laws, unless the state law has determined otherwise.

As a consequence the level on which law has been be created is determines to a large extent the territorial scope of rules, and therefore also the degree of uniformity of the way in which a topic is regulated in a larger territory. If the rules on a particular topic are created on a central level, with a large territorial scope, the way in which this topic is regulated will in principle[13] be the same over the broad territorial scope of the regulation. If, on the contrary, rules on a topic are created on a highly decentralized level (e.g. contract partners) then the way in which the topic is regulated will normally be highly diverse.

Because circumstances vary from one person to another, from one municipality to another, and from one country to another, the best rules may be different

[13] This may be different for open-ended rules, because their effect may depend on local circumstances, such as customs and legitimate expectations. Moreover, although it is not usual, it is not in principal impossible that a national law maker creates rules that only apply in a particular region of a country, or that a supranational body creates rules that only apply in one particular state.

from one unit to another. This may be a reason to make rules that are adapted to the local circumstances and, assuming an automatic 'translation' from the scope of the rule to the level of regulation, therefore also a reason to make rules on decentralized level.

Obvious as this may be, there is still a major complication, namely that the size of the units is not something given. What should we take as the units when it comes to deciding whether the rules of one unit should differ from those of another unit? It is tempting to think in terms of states, because for historical reasons those are seen as the bearers of sovereignty. If we set aside these historical contingencies, states are not a priori in an advantaged position relative to sub-states (*Länder*; *gewesten*; *Kantons*), districts, provinces, municipalities, families, or individual persons. One street differs from another street. Should this be a reason why every street should have its own rules, and that therefore at least some rules should be made on the level of streets? There are no two persons who are in exactly the same position. Is this a reason to let every person make his own rules? Obviously not, but the difference between persons is at least a reason for personal autonomy which must be outweighed by other reasons if autonomy is not to decide the issue about the level of regulation.

The main reason for having uniform rules is also a reason for having rules in the first place. Following Westerman[14] it is possible to distinguish between the guiding, the coordinative, the predictive, the evaluative and the institutional function of rules. In their guiding function, rules assist people in deciding what to do. They facilitate the decision making procedure by limiting the amount of possible choices.

In their coordinative function, rules make it possible for agents to coordinate their behaviour. For instance, the owner of a good expects that others will not damage it, while the others will not damage the good because as non-owners they are not allowed to do so.

In their predictive function, rules enable people to predict the behaviour of others. This makes it possible for a landlord to invest money in a house, because he can predict that the lessor will pay the rent.

In their evaluative function, rules make it possible to evaluate or justify behaviour after it was performed. Damaging a good that belongs to somebody else will be evaluated as unlawful, while a landowner will normally be justified in removing buildings that were erected on her land by somebody else without permission.

In their institutional function, finally, rules aim to secure that a particular state of affairs will be accomplished. For instance, car producers must make sure that their cars satisfy a particular safety standard.

In particular in their coordinative, predictive and evaluative functions, rules deal with the relations between different agents; these three functions concern the interaction between persons or organizations. Let us therefore call these three functions the interaction functions of rules.

14 Westerman 2012, p. 720-728. In translating Westerman's expressions into English the terminology was slightly changed.

Rules cannot fulfil their interaction functions well if the group of people within which they function is too small. Take as an extreme example a rule that tells car drivers to drive on the right. If this rule only holds for two car drivers, or only for the drivers in a tiny village, it will hardly function unless there are no other car drivers, or the village is not visited by drivers from outside. The bigger the group of people who use this rule to guide their own behaviour, but also to predict the behaviour of others, the better the rule can fulfil its interaction functions. Since a wider territorial scope normally means a bigger set of people who use the rule, the interaction functions of rules plead for a scope that is as wide as possible. And, assuming again a translation from the scope of rules to the level of regulation, the interaction function also pleads for central regulation.

Transaction costs provide still another reason for a wide scope of rule application and therefore for central regulation. The smaller the territorial scope of rules, the more often legal actors will have to deal with other rules than the ones they are accustomed too. This leads to transaction costs which make that transactions which would have been economically viable without these costs lose their viability. This is an economic loss and in the end normally also a loss in welfare, and - on the assumption that welfare increases happiness - a loss of happiness.

5. Autonomy

In section 4 we looked at the desirable level of rule production in the light of the quality of the rules produced. A completely different approach is possible, though. This approach does not focus on the quality of law, but on the authority of the law creating agent. The question is not so much who will make the best law, but who is entitled to make law: who is to decide? This question who is entitled to decide seemingly does not make much sense from the utilitarian point of view, because it apparently ignores the consequences of the level on which law is created. The focus is completely on the type of the act, rule creation by agent A, instead of its consequences.

Completely disregarding this authority-based approach would be a bridge too far, however. Several centuries ago Rousseau[15] pleaded for autonomy of the people which would be free if it obeyed its own rules. The underlying assumption here is that it is good for people to be free, or - cast in utilitarian terminology - that being free makes people happy. There is certainly something to be said for this view: most people like to be free, and lack of freedom may cause unhappiness.

However, in its extreme version this view leads to autonomy for every single person. This extreme version is unattractive if only because it completely ignores the interaction functions of rules. Also the less extreme version that pleads for autonomy of a people, rather than of individual persons, has its drawbacks. The fact that a people wants something is insufficient proof that it is also good for the people. Because of false beliefs and irrational attitudes, people often want things that are not good for them. In those cases, following the will of people is not the best

15 Rousseau 1797.

way to further their interests, or – to stay in the utilitarian framework – to promote happiness. Giving people what they want is a good idea if people tend to want what makes them happy in the long run, or if they are at least better judges of what will make them happy than the agent that would otherwise make the rules for them. At this point, the argument from autonomy has merged with the argument from expertise that was discussed above (section 4.2).

6. Side-Constraints and Transition

The argument thus far may have stricken some readers as highly theoretical. It hardly mentioned the EU-oriented setting within which the actual discussion about the best level of regulation takes place, and neither does it pay attention to the practical implications if some field of law will have to be regulated by a rule creating agent which is allegedly 'better', but which is not the same as the agent that actually creates the law in this field. Can such a theoretical argument have any practical relevance?

It can, because it is useful to know which ideal to strive for, even if there is no guarantee that it can actually be achieved. Even unachievable ideals can indicate into which direction the actual situation should be developed. However, the relevance of ideals is heightened if attention is paid to side-constraints and to transition. Side-constraints are limits on the number of alternatives that are considered in deciding what is the best course of action, or – in our present discussion – what is the best level of rule creation. In a sense, the above argument made use of side-constraints by limiting the alternatives to three levels of rule creation: the EU, national states and private agents. The reason behind this limitation was that these three are the most likely alternatives given the actual legal practice. However, the actual practice was not taken at face-value, but merely as an indication of the alternatives that should by default be taken as the relevant ones. It is still possible to present reasons for making additions to the list of alternatives that should be taken into account.

Whether this approach, in which the number of alternatives is limited by default, is the right one depends on the kind of enquiry one is engaged in. If this enquiry is from the beginning limited to the alternatives that are available within the framework of actual positive law, a different list should be considered than if the enquiry aims at finding the best level of rule creation in general. For scientists the latter enquiry seems more appropriate than the former; for politicians it is probably the other way round.

There are at least two ways to approach a society in which the average amount of happiness is maximal. The one, implicitly adopted above, is to sketch an ideal situation, or the ideal answer to a particular question, from scratch, and then try to change the current situation into the direction of the ideal. The other approach takes the current situation as its starting point and aims at making continuous improvements that increase the amount of happiness. Both approaches to deal with the transition from the current situation to a hopefully better one have their advantages and disadvantages. Starting from scratch opens one's eyes for what is theoretical possible and allows to take a step backward in order to take a different road which is better suited to reach the ideal (avoidance of local optima). It has the disadvantage that it easily leads to 'daydreaming' and underestimating the constraints that are imposed by what is actually the case. Starting from the actual situation has the corresponding advantages and disadvantages: the risk of being unrealistic concerning what is practically manageable is minimized, but at the cost of possibly losing sight on what might be reached because the complications of the actual situation blind one's view.

Utilitarianism offers, at least in theory, a solution for this dilemma, because it aims at maximizing happiness in the long run, with a probability discount for future happiness. Any project that moves from one way to organize society to a different way brings costs with it, costs which can in the end be expressed in terms of (a loss of) happiness. These costs are justified by the increase in happiness that results from having the better organization, but only if the costs of change are not too high in comparison to what is to be gained. The happiness calculus does not only provide us with a tool to compare future states of affairs, but also to compare courses of change. As sketched above (section 2), comparative reasoning demands that some alternative courses of change are preliminary selected and that the happiness effects of these courses are calculated. The usual problem of lack of relevant data will present itself, and the usual way to deal with this problem - search for default solutions - will be appropriate.

Which courses of possible change in the current situation concerning the level of rule creation should by default be considered, and which possible solution should be default be adopted are questions beyond the scope of this contribution. The important finding that remains is that the question what is the best level to create law should be replaced by the question what is the best course of transition from the current situation to some better situation.

7. Summary

What is the best level to create law? Ideally we should now be able to answer this question, but our investigations so far have mainly made it clear how much information that is required to answer this question is still lacking. And - perhaps more surprising - it has also made clear that the research question that underlies the present contribution was wrongly formulated from the beginning. It should not have been what is the best level to create law, but what is the best course of transition toward a situation in which the level of law creation is handled appropriately.

That the relevant information is still lacking could only be established in the light of an evaluative standard at the hand of which the question after the appropriate level of rule creation is to be answered. In this contribution the utilitarian standard that happiness should be maximized was more or less taken for granted. Given this standard, the relevant information concerns *in last instance* what makes people happy and what are the consequences, including the future consequences, of creating law on a particular level. Noteworthy in this connection is that for practical reasoning purposes the happiness standard should be replaced by more concrete standards that are pinpointed towards specific issues and which require data that can relatively easily be obtained. The role of the utilitarian standard is then confined to the justification of these more concrete standards.

Since the lack of much relevant information made it impossible to deal with very concrete issues in connection with rule creation, the main line of the argument had to remain rather abstract. Five factors were identified as relevant for the best level of regulation: the availability of expertise, the willingness to use this expertise to make the rules that maximize overall happiness rather than further the interests of special groups (no externalities), the coherence of the rules that result from the rule creating process, the scope of the rules that are being created, and the actual situation concerning the level on which law is being created. The relevance of the actual situation occasioned the change in the question that was to be answered.

It should be emphasized that these findings are only a first step on the road to a satisfactory theory on the best level of creating law. The more important findings are that our present insights are no more than a starting point for the formulation of hypotheses that can be tested empirically and that the agenda for legally relevant research should contain questions that can to a large extent be answered by empirical research.

8. Comparison

It may be worthwhile to compare the results of the present contribution with those of Smits, who raises the question 'how viable criteria can be found for the optimal distribution of competences among the EU and the member states'.[16] In this connection Smits limits the number of alternative levels of law creation to two levels that were also taken into account in the present contribution. The level of law creation by private agents is ignored, presumably because that level does not play a role in the present discussion about the division of competences within Europe.

It is noteworthy that Smits does not focus on the best distribution of competences, but on 'viable' criteria for the optimal distribution of competences. This formulation suggests that what Smits is after consists of the 'concrete', or 'more specific' standards mentioned above (section 2.3). The present contribution mentioned in this connection three factors, namely whether the standard

- is sufficiently pinpointed to the rule creating act;
- requires data that can relatively easily by acquired;
- is justified in the light of the utilitarian demand that happiness should be maximized.

8.1. Arguments from the Existing Literature

Smits' introduction is mainly devoted to stage setting, to illustrate that the central research question does not only have scientific significance, but also addresses a 'hot' issue. After this introduction Smits first points out that the existing literature

16 Smits 2015.

on competences hardly deals with the normative question of which competences belong at which level of government. He points out that political scientists aim to describe and to explain the emergence of authority beyond the state, and that legal scientists seek to classify the competences and try to answer the question how conflicts between the different levels of government should be solved, and arrives at the conclusion that these sciences have little to say about his research question.

This is different for the economic approach. Smits points out that the theory of (fiscal) federalism provides a general normative framework for the assignment of functions to different levels of government. The finding is that 'things must be dealt with at a higher level if they create cross-border effects ... or if economics of scale can be achieved'. This result seems related to the finding of the present contribution that the avoidance of externalities and the coordination function of rules (may) plead for central regulation.

A further result would be that 'Lower levels of government must provide goods and services of which the consumption is limited to the own jurisdiction because the efficient level of output of a public good will vary across jurisdictions.' This argument was discussed in section 4.2, where the outcome was that it would be too hasty to draw the conclusion that rules should be made regionally if the best rule for one region might differ from the best rule for another region. There is no automatic translation from a difference in rules to a difference in rule makers.

Another 'economic' argument pleading for local government would be that local governments have better knowledge of the preferences of local people and of the local conditions. Apart from the fact that local preferences should according to Utilitarianism not automatically determine what the best rules are, it was found above (section 4.2) that there is no deep reason why knowledge about local circumstances should be better available to local governments.

The economic argument for local government that a central government cannot vary levels of public output across jurisdictions because it is expected to treat everyone as equal is not convincing. Unequal cases should be treated unequally. The issue is which inequalities should be taken into account and in what manner.

The economic argument that local government leads to competition between governments and thereby to limitation of monopolist behaviour by the central government may be true, but local government may also lead to competition which in extreme cases may amount to war. It depends on the circumstances which reason is the strongest. What seems to be lacking in this discussion is a clear higher level criterion at the hand of which sub-criteria such as balance of powers and avoidance of war can be measured. Utilitarianism provides such a higher level criterion.

Having mentioned the economic arguments, Smits concludes that the general insights do not offer much guidance because the optimal solution depends completely on the specific circumstances.

8.2. *Parameters*

Having found that existing political, legal and economic science is not very helpful for answering his research question. Smits continues to develop his own research agenda. He distinguishes two elements: mapping the existing distribution of authority among the EU and the Member States, and developing normative criteria for the optimal assignment of competences for various policy fields. This first element is important because knowledge about the legal status quo is relevant for the comparison of transition courses (cf. section 6 above).

The development of normative criteria is exactly what Smits' research question asked for and the section of his contribution devoted to this topic (most of section 3.2) may therefore be branded as the core of his paper. Smits identifies two methodological challenges in this connection. The one is the dependence of what is optimal on '... valuation of the relevant policy arguments that one aims to achieve in a certain field'. And, Smith continues, one can reasonably argue about which goals are more important in the circumstances of the case. Actually, there are two issues at stake here:

- it must be determined which goals should play a role in determining the best level of regulation; and
- the relative importance of these goals must be established.

In the present paper, the adoption of the utilitarian standard determines how these two questions should be answered. Smits does not adopt that approach, but nevertheless mentions five 'parameters' that are relevant for the optimal assignment of competences. One parameter, called 'dimension', is whether the competence concerns rule setting, implementation or enforcement.

The second parameter actually consists of nine sub-parameters which mention factors that are relevant for the assignment of competences. These factors are local preferences, responsiveness, the desire to internalize externalities, the capacity of governments at different levels to effectively set, implement and enforce rules, achieving economies of scale, the desire to experiment with different solutions, the risk of a race to the bottom, legitimacy, and legal-systematic arguments. These factors sound plausible, but what is lacking is a general view of what makes them relevant. Lacking such a more general view, it is difficult to determine whether the list is complete, and what might be possible other candidates if the list is not complete. Moreover, it is unlikely that all these sub-parameters are relevant for all different cases, and lacking a more general view, there is no criterion for determining what makes a factor relevant. Smits' list is useful to get an impression of factors that might be relevant, but it also makes clear why a general view, such as the one offered by Utilitarianism, is crucial.

The third parameter mentioned by Smits is the need to balance the sub-parameters mentioned under two. Smits states that it may be hard to find a common standard on which these factors can be measured, but correctly assumes that rational reasoning about this is still possible. He is correct in this last view,[17] but if Utilitarianism is adopted even a common standard becomes available.

The fourth parameter would concern the goals of European integration, which would influence the balancing of the factors. That these goals are relevant is far

17 See the discussion of comparative value judgments in Hage 2015, section 9 and the literature mentioned there.

from obvious, certainly if one has adopted Utilitarianism. But also if one does not embrace this ethical theory, it is not immediately clear that the balancing of the sub-parameters depends on the goals of European integration.

The fifth parameter rightly mentioned by Smits 'concerns the extent to which the existing division of competences stands in the way of achieving an optimal distribution'. This is the transition issue, discussed in section 6. The 'solution' proposed there (adapted to the terminology of Smits) was to replace the question after the optimal assignment of competences by the question after the optimal course of transition.

8.3. *Conclusion*

Perhaps the most interesting conclusion to be drawn from the comparison between Smits' approach of the question after the optimal assignment of competences and the approach of the present contribution is that Smits does not adopt an abstract criterion for the evaluation of levels of regulation. In the absence of such a choice it becomes hard, if not outright impossible, to justify any concrete criteria for the assignment of regulatory tasks or competences. Smits mentions nine factors, but many questions (is this list complete; are all factors relevant under all circumstances; how should they be balanced in case of a conflict?) are hard to answer in the absence of an abstract criterion.

Formulating an ultimate evaluative standard such as the utilitarian one cannot be uncontroversial. However, a legal science which sees it as one of its tasks to answer normative or evaluative questions *must* deal with a standard, and it also *must* deal with empirical research to acquire the data to which this standard and its specifications refer. It may be difficult to make the proper choice and to obtain the relevant data, but these difficulties should not withhold us from leading legal science in the right direction. Legal scientists should not become like the man who looked for his car keys under the lamp, rather than where he lost them.

Bibliography

Dolan & Peasgood 2010
Dolan, P. & Peasgood, T., 'Measuring Well-Being for Public Policy: Preferences or Experiences?', in: E.A. Posner & C.R. Sunstein (eds.), *Law & Happiness*, Chicago: The University of Chicago Press 2010, p. 5-31.

Hage 2015
Hage, J., 'The Justification of Value Judgments', in: J.M. Smits, J. Hage, N. Kornet & B. Akkermans (eds.), *Who does What? On the Allocation of Competences in European Private Law*, Antwerp: Intersentia 2015, p. 3-44.

Layard 2003
Layard, R., *Happiness. Lessons from a New Science*, London: Penguin Books 2003.

Rawls 1972
Rawls, J., *A Theory of Justice*, Oxford: Oxford University Press 1972.

Rousseau 1797
Rousseau, J.-J., *Du contrat social*, many editions.

Smits 2015
Smits, J.M., 'Who Does What? On the Distribution of Competences among the European Union and the Member States', in: J.M. Smits, J. Hage, N. Kornet & B. Akkermans (eds.), *Who eoes What? On the Allocation of Competences in European Private Law*, Antwerp: Intersentia 2015, p. 45-60.

Westerman 2012
Westerman, P., 'Ruimte door regels', 61 *Ars Aequi*, 2012, p. 720-728.

PART II

SPECIFIC PERSPECTIVES

William Bull
Jiangqiu Ge
Catalina Goanţă
Mark Kawakami
Jan Smits

WHO DOES WHAT IN CONSUMER LAW: A SEARCH FOR CRITERIA FOR CENTRALIZED LAWMAKING

1. Introduction

There is little doubt that consumer law is a field that is highly affected by European influence. Consumer policy has long been one of the main fields of interest of the European legislator, which frequently enacts new and updates existing legislative instruments in this area.[1] The European Commission also regularly publishes new documents on its consumer policy strategy.[2] This puts the consumer *acquis* at the heart of European private law.[3] The European Union has even had such a profound influence in this area that it is difficult to imagine consumer law without European intervention. In the view of the European institutions, consumers are central to the development of the internal market: by granting them well-defined rights and providing extensive information on these rights and other essential elements of the contract, consumers are supposedly able to boost cross-border trade throughout the European Union.[4] This explains why the 15 or so existing Directives in this field are based on (the present) Article 114 TFEU, which allows the European legislator to harmonize national rules which have as their object the establishment and functioning of the internal market.

In line with the aim of this book, this contribution will critically assess the present distribution of competences in the area of consumer law. According to Article 4 TFEU, consumer protection is a shared competence of both the European Union and the Member States. Despite the apparent success of European consumer law, it will be investigated to what extent consumer protection should indeed be a matter for both geographical levels of government. We have organized our argument as follows: The next section (section 2) is devoted to an explanation of our starting point, which is the rebuttable presumption that consumer law, as any other field, should primarily be a competence for the Member States. After having set out

1 An updated overview of these Directives can be found in Smits *et al.* 2014.
2 See most recently the Commission's communication on A European Consumer Agenda: Boosting confidence and growth, COM(2012) 225 final.
3 An overview of the field is provided by Micklitz, Stuyck & Terryn 2010.
4 See (critically) Wilhelmsson 2004, p. 317 *et seq.*

the arguments in favour of this presumption, section 3 will discuss the possible arguments that merit a higher geographical level of rule-setting. Sections 4 and 5 subsequently apply these findings to two specific case studies: doorstep selling and the European market for business-to-consumer e-commerce (the so-called virtual internal market). Section 6 concludes.

This contribution does not deal with all possible aspects of consumer law. Consumer law is a functional field, which means that it deals not only with private law rule-setting, but also with public and collective enforcement of the relevant rules. We choose to focus on the substantive rules in the field of consumer contract law, so the part of European consumer law that has gained most attention from the European legislature.[5]

2. The Starting Point: Consumer Law must be dealt with at the National Level

The implicit starting point in both the political and the academic discussion about harmonization of consumer law is that the national level is the most appropriate *locus* to deal with consumer law. European intervention would merit an explicit justification. However, this does not mean that the arguments in favour of the national level are usually clearly spelled out. To the contrary: the usual way of reasoning is that the arguments *in favour of* harmonization are put forward by, for example, the European Commission, which is subsequently followed by a rebuttal of these arguments by others. This section attempts to shy away from this approach by mentioning the positive arguments in favour of regulation at the national level. This is in line with our view that, in the absence of good reasons to deal with private law at a higher geographical level of government than the national one (discussed in detail in section 3), consumer law should remain a matter for the Member States.

The first traditional argument in favour of the national level is well-known and follows from the economics of federalism.[6] If national states are seen as communities with their own proper set of preferences, these communities should be allowed to satisfy these preferences. This allocation at the lowest possible level of government can be motivated by the view that local government is close to its constituency and has therefore better knowledge of the preferences of local people and of other local conditions.[7] Decentralized regulation will thus better involve citizens in the democratic process. The second, related, argument is that decentralization will also effectively constrain monopolist behaviour by the central government and make government more responsive.[8] Finally, regulation at the national

[5] We believe that our arguments can equally extend to the international level. However, given the lack of an institution that parallels the authority of the European Union at this level, we limit our discussion to the European governance context.

[6] See Tiebout 1956, p. 416 and, applied to the present field, Wagner 2005, p. 1 *et seq*.

[7] Oates 2005, p. 349.

[8] See in more detail the contribution of Jan M. Smits to this book.

level instead of at the European one will allow for better experimentation with innovative solutions.[9]

While these three arguments are often invoked in general in favour of regulation at the lower level of government, it is usually left open how they should be applied to the field of consumer law. This is why we want to look at each of these arguments in more detail.

The first argument that different communities have different preferences is not difficult to discern in the area of consumer protection. It is generally assumed that some countries are in favour of more protection than others. For example, Nordic countries are known for their high level of protection while the Southern member-states usually have less consumer-friendly rules in place. It is true that these differences have been gradually evened out as a result of European legislation, but this does in itself not say much about the still existing preferences as to what is *desired*. This becomes clear if one scrutinizes the political process through which new European directives are enacted. The current desire of the European Commission to create more maximum-harmonization is usually met with much scepticism by the Nordic countries and Western-European member-states such as the Netherlands or Germany. The adoption of the Consumer Rights Directive[10] is a clear example of this. Even though the European Commission wanted to ensure a 'high level of consumer protection' with this Directive, there is no real criterion on how to establish what a high level for the entire European Union would actually be. This level is likely to be always too low for some Member States, while being always too high for others. This is what Frank Easterbrook referred to when he wrote that 'producing a level playing field by chopping down the heights, forcing all of us to live in the valleys, has nothing to recommend it'.[11] The European Commission's argument that regulation at the European level will lead to higher protection than leaving consumer law to the Member States is thus not true. This may be true for those countries that would, without European intervention, have a level of protection that is below the European minimum-level, but in the end the real question is whether this argument should outweigh the argument of satisfying different preferences of the Member States. As mentioned before, there is not one criterion with which to establish what is the 'best' level of protection for the whole of the European Union.[12]

An important question to ask is why the national level should be the lowest possible level of government and not an even lower level such as that of a province or municipality. We are assuming in this contribution that there is indeed a need for protection of the consumer,[13] but why organize this at the level of the national State instead of at a lower level? In our view, this follows not so much from the higher

9 Hayek 1968.

10 Directive 2011/83 on consumer rights, L 304/64.

11 Easterbrook 1994, p. 132. See also Faure 2008, p. 433, 441-442 who refers to Ronald Coase's argument that the higher the level of protection, the higher the price the consumer has to pay for the product or service.

12 See e.g. Van den Bergh 2007, p. 184.

13 This is an assumption that is not self-evident: see Epstein 2013, p. 207.

quality of the democratic process at the national level (local democracy may in fact be much more effective), but rather from the desire to create economies of scale (the number of people affected by the law must merit the investment of making a coherent system of rules) and from the fact that people's preferences in this field are more likely to be influenced by national than by local culture.

The second argument in favour of the lower level of government is that the diversity of 28 different consumer laws within the European Union will constrain monopolist behaviour and make government more responsive. Using minimum-harmonization by way of EU-directives is no doubt conducive to this goal. Allowing Member States to choose their own method of implementation and to provide for a higher level of protection guarantees that consumer law is more in tune with the national needs.

The third argument is the Hayekian view that diversity allows experimentation. This is something that can again be readily seen in European consumer law. Ever since the rise of the field in the 1970s, countries have been eager to 'borrow' solutions adopted elsewhere, or to explicitly reject these because of negative experiences. Thus, the use of lists of terms that are presumed or deemed to be unfair in consumer contracts was first adopted in Germany,[14] and subsequently taken over by for example the Dutch and European legislator.[15] The French solution of leaving the control of unfair terms primarily to a public body[16] failed in France and was not taken over anywhere else. In particular Central and Eastern European Member States have recently made extensive use of this method when they adopted new civil codes, or amended existing ones.[17] In particular in consumer law a strong argument can be made for allowing diverse solutions. This is because we know very little about the effect of specific rules on consumer behaviour. Is it really the right rule that liability for a lack of conformity of a good should be limited to two years or that the consumer shall inform the trader of the lack of conformity within two months after he detected it (Art. 5 Directive 99/44 on Sale of Consumer Goods)? We can only tell if other jurisdictions are allowed to adopt different solutions.

In our view, these three arguments are a sufficient basis for the presumption in favour of regulating at the lower level. We now turn to an account of the factors that we like to put forward as possibly meriting regulation at a higher level.

3. Centralization of European Consumer Law: Justifying the Departure from the Starting Point

The question addressed in this section is whether the fundamental arguments in favour of legal diversity in the area of consumer law can be rebutted for other reasons than those mentioned by the European Commission. For sure, the growing populist belief that Brussels and the European Union are to blame for problems

14 German Act on General Conditions (AGBG) of 1976.

15 In resp. Arts. 6:236-237 of the new Dutch Civil Code of 1992 and in Directive 93/13 on Unfair terms in consumer contracts.

16 The *Loi Scrivener* of 1978 created the *Commission des clauses abusives*.

17 See e.g. Schulze & Zoll 2013.

currently plaguing Europe[18] has made it more difficult - at least in various political circles - to justify the argument that further centralization at the European level is necessary. Nevertheless, many rebuttal arguments to these anti-European voices have been made, one in particular by the European Economic and Social Committee (EESC), which goes as far as to suggest that many of the problems that the EU is currently facing - ranging from economic woes to increasing social unrest - are actually created by the fact that the European integration is 'fundamentally incomplete'.[19] The EESC argues that a more completely integrated Europe through a more centralized coordination at the European level, vis-à-vis an approach that would give more autonomy and control to the Member States, is the solution rather than the problem.[20] If what the EESC claim is true, centralization ought to reduce costs, optimize expenditures and maximize opportunities.[21]

In some cases, this debate has become heated with pro-EU factions pointing fingers at the anti-EU faction (and vice-versa): In the words of the EESC, however, it is the fault of

> 'the shameful disinterest displayed by Member States and the European institutions, constantly putting off the work necessary to achieve genuine economic integration and the process necessary for legitimate and democratic decision-making in the Member States have ended up ... causing a spiraling lack of confidence in the markets'.[22]

In other words, the proponents of the EU and centralization seem to - rather undiplomatically - blame the Member States for their failure to fully buy into the EU.

Now while - for the reasons explained in the preceding section - our starting point is that legislative intervention should in principle take place at the lowest appropriate level of regulation, the position of the EESC and others in favour of deeper EU integration is a noteworthy reminder of the point that centralization may be desirable. The general arguments for centralization, as posited by Van den Bergh, are (i) that centralization reduces transaction costs by eliminating barriers and (ii) that it regulates interstate externalities that Member States by themselves may not be competent to handle.[23] For both arguments, the economy of scale available for the EU (but not necessarily for the Member States) is the underlying reasoning. This suggests that there may be at least some circumstances in which a higher level of regulation than that initially supported may be justified. Yet whether these arguments hold true in concrete cases will clearly depend on the given legislative intervention and area of law. So the question for us becomes whether these general

18 As evidenced by the rise in popularity of parties like UK Independence Party and its eccentric anti-EU leader Nigel Farage, who is also a member of the European Parliament.

19 Dassis & Jahier 2012, para. 4.1.

20 Dassis & Jahier 2012, para. 1.5.

21 Dassis & Jahier 2012, paras. 1.6 and 4.1 (EESC also argues the converse, stating that the failure for the Member States to buy into this philosophy will lead to a loss in competitiveness, decrease in available jobs, social adhesion and loss of democratic legitimacy).

22 Dassis & Jahier 2012, para. 4.1.

23 Van den Bergh 2007, p. 6.

arguments for centralization apply with regards to consumer law and, if so, under what circumstances? Our novel approach is that we do not frame this discussion by way of the economic arguments used by Van den Bergh, but by way of two other criteria.

The existing method for allocating competences between the EU and the Member States is subject-specific (i.e. the EU has exclusive competence over customs union, monetary policy, etc.).[24] However, what if this method was replaced with dividing up competences according to the following two criteria: (i) the level of fragmentation amongst the Member State, and (ii) the permeability of the matter being regulated. Our working theory is that the more fragmented and more permeable the matter is, the stronger the argument that the issue should be regulated at the EU level. This section will subsequently elaborate on how these two criteria interplay with factors such as maintaining and strengthening the internal market, empowering consumers and levelling the playing field for businesses.

3.1. *Fragmentation Criterion*

The fragmentation criterion is closely related to the notion of transaction costs and the various barriers that allegedly impede consumers from conducting cross-border transactions (thus preventing the internal market from reaching its full potential).[25] The obvious assumption here is that if left only to the Member States, the legislations that they promulgate will differ from one another (thus reducing the consumer incentive to conduct cross-border transactions); whereas if the process was centralized, the transaction costs would be reduced and barriers removed (thus incentivizing consumers to conduct more cross-border transactions). Relying on this assumption, this section argues that the fragmentation criterion is a relevant criterion for answering our question of 'who does what', while elaborating on how factors such as 'consumer confidence' and 'novelty' are related to the fragmentation criterion.

3.1.1. Consumer Confidence Factor

As previously noted, fragmentation is not limited to the fragmentation of laws, but relates to the fundamental differences in culture and language amongst the Member States.[26] Our assumption here is that this fragmentation decreases consumer confidence in cross border transactions, thus making consumers reluctant to make cross-border purchases and weakening the internal market in the process. Therefore, an argument could be made that consumer confidence is a factor that correlates with fragmentation: The more fragmented the Member States' regulations are or more

24 Art. 3 TFEU.

25 See generally Van den Bergh 2007, p. 186-195.

26 See e.g. Cseres 2005, p. 233; see also, Wilhelmsson 2004, p. 317; our use of the notion of 'fragmentation' corresponds to what is sometimes referred to as 'legal diversity', and should not be confused with the issue of fragmentation pertaining to the consumer *acquis* (the piecemeal approach).

distinct their consumer protection mechanisms are, the lower the consumer confidence will likely be when it comes to conducting cross border transactions.

One of the main arguments for centralized decision making - or the promulgation of regulation at the EU level - especially with the internal market and consumer rights in mind, is based exactly on this fact: These differences in legal rules and cultures hinder firms from 'extend[ing] their operations beyond national borders' and that the existence of fragmentation may cause consumers to 'refrain from cross-border shopping' especially if they do not 'enjoy the same legal protection abroad'.[27] This is why the European Commission believes that full harmonization 'will considerably increase legal certainty for both consumers and business'.[28] According to an EU-backed study, the eradication of these fragmentations in the past - through centralization of regulations at the European level - is said to have led to an increase between 4.5% and 7% of the EU's GDP with the projected creation of a further 2 to 5 million jobs in the unified area.[29] These figures suggest that consumer confidence is higher and that they are willing to spend more money (thus strengthening the internal market) when fragmentation is eradicated and regulations are centralized at the EU level.[30]

If we accept these statistics *prima facie*, our hypothesis that 'fragmentation is an important criterion' can be substantiated. A more specific example of this can be illustrated by looking at withdrawal rights in the context of consumer contracts. If the cooling off period for returning a good purchased online is 7 days in one Member State and 30 days in another, a strong argument could be made that the EU should step in to find a reasonable compromise that is applicable for all Member States, say 14 days. This would arguably clarify the standard, provide legal certainty, level the playing field and possibly strengthen the internal market. In fact, this is precisely why the EU promulgated the Consumer Rights Directive, which harmonized the cooling off period at 14 days for online sales. While the maximum harmonization that the Directive imposed drew some legitimate criticisms,[31] the Directive will likely reduce transaction costs associated with cross border trade and ultimately minimize the legal fragmentation, which in turn will strengthen the EU as a whole and its internal market.

We still wish to mention one possible counterargument. It is that regardless of how much the EU attempts to harmonize various aspects of private law, significant differences will always remain in areas such as tax, infrastructure, safety standards,

27 Van den Bergh 2010, p. 59 (noting some of the common arguments for centralization and decision making at the EU level).

28 Proposal for a Directive on consumer rights, 8 October 2008, COM(2008) 614 final, preamble, No. 8: 'These barriers (i.e. barriers stemming from the fragmentation of rules, *authors' comment*) can only be eliminated by establishing uniform rules at Community level.'

29 See Dassis & Jahier 2012, para 2.2; cf. Hubbard 2012, p. 18-20 (noting that the surveys conducted on behalf of the EU does not actually substantiate its justification).

30 This is assuming that with the increase of GDP, there was a relative and proportional increase in consumer spending as well, which is one of the factors that go into calculating GDP.

31 Smits 2010, p. 14 (noting that 'diverging preferences about the desired level of consumer protection should be kept intact').

level of wages and many others.[32] There is certainly some truth in this. The shopping behaviour of consumers may not be influenced too much by differences in contract law. And non-legal factors such as language, culture,[33] distances and differences in technical rules[34] may be important as well. Even more important is the possibility for the consumer, in case he would anticipate his dissatisfaction with the product, to have relatively easy recourse to the seller. This would explain why the consumer usually does not shop in a location too distant from his place of residence. This is of course different in the case of products for which no after sales service is needed (such as books and CD's): here, the Internet does offer a convenient possibility for cross-border shopping. Interestingly, though, this international market already came into being, even without a uniform (consumer) law.[35]

3.1.2. Novelty Factor

Also in the context of the fragmentation criterion, a specific factor that can significantly impact the creation of fragmentation is 'novelty'. The concept of novelty is related to innovation and breakthrough developments that could alter the existing framework or technology that drastically change the existing paradigm. The advent of the Internet is the perfect example of novelty, where – in the context of consumer law – it largely changed the consumers' shopping habits. The question of 'who does what' becomes particularly important in this context, because it has often been argued that excessive regulation could stifle innovation.[36] If we are to assume that regulations could possibly create a chilling effect to freeze innovation, then the type of regulation and our question of 'who does what', becomes a very important one. While lawmakers – both at the EU and Member States levels – have been adapting to the advent of the Internet, more recently, novelties such as digital content and 3D-printed goods have entered our global stream of commerce, which has created fragmentation amongst the Member States in terms of how they aim to regulate these novelties.

For example, piracy of digital content was something that was initially dealt by the individual Member States, which resulted in downloading of mp3 being 'permitted' in some Member States, while not in the others. This clearly led to fragmentation of rules and created confusion amongst the 'consumers' of what was legal and what was not. Our argument here is that if the EU, at the onset, provided a centralized policy regarding purchasing, downloading and sharing of digital content, this confusion and the proceeding fragmentation that ensued could possibly

32 See e.g. Faure 2008, p. 437, 439-40 (arguing that harmonization efforts aimed at maximum harmonization are 'impossible' or impracticable because of these fundamental differences).

33 Wagner 2002, p. 1016 refers to a Swiss survey showing that the average consumer travels 6,8 km to satisfy his needs.

34 Cf. Faure 2008, p. 438.

35 See also Wagner 2002, p. 1016 *et seq.*; Faure 2008, p. 439.

36 Venturelli 2002, p. 69-90 (noting that 'As nations enter the Global Information Society, the greater policy concern should be for forging the right environment (policy, legal, institutional, educational, infrastructure, access, etc.) appropriate to this dynamism as opposed to engaging in a strategic defense of cultural legacy or of the industrial base').

have been avoided. Given that legal certainty is hailed as a matter of paramount importance by some, the EU providing a clear, centralized guidance when some paradigm shifting event occurs could provide useful guidance to the Member States and potentially minimize fragmentation.

To summarize, the argument put forth here is that when it comes to legislating and regulating 'novelties', given the high probability that it will render some level of fragmentation if left solely to the Member States, novel matters should be regulated at the EU level *ex ante*,[37] rather than allowing Member States to create their own set of standards, only for the EU to come in *ex post* to 'require' them to assimilate to their standards. In other words, the more novel an issue is, the stronger the argument that it should be regulated at the EU level.

3.2. *Permeability Criterion*

Before discussing our second criterion of permeability, it must be noted that centralization – or a top-down European intervention – is not just preferred, but almost necessary when a law of one Member State fails to regulate the conduct of its inhabitants, which creates negative externalities to those in the other Member State. In such cases, centralization and coordination at the European level could ensure that the negative externalities are internalized where it is supposed to be and that no harm is brought to the inhabitants of the other Member State.

The most obvious example to illustrate this point on interstate negative externality is pollution, which is a subject that goes hand in hand with preventing a 'race to the bottom'. With regards to pollution, absent some centralized authority establishing a uniform standard, the Member States would be left to set their own emission standards at a level that they see fit. This being the case, pollution rendering businesses would flock to the Member State with the most lenient pollution regulation, which could create a domino effect of Member States all lowering their emission standards to attract businesses (in order to boost their economies), thus triggering a race to the bottom. Van den Bergh refers to these externalities as 'trans-boundary effects' and when national rules cannot competently contain these negative trans-boundary effects, the EU ought to step in.

Van den Bergh also offers trans-boundary tort product liability – which is more closely related to our subject of consumer law – as another example where the laws should be promulgated and enforced at the European level, reasoning that '[s]ellers of defective products should not escape liability when harm occurs outside the territory of the exporting state'.[38] While tort product liability falls under the general scope of consumer law, it does not fall under the category of consumer *contract* law, which is the specific focus of this paper. In the interest of full disclosure, it is worth noting here that it is rather difficult to come up with an example of an interstate negative externality with trans-boundary effect in the context of

37 This *ex ante* intervention need not necessarily be a hard regulation, but can also be an advising or guiding soft law.

38 Van den Bergh 2010, p. 82 (noting some of the common arguments for centralization and decision making at the EU level).

consumer contract law, which required us to come up with more suitable criteria. This is precisely the reason why we selected permeability as one of our criteria.

Permeability – a term borrowed from physics and earth sciences – measures how much fluids or gasses (usually) a porous material allows to pass through. To provide a non-legal example, things such as water-proof jackets or bike tires are preferred to be *impermeable* so as not to let water in or air out, thus preventing unwanted results (i.e. being wet or having a flat tire). In a legal context, one can think of the tires as the national law and its enforcement and the air being the matter that the Member States are attempting to contain or regulate. For the same reason that we do not want water-proof jackets to be made out of paper (an example of a permeable material), we should not leave it to the Member States to regulate matters that they cannot adequately contain or prevent from causing unwanted results outside of their borders.

With this in mind, we argue that if Member State legislations are permeable, in other words, they fail to constrain or restrict the matter that it is supposed to, then the matter in question ought to be regulated at the EU level. This criterion seems similar to 'trans-boundary effects' or 'negative interstate externalities', but it is slightly different in a very crucial way: If a particular Member State legislation and its enforcement with regards to a matter is said to be permeable, then by definition there are trans-boundary effects and likely interstate externalities as well. The converse of this statement, however, does not necessarily have to be true because if something has trans-boundary effects and therefore could create negative interstate externalities, but that something can still be contained and adequately dealt with by the Member State legislation and its enforcement, then there is no permeability. In such cases, the Member State legislation could be described as being 'impermeable'.

We opt for this criterion rather than for the more traditional criterion of 'trans-boundary effects' because the argument that we are attempting to make is not to Europeanize all decision making if the matter in question has any trans-boundary effects or if it has any possibility of creating negative interstate externalities. The criterion of trans-boundary effects is a criterion in name only as one could argue that anything and everything has trans-boundary effects.[39] Permeability, on the other hand, would require some level of proof by the EU to substantiate its claim that the Member State legislations cannot adequately contain or restrict said trans-boundary effects. If there are trans-boundary effects or possible negative interstate externality, but the Member State legislation and its enforcement can adequately contain them, then we should not depart from our starting point and leave it to the Member States to deal with that matter.

Member State legislation of the Internet – a tool that allows a German seller based in Stuttgart to market and sell goods online to a French buyer in Lyon – is likely to meet the permeability criterion, but not necessarily so. This is because the

[39] This point can be evidenced by the legal debate that the US courts perpetually struggle with on what exactly constitutes 'interstate commerce' as enumerated in Art. I, Section 8, Clause 3 of the US Constitution. When read together with the Necessary and Proper Clause, this authorizes the US federal government, vis-à-vis the States, to legislate on a wide assortment of 'interstate commerce' matters ranging from wheat production to gun control.

Internet is something that can 'penetrate' through borders and have trans-boundary effects, but some Member State legislations could regulate what people can access and thus adequately constrain what it lets in and what it lets out through its territorial borders. For example, access to certain websites can be restricted at the Member State level if a particular website is likely to cause 'harm' to its inhabitants. Member State legislations could also prohibit consumers within that territory from buying certain types of goods that are available in other jurisdictions (i.e. firearms, fireworks, etc.). The two examples, which will be elaborated upon further in sections 4 and 5 below, will provide a good illustration of how the permeability criterion can be applied.

To summarize this criterion as a way to conclude, when Member State legislations and their enforcement are permeable, that is, when they cannot contain or regulate the trans-boundary effect and/or the negative interstate externality that the matter in question could create, then our argument is that that matter should preferably be regulated at the EU level.

3.3. *Application of the Criteria*

The two cumulative criteria noted above – fragmentation and permeability – should provide guidance to answering our fundamental question of 'who does what?'[40] If the two criteria are met, then there is a strong argument that the issue should be dealt with at the EU level. If not, then we argue against deviating from the starting point and the decision should be made at the Member State level. This means that if there is fragmentation, but the Member State legislation is not permeable, or vice-versa, then that issue should be regulated at the Member States level. The following two sections will show how the two criteria can be applied using doorstep selling (section 4) and the virtual market (section 5) as examples.

4. Doorstep Selling: Example of when Decision Making at Centralized Level is not Appropriate

As has already been explained, the starting point we advocate in determining the most appropriate level of regulation in the European Union is the decentralized level. However, as has also been made clear, being merely a point of departure this approach recognizes that in various areas of law there will be at least some aspects for which more centralized regulation – that is, action taken at the European- (if not the international-) level – would be more appropriate. The question this gives rise to in relation to each of these areas of law, is therefore *which* aspects warrant such a shift to a more centralized level of legislation. Or, framed more precisely in the context of our analysis, in respect of which aspects of consumer law do the general arguments for centralization hold true?

40 The question of how much guidance these criteria could provide is of course an entirely different matter, given the potential difficulty in measuring them.

As far as the area of consumer law (and particularly consumer contract law) is concerned, it can certainly be maintained that that there are a number of aspects of this field that necessitate some form of legislation promulgated at EU-level. Of course it is well known that the European legislator has asserted the need to regulate an array of aspects of consumer law, from doorstep selling and distance selling to package travel and timeshare agreements. This has resulted in the development of a body of EU law commonly referred to as the 'consumer *acquis*', comprising a series of directives introduced from 1985 onwards. However, this does not necessarily mean that all of the aspects of this area of law that have been regulated by the European legislator *should have* been regulated at Union-level. Indeed, as has previously been stated, the existing distribution of competences between the EU and the Member States says little (if anything) about the optimal distribution of such competences. Rather, the normative question of which aspects of consumer law should be addressed at EU- and which at national-level depends on the elaboration of a set of criteria that can be applied to different situations. In other words, one should seek to arrive at a reasoned division between those aspects of consumer law (and particularly those types of consumer contracts) that are of such a nature as to require centralized intervention by the European legislator, and those that may be satisfactorily addressed by the Member States.

Now, recalling the general arguments for centralization outlined in the preceding section, we argue that there are some aspects of consumer law that have been regulated at EU-level that do *not* satisfy the criteria of fragmentation (taking into account also the factors of consumer confidence and novelty) and permeability delineated above. We illustrate this by reference to the case of consumer contracts negotiated away from business premises (i.e. what is typically referred to as doorstep selling).

Firstly, regarding the criterion of fragmentation, it is true that this may at first sight appear to be met in the case of doorstep selling, since there may well exist some potential for obstacles to cross-border trade (and associated transaction costs) caused by differences between domestic laws also in this context. It therefore follows that by centralizing the process of legislating in this area, barriers to cross-border activities (particularly of businesses engaged in doorstep selling in different Member States) could be removed, and transaction costs reduced. However, it is questionable whether such barriers are really so significant as to impede the internal market from reaching its full potential. This is because the potential for obstacles to cross-border trade in the area of doorstep selling appears at any rate to be relatively low, considering the relative difficulty with which contracts negotiated away from business premises may be entered into across borders. In this sense, doorstep selling is arguably the antithesis of online sales, insofar as it entails being physically present at the consumer's place of residence. So it is hard to see how the harmonization of this aspect of consumer law could be expected to achieve the elimination of *significant* obstacles to trans-frontier trade within the EU, and, in turn, a *notable* decrease in associated transaction costs. Furthermore, the case against centralized legislation on doorstep selling is strengthened if we take into account the additional factors of consumer confidence and novelty.

Consumer confidence may well increase through the approximation of domestic laws regulating business activities based on doorstep selling, as consumers would enjoy the same legal protection in each of the Member States. But here too the question is whether centralized regulation of these activities would lead to a *significant* increase in consumer confidence, such that the result would be a considerable improvement in the functioning of the internal market. And, considering once more the fact that the scope for cross-border transactions based on doorstep selling is rather limited, the answer is again likely to be that it would not have such a result.

In addition, with respect to the factor of novelty, even at the time the Doorstep-selling Directive was adopted in 1985, it could hardly be described as a novel business model. On the contrary, the 'door-to-door' market is generally characterized as a traditional or classical one, since it is a market in which '[m]ost of the companies have been in business for decades…'.[41] In fact the European legislator recognized as much in the preamble to the Directive, where it affirmed that 'it is a common form of commercial practice in the Member States for the conclusion of a contract or a unilateral engagement between a trader and a consumer to be made away from the business premises of the trader…'.[42] Therefore, unsurprisingly, legislation governing this activity had already been adopted by individual Member States. Indeed, as the European legislator also stated in the preamble, the aim of the Directive was to approximate these existing national regulations, because 'such contracts and engagements are the subject of legislation which differs from one Member State to another…'[43] For this reason, the novelty factor clearly does not point in the direction of centralized lawmaking when it comes to the field of doorstep selling.

Secondly, we argue that the criterion of permeability is not satisfied either in the case of doorstep selling, and again for similar reasons to those mentioned thus far. As already indicated, businesses engaged in doorstep selling may operate (or wish to operate) in multiple Member States; so, in this sense, it is an aspect of consumer law that may be described as 'permeable', insofar as it can penetrate through national borders. However, given the very nature of doorstep selling, the potential for trans-boundary effects in this area is also limited. Therefore, it is improbable that the Member States' authority (restricted as this is to territorial borders) would not have been capable of adequately dealing with the issue of doorstep selling, since its trans-frontier implications are inherently circumscribed.

In short, for these reasons, the need for centralized lawmaking on this aspect of consumer law seems to be questionable at best. Hence doorstep selling is arguably a good example of an area of consumer law where the arguments for centralization fail. We will now continue to see whether this is any different in the area of the virtual internal market.

41 Micklitz 1999, p. 4.

42 Council Directive 85/577 EEC of 20 December 1985 to protect the consumer in respect of contract negotiated away from business premises, Recital 3.

43 *Ibid.*

5. The Virtual Internal Market: Example of when Decision Making at Centralized Level is Appropriate

To further illustrate how centralization arguments perform when applied to consumer contract law, our second example will focus on the virtual internal market – that is, in a nutshell, the common market created by B2C e-commerce.[44] As the largest market in the world, the European Union is still expanding its e-commerce scale at a rapid rate. Compared to 2011, when the market value reached €254 billion, the e-commerce turnover of products and services in 2012 has grown by 20% and reached approximately €305 billion. In comparison: in 2012 the US e-commerce market reached €280 billion, while the size of the Chinese online shopping market achieved a rough €157 billion.[45] This increase in the European market was the effect of 240 million consumers shopping online around the EU as Internet penetration into European households or mobile devices was on the rise. Within e-commerce, the booming m-commerce (mobile commerce) subcategory is also noteworthy. Predictions show that global spending on mobile apps will reach €26.82 billion in 2015 and smartphones will account for 40% of Internet traffic, while tablets for 26%.[46]

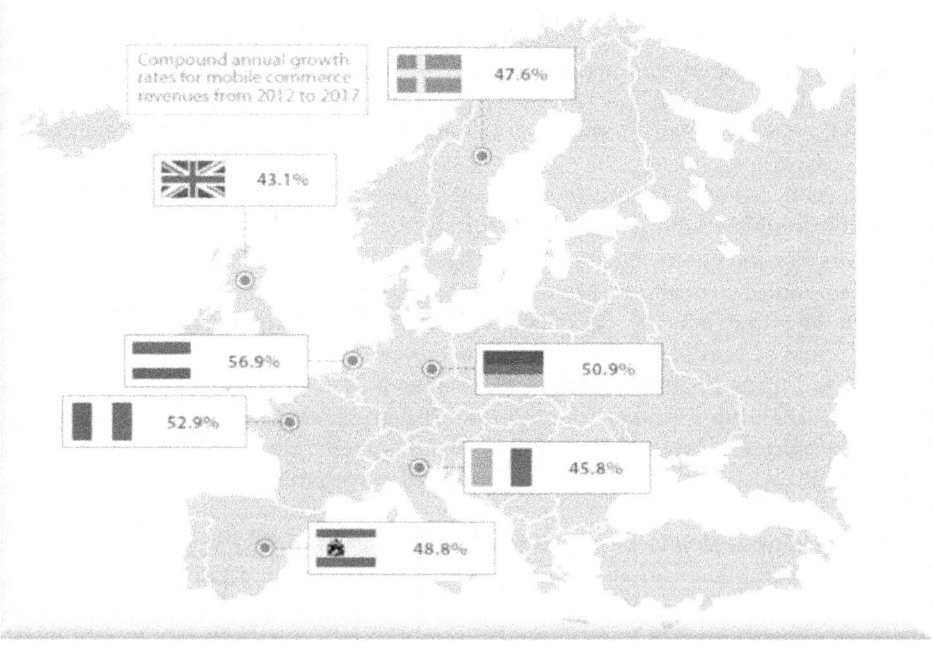

Figure 1. M-commerce revenues 2012-2017 (Source: Forrester Forecast)

44 In terms of the reason why e-commerce is a good example that perfectly fits the criteria we suggest, see, previously mentioned, the third paragraph of Section 2.2.

45 CNNIC 2013.

46 These statistics were mentioned at the European Consumer Summit in 2013: Nöthlichs 2013.

We will consider the virtual internal market example in the light of the criteria elaborated upon earlier. In order to do so, this case study starts with asking the question 'who is the consumer who shops online?', which we endeavour to answer by creating a profile for the average user anecdotically called 'Joe the consumer' on the basis of statistical data stemming from consumer practices as recorded by various EU and non-EU actors and of case law of the Court of Justice of the European Union (CJEU) in the field of distance selling.[47] The fragmentation and permeability criteria will then be applied to the consumer profile to determine the need for centralization. Subsequently, e-commerce issues arising out of the consumer profile will be dealt with under the concluding recommendation on a future European policy concerning trustmarks.

5.1. *Joe the Consumer (Number Profile)*

As Flash Eurobarometer #358 shows, in 2012 53% of all EU consumers had made at least one purchase via the Internet,[48] which reveals an increase when compared to 2006 (27%) and 2010 (37%).[49] As more consumers get access to the Internet, their likelihood to purchase goods/services online grows.[50]

However, the consumer online shopping enthusiasm that seems to drive these numbers up has a national origin. In 2012, a mere 11% of EU consumers had conducted Internet purchases from a seller or provider located in another EU Member State.[51] However, this proportion increased since 2010 (7%).[52] One of the leading reasons for this limitation seems to be the issue of consumer confidence: approximately 5 out of 10 EU consumers did not agree with feeling confident about purchasing goods or services via the Internet from retailers/providers in another EU country (28% 'Disagree' and 21% 'Strongly disagree').[53] According to Flash Eurobarometer #299, 62% of the respondents were not interested in making a cross-border transaction because they were worried that they 'could fall victim to scams or frauds when purchasing goods or services' (36% 'Totally agree' and 26% 'Tend to

47 The Distance Selling Directive is currently the main piece of European legislation dealing with consumer contracts concluded over the Internet.

48 Flash Eurobarometer 2013, p. 5.

49 Flash Eurobarometer 2011, p. 5: '37% of all EU consumers made a distance purchase on the Internet, 21% used the post (catalogues, mail order, etc.) and 13% made a distance purchase by phone'.

50 Online shopping and the Internet penetration rate seem to be correlated - in countries where the level of Internet access is higher, online shopping tends to be more widespread. This is the case for the Netherlands (74% purchased via the Internet/household Internet access 93%), Denmark (71%/86%), the UK (68%/74%), Ireland (66%/67%) – Flash Eurobarometer 2013, p. 10.

51 Eurostat, 'Individuals using the Internet for ordering goods or services from other EU countries', code tin00003, retrieved on 02 May 2014; however, it must be noted that Flash Eurobarometer No. 358 claims that the number of individuals who entered into a transaction with a seller/supplied from a different Member State via the Internet is 15%.

52 Flash Eurobarometer 2013, p. 16.

53 Flash Eurobarometer 2013, p. 23.

agree').[54] Among the other concerns that show why consumers would not be cross-border-friendly is that only 39% of the consumers interviewed for Eurobarometer #299 were willing to shop in another EU language;[55] 47% quoted problems with delivery; or 57% mentioned that they would fear having to deal with difficulties relating to the return of faulty products and complaints. At this point, it is note-worthy to acknowledge to the reader that consumer confidence is not treated here as the main issue deterring consumers from shopping on other European websites, although this is what European surveys like the ones just cited might advertise. Hubbard has recently shown that some empirical findings included in Eurobarometers are biased and favour a specific policy-making purpose.[56] However, the way in which our analysis features consumer confidence is by qualifying it as a factor that may show the effects of legal fragmentation.

What do these numbers mean for the profile of the consumer? There are two different arguments that can be made to answer this question: first, that European consumers are prone to shop online, as their internet access and inclination to own smartphones increase and second, that shopping online does not mean shopping across borders, because of a general lack of consumer confidence.

As far as the first argument is concerned, consumers are indeed more willing than ever to engage in online behaviour. One way to look at this willingness is to acknowledge the benefits gained by consumers when shopping online, whether they are utilitarian shoppers (persons who see shopping as a necessity and want to minimize the time spent and importance given to such an activity) or hedonistic shoppers (persons who derive emotional benefits from the shopping process), rational shoppers or impulse shoppers: saving time and gaining comfort for not having to queue in a real store;[57] researching information regarding the product by using price-comparison websites and apps;[58] having access to consumer reviews and opinions on social media;[59] etc.

The second argument relates to the fact that among others, survey-based consumer confidence findings helped trigger the maximum harmonization trend in European consumer contract law, which by itself may be perceived as increasingly protective, and on the other hand does not allow Member States to impose rules that go beyond or below it. But how has the Court of Justice of the European Union received this development?

54 Flash Eurobarometer 2013, p. 32.
55 Even by the end of 2012, this proportion has not significantly increased (41%); Flash Eurobarometer 2013, p. 33.
56 See Hubbard 2012.
57 Scarpi 2006, p. 224.
58 One example of such a website is Google Shopping: <www.google.com/shopping>.
59 DeMers 2013.

5.2. *Joe the Consumer (Case Law Profile)*

Judging the several interpretations issued by the CJEU on the applicable legislation to the field of virtual shopping, namely the Distance Selling Directive (DSD),[60] it can be argued that these too can help put together features to profile the consumer. The classical rationale of the DSD entails giving the consumer the confidence he needs to engage in distance shopping, in spite of the fact that his purchase is considered to be made 'in the dark',[61] meaning that the consumer is vulnerable before unreliable sellers. Recent interpretations of the CJEU add more characteristics to this profile.[62]

The fact that the CJEU interprets consumer directives in a pro-consumer manner is nothing new as it has been well addressed in academic literature.[63] Nonetheless, the *Content Services* judgment sheds new light on how the Court profiles Internet consumers: as vulnerable, passive and uninformed. The case concerned the seller's duty to confirm information according to Article 4(1) DSD in general and the interpretation of the novel notion of 'durable medium' in particular.[64] The Court determined that by clicking a link, the consumer is denied the absolutely passive role promised under the Directive - a role entailing the seller's exclusive obligation to confirm the necessary information regarding the transaction but general consumer rights.

In the light of such a consumer-biased interpretation, it can be stated that the Court of Justice raises the bar for consumer protection even further. Although there are indeed categories of consumers who are more likely to be affected by the aggressive business practices of a business like Content Services, such as the elderly or children,[65] the question still to be answered is whether in its judgment the Court looks at the average or the most vulnerable consumer.[66]

Using a very high standard of consumer protection does not only impact further case law under the preliminary reference procedure, but it also impacts business practice. Online trade is strengthening the internal market; still, this only holds true if Internet sales are also attractive to businesses. To take business interests into account is not uncommon in the interpretation of the DSD. After all, in both *EasyCar*[67] and *Messner*[68] the CJEU looked at the balance of interests between both parties to the contract. However, if based on the *Content Services* case it can be

60 Directive 97/7/EC on the protection of consumers in respect of distance contracts, L 144.

61 Dickie 1998, p. 217; Borges & Irlenbusch 2007, p. 85; Rothchild 1998, p. 295; Eidenmueller *et al.* 2011, p. 1085.

62 As of June 1014, the Distance Selling Directive is replaced by the Consumer Rights Directive; however, the first is still relevant for our analysis because of the available case law.

63 Mak 2012, p. 8; Unberath & Johnston 2007, p. 1237; Reich 2006, p. 43.

64 See Goanță 2013, p. 653.

65 European Parliament, Resolution on a strategy for strengthening the rights of vulnerable consumers (2011/2272(INI)), 8 May 2012.

66 See Waddington 2013, p. 759.

67 Case C-336/03, *EasyCar (UK) Ltd* v *Office of Fair Trading*, Reference for a preliminary ruling from the High Court of Justice of England and Wales, Chancery Division, ECR [2005], I-01947.

68 Case C-489/07, *Pia Messner* v *Firma Stefan Krüger*, Reference for a preliminary ruling: Amtsgericht Lahr - Germany ECR [2009] I-07315.

held that asking the consumer to click a hyperlink actually means that he will be deprived of information, the Court clearly founded its ruling on a more vulnerable consumer profile. The higher this standard, the more burdensome it becomes for businesses. However, at this point it must be mentioned that existing case law only reflects the minimum harmonization policy behind the Distance Selling Directive. It remains to be seen how the Court will interpret and apply maximum harmonization as proposed in the Consumer Rights Directive. However, we have serious doubts that the implementation of a new directive, irrespective of how much protection it allegedly offers, or its subsequent interpretation by the European court will actually trigger more trust in consumers. At the end of the day, consumers seem to be uninterested as to what legal regime applies to their contracts - what they do care about is for their products to be delivered, to meet their expectations, and in case of problems, to have a way of protecting their investment. These features are what actually impacts the reason why consumers are reluctant to get involved in cross-border trade: if a Polish consumer never used a Finnish website to buy electronic devices, why should she consider it as a more beneficial alternative to purchasing the same good nationally? Here is where non-legal aspects will start playing an important role. Let us mention a few: the reputation of the company, the looks of the website, its user-friendliness, reviews by other consumers, etc. Ruling all these aspects is of course the issue of price, but price determination elements (e.g. taxes, etc.) find themselves outside the ambit of this paper.

To connect our attempt to profile the consumer with the earlier discussion on the need for centralization, it can be stated that the Internet offers insights into a field of law - consumer law - that in the view of the authors is better off with centralized rules. One of the aspects that we have explored in this section is the fact that globalization and the rise of technology lead consumers around the world in the same direction - regardless of their preferences, whether based on cultural or geographical considerations, they will all choose Internet shopping for more or less the same reasons.[69] In other words, consumer profiles show that regardless of origin or preferences, technology shapes common features in consumers. In turn, these common features need common rules to govern them.

Having mentioned that consumer decisions might be triggered by factors other than law, the next step is to investigate whether there is any user-friendly way to combine law with behavioural characteristics of consumer decision-making. In our view, the introduction of a European trustmark might achieve just that.

5.3. *Centralization Criteria are Met*

So far, the focus was on understanding the general features of the European online shopper, and in order to define such features attention was paid to various statistics as well as to case law from the Court of Justice. In the following paragraphs we will first address *why* rules should be made at centralized level, and subsequently go into the details of *how* this could be achieved.

69 See section 5.1.

Let us first discuss why online shopping should be governed by centralized rules. As we have seen above, our analysis determined that unless our criteria are met – that is, fragmentation and permeability – rule-making should be made at national level. We argue that Internet shopping is an example that fully meets both criteria by featuring consumer confidence and novelty as factors influencing legislative policy while displaying characteristics of permeability. Each of the factors will be elaborated upon in what follows.

In section 3 of this paper, it was stated that fragmentation is generally detrimental because of the resulting increase in transaction costs. For businesses, this means resources spent on synchronizing with different environments (information costs, dispute management, etc.),[70] while for consumers it might very well translate into trust issues (diverging fairness standards and practices that stem from different legal cultures), which as we have noticed, have the power to hinder cross-border trade.

Similarly, we have also shown that not only are Internet shopping rates on the rise, but so is the use of new technologies that might support it, such as shopping on mobile phones (m-commerce) whenever, wherever.[71] Since technology is advancing rapidly, it is difficult to assume that 28 individual member States will simultaneously be on the lookout to design and introduce consumer-specific legislation every time new devices shape consumer behaviour.[72] This points to the conclusion that if left to the European Union, legislation on technological developments will lead to more uniform practice. What illustrates this thought is the consideration that the Internet does not have any borders, but reflects a post-territorial reality;[73] and if we accept that idea, we must ask ourselves – why should we fragment it rather than allow it to be governed by the same rules? A speaking example of potential fragmentation issues may be seen in the French landmark case *LICRA* v *Yahoo! Inc.* The already 13 year-old case tackled jurisdictional issues arising out of Internet use by consumers in France who were able to bid for Nazi memorabilia sold on the American website of the communication giant.[74] In the light of cases like this, if it is a steady trend that consumers are turning into iConsumers and are enhancing their online presence,[75] it seems reasonable to assume that applying a unified standard to their activity might support technological revolutions rather than hinder them.

Additionally, as it was illustrated already in section 3.2, the Internet is a tool that allows a German seller based in Stuttgart to market and sell goods to a French buyer in Lyon. The fact that an action of a German cannot be restrained or constrained by the strict application of German law (or French law for that matter) makes online sales a perfect illustration of permeability.

70 Wagner 2007, p. 39.
71 The Huffington Post 2012.
72 It is, however, true that European legislation was only updated in 2011 when the new Consumer Rights Directive was adopted, and that until its entry into force Internet matters are still governed by the decrepit Distance Selling Directive.
73 Goldsmith & Wu 2006, p. 5.
74 *UEJF & LICRA* v *Yahoo!, Inc. & Yahoo!*, Tribunal de Grande Instance Paris, 22 May 2000; see also Greenberg 2003, p. 1191; Okoniewski 2002, p. 295.
75 See McKinsey & Company 2013.

5.4. *Online Shopping – the Next Step in Terms of Trust*

The above implies that binding rules on consumer protection for online shopping must be set at the European level. But this is not the full story. Once it is established that centralization is needed, this still leaves open what type of harmonization is to be put into place. Experience shows that it is politically difficult to reach anything other than minimum harmonization. What is more, this is also not desired in view of the need to satisfy different preferences: even when the two criteria for centralist lawmaking are met, there still has to be a trade-off with the need to satisfy these preferences. Minimum-harmonization allows this. We therefore propose a dual system in which minimum-harmonization in the field of online consumer sales law is combined with the use of a European trustmark. Trustmarks are logos displayed on websites of suppliers reflecting that the supplier is following certain practices of the organization issuing the quality label. Within the framework of the European Commission's Digital Agenda for Europe, several studies mapped the existing trustmarks in Europe and found this field to show one main feature: diversity – in terms of issuing organizations, characteristics of the trustmark, rights and obligations of the issuer/supplier, etc.[76]

For instance, displaying a logo might simply point to a supplier's affiliation to a business organization. However, there are cases when using these markings provides suppliers with services: the Norwegian trustmark *Nsafe* offers dispute settlement services and the Finnish *SafeShop* offers insurance.[77] In most of these cases what lays behind trustmarks is a system of rules stemming from codes of conduct.

The European Commission has also been looking into a roadmap for such codes, and went as far as to try and determine the feasibility of an eventual EU trustmark. This is only one of the five policy options it is currently looking into; the other four include: (i) no intervention; (ii) encouraging self-regulation; (iii) co-regulation; and (iv) establishing an EU trustmark accreditation scheme. The EU-commissioned research mapped many of the existing features of various types of trustmarks.[78] We do not aim at matching the level of detail, but rather at furthering the discussion on this topic.

We envisage an EU trustmark to operate as a voluntary accreditation system which would synchronize business practices with the Consumer Rights Directive and add other services such as online dispute resolution, insurance or centralized user reviews for a separate fee. We consider such trustmark to have two fundamental features: reflecting a European standard of consumer protection and educating the consumer visually by associating a logo with quality of goods and services. This means that on top of the mandatory minimum-rules set by the Directive, the European trademark reflects compliance with a higher level of protection that is well defined by the European legislator.

76 DG Internal Policies 2012, p. 70.
77 Nordic Council of Ministers 2001, p. 14.
78 Intrasoft International & TNO 2012.

First, instead of being linked to a code of conduct, businesses signing up for the trustmark would instead vouch to respect the higher level of European legislation in the field of online shopping, focusing primarily on information duties leading to more transparency for the consumer, and the withdrawal right. Further rules on conformity with the contract (Consumer Sales Directive) would be equally applicable and would be part of the checklist. Evaluating adherence to some of these rules - such as information provided prior to the conclusion of the contract - is highly objective and can be done consistently by simply visiting the websites in question. As for business practices relating to, for instance, how the business deals with withdrawal rights or if they follow the consumer remedy hierarchy in cases on non-conformity a mixed evaluation can be put into place. One option might be to bring together the review of the expectations the seller or supplier raises in his communication (whether it is information posted online or standard e-mails sent to consumers) and information obtained from user reviews.

Second, current trustmarks have the downside of multiplying their number exponentially because of the reality that any business or consumer organization may issue one such logo. For this reason, the visual element would be highly important. Creating an umbrella logo (the main EU trustmark) creates the strong, non-verbal communication of a standard that consumers may understand to govern their transactions in the entirety of the European Union.

Indeed, as stated earlier in section 2, differences in culture, language, etc. might be used as arguments against the viability of a European trustmark. However, behavioural science shows that consumers can be nudged or, in other words, the architecture of their choice can be influenced. It cannot thus be ruled out that preferences for the unfamiliar may develop with time. Take, for instance, the example of trying out exotic food for the first time - in the view of Thaler and Sunstein, 'even in less exotic locales, it can be smart to let someone else choose for you'.[79]

6. Conclusion

This paper strived to bring together arguments addressing how competences in the field of consumer contract law may be divided. We started out with the presumption that national rules should govern this field because of the diversity that they can protect. The three arguments presented in this sense related to the economics of federalism, reducing monopolist behaviour and experimenting with diversity. We then proposed two main criteria, which if cumulatively fulfilled, would legitimize centralized rule-making: fragmentation (including consumer confidence and novelty as determining factors) and permeability (including negative externalities and race to the bottom as factors).

This framework was subsequently applied to two case studies. In case of doorstep selling, the criteria for centralized lawmaking are in our view not fulfilled, and thus centralized action is not justified. However, not the same can be said about

79 Thaler & Sunstein 2009, p. 77-78.

Internet shopping. The virtual internal market brings together iConsumers from across the EU who tend to have the same habits: they increasingly rely on the Internet in their lives, including shopping. The fact that the majority of these consumers do not look beyond the realm of their own national domain URLs shows that they might be afraid – of dealing with fraud, of putting up with unnecessary hassle, overall of having negative experiences – in a nutshell, of the unknown. And the unknown means 27 other legal systems. This means that consumer confidence is a factor that definitely influences online shopping. Moreover, we have also determined that given the Internet's growing impact on daily life, the novelty factor is also met – consumers from France should not have different (minimum-) rules and standards imposed on them simply because they have the freedom of visiting <amazon.de> or <amazon.fr>; they do not even move from their chairs when making this choice, so why should the law move for them? A European trustmark would be the necessary complement of minimum-harmonization. All in all, these two factors are strong indicators of how fragmentation operates. As Bill Gates is reported to have said, the Internet is becoming the town square for the global village of tomorrow – there is probably a reason why he did not mention anything about multiple town squares.

In the end, it remains unresolved whether the failure to complete the European integration process is the source of the problems currently burdening the EU or whether the attempt to integrate Europe in and of itself is the problem. However, this paper was able to illustrate that there are circumstances where centralized decision-making at the EU- (if not even international-) level is more appropriate than our starting assumption of allowing legal diversity.

Bibliography

Borges & Irlenbusch 2007
Borges, G. & Irlenbusch, B., 'Fairness Crowded Out by Law: An Experimental Study on Withdrawal Rights', 163 *Journal of Institutional and Theoretical Economics*, 2007, p. 84-101.

CNNIC 2013
China Internet Network Information Center (CNNIC), *Research on Chinese Online Shopping Market in 2012*, March 2013, available at: <www.cnnic.cn/hlwfzyj/hlwxzbg/dzswbg/201304/P020130417543965742695.pdf>.

Cseres 2005
Cseres, K.J., *Competition Law and Consumer Protection*, The Hague: Kluwer Law International 2005.

Dassis & Jahier 2012
Dassis, G. & Jahier, L., *Opinion of the European Economic and Social Committee on Towards an Updated Study of the Cost of non-Europe* (SC/035 (2012), Brussels 2012.

DeMers 2013
DeMers, J., 'How Social Media is Changing the SEO Industry', *Search Engine Journal*, 2013, available at <www.searchenginejournal.com/how-social-media-is-changing-the-seo-industry/63060>.

DG Internal Policies 2012
DG Internal Policies, *A Pan-European Trustmark for E-Commerce: Possibilities and Opportunities*, Brussels: European Union 2012, available at <www.europarl.europa.eu>.

Dickie 1998
Dickie J., 'Consumer Confidence and the EC Directive on Distance Contracts', 2(21) *Journal of Consumer Policy*, 1998, p. 217-229.

Easterbrook 1994
Easterbrook, F., 'Federalism and European Business Law', 14(2) *International Review of Law and Economics*, 1994, p. 125-132.

Eidenmueller et al. 2011
Eidenmueller, H., Faust, F., Jansen, N. Wagner, G. Zimmermann, R., 'Towards a Revision of the Consumer Acquis', 48(4) *Common Market Law Review*, 2011, p. 1077-1123.

Epstein 2013
Epstein, R., 'Harmonization, Heterogeneity and Regulation: CESL, The Lost Opportunity for Constructive Harmonization', 50(1/2) *Common Market Law Review*, 2013, p. 207-223.

European Parliament 2012
European Parliament, *Resolution on a Strategy for Strengthening the Rights of Vulnerable Consumers* (2011/2272(INI)), Strasbourg, 8 May 2012.

Faure 2008
Faure, M., 'Towards a Maximum Harmonization of Consumer Contract Law?', 15(4) *Maastricht Journal of European and Comparative Law*, 2008, p. 433-445.

Flash Eurobarometer 2011
Flash Eurobarometer No. 299, *Consumer Attitudes towards Cross-Border Trade and Consumer Protection: Analytical Report*, March 2011.

Flash Eurobarometer 2013
Flash Eurobarometer No. 358, *Consumer Attitudes towards Cross-Border Trade and Consumer Protection: Report*, June 2013.

Goanță 2013
Goanță, C., 'Information Duties in the Internet Era: Case Note on Content Services Ltd v. Bundesarbeitskammer', 21(2) *European Review of Private Law*, 2013, p. 643-659.

Goldsmith & Wu 2006
Goldsmith, J. & Wu T., *Who Controls the Internet? Illusions of a Borderless World*, Oxford: Oxford University Press 2006.

Greenberg 2003
Greenberg, M.H., 'A Return to Lilliput: The LICRA v. Yahoo! Case and the Regulation of Online Content in the World Market', 18 *Berkeley Technology Law Journal*, 2003, p. 1191-1258.

Hayek 1968
Hayek, F.A., *Der Wettbewerb als Entdeckungsverfahren* (Kieler Vorträge N.S. 56), Kiel: Universität Kiel 1968.

Hubbard 2012
Hubbard, W.H.J., *Another Look at the Eurobarometer Surveys*, Chicago Institute for Law and Economics Working Paper, No. 615, 2012.

Huffington Post 2012
The Huffington Post, 'More Than 38 Million Americans Shop While On The Toilet, Survey Says', 19 November 2012, retrieved from <www.huffingtonpost.com/2012/11/19/americans-shop-on-the-toilet_n_2160767.html>.

Intrasoft International & TNO 2012
Intrasoft International & TNO, *EU online Trustmarks Building Digital Confidence in Europe* (A study prepared for the European Commission (DG Communications Networks, Content & Technology)), 2012, available at <www.ec.europa.eu/digital-agenda/en/pillar-i-digital-single-market/action-17-stakeholder-platform-eu-onli ne -trustmarks>.

Mak 2012
Mak, V., 'The Myth of the "Empowered Consumer". Lessons from Financial Literacy Studies', 4 *Zeitschrift für Europäisches Unternehmens-und Verbraucherrecht*, 2012, p. 254-264.

McKinsey & Company 2013
McKinsey & Company, *iConsumers: Life Online*, New York 2013, available at <tmt. mckinsey.com>.

Micklitz 1999
Micklitz, H-W., *Door to Door Selling – Pyramid Selling – Multi Level Marketing*, Study Commissioned by the European Commission, Brussels: 1999, available at: <www.ec. europa.eu/consumers/cons_int/safe_shop/door_sell/sur10_01.pdf>.

Micklitz, Stuyck & Terryn 2010
Micklitz, H.-W., Stuyck, J. & Terryn, E. (eds.), *Ius Commune Casebooks: Cases, Materials and Text on Consumer Law*, Oxford: Hart Publishing 2010.

Nordic Council of Ministers 2001
Nordic Council of Ministers, *Self-regulation of Electronic Commerce in the Nordic Countries: Trade and Industry Sector Ad Hoc Working Group for Electronic Commerce and Trade and Industry Related IT Issues*, Copenhagen: Nordic Council Of Ministers 2001.

Nöthlichs 2013
Nöthlichs, J., *E-Commerce Trends of Today and Tomorrow*, 18-19 March 2013, available at <www.european-consumer-summit.eu/presentation/3%20Workshop%20-%20e-Enforcement/1%20facts%20&%20figures%20E-commerce%20trends%20-%20Janine %20No | êthlichs.pdf>.

Oates 2005
Oates, W.E., 'Toward a Second-Generation Theory of Fiscal Federalism', 12 *International Tax and Public Finance*, 2005, p. 349-373.

Okoniewski 2002
Okoniewski, E.A., 'Yahoo!, Inc. v. LICRA: The French Challenge to Free Expression on the Internet', 18 *American University International Law Review*, 2002, p. 295-301.

Reich 2006
Reich, N., 'Protection of Consumers' Economic Interests by EC Contract Law: Some Follow-up Remarks', 28(1) *Sydney Law Review*, 2006, p. 37-62.

Rothchild 1998
Rothchild, J., 'Making the Market Work: Enhancing Consumer Sovereignty Through the Telemarketing Sales Rule and the Distance Selling Directive', 21 *Journal of Consumer Policy*, 1998, p. 279-313.

Scarpi 2006
Scarpi, D., 'The Fun Side of the Internet', in: S. Zappalà & C. Gray (eds.), *Impact of E-Commerce on Consumers and Small Firms*, Hampshire: Ashgate Publishing Ltd 2006, p. 223-234.

Schulze & Zoll 2013
Schulze, R. & Zoll, F. (eds.), *The Law of Obligations in Europe: A New Wave of Codifications*, München: Sellier 2013.

Smits 2010
Smits, J.M., 'Full Harmonization of Consumer Law? A Critique of the Draft Directive on Consumer Rights', 18 *European Review of Private Law*, 2010, p. 5-14.

Smits et al. 2014
Smits, J., Bull, W., Goanţă, C. & Kawakami, M. (eds.), *Ars Aequi wetseditie European Private Law 2014-2016* (4th edition), Nijmegen: Ars Aequi 2014.

Thaler & Sunstein
Thaler, R.H. & Sunstein, C.R., *Nudge – Improving Decisions about Health, Wealth and Happiness*, New Haven: Yale University Press 2009.

Tiebout 1956
Tiebout, C., 'A Pure Theory of Local Expenditures', 64(5) *Journal of Political Economy*, 1956), p. 416-424.

Unberath & Johnston 2007
Unberath, H. & Johnston, A., 'The Double-Headed Approach of the ECJ Concerning Consumer Protection', 44(5) *Common Market Law Review*, 2007, p. 1237-1284.

Van den Bergh 2007
Van den Bergh, R., 'The Uneasy Case for Harmonizing Consumer Law', in: K. Heine & W. Kerber (eds.), *Zentralität und Dezentralität von Regulierung in Europa*, Stuttgart: Lucius & Lucius 2007, p. 183-205.

Van den Bergh 2010
Van den Bergh, R, 'Private Law in a Globalising World: Economic Criteria for Choosing the Optimal Regulatory Level in a Multilevel Government System', in: M. Faure & A. van der Walt (eds.), *Globalization and Private Law*, Cheltenham: Edward Elgar 2010, p. 57-96.

Venturelli 2002
Venturelli, S., 'Inventing e-regulation in the US, EU and East Asia: Conflicting Social Visions of the Information Society', 19 *Telematics and Informatics*, 2002, p. 69-90

Waddington 2013
Waddington, L., 'Vulnerable and Confused: the Protection of "Vulnerable" Consumers under EU Law', 38 *European Law Review*, 2013, p. 757–782.

Wagner 2002
Wagner, G., 'The Economics of Harmonization: the Case of Contract Law', 39 *Common Market Law Review*, 2002, p. 995-1023.

Wagner 2005
Wagner, G., 'The Virtues of Diversity in European Private Law', in: J.M. Smits (ed.), *The Need for a European Contract Law*, Groningen: Europa Law Publishing 2005, p. 3-24.

Wagner 2007
Wagner, G., 'Transaction Costs, Choice of Law and Uniform Contract Law', in: UNCITRAL (ed.), *Modern Law for Global Commerce*, Proceedings of the Congress of the United Nations Commission on International Trade Law Held on the Occasion of the Fortieth Session of the Commission, 9-12 July 2007, Vienna: United Nations English, Publishing and Library Section, p. 39-45.

Wilhelmsson 2004
Wilhelmsson, T., 'Abuse of the "Confident Consumer" as Justification for EC Consumer Law', 27 *Journal of Consumer Policy*, 2004, p. 317-337.

Anna Beckers
Nicole Kornet
Janwillem
Oosterhuis

WHO DOES WHAT IN COMMERCIAL LAW? THE CASE FOR A MULTI-LEVEL & MULTI-ACTOR APPROACH TO REGULATING COMMERCIAL TRANSACTIONS

1. Introduction

Commercial law constitutes the backbone of economic activity and as such it has been coined the 'engine for trade.[1] As a field, it is very broad and its scope is not clearly defined.[2] It comprises a body of law regulating all aspects of commercial relations, such as commercial contracts (e.g. sales, services, agency and distribution, leasing, carriage, insurance), payment and financing mechanisms (e.g. documentary credits, bills of exchange, guarantees) and covers the trade in goods and services that takes place on a variety of markets, including, for instance, commodity exchange markets, financial and securities markets, energy markets, manufacturing markets, and agricultural markets. Commercial law also covers a variety of dispute resolution mechanisms including negotiation, mediation and arbitration. It is clear that although the contract for the sale of goods or supply of services is at the core of a commercial transaction, commercial law goes beyond the field of contract law, and incorporates property, tort, restitution, company and insolvency law. A clear definition of the scope of commercial law is further complicated by the fact that the markets on which commercial actors trade can be truly global, as well as specifically local. Hence, a comprehensive answer to the question of 'who should do what in commercial law?' must remain an impossible undertaking.

In this contribution, we therefore confine ourselves to developing an approach to the desirable regulation of commercial transactions in the sense of trade in goods and services. In doing so, we will address two main questions. Firstly, what are the normative criteria to decide upon the appropriate design of commercial contract law? Secondly, in light of these criteria, we seek to develop an answer to the questions of *who* should set the rules in commercial law, or, in other words, which

1 See Irvine 2001.

2 See e.g. Goode 2010, p. 1347: 'the totality of the law's response to the needs and practices of the mercantile community'; also see Twigg-Flesner & Villalta Puig 2011, p. 1: the law dealing with the sale and supply of goods and services and 'the various means by which this is done and financed'.

regulatory actors, i.e. private or public actors, and *where* should these rules be set, or, in other words, at what regulatory level, i.e. local, national, regional or global.

Before addressing how the law concerning cross-border commercial transactions should be regulated, we will sketch, in section 2, the current regulatory landscape in commercial law - including some historical context - and analyse it with a view to our two main topics, namely who regulates and where does regulation exist. This historical overview will reveal that commercial law can be considered a complex amalgamation of regulatory frameworks, produced by different actors and at different levels of governance and seeks to underline why an approach is needed to determine the desirable form of regulating commercial relations. Following this initial sketch of the field, the contribution will continue to explore how commercial contract law should be regulated in section 3. In developing our normative criteria we will first discuss our basic assumptions, which are that commercial law should facilitate the exchange of goods and services, and that facilitating the exchange of goods and services can best be achieved through the exercise of party autonomy. Therefore, we posit that commercial contract law should primarily facilitate the exercise of party autonomy and enforce agreements voluntarily entered into by private actors. It is our position that further regulation is only needed when either the actions of private actors jeopardize the exercise of party autonomy, or the exercise of party autonomy could have negative effects on the market or on society. Given these criteria, we will subsequently discuss more specifically who should regulate and at what level regulation should take place. In section 4, we present three cases studies analysing the appropriate role of private and public actors at different governance levels with a view to illustrating the approach forwarded in this contribution. The case studies adopt three different perspectives. A first case study looks at the law relating to bills of exchange from a historical perspective with a view to drawing lessons for our approach from the past. The second case study addresses the core of commercial exchange - the contract of sale - to illustrate how commercial sales law ought to be regulated according to our analysis. The final case study addresses the appropriate actor and level for regulating commercial transactions to prevent a negative impact on fundamental societal interests.

In our conclusion we will summarize what our findings mean for the development of commercial law, and in particular what the insights provided by our analysis contribute to the discussion on the distribution of competences. In particular, we highlight that our findings have implications for the debate on the distribution of competences in European Private Law, which remains incomplete if two other regulatory levels, the broader global regulatory perspective on private relations as well as the specific locally shaped practices of sectors and trades are not taken into consideration. Moreover, our contribution can be read as contributing to the general debate by emphasizing the need to take into account as 'competences' not only national, European or global politics, but also the productive potential of the private sphere to develop effective self-regulation.

2. A Sketch of the Current Regulatory Landscape for Commercial Transactions

Commercial law can be considered as a multilevel, multi-actor system, in the sense that it is produced by different actors, at different levels of governance, and in different forms. A historical introduction is chosen to discuss and place into context some examples of commercial law in Europe.

Currently, commercial relations in which goods or services are exchanged between businesses are still importantly governed by national legislation. This, however, was not always the case. It was merely the eighteenth and nineteenth centuries that witnessed the emergence of nation states, i.e. public actors, many of which tried to establish legal unity within their territories, including legal unity in commercial matters.[3] Legal rules regulating contractual relations - including, for example, commercial sales - were, inter alia, laid down in general Civil codes such as the Prussian *Allgemeines Landrecht* of 1794, the French *Code civil* of 1804, and the Dutch *Burgerlijk Wetboek* of 1838 - essentially a copy of the French *Code civil* valid until then - later replaced by the new *Burgerlijk Wetboek* of 1992, or in separate statutes confined to a particular area, such as the English Sale of Goods Act 1893, succeeded by the Sale of Goods Act 1979. Legal rules on typical commercial customs, contracts, and institutions - such as commercial records, partnerships and companies, bills of exchange, and maritime commerce - were often laid down in separate Commercial codes such as the French *Code de commerce* (1807) and the Dutch *Wetboek van Koophandel* (1838) - the latter again more or less a copy of the French *Code de commerce* valid until then.[4] The German *Allgemeines Deutsches Handelsgesetzbuch* of 1861 was a mix of provisions on general contract law and specific commercial rules: no common German codification existed yet.[5] With the German *Bürgerliches Gesetzbuch* of 1900 this lacunae disappeared, and the *Handelsgesetzbuch* of 1896 had thus more a specific commercial character than its predecessor, the *Allgemeines Deutsches Handelsgesetzbuch*.[6] Many of these commercial codes were - at least partly - a codification of existing commercial usages[7] or drawing upon even earlier codifications of such usages, like the French *Ordonnance sur le commerce* (1673) and *Ordonnance de la marine* (1681) of Jean Baptiste Colbert (1619-1683) and Louis XIV (1638-1715).[8]

Content-wise, these codes were primarily a continuation of previous existing commercial and mercantile usages, including certain international maritime usages.[9] These mainly local customs were thus made by private actors, the merchants, even if public actors, such as city councils or lords, recorded and - to a certain

3 E.g. Bergfeld 1987, p. 101–103; Kanning 2003, p. 61.
4 E.g. Flume 2014, p. 53-56; Klomp 1998, p. 13-24.
5 Flume 2014, p. 56-59.
6 Flume 2014, p. 65-67.
7 E.g. Flume 2014, p. 50-51, 56-57; Rückert 1993, p. 24-25.
8 E.g. Gelderblom 2013, p. 133-139; Flume 2014, p. 49-50; Klomp 1998, p. 94-97.
9 Gelderblom 2013, p. 133-139.

extent - transformed them.[10] However, since the French revolution, states generally abolished different classes in society, including a 'merchant class'. This is reflected in civil and/or commercial codes after the French revolution - such as the *Code de Commerce* (1807) and the *Allgemeines Deutsches Handelsgesetzbuch* (1861) - where commercial law was regulated as the professional law of a business community, and no longer as the law of a 'merchant class'.[11] Also, these civil and/or commercial codes were to create legal unity for emerging national markets - like in France - or interregional markets - like in the German Confederation.[12] Because these codes are embedded in the national legal systems, they also imply the enforcement of agreements between private actors.[13] Moreover, in the eighteenth century a *laissez-faire* policy replaced the mercantilism of, for instance, Colbert of the previous century.[14] For these civil and commercial codes - and for Europe obviously many more could be listed here - the regulation of commercial relations thus took place by a public actor - the national legislator - on a national level in the form of legislation. Indeed, cross-border commercial relations were increasingly governed by national codifications - such the *Code de commerce* (1807), the *Wetboek van Koophandel* (1838), the *Allgemeines Deutsches Handelsgesetzbuch* (1861), and the Sale of Goods Act 1893 - which in turn underlined the importance of rules on conflicts of laws, i.e. private international law, for which the Hague Conference on Private International Law was first held in 1893.[15]

In the second half of the nineteenth century and at the beginning of the twentieth century, many European states faced an enormous increase in trade, internally as well as internationally. Internally, this increase in trade, but also its changing character, was due to, inter alia, the expansion of railway networks that started to connect once isolated markets effectively creating unified national markets.[16] The challenges faced due to the increase and changes in internal trade had to be met by the above-mentioned national civil and/or commercial codes, many of which were modified in the course of the nineteenth and twentieth century.[17] The increase in international trade was not only due to, for instance, technological progress, but also stimulated by an important liberalization of trade towards the end of the nineteenth century through a series of bilateral and sometimes multilateral treaties.[18] Several international, private organizations were set up to facilitate this globalizing

10 See Van Hofstraeten.

11 Flume 2014, p. 53-54, 59-60.

12 E.g. Bergfeld 1987, p. 101–103; Kanning 2003, p. 61.

13 See e.g. North 1991, p. 97; Greif 2004, p. 109-110.

14 See e.g. Screpanti & Zamagni 1993, p. 25-27, 42-43.

15 Although the activities of the Hague Conference are also extended to family law and the law of succession. See Schmitthoff 1981, p. 26-27.

16 See e.g. for England: Deane 1973, p. 209-216; Deane & Cole 1969, p. 238-241; Aldcroft 1992, p. 66-69; Mathias 1983, p. 261-262; for Germany: Hoffmann 1963, p. 104-105; Pierenkemper & Tilly 2004, p. 58-68, 76-80; Henderson 1975, p. 51; for France: Labrousse 1954, p. 9; Price 1981, p. 20-26, 27-37, 109-119; Bouvier 1997, p. 652, 668-669.

17 Flume 2014, p. 56, 64-65.

18 See e.g. Deane & Cole 1969, p. 47; Wintle 2000, p. 147-150; Van Zanden & Van Riel 2004, p. 183-187; Bairoch 1989, p. 36-45.

trade, such as the International Law Association (1873), the International Maritime Committee (1896), and the Hague Conference of International Law.[19] The First World War abruptly put these initiatives on hold.

In the wake of the war, a first wave of international regulations and instruments that still remain in force was created. Again, several international organizations were set up, most notably the League of Nations in 1919, a public actor, but also, for instance, the International Institute for the Unification of Private Law (UNIDROIT) in 1926 as an auxiliary organ of the League of Nations, and the International Chamber of Commerce (ICC), founded in 1919, which are essentially private actors.[20]

Several international treaties regulating certain commercial transactions were concluded, for example the International Convention for the Unification of Certain Rules of Law relating to Bills of Lading ('Hague Visby Rules', 1924, amended in 1968 and 1979), which has as its premise that a carrier has greater bargaining power than the shipper, and that to protect the interests of the shipper/cargo-owner, the law should at least impose a set of minimum obligations upon the carrier.[21] Unlike the national civil and commercial codes, these regulations are more specific and thus limited in application to specific (aspects of) commercial relations, but on the other hand they are meant to regulate matters at a global level.

It is also important to emphasize the relevance of regulatory efforts developed by private actors, such as, for instance, the ICC. The ICC published several model contracts and standard conditions such as the Uniform Customs and Practice for Documentary Credits (UCP) (1933, latest, 6th version 2007, UCP 600) - a set of rules on the issuance and use of letters of credit - and the International Commercial Terms (INCOTERMS) (1936, latest, 8th version 2010) - a series of pre-defined commercial terms widely used in international commercial transactions. These efforts have often filled regulatory gaps with a view to providing commercial parties with clear rules that offer predictability in a way that aligns with their commercial interests. In addition, trade associations, such as the Grain and Feed Trade Association (GAFTA, 1871) or the International Air Transport Association (IATA, 1945), are involved in providing model contracts and rules for the transactions that take place within their trade. In this context, the development of corporate codes of conduct also should not be forgotten.

The Second World War interrupted the increase of international trade once more, but after the war a second wave of international instruments was created. These include, for instance, the OECD Guidelines for Multinational Enterprises (1976, latest, 7th version 2011), which was initially designed as an annex to the OECD Declaration on International Investment to regulate mainly foreign direct investment, but over time transformed into a self-standing global framework for globally operating companies and international trade. These instruments aim to codify the expectation of countries that commercial parties respect fundamental social values. In the area of carriage of goods, the United Nations created the

19 Schmitthoff 1981, p. 26-29.
20 Schmitthoff 1981, p. 24-26.
21 See e.g. Goode 2010, p. 1144.

Hamburg Rules (1978) to offer an alternative to the Hague Visby Rules, which was perceived to be too carrier-friendly, and the Convention on Multimodal Transport (1980) in response to the changing nature of transportation modalities.[22] Following the demise of the League of Nations, the UNIDROIT was re-established in 1940. Initially the Institute directed its activities again mainly towards international conventions, such as the Hague Uniform Laws on the International Sale of Goods (1964). The United Nations Commission on International Trade Law (UNCITRAL), established in 1966, subsequently used the Hague Uniform Laws (1964) as a source of inspiration for the UN Convention on the International Sale of Goods (CISG) (1980).[23] In 1994 UNIDROIT published general principles on commercial contract law at a global level, the UNIDROIT Principles (1994, 2004, 2010). Only recently, the regulation of commercial relations became also an issue at the United Nations. In the recently adopted UN Guiding Principles on Business and Human Rights (2011), the expectation towards companies to respect human rights has been extended to cover also business partners.

In the aftermath of the Second World War, the forerunners of the current European Union were created, inter alia, establishing a common European market. In the creation of this common market, the European Union promulgated several directives regulating commercial relations in which goods or services are exchanged between businesses, inter alia, the Commercial Agency Directive (1986), Financial Instruments Directive (2004), and the Late Payments Directive (2007). These Directives cover a range of subjects that either had been regulated by national governments or at least traditionally belonged to their competence. Whether or not the European Union is the right - public - actor is amongst others extensively discussed in literature on proportionality and subsidiarity.[24] Most recently, in 2011, the European Commission proposed the adoption of a Common European Sales Law (CESL) (2011), which has an opt-in character.

The developments within the European Union have been further supported by non-legislative initiatives involving private actors, primarily academics. In 1995, the Lando Commission published general principles on contract law at a European level, the Principles of European Contract Law (PECL) (1995, 1999, 2003), which had a follow up in the more extensive and scholarly Draft Common Frame of Reference (DCFR) (2009). The DCFR had been supported by the European Union. Other activities at the European level directed at commercial relations can be identified in the form of, for instance, the Principles of European Law on Commercial Agency, Franchise and Distribution Contracts (2009) and the Principles of European Law on Service Contracts (2007).

This brief historical overview of the current regulatory environment for commercial contracts is not comprehensive, many other instruments and initiatives could be mentioned, but it serves to illustrate that commercial law constitutes a

22 The Hague Visby Rules and the Hamburg Rules are eventually to be replaced by the Rotterdam Rules (2009, not yet in force). The Convention on Multimodal Transport never entered into force.

23 See Schmitthoff 1981, p. 24-26; Hartkamp 2011, p. 240-241.

24 See for an overview, instead of many, Jansen & Rademacher 2012, p. 299-313.

complex amalgamation of private and public actors at different levels of governance developing rules for different types of commercial contracts. We detect certain waves with respect to who develops the rules for commercial transactions. It can be seen that historically, private actors have borne responsibility for creating rules to regulate their transactions and that this private regulation has been supported and subsequently codified by public actors. We highlight, however, that as European and global trade increases and economic integration progresses, there is not only renewed attention for regulation of commercial transactions at a level other than the national, but also a revival of rules created by private actors that suit with their commercial activities, although these rules must fit within the frameworks primarily provided by public actors. What the proper role of the public actor, whether the European Union or international political institutions, is in this context is the subject of much discussion in the literature, an example being the proposed CESL that would apply to cross-border business-to-business sales contracts.[25] In light of the complexity and fragmentation of the current regulatory environment as well as the suggestions made by European and international actors, it is highly relevant to consider who is best qualified to develop the rules for commercial contracts and at what level such rules should be implemented. The following section aims to assist this debate by identifying normative criteria for assessing which actor should regulate and at what level.

3. How should Commercial Law be Regulated?

3.1. *Introduction*

In order to develop the normative criteria for determining at what level commercial law should be regulated and by whom, we start by addressing the primary purpose of the subject matter of commercial transactions as well as the role and function of the law in this context.

The basic assumptions made in this contribution are, firstly, that commercial law exists to facilitate the exchange of goods and services between commercial parties in a free market economy and, secondly, that facilitating such exchange of goods and services can best be achieved by means of exercising party autonomy. Commercial law should therefore facilitate the exercise of party autonomy and enforce agreements freely made between commercial actors. Having said this, further regulation may be needed in certain circumstances. This can be the case when the actions of private actors jeopardize the exercise of party autonomy, for instance, in the case of fraud or where one party takes illegitimate advantage of an inequality of bargaining power.[26] In such cases, further regulation is needed to safeguard party autonomy. Moreover, further regulation may be called for when the exercise of party autonomy has negative effects on the market or on society at large. Regulation may then be needed if the result of the exercise of party autonomy interferes with

25 See, e.g., Schwenzer 2012; the various contributions to Magnus 2012; Kornet 2012.

26 Irvine 2001, p. 343: 'the first danger of an unregulated market: the inevitable temptation to perpetrate fraud'.

the proper functioning of the market or results in non-compliance with fundamental societal values.

3.2. *Facilitating Party Autonomy*

We start from the basic presumption that commercial law should be guided by the fundamental principle of party autonomy and, hence, be directed towards enforcing the agreements and declarations that commercial actors autonomously create. This presumption can be justified with a view to the core function that commercial law fulfils, which is to regulate the relationship between two private actors that enter into a transaction with the primary purpose to successfully complete an exchange of goods or services between them. From this follows, in our view, that commercial law must be directed towards facilitating this objective.

In this context, two core arguments, an economic and a sociological, support our understanding that facilitating the exchange of goods and services is best achieved by adhering to the principle of party autonomy. If one takes an economic perspective, one would start from the assumption that the parties that enter into the transaction are guided by the objective to improve their welfare and seek primarily to conclude agreements that are beneficial for them. This is in particular the case in the context of commercial transactions, since commercial parties' primary objective is the pursuit of profits and thus they enter into exchanges that allow them to realize this objective. From this economic perspective, the function of contracts and contract law is to facilitate efficient exchanges and promote gains from trade by making it possible for commercial parties to improve their welfare through voluntary exchange.[27] It is assumed that the parties will only agree to terms that make each of them better off, and that the agreements they conclude consequently will lead to mutual gain. In international trade practice, the recognition of party autonomy is paramount, since the process of voluntary exchange promotes economic growth through competition and the efficient allocation of resources. An important function of contract law is therefore to facilitate exchange by enforcing contractual commitments and to sanction parties that engage in opportunistic behaviour by means of breaching these voluntary agreements in the future.[28]

Yet, the justification for party autonomy on the ground of an economic perspective requires additional backing from the sociological perspective on the commercial relation. This is due to the fact that markets and thus the perceived individual pursuit for interest-driven and eventually welfare-improving exchange is dependent on contextual factors in order to function properly.[29] From the perspec-

27 See e.g. Schäfer & Ott 2004, p. 5; Posner 2003, p. 94; Cooter & Ulen 2004, p. 196 *et seq*.

28 Compare with further references Kornet 2006, p. 290 *et seq*.

29 Etzioni 1988, pointedly p. 199: '(...) neoclassicists have valiantly tried to deal with the need for rules of the game (...) by generating them internally, by viewing them as having emerged from rational, self-maximizing individuals, who are seeking to improve their relationships. However, (...) there is no historical or logical reason to assume that fully formed individuals preceded the community or shared rules. Indeed, (...) individuals would not exist, if there were no community and no rules.'; Streeck 1997, p. 199 ('(...) an economy can perform well only to the extent that it is embedded in a well-integrated society (...).').

tive of economic sociology, the individual's pursuit for interest-driven exchange is understood as embedded in the broader social context of the market. In this specific context, parties are only capable of pursuing their interests thereby improving overall welfare by means of exchanging goods and services if certain underlying contextual factors are present, such as a specific morality,[30] the existence of social relations that reinforce trust between the parties,[31] but also, and very important for our discussion, legal rules set by governments[32] that institutionalize specific expectations. One crucial contextual factor for markets to function properly is in this respect the need to institutionalize and uphold the expectation that an agreement that parties on the market conclude will be adhered to even if it eventually turns out not to be beneficial for one party.[33] Hence, as a core of being able to engage in economic behaviour, it is necessary that parties in the first place can trust that the agreements they intend to make are adhered to and upheld. This can partly already be achieved by the presence of a social relation between the parties to a contract, an underlying 'ethic on the market', or a social convention from which follows that agreements should eventually be upheld and not deviated from, but it requires as last resort also the coercive power of the state in the form of legal enforcement.[34]

One can add in this respect that our suggestion to take as the starting point for the regulation of commercial law the respect for party autonomy is also by no means a novel understanding in private law scholarship. Quite the contrary, it merely embraces the traditional theoretical understanding about the core function of private law. Historically, private law in general was initially perceived as the specific field of law that deals with the concrete relationship between two private parties and takes their private interests as the ultimate benchmark when deciding about the enforcement of private agreements.[35] Hence, an integral part of private law in general is in fact the freedom of contract and the respect for party autonomy.

From what has been said so far, one can draw the preliminary conclusion that the role of the law in regulating commercial transactions is in the first place reserved to enforcing what private actors autonomously agree upon. As a result, legal intervention beyond this facilitative role on whatever level merits explicit justification.

30 One of the most influential sociological attempts to reveal an underlying morality as a significant factor for the capitalist economic system is still Weber's study on the impact of protestant ethic on capitalism, i.e. Weber 2002 [1920].

31 Granovetter 1985, p. 487 *et seq.*

32 Etzioni 1988, p. 211 *et seq.*; Streeck 1997, p. 202 and *passim*.

33 Streeck 1997, p. 201 *et seq.*; Beckert 2012, p. 250 *et seq.*

34 Etzioni 1988, p. 212; Streeck 1997, p. 202: 'Social constraints on rational behavior can reinforce trust, and thus facilitate the rational pursuit of economic objectives (...) they may consist of impersonal rules, especially formal law, that provide for sufficiently strong sanctions to make opportunistic withdrawal from reciprocal obligations highly unlikely or factually impossible.'

35 The historically most influential proponent of this understanding of private law is probably Savigny 1840, Volume I, p. 22, but it also appears in the famous understanding of 'private law society' as suggested by Böhm 1966. More recent prominent proponents of this understanding are, despite important differences in detail, Simmonds 1984; Weinrib 1995.

3.3. *Setting the Limits - Regulating Negative Externalities*

While we have so far argued for a strong role of party autonomy in the regulation of commercial relationships, we nonetheless agree that there are indeed situations where legal intervention in the agreements of private parties can be justified on substantive grounds. There are, to our understanding, two core constellations, in which the fundamental principle of party autonomy requires limitation in the form of legal intervention in the commercial relation.

Firstly, legal intervention is necessary whenever the parties themselves or one of them jeopardizes the exercise of party autonomy. This may happen in the form of fraud or if one party exploits an actual or structural inequality of bargaining power. The argument in favour of legal intervention for this constellation is already a very well-known justification for an interventionist approach in consumer law.[36] Party autonomy can, however, be equally jeopardized in a commercial relation and legal regulation in the field of commercial law needs to be directed towards safeguarding and establishing party autonomy. This implies concretely that legal rules need to be in place which allow rendering agreements or single negotiated provisions in a contract void if these have been entered into on the basis of fraud, an actual or structural imbalance of bargaining power, or unfair behaviour. Yet, what criteria should be guiding when determining whether or not interventionist rules should be applicable? One could of course argue that general criteria, such as the size of the company, provide an indication for structural inequality and thus serve as a justification for intervention. This is currently specifically suggested in the form of providing legal protection to small and medium-sized in a similar way as it is offered to consumers.[37] We, however, argue that such general criteria, in particular the size of the company are not useful in this respect. The size of an enterprise says often little about its actual bargaining power. On the contrary, a very small company can, due to its specific expertise or its highly-demanded niche products, have in fact structural power. Empirical research into the functioning of cross-border commercial contracting supports this. In some sectors, one can in fact observe that contractual supply-chains are organized as supplier-driven with small and medium-sized enterprises as the dominating actors.[38] Against this background, the decision of whether legal intervention is required to safeguard party autonomy, can only be taken with a view to, firstly, the specifics of the relation as such, and, in order to identify whether structural imbalances exist, with a view to the relevant sector or market.

This focus on the concrete commercial relationship notwithstanding, we explicitly also argue for a broader perspective when conceptualizing the normative criteria that should guide legal regulation of commercial relations. As already indicated above, agreements of commercial parties are not concluded in a vacuum, but they function in a broader economic and social context.[39] This implies that they

36 See, e.g., Wilhemsson 2004, p. 719 *et seq.*

37 Compare the contributions in Loos & Samoy 2014.

38 See extensively on the sectoral differences between contractual relations in global value chains: Gereffi, Humphrey & Sturgeon 2005.

39 See above section 2.3.

may have effects on this context, positive as well as negative. Given this embedding, it is indispensable that the commercial relation needs to give due respect to the interests that derive from this social context. This is why legal regulation is needed whenever the interest of the commercial parties are likely to jeopardize social interests, with the aim to stabilize the expectation that such destructive behaviour is legally not accepted.

To that end, legal intervention into the agreement of private actors becomes indispensable once the commercial relationship negatively affects the functioning of the economy and the competitive market as its organizing paradigm. Otherwise, commercial parties risk by means of executing a contract destroying the economic basis of their relation. To be more precise, legal regulation may be required when voluntarily agreed commercial agreements produce inefficient market outcomes or when parties act contrary to the internal fairness standards on the market. A prominent example in which legal intervention is required is agreements between companies on price fixing that seek to undermine competition. Such agreements may not only be regulated by public law with the help of criminal or administrative law; it is also commercial contract law that is considered to play a role here. It may require provisions in commercial law that determine the enforcement of agreements between parties with a view to whether its outcome complies with the social interest of maintaining a competitive market.[40]

Next to the need of regulatory elements in commercial law that aim at safeguarding the institution of the competitive market, commercial law should, in our view, also intervene into private relations when the agreements between commercial parties are both in the interest of the contracting parties and respect the rules of competition, but nonetheless have negative effects on society. This is due to the fact that even the competitive market is not the ultimate frame of reference for a commercial relation to function properly. The competitive market, in turn, operates in a broader context of society and in order to sustain in the long run needs to maintain its legitimacy, namely its 'licence to operate'.[41] This claimed necessity for the market to maintain its legitimacy in society derives from the understanding that markets cannot function stably without an overarching social structure; instead, they remain embedded in a broader social context.[42] Hence, in order to function on a stable basis they necessarily must respect these interests. This, as a result, suggests that markets and thus commercial relations as their core structure require regulatory elements that restrict commercial activity in the interest of society.[43] In this context, one can distinguish between different directions that such market-restricting legal regula-

40 See on this point Wielsch 2013, p. 102 *et seq*.

41 This term has been coined by Gunningham 2007.

42 *Locus classicus* in economic sociology: Polanyi 2001 [1944]; Granovetter 1985.

43 Pointedly for this argument Joerges 2011, p. 472: 'The proponents of the self-regulating market, he warns us, expose "economy and society" to economic and social risks, which will provoke, and, indeed, may be dependent upon, counter-movements striving for stability and protection. There is neither an invisible hand at work, which would ensure prosperity and social integration as a lasting effect of the expansion of market rationality, nor will the double movement somehow find some stable social equilibrium automatically. Stability will, in the last resort, be dependent upon political action.'

tion can have. There are, on the one hand, societal interests that may already be jeopardized once they become subject to the interest-driven logic of the market.[44] Hence, an appropriate protection of these interests requires legal intervention in the form of keeping them entirely free from the market logic. The prominent examples for such comprehensive market-restricting rules are, for instance, rules prohibiting a market for human organs, which in commercial law, would be reflected in the form of mandatory rules prohibiting the enforcement of such agreements. Controversially debated cases would, for instance, be prostitution, or the employment of children. On the other hand, there are also social interests that are not jeopardized by becoming subject to an economic exchange as such, but nonetheless require protection against becoming subject to unrestricted market logic. For such constellations, regulation in commercial law needs not to be directed towards prohibiting the commercial exchange, but rather to impose restrictions on how the commercial exchange should be performed in light of the social interest affected. The paradigmatic examples for such constellations are corrective intervention into market relations in order to safeguard respect for human rights when conducting commercial transactions or the claim for a *democratic* capitalism, which would include the political empowerment of certain interest groups, such as labour.[45] Regulation to safeguard these social interests are of course in the first place relevant with respect to areas of the law other than commercial law. They provide the normative justification for legal intervention in the form of laws protecting the rights of employees or consumers. Yet, they are also indirectly relevant for the regulation of commercial relations, to be more precise, to the extent the commercial relation has negative impact on the rights of these parties when performing cross-border contracts.[46] Another noteworthy social interest that is prone to be jeopardized by commercial relations and that is currently debated as to whether it requires protection by legal regulation could be the protection of the natural environment[47] and thus legal regulation in case the performance of commercial contracts causes or contributes to environmental pollution.

To conclude, we have identified three main interests that regulation in commercial law should be oriented towards. In the first place, commercial law needs to be oriented on the commercial interest of the parties and their pursuit of commercial activity with a view to realizing mutual gain through voluntary exchange. Secondly, commercial law would need to be based on the market interest in the sense of maintaining a properly functioning market. Thirdly, we recognize that commercial

44 Compare for this argument, the similar observations of Shleifer 2004 and Sandel 2012 and their different conclusions on how to deal with these problems.

45 Streeck 1997, p. 203 *et seq*.

46 This is recently emphasized by Collins 2014, who suggests ultimately, however, to regulate the violation of such social interests with the help of consumer contract law. Some aspects of regulating social interests in commercial contract law are dealt with by Schwenzer & Leisinger 2007 and Schlechtriem 2007.

47 The relevance of the environment as an interest of society that informs regulation has already gained some prominence with respect to regulation in consumer contract law (see, e.g., Wilhemsson 1998; Wilhelmsson 2002-2003; Wilhemsson 2004, p. 723) and company law (see, e.g., Sjåfjell 2011).

activity can affect the broader the interests of society by violating its fundamental values. Hence, the decision, which rule-maker is most appropriate for enacting legal rules for commercial transaction depends, primarily, on which actor is best able to foster the commercial interest by safeguarding party autonomy and enforcing voluntary agreements and declarations while at the same time maintaining a proper functioning of the market and protecting fundamental social values. As we seek to show below, there is, however, no such all-encompassing competent actor. Commercial law would therefore need to be developed by the interplay of different actors, the competence of which is determined with a view to the interest that a specific regulatory element fulfils.

3.4. *Criteria for Determining Who should make Rules for Commercial Transactions*

In the introduction, we already presented the field of commercial law as a multi-level and multi-actor system. Commercial law has evolved on different territorial levels - regional, national, European and global - and with the involvement of various actors, coming from the public as well as the private sphere.

As a useful starting point for the analysis on the actors that should set the rules in commercial law, we start by drawing a general distinction between two different general types of actors. As has been set out before, commercial law encompasses, firstly, the rules that are created by public actors, in particular national laws dealing with the rules on commercial contracting, European directives and regulations and legal instruments developed by international political organizations. Secondly, commercial law is equally influenced by the informal rules of private actors. This refers, on the one hand, to the contracting parties that create the rules that govern their relation by means of the individually negotiated contract. On the other hand, the private rules in the area of commercial law encompasses, as prominently emphasized by scholars that analyse business contracts from a sociological perspective, also the rules of the contracting community, such as codified self-regulatory frameworks of a specific sector, trade, or industry, customs or implicit understandings between the contracting parties that shape the way in which commercial relations are performed.[48] Given the significance of such private rules in influencing the parties' behaviour, it is important not to ignore such elements, but to take them seriously as regulating commercial relations. When determining the appropriate actor to develop a particular regulation, we suggest taking the substantive interest to serve as the core criterion. This has several consequences for the appropriate regulation in the area of commercial law. It involves regulatory elements from different actors depending on whether the regulation is oriented on the commercial interest, the market interest or the social interest and thus results in what we define as a multi-actor system. Moreover, it also has an influence the level of regulation, which accordingly needs to be determined with a view to where the interest that a specific regulation aims to protect is dealt with best.

48 See, instead of many, Campbell, Collins & Wightman 2003.

3.4.1. Regulation Serving the Commercial Interest

To the extent that the rules in commercial law should be oriented on the principle of party autonomy and seek to protect the commercial interest, it is the parties to the transaction that have the most relevant expertise and legitimacy to decide about their interests. The core of commercial law is thus to leave the parties a great deal of autonomy in regulating their transactions and to understand the role of public bodies as merely facilitative and supportive. We posit that the appropriate regulator for commercial law depends on which actor can facilitate and give effect to the exercise of party autonomy by providing rules that are (i) clear and predictable, (ii) reflect the needs, interests and expectations of commercial actors in a particular contracting community, (iii) are capable of adaptation to new developments and practices, and (iv) and promote a coherent system.

In the first place, commercial actors need clarity and predictability with respect to the rules that govern their transactions. Lord Mansfield's statement in *Vallejo* v *Wheeler* is illustrative of this:

> 'In all mercantile transactions the great object should be certainty: and therefore, it is of more consequence that a rule should be certain, than whether the rule is established one way or the other. Because speculators in trade then know what ground to go upon.'[49]

Certainty and predictability are not there for their own sake, but they serve an instrumental goal. Commercial actors use contracts to plan and coordinate their commercial activities with others and to manage the risks associated with their transactions. To be able to do so effectively, they must know with some clarity and predictability the rules to which they are legally bound. Where rules that apply to the contract are unclear, vague or open-ended, predictability is undermined, and contracting parties will be required to incur the transaction costs that are associated with negotiating and drafting provisions in the contract that restore such clarity and predictability. Clarity and predictability play a particularly important role in certain types of commercial arrangements, in particular where third parties become involved, for example in the context of complex construction projects where multiple parties are involved such as suppliers and subcontractors, or in the context of financing arrangements, for example bills of exchange. A particular contractual arrangement cannot simply be viewed in isolation, but impacts on other transactions and contractual arrangements, which means that clarity and predictability becomes important not only in the context of assessing the individual risks associated with a particular transaction, but also in the context of the broader commercial activities in which the commercial actor is involved. In line with this criterion, it has to be identified whether private or public actors are best able to provide rules that

[49] *Vallejo* v *Wheeler* (1774) 1 Cowp. 143, 153; 98 E.R. 1012, 1017. Also see e.g. Scott 2000, p. 149: referring to certainty, predictability and stability as the 'bedrock desiderata of commercial law'. Also see e.g. Orgalime's Position Paper on the Commission's Proposal for a New Regulation on a Common European Sales Law (2011/0284) of 23 July 2012, which emphasizes the need for legal certainty. Available via <www.orgalime.org>.

are clear and predictable and at which level of regulation clarity and predictability can best be achieved.

The second criterion stems from the economics of federalism literature, according to which decentralized, local decision-making is preferred and regulation at a higher, centralized level requires an explicit justification. It is assumed that regulation should take place at the lowest level since it is then able to reflect the local preferences of a particular community.[50] Within a particular community, the preferences tend to converge due to shared underlying values and norms, and such preferences are reflected in various social institutions, including the law, and reinforced through the democratic process. It is suggested that if a person has different preferences than those prevalent in the community, they can 'vote with their feet' and move to another community where the law reflects their preferences. In the context of this contribution, we do not conceive this argument as concerning exclusively territorial preferences, in the sense of possibly varying preferences of commercial actors in different jurisdictions. Instead, commercial actors can be seen to participate in contracting communities that are defined by the characteristics of a particular type of transaction and the sector, trade or industry within which the commercial activity takes place.[51] It has previously been highlighted that commercial transactions are diverse and cover a wide range of activities, for instance, sales, carriage, insurance, finance, lease and so on and so forth. Each type of transaction has its own characteristics, different needs and interests. Furthermore, the characteristics, needs and interests may also differ from one market – in the sense of sectors, trades or industries – to another. In this light, our reference to 'local preferences' does not necessarily only relate to differences between territorial units, but also differences in preferences between markets. We suggest that rules aimed at facilitating commercial transactions should reflect the specific preferences of a particular contracting community, addressing the particular needs and interests of specific markets. Following the reasoning underlying the economics of federalism, we therefore suggest that commercial law should be made at the lowest level, the level that is most closely connected to the relevant contracting community or market, and therefore regulation at a higher level requires explicit justification. Such justification could exist where the preferences of different markets converge.

Providing solutions that reflect the needs, interests and expectations of a particular contracting community leads to efficiency, since the rules that are made meet the preferences of the majority of parties within a particular contracting community and thereby reduce transaction costs, because they do not incur the costs of 'moving' to a system of rules that does reflect their preferences. Of course, in contract law, commercial actors do not have to physically move to another jurisdiction, they can utilize their party autonomy to opt into another system through, for instance, a choice of law clause. However, this does lead to the additional transaction costs of finding the set of rules that does reflect the individual preferences. In commercial contract law, this means that the appropriate law-maker is the law-

50 See Tiebout 1956; also Wagner 2005; and the explanation provided in the contribution by Bull, Ge, Goanţă, Kawakami & Smits in this book.

51 See Wightman 2003.

maker who is capable of creating solutions that reflect the preferences of its contracting community, in the sense of providing standardized solutions that the majority of contracting parties within a particular contracting community would agree upon.[52] In this way, the transaction costs for the majority of contracting parties are reduced, because they do not have bear the costs of negotiating contract terms that reflect their needs and interests. Only those commercial actors with atypical requirements would need to incur the costs of either finding a system of rules that reflect their preferences, or negotiating and drafting terms that reflect their specific requirements.

In accordance with our third criterion, the rules should be capable of adaptation to new developments and practices within the commercial community in order to continue to meet the needs and interests of commercial actors and remain relevant. Where the rules lose their relevance, commercial parties will need to incur the costs of exercising their party autonomy to negotiate appropriate terms. Rules that are set in stone and incapable of, or difficult to, change, will be contracted out of and lose their relevance and undermine the objectives of facilitating the contracting process and reducing transaction costs. Commercial actors are constantly looking to streamline, refine and improve their operations in order to create opportunities to improve efficiency and maximize their gains. Their contractual arrangements will need to adapt to these changes and therefore commercial law needs to remain dynamic and adaptable to new developments and practices within the contracting community. This implies the need for an effective rule-maker who is capable of reacting to new developments and adapting the law appropriately.

With our fourth criterion, we posit that commercial law should ideally avoid regulatory fragmentation and maintain a consistent and coherent system.[53] In our view, it is necessary to avoid an approach whereby certain rules are, for instance, offered at a global level and others at a regional or national level for one and the same transaction. This approach leads to regulatory fragmentation and requires effective conflict rules in private international law to establish which legal issues are to be attributed to which legal framework. Such fragmentation of the legal regimes, where competing and overlapping systems apply to a single contractual relationship, could lead to inconsistent results and consequently undermine the need for clarity and predictability. It is therefore necessary to identify which rule-maker is able to provide a consistent and coherent system.

3.4.2. Regulation Serving the Interests of the Market and Society

As far as regulation should be in place to safeguard that the interests of the market and society are not jeopardized, the situation is different. Whereas for safeguarding party autonomy a strong role for private parties and a facilitative role of public actors was considered appropriate, regulation to restrict party autonomy to safeguard respect for social interest can certainly not be enacted with the same distribu-

52 See Kornet 2006 and the literature referred to there.

53 On fragmentation of the regulatory framework see, e.g., Smits 2010; Kenny, Gillies & Devenney 2011; Kornet 2012.

tion of competences. To the contrary, party autonomy, if allowed to reign freely, may create dangers of barriers to entry and the potential for collusion and monopolistic price-fixing. For instance, if business organizations operate as closed networks, which might be beneficial for them to reduce transaction costs, they can create barriers to entry to newcomers who must, for instance, establish a good reputation to gain entry to a particular trading network. There is potential for collusion and monopolistic pricing where the relative bargaining power between buyers and sellers is altered or pushed 'out of balance'. Competition law as enacted by public bodies therefore plays a vital role in providing regulatory measures that address concerted practices and anti-competitive behaviour and promote open and competitive markets, but also securities regulation, insolvency regulation, or intellectual property laws are needed. In order to determine at what level these rules should be set by a public body one would need to identify the proper market that needs to be protected. Next to public competition law, for which the distribution of competences is dealt with in a specific chapter of this book,[54] the interest of a competitive market and its protection against the anti-competitive behaviour of commercial parties in exercising their party autonomy also needs to be reflected within the core of commercial contract law as focussed upon in this chapter. On that point, it is necessary to have in place rules that can influence the decision on the enforcement of agreements that parties in their mutual benefit make with the objective to prevent competition. Such rules can be flexible as to the appropriate consequence, i.e. denial of enforcement or enforcement of the contract against the party having the stronger bargaining position in order to sanction its anti-competitive behaviour. The important element of the rules in commercial law is, however, that they be oriented on the objective to protect to the largest extent possible the interest of a competitive market and thus deter the private parties' from engaging into anti-competitive behaviour with the use of party autonomy.[55]

Insofar as the rules of commercial law are guided by the legitimate interest of society to have its fundamental values respected by the agreements of commercial parties, the situation differs again. Being oriented on an interest of society, regulation must in this constellation be conceptualized by the affected society and not the commercial parties. However, for this type of regulation, an important distinction would need to be introduced. Intuitively, it is for this type of regulation certainly a public body, namely the political legislator that would seem the most competent actor to enact regulation. It is generally perceived as the institutionalized representation of society. Yet, one should, to our understanding, equally not forget that there is also a productive potential in society outside the state, in the social sphere to further that public interests are respected in the shadow of institutionalized poli-

54 Cauffman & Philipsen in this book.

55 For such rules with respect to the interest of protecting the internal European Market, see the ruling of the Court of Justice C-453/99, *Bernhard Crehan* v *Courage Ltd.* [2001] I-06297, on this ruling and its influence on national rules on the enforcement of contracts (with a view to England), Collins 2003, p. 51 *et seq.*

tics.[56] In this regard, this social sphere has already proven on manifold accounts that it is capable of enacting regulation, in the form of 'privatized private [or commercial] laws'.[57] Of particular importance for such privatized regulation are the results of manifold pressures deriving from civil society,[58] pressure from industry peers,[59] consumer pressure,[60] and the voluntary undertaking of commercial parties to fulfil the role of a political actor.[61] These pressures can result in self-regulation whenever it appears in the agreements or commitments made by private actors or self-regulatory guidelines, which exhibit the aim to safeguard respect for the interests of society. Having established this distinction between essentially two types of public actors that are capable of enacting regulation that serves the interests of society, the competence and thus the weight in the law-making process of each, institutionalized politics and the politicized social sphere, requires further attention. With the recognition of the politicized private sphere, a decision as to who we deem the *ultimately* competent actor to develop rules for commercial parties that aim to safeguard social interests becomes indispensable. Although this might seem in the first place unsatisfactory as an answer, we accept that there is no clear-cut and overall valid answer. Since both regulatory instances have their advantages and disadvantages, we argue that the question of who is competent would need to be answered by advocating a combination of both regulatory elements. On the one hand, regulation enacted by private actors, in particular by the commercial parties themselves and by trade associations, certainly has the advantage that these actors have the best expertise on how to effectively regulate commercial relations.[62] They know the specifics of the sector and the individual relation and thus are better able to develop regulation that fits their needs. Yet, regulation by these actors exhibits, at the same time, the greatest risk of enacting regulation that is 'biased' and influenced by private interests and therefore not truly serving the interest of society at large.[63] One may accordingly say that the politicized private sphere has, so to say, the best competence to enact effective regulation, but the least motivation to enact regulation serving the social interest.[64] The political legislator may, conversely, due to its legitimatory capital of democratic elections ultimately be viewed as the more competent actor to

56 On this public dimension in the social sphere and its relation to the state and private sphere with a historical and critical perspective, fundamentally Habermas 1989.

57 Michaels & Jansen 2006, p. 868.

58 Among others: Levy & Kaplan 2008, p. 443 *et seq.*; Anderson 2013.

59 Gunningham & Rees 1997.

60 On this political potential of consumers, see amongst others Micheletti 2003; Stehr, Henning & Weiler 2006.

61 See already Haufler 2001 and more recently (with, however, differences in the approach) Flohr *et al.* 2010.

62 For this argument, see amongst others Cutler, Haufler & Porter 1999, p. 18 ('Private Authority can (...) achieve a high degree of acceptance through recognition by others of specific knowledge, expertise, and representational skills.').

63 Christodoulidis 2013.

64 Teubner 2012, p. 92 frames this as the 'motivation-competency dilemma'.

enact regulation that serves the interest of society.[65] Simultaneously, it does not in every respect have the relevant expertise on how to effectively regulate commercial relations and thus may be less well equipped to enact effective regulation.[66] Against this background, a suggestion of a desirable distribution of competences between private self-regulation serving the interests of society and interventionist regulation by a political regulator can hardly be an overall decision for one regulatory actor or the other. Instead, the focus should be set on the more differentiated forms of regulation, which seek to overcome this dilemma by suggesting the recognition of effective self-regulation, but simultaneously requiring an external regulation by politics in order to avoid private interest biases. An appropriate way out could here be the interaction between the politicized private sphere and external regulation by the legislator, as it has been suggested in the regulation literature in the form of responsive[67] or reflexive[68] regulation, meta-regulation,[69] or enforced self-regulation.[70] For this undertaking of combining self-regulation and regulation, one can refer specifically to the successful attempts in commercial law to generally recognize non-state laws by private actors as a source of enforceable legal obligations in specific areas, but, in the course of doing so, to subject them to legal rules enacted by the public actor that aim to safeguard that the private rules remain oriented on the interests of society. One prominent example for this approach is the legal approach to standard contract terms, which can be viewed as a combination of recognizing such terms legally binding for commercial relations and legislative regulation that specifies conditions under which the enforcement needs to be denied due to its negative effects on society.[71]

To argue for a combination of self-regulation and political intervention as the desirable distribution of competences for regulation in commercial law to the extent it needs to be oriented on the interests of society is, however, still not sufficient as an answer to the question of 'who should do it?'. So far, we have refrained from answering the question of who should enact ultimately the regulatory rules for commercial relations. Is it the political legislator, which should have the monopoly as to the decision on whether or not to recognize private self-regulation? Or should there be in commercial law, conversely, a primary reliance on societal self-regulation with only a corrective intervention of the political legislator? In other words, how should the competences *between* these two political actors be distributed? An answer to this question is in fact closely related to the envisaged level of regulation. As to the level of regulation, we can rely on another variation of the already afore-

65 The case for viewing national institutionalized politics as the most legitimate actor to regulate global trade is made prominently Rodrik 2011. It can also be taken from the 'local preferences' argument as explained above. See *supra* section 3.4.1.

66 On this problem in relation to national legislators and the increase of delegated law-making to the administration and the private sphere taking a historical approach Taggert 2005.

67 Nonet & Selznick 1978.

68 Teubner 1983.

69 Parker 2007 with further references, p. 208, note 6.

70 Braithwaite 1982.

71 For this interaction between private self-regulation and the private law system with amongst others the example of standard contract terms, see Wielsch 2012, *passim*.

mentioned 'local preferences' argument. In the previous section, we have already argued that the level on which regulation would need to be enacted would not need to be oriented on the territorial unit, but on the relevant market with a preference for regulation at the lowest level possible.[72] This argument is equally relevant for regulation that serves the societal interests, but in its traditional form. As this regulation serves the social interest, the appropriate level would consequently depend on the character of the social interest that ought to be protected. Comparable to the regulation of the commercial interest, this implies that for the interests of a global society regulation on a global level would be preferred,[73] whereas for interests of a national society, a preference for regulation on a national level is expressed[74] and the core interests of local communities would be best served by regulation on a local level.[75]

Turning back to the question of how the competences between institutionalized politics and the politicized private sphere are distributed, this claimed appropriate level has an influence. Taking a closer look at the regulatory levels, one can also identify a crucial difference between how the different political actors are institutionalized. The political legislator proves to function very well within territorial national boundaries as the authority to enact regulation with collectively binding effect and in the interest of national society. Self-regulation has in this context evolved as being dependent on the mercy of the state-legal order to be recognized as relevant.[76] However, at the other side of the spectrum, on a global level, the situation seems to be reversed. In this case, the authority of the political legislator seems increasingly erupted by the possibility of commercial parties to choose the law governing their relation and the forum to enforce it, and the lack of an overall political authority on an international level that is competent to enact mandatory regulation for commercial parties. On this level, the diminishing role of a state-like public authority has resulted in an increasing reliance on the value of social pressures and the evolving private rather than public regulation. As Michaels and Jansen pointedly observe: 'In the domestic sphere, all law may really be public; in the global sphere, all law is, arguably, really private'.[77] Consequently, the question

72 See *supra* section 3.4.1.

73 For attempts to frame 'interests of world society' by defining genuine global problems, see Scherer & Palazzo 2008, p. 418, 423 *et seq.* Michaels 2011, p. 166 *et seq.* (p. 167: 'Global problems are characterized by two qualities. First, they concern the world at large, not just one country or one region, or the relations between only a few countries (…). Second, they cannot be separated into different sub-problems that can be solved individually. Rather, an adequate response has an effect on the whole problem.').

74 A prime example for such national interests would be labour standards and the legal regulation of industrial relations, which are perceived differently in national political economies, see on this aspect Rodrik 2011, p. 222 *et seq.*

75 Such interests of local societies could, for instance, be the rights of indigenous communities and their access to traditional knowledge, which can conflict with the interests of global trade (see on this constellation Fischer-Lescano & Teubner 2008) or the need of local communities to give informed consent on community development agreements on the protection of natural resources against unrestricted global trade (see on this constellation Cafaggi 2013, p. 1568).

76 For a typology of these different recognition strategies of states: Michaels 2005, p. 1227 *et seq.*

77 Michaels & Jansen 2006, p. 872.

of who should have the ultimate competence to enact regulation aimed at safeguarding the interest of society becomes linked to the question of who is actually present and capable of regulating effectively and in the interests of the relevant society on the level that we deem appropriate. On the most general level, one would probably therefore need to distinguish between regulation on different levels. In the former constellation of interests of a national society, a stronger role for national institutionalized politics seems feasible,[78] whereas on a global level the adoption of mandatory regulation seems, firstly, less feasible to be adopted and to operate effectively, and, equally important, also difficult to legitimize given the different political preferences of regulating commercial relations on a national level.[79] Politicized private actors and their own self-regulatory mechanisms may for this constellation be the more effective tools to develop regulation for commercial relations, they might even be considered more appropriate to reflect what is of concern for global societies and institutionalize it properly,[80] which would then require a merely coordinating, facilitating and correcting role of the political legislator.[81]

3.5. *Conclusion*

In the previous part, we sought to develop the normative foundation and the criteria for law-making in the field of commercial law in terms of who should set the rules and at what level should the rules be set. To that end, we can summarize our proposals as explicitly refraining from declaring one actor and one level appropriate, and, instead, to decide about the distribution of competences between public and private, but also between regional, national, European, and global with a view to the characteristics of the commercial relation and their regulation, and for market-restricting regulation with respect to the interests of the market and the broader social context in which the commercial relation takes place. This core understanding on the distribution of competences explains why we suggest characterizing our regulatory approach as 'multi-actor' and 'multi-level'. This general approach towards favouring a mix of different regulatory actors and levels notwithstanding, one can take from our analysis also the emphasis on two tendencies. When it comes to the relevant actor, one can identify a tendency of relying for regulation in commercial law on private actors and viewing the role of public actors merely in correcting negative impact of commercial relations on markets and society. As far as the level of regulation is concerned, we suggest regulating the relation on the lowest and most specific level possible.

78 Compare for this assumption in relation to consumer contract law also Smits, Bull, Ge, Goanță & Kawakami in this volume.
79 Rodrik 2011, p. 222 *et seq.*, 236 *et seq.*
80 See on this perspective in detail Backer 2011.
81 Abbott & Snidal 2009, p. 564 *et seq.*

4. Case Studies

With this 'multi-actor' and 'multi-level' approach in mind, we now seek to turn to our case studies in which we explain what our suggestions would mean for the analysis of historical developments and what they can offer for the regulation of two constellations, namely the general regulation of the contract of sale and the regulation of constellations where commercial parties violate fundamental human rights.

4.1. *Bills of Exchange - A Historical Perspective*

In this first case study, we offer a historical perspective of the development of the law concerning bills of exchange with a view to identifying lessons that can be learnt about the appropriate design of commercial law.[82] The history of the law of bills and notes provides an example of the interaction between private and public actors. This case study illustrates that private actors appear to be pre-eminently suited to creating relevant legal rules, regardless of the level - local, regional, global - where these rules are used, provided a relatively efficient enforcement mechanism exists.

Between the thirteenth and seventeenth centuries merchants developed their own, varying customs to solve commercial problems,[83] one of them being the fact that trade to a distant place necessarily requires a return trade. Traditionally merchants sold their goods at a fair, such as those of the Champagne in the high Middle Ages, bought a return cargo with proceeds, and sold this cargo at home with a view to making a profit. Bills of exchange have their origins in a new mechanism for making returns that became possible with the transition to a regime of sedentary merchants and the development of an agency merchant system between the thirteenth and seventeenth centuries.[84] For the sake of clarity a basic example: a merchant from Venice could ship spices to his representative in Bruges, who would sell the spices. To obtain payment from the buyer in Bruges, the Venetian merchant would ask his representative (the remitter or deliverer) in Bruges to have the money delivered to a merchant in Bruges, e.g. trading wool to Venice, who, importantly had a representative in Venice. This wool merchant of Bruges (the drawer), who was required to transfer the payment to the Venetian merchant, would draw a bill of exchange on his representative in Venice (the drawee), ordering the Venetian representative to pay a certain sum of money upon presentation of the bill at

82 For critical remarks on the history of bills of exchange in the Early Modern Period, we would like to thank Bram van Hofstraeten.

83 It is submitted that no *lex mercatoria* existed in the sense of 'an autonomos system of legal rules applying to merchants throughout the civilized world, akin in status to civil or canon law', or 'a corpus of international rules accepted by merchants everywhere, and was for that reason part of the *jus gentium* or law of nations', Baker 1999, p. 81. See for other rebuttals of such a *lex mercatoria*, i.a. Ewart 1903; Epstein 2004; Donahue 2004; Kadens 2004; Kadens 2012.

84 See De Roover 1953, p. 29-42; Posnan 1973, p. 54-64; Spufford 1987, p. 825-826; Rogers 1995, p. 32-33.

maturity. The representative of the Venetian spice merchant in Bruges would then send this bill of exchange to the Venetian merchant (the payee), who would present the bill to the wool merchant's Venetian representative upon its maturity to obtain payment.[85] Likewise, when the merchant from Bruges would ship wool to Venice and have it sold there by his representative, a similar set of transactions could be made. The problem of making returns could thus be solved by relying on a system of bills of exchange.[86] Apart from facilitating payment between merchants trading at a distance, the advantage of these bills of exchange was that since around the seventeenth century and particularly in Antwerp, they became negotiable instruments.[87] In the abovementioned example, the Venetian merchant could, instead of obtaining payment himself, transfer title to the bill and thereby all rights under it to another merchant who would become the holder of the bill in order to meet his own payment obligation. This subsequent holder would then be entitled to obtain payment under the bill from the drawee upon its maturity.

Although a similar - functional - problem thus had to be solved by medieval merchants in different locations, no universal commercial custom arose: the law of bills of exchange varied from country to country, or rather even from city to city.[88] In the early Modern Period, many cities of commerce started to codify or at least record their laws, including commercial customs, to avoid the time-consuming judicial investigations by a group of sworn witnesses (turben) to confirm the validity of a contested (commercial) practice.[89] Famous examples are customs of Italian city states, such as Genoa and Venice, but since around 1300 customary law also started to be privately recorded in towns in Flanders and Brabant. In certain cities, such as Bruges, and initially also Antwerp, foreign merchants of some privileged nations could have their commercial disputes decided before their own consular courts relying on their own customs. However, in Antwerp, and since 1413 also in Amsterdam, local customs were aligned to business practice by frequently using turben, produced by local and foreign merchant. Contrary to ordinary testimonies by witnesses a turbe had legal force.[90] Particularly in Antwerp the city's local customs seem to have universal acceptance by local and foreign residents. A first full set of the Antwerp customs was edited in 1547. This first edition was rejected by the government and edited again in 1570, 1582, and 1608.[91] In recording these customs both local and foreign merchants - private actors - thus played a vital role, though the actual rule setting was done by a public actor - the city - at a local level. The Antwerp customs, however, had a more regional impact, as it was one of the sources of Amsterdam's commercial customs, also regarding the law of bills of

85 See Rogers 1995, p. 33-34; Goode 2010, p. 516-517. See also Asser 1987, p. 112-114.
86 Rogers 1995, p. 34.
87 Van der Wee 1977, p. 328-332, 348-350. See also Rogers 1995, p. 94; Asser 1987, p. 122; De ruysscher 2009b, p. 265-277.
88 See e.g. Kadens 2004, p. 57-58; Baker 1999, p. 85; Ewart 1903, p. 152; Asser 1987, p. 116-122, 124-130.
89 Gelderblom 2013, p. 135-136.
90 Gelderblom 2013, p. 135.
91 Gelderblom 2013, p. 135; Asser 1987, p. 106.

exchange.[92] Since the fifteenth century, the Amsterdam magistrate treated all merchants, foreign and local, as equal before the law.[93] Similar developments took place in, for instance, Genoa and Venice.[94] For England it appears that between the thirteenth and seventeenth centuries in general commercial transactions were adjudicated by common law courts,[95] but also the courts of fairs (piepowder), markets, and towns,[96] including transactions which involved exchange transactions.[97] In England too a survey of local and foreign commercial customs appeared, the *Consuetudo, vel Lex Mercatoria* of 1622 by Gerard Malynes, pointing out the great variety in customs as to bills regarding formation, times of running, falling due, days of grace, etc.[98] In England, from the seventeenth and eighteenth centuries onwards, bills of exchange were no longer considered just a contract between deliverer and taker, but an instrument that created and embodied an obligation for the drawee to pay money to the payee or other holder - as had been earlier the case in Antwerp.[99]

This historical development shows that with the backing of the local courts and city councils, merchants were perfectly capable of developing their own rules to resolve a particular their commercial problem.[100] Bills of exchange are, therefore, indeed an example of law developing from commercial practice, into local and regional customs. It also shows that despite the diversity of local rules on bills of exchange, the system of bills of exchange could function effectively for merchants trading throughout Europe.

In the course of the eighteenth and particularly nineteenth centuries, many nation states tried to establish legal unity in commercial matters.[101] Earlier, Louis XIV had pursued the same goal with his *Ordonnance sur le commerce* (1673) that also had rules on bills of exchange. The origins of these rules were partly based on the customs of Amsterdam and thus Antwerp.[102] But as late as the eighteenth century, there were wide divergences in practice on the most basic principles of law relating to bills of exchange in e.g. Dutch, French, and English law.[103] These varying rules on bills of exchange were, inter alia, laid down in civil and commercial codes - the Prussian *Allgemeines Landrecht* (1794), the French *Code de Commerce* (1807), the Dutch

92 See Lichtenauer 1956, p. 87-88; Asser 1987, p. 106-107; De ruysscher 2009a, p. 478-479. See also Van der Wee 1977, p. 328-332, 335-336, 344.
93 Gelderblom 2013, p. 136-137.
94 Gelderblom 2013, p. 138.
95 Rogers 1995, p. 12-20.
96 See Bakers 1999, p. 85-86; Rogers 1995, p. 20-31.
97 See Rogers 1995, p. 44-68; Baker 1979, p. 308-313.
98 See Bakers 1999, p. 85; Gelderblom 2013, p. 138; Ewart 1903, p. 152.
99 See Rogers 1995, p. 94, 194-195; Van der Wee 1977, p. 328-332, 348-350 and De ruysscher 2009b, p. 265-277.
100 See Gelderblom 2013, p. 138; Kadens 2004, p. 51-54; Epstein 2004, p. 16-20. For the high Middle Ages impartial legal enforcement is more problematic, see e.g. Greif 2004, p. 116-119.
101 Bergfeld 1987, p. 101-103; Kanning 2003, p. 61.
102 For instance, via the French translation book of Johannes Phoonsen (1631-1702) on the customary exchange law and practice of Amsterdam. See Asser 1987, p. 107; Gelderblom 2013, p. 138-139.
103 Baker 1999, p. 85; Ewart 1903, p. 152; Asser 1987, p. 116-122, 124-130.

Wetboek van Koophandel (1838) – or even separate codes – such as the German *Allgemeine Deutsche Wechselordnung* of 1869,[104] and the English Bills of Exchange Act 1882.[105] Although content wise these codes were generally a continuation of the – now nationally – existing rules on bills of exchange, formally and eventually it was now the nation state that acted as the rule-maker, and not just in the marginal sense of recording rules made by private actors. The national law-maker actively shaped the rules applicable to bills of exchange. In particular, in light of the negotiability of bills, legislation was able to secure the reliability of the system of bill of exchange, for instance, by protecting the legitimate interests of subsequent holders of the bill. In this way, the public actor can be seen to promote the market interest.

However, the flexibility of the national lawmaker in adapting rules to changing economic circumstances is by definition more limited than an evolving custom itself, but also more limited than the earlier city councils. Also the level became more pronounced, namely a level defined by national boundaries.[106] Consequently, private international law, in the sense of conflict rules on the applicability of national laws became increasingly important when nation states took over the regulation of bills of exchange. The rise of and need for private international law is illustrated by the Hague Conference on Private International Law, first held in 1893, which aimed to unify national rules on conflict of laws, including those in the field of commercial law.[107] However, with the enormous increase in international trade since the 1870s – though interrupted at the end of the nineteenth century by protectionism and two global wars in the twentieth century – it was thought necessary to create unified rules dealing with bills of exchange.

To facilitate the increasing international trade since the end of the nineteenth century, the documentary credit, including the use bills of exchange, became a truly global phenomenon, in need of international instruments.[108] In the wake of the First World War, this need was addressed by both public actors, in particular the League of Nations (1919) and the United Nations Commission on International Trade Law (UNCITRAL, 1966) and private actors, in particular the International Chamber of Commerce (ICC, 1919).

Under the auspices of the League of Nations, the Geneva Convention providing a Uniform Law for Bills of Exchange and Promissory Notes (1930) was adopted. However, this resulted in the harmonization of the negotiable instruments laws of only a limited number of civil law jurisdictions. The common law rules relating to bills of exchange, cheques, and promissory notes had been codified in the Bills of Exchange Act 1882, and this Act was subsequently adopted throughout the common law world and continued to be applied.[109] Therefore, after the Second World War and the demise of the League of Nations, UNCITRAL drafted the

104 Before the *Allgemeine Deutsche Wechselordnung* of 1869/71, numerous local laws on bills existed, more than fifty in 1847, Brox 2005, p. 228-229.

105 Although it had already a predecessor in the Bills of Exchange Act 1704. See Goode 2010, p. 521.

106 Schmitthoff 1981, p. 6-7.

107 Schmitthoff 1981, p. 26-27.

108 See e.g. Goode 2010, p. 1353.

109 See Goode 2010, p. 521.

United Nations Convention on International Bills of Exchange and International Promissory Notes (New York, 1988) with a view to 'overcom[ing] the major disparities and uncertainties that currently exist in relation to instruments used for international payments'.[110] The Convention was adopted by the General Assembly on 9 December 1988, however, by October 2014, only five states have acceded to the Convention (Guinea, Gabon, Honduras, Liberia, and Mexico) and consequently the convention has not yet entered into force.[111] The idea that commercial actors are in need of an international regulation of the law concerning bills of exchange, has so far proven to be false.[112]

From this concise history of the bills of exchange, it is possible to draw three main conclusions in relation to the normative framework discussed in the previous section. Firstly, the example of the bills of exchange shows that private actors are capable of creating clear and predictable rules themselves through practice resulting in the development of customs, however, these rules can only exist and function with the recognition and support of an effective enforcement system, previously courts at fairs, city councils, and later national courts.

Secondly, the historical development shows that while private actors have essentially been responsible for the creation of a solution to a commercial problem, in this case study the creation of an effective payment mechanism between merchants trading with each other at a distance, these rules are often subsequently codified by public actors with a view to promoting clarity and predictability. However, such legislative action can lead to the rules becoming entrenched and due to the formalities of the codification process render them less adaptable to new developments and practices. Nevertheless, such rule-making can have the positive effect of supporting the system created by merchants, and thus promote the interests of the market.

Thirdly, the case study demonstrates that the level at which rules are made or set appears to depend on the market for which these rules are meant. In the Middle Age and the Early Modern Era, the level was local, with occasional regional – European – implications, parallel to the commercial ties that existed in those days. They reflected the local preferences of the particular market, which is illustrated by the diversity of local customs that existed for different fairs and cities. As the local preferences of a commercial community converged, through increasing trading ties but also through the unification of nation territories, regulation took place at an increasingly higher level. The Geneva Convention providing a Uniform Law for Bills of Exchange and Promissory Notes (1930) led to a further convergence of laws in a number of civil law systems possibly demonstrating a further convergence of preferences. However, the failure of the United Nations Convention on Internation-

110 See II. Explanatory Note by the UNCITRAL Secretariat on the United Nations Convention on International Bills of Exchange and International Promissory Notes, p. 42 (<http://www.uncitral.org/pdf/english/texts/payments/billsnotes/Bills_of_Exchange_expl_Note.pdf>); Goode 2010, p. 521; Schmitthoff 1981, p. 25.

111 <http://www.uncitral.org/uncitral/en/uncitral_texts/payments/1988Convention_bills_status.html>.

112 See Schmitthoff 1981, p. 31. See also Goode 2010, p. 1354.

al Bills of Exchange and International Promissory Notes (New York, 1988) could be interpreted as evidence of continuing divergence of preferences between, broadly speaking, common law and civil law countries and therefore the appropriate level of regulation.

4.2. *The Core of Commercial Exchange: Commercial Sales Transactions*

In our second case study we focus on the core of commercial exchange, the contract of sale. The inquiry explores the appropriate roles of private and public actors at various levels of governance to identify which rule-maker has the expertise and legitimacy to create a system of rules that recognizes, safeguards and enforces the exercise of party autonomy, whilst protecting the legitimate interests of the market and society within which the commercial transaction is embedded. As previously outlined, the rule-maker should provide a coherent system of rules that are clear and predictable, reflect the preferences of the contracting community and are adaptable to new developments and practices.

It should be clear that the commercial actors themselves are in the best position to decide on what is in their best commercial interest, which means that commercial actors – individually or collectively within a contracting community such as a trade, industry or sector – themselves possess the necessary knowledge and expertise to regulate their commercial transaction. However, it is recognized that the private agreements and regulatory frameworks they create cannot exist in a vacuum and require, for their legitimacy, a public actor to attribute legal recognition, and ultimately enforce such agreements.[113] This is something only the public actor is competent to do. Consequently, the primary role for the public actor is to create a general framework that allows commercial actors to exercise their autonomy and enter into sales transactions. This framework requires rules that give effect to the general principles that underlie the commercial interest, in particular freedom of contract – the cornerstone of an open, market-oriented and competitive economic order[114] – consensualism, and the sanctity of contracts (*pacta sunt servanda*). These principles are of particular importance in an open market economy, and therefore well-established in all systems of contract law, as they ensure that commercial parties are free to decide to whom they will offer their goods, and by whom they wish to be supplied, as well as to freely agree on the terms of those transactions. Once such voluntary agreements have been reached, security of the transaction requires that they are enforced. Apart from rules identifying when a valid contract is concluded, the public actor must also provide rules to protect the exercise of autonomy and ensure that consent has been freely given, in the sense that there are rules sanctioning, for example, fraud or the illegitimate exercise of pressure. In line

113 See e.g. Wagner 2005, p. 5: 'Of course, markets do not function well in the state of nature but are in need of a legal framework, if only to guarantee that promises may not be broken with impunity.'

114 See UNIDROIT, *Unidroit Principles of International Commercial Contracts*, Official Comments to Article 1.1.

with the criteria we have established previously, these rules need to be clear and predictable and form a coherent system.

Such general legal frameworks that recognize and enforce validly entered into commercial contracts currently exists at different governance levels. All national contract laws have rules recognizing and safeguarding the exercise of party autonomy and enforcing validly entered into private agreements. Such rules are contained in a single, coherent system that governs the full life-cycle of the contract. Comparative research reveals, however, that they diverge to varying degrees.[115] In the context of commercial sales contracts, these divergences do not, in our view, reflect fundamental choices that indicate different preferences concerning the content of these rules. Their aim is to provide an effective framework with clear and predictable rules that commercial actors can rely on to engage in commercial activity. Consequently, we posit that, in light of the shared underlying objective of these rules to recognize, safeguard and enforce the exercise of party autonomy, such rules could be provided at a higher level.

Two instruments at an international level already exist that could be applied to commercial sales contracts, in particular, the UN Convention on Contracts for the International Sale of Goods (CISG, 1980) and the UNIDROIT Principles on International Commercial Contracts (UPICC, 2010). However, both instruments have limitations when it comes to providing a general legal framework for commercial sales contracts. Although the CISG contains rules recognizing the exercise of party autonomy and securing the sanctity of the agreement, it is incomplete. The CISG does not contain rules safeguarding the exercise of party autonomy in the form of rules concerning e.g. mistake, fraud or the illegitimate exercise of pressure. Consequently, when a contract is governed by the CISG, the applicable national law will continue to govern those issues not regulated in the Convention. This inevitably leads to fragmentation in the applicable legal regime, which may lead some commercial actors to opt solely for a national regime with a view to ensuring a single coherent system is applicable to their contract.[116] The UPICC provide rules for recognizing and safeguarding the exercise of party autonomy and thus constitute a single, coherent legal framework. However, it must be noted that these Principles do not originate from a public actor with competence to legislate, and therefore they ultimately remain dependent on recognition by national courts and arbitral tribunals. In the absence of a global legislator with competence to regulate contract law at a global level, an international framework would need to be laid down in an international convention, which then depends on the political willingness of states for its success. The existence of the UPICC shows, nevertheless, that it is possible to create a coherent set of rules that provide a framework for recognizing, safeguard-

115 See e.g. Kötz & Flessner 1998; Smits 2014.

116 See e.g. Spagnolo 2010; Koehler & Yujun 2008; Philippopoulos 2008; Ziegel 2005. On the CISG, see recently DiMatteo 2014. Also see the survey on applicable law by Vogenauer: *Civil Justice Systems in Europe*, A Business Survey conducted by the Oxford Institute of European and Comparative Law and the Oxford Centre of Socio-Legal Studies, 2008, <http://denning.law.ox.ac.uk/themes/iecl/pdfs/Oxford%20Civil%20Justice%20Survey%20-%20Summary%20of%20Results,%20Final.pdf> (last visited, 9 December 2024).

ing and enforcing the agreements that result from the exercise of party autonomy by commercial parties.

When it comes to regulating the content of the sales contract, the foundation of an open, market-oriented and competitive economic order dictates that party autonomy should prevail. It is assumed that commercial actors enter into their transactions on an equal footing - or that the general legal framework provides safeguards against the use of illegitimate pressure in case of inequality - and that their exchange therefore results in mutual gain. Intervention in the resulting contract by regulating its content is therefore not necessary in order to protect the commercial interest, suggesting no further regulatory role for the public actor. Further intervention only seems justified with a view to the negative effects of such private agreements on the market or societal interests. Having said this, it has to be recognized that leaving the parties to negotiate and draft the entire content of their contract can lead to inefficiency due to the transaction costs involved in providing for every possible contingency that could arise. Such an approach does not facilitate commercial exchange and would thus be contrary to the interests of promoting a functioning and efficient market. The creation of standardized contracting solutions that facilitate the exchange while leaving the parties free to adapt the solutions to their own needs is therefore necessary. This is in essence the purpose of the default rules provided by contract law. We suggest, however, that the further away from the transaction such facilitative default rules are made, the less likely they will be adequate to the specific needs of the commercial actors who would rely on them, requiring them to incur the transaction costs to provided tailored solutions.

When it comes to standardizing solutions, we observe that commercial actors are very capable of doing so themselves, and sales contracts are particularly amenable to such standardization. Through standardization, commercial actors encounter the one-time transaction costs of drafting a comprehensive and detailed contract that can be used in a multitude of sales transactions, thereby allowing them to focus their resources on negotiating the key issues specific to a particular sales transaction or those specific points in the standardized contract that the parties do not agree upon. They are also able to adapt the standardized contract to new developments and their changing needs and interests, and in light of experience gained through repeat dealings of the nature of contingencies that can arise.

It is recognized, of course, that when drafting the standardized contract, a commercial actor is primarily guided by its own the needs, interests and expectations. The seller will be driven to strengthen its position, for instance, by limiting the time available to inspect the goods, the warranty that is given, or the nature of the damages that will compensated in case of defects. Conversely, the buyer will aim to impose upon the seller an extended warranty, expand its rights in relation to inspection and notification of defects, and broaden the scope of the damages that are to be compensated in case of breach. A comparison of the standardized contracts offered by the seller and the buyer will consequently reveal major discrepancies. This would require parties to negotiate which terms are to be included in their particular contract, thereby incurring the costs they were seeking to avoid through standardization. Alternatively, it could lead the party with the stronger bargaining position to insist upon its terms. In that case, the regulatory framework provided by the public actor will need to step in to ensure that such insistence on terms is not illegitimate with a view to safeguarding the exercise of party autonomy by both parties.

To avoid such discrepancies in standardization and the problems associated with it, a better solution could be the involvement of representative organizations of the contracting communities commercial actors participate in, in the sense of trades, sectors or industries at national, European or international level.[117] We suggest that a private regulator is in a better position than a public legislator to provide a coherent system of clear and predictable rules that meet the preferences of the members of their contracting community, and that are adaptable to new developments and practices. Such a private regulator is able to channel the shared specialist and technical knowledge about the characteristics of a product, and accumulate collective knowledge and experience about what can typically go wrong and how typical problems are usually dealt with in the particular contracting community.[118] In this way, regulatory responsibility is attributed on the basis of sectoral boundaries as opposed to territorial boundaries.

Through these private organizations the members of the contracting community can combine efforts to develop a private regulatory framework that provides a comprehensive set of clear and detailed contracting solutions that reflects the preferences of the contracting community and balances the needs and interests of its various members, whilst leaving individual commercial actors the freedom to customize the solutions to their particular transaction. These private regulatory frameworks are to be viewed as specialist 'statutes' that reflect the preferences of a particular contracting community. Commercial actors transacting within the contracting community are likely to prefer such private regulation to the less tailored contract law provided by public legislators. This preference would be strengthened further if the private regulatory framework would provide an alternative form of dispute resolution, such as arbitration by a sectoral panel. It should be noted that what we depict here is not novel. In a number of empirical studies, Bernstein has shown that various trades and industries opted out of the Uniform Commercial Code (UCC) in the United States,[119] substituting it with their own private regulatory framework.[120] Commercial transactions are then governed by the private regulatory

117 Wightman 2003, p. 149, describes a contracting community model as referring to 'contractual relations which occur within a market sector where there are established practices for carrying on trade which any firm wishing to participate in the trade will normally have to take part in'.

118 Wightman 2003, p. 150; Epstein 1999, p. 828.

119 The UCC has been enacted in 49 states (with some local variations), as well as partially in Louisiana. §1-103 lays down the objective of the UCC is '(1) to simplify, clarify, and modernize the law governing commercial transactions; (2) to permit the continued expansion of commercial practices through custom, usage and agreement of the parties; and (3) to make uniform the law among the various jurisdictions'.

120 Bernstein 1996; Bernstein 1999; Bernstein 2001; also see Richman 2009. Bernstein 1998 outlines that private regulatory frameworks exist in over more than fifty industries in the US, such as diamonds, grain, feed, independent films, printing, binding, peanuts, rice, cotton, rubber, hay and tea.

framework as opposed to the publicly provided UCC. Another example is provided by GAFTA, which provides a range of 80 standard contract forms for every link in the supply-demand chain from the farmers whose crops are processed to specialists in malting, brewing and distilling, milling, feed and food processing who together with exporters, importers and other commercial actors trade in the vast bulk commodity crops that are transported around the world.[121] All these contracts include an arbitration clause submitting disputes to arbitration under the GAFTA arbitration rules, which is specifically focused on settling disputes relating to the GAFTA standard contracts. Provided the private regulatory framework balances all interests, including buyers and sellers at all levels of the supply chain, the public legislator does not need to intervene further in the content of such regulations, at least not for the purpose of protecting the commercial interest. The role of the public actor is consequently to provide a framework or infrastructure that attributes legitimacy to this private framework, recognizes contracts concluded within its framework and enforces awards rendered by the arbitration panel, in case an internal sanctioning method such as reputational sanctions, is not capable of ensuring compliance.[122]

It is necessary to recognize that there are concerns relating to private regulation, however, and therefore a role for the public actor can be envisaged with a view to protecting market and societal interests.[123] Economists in particular warn of the dangers of barriers to entry and the potential for collusion and monopolistic price-fixing.[124] Trade organizations that operate as closed networks create barriers to entry to newcomers, who must, for instance, establish a good reputation to gain entry to the contracting community. This problem does not exist in the case of an open network, allowing open entry and exit. The private regulatory framework should therefore be available to new members of the relevant contracting community, as well as commercial actors who only incidentally transact in the particular market. Where there is confidence that the private regulatory framework reflects a balanced assessment of the needs, interests and expectations of parties on both sides of the transaction, these incidental actors should accept the standardized solutions. The second concern arises where the relative bargaining power between buyers and sellers is altered or pushed 'out of balance' giving rise the possibility of collusion and monopolistic pricing. The power to fix prices will depend, however, on the nature of the organization. Collusion and monopolistic pricing will in particular take place if the organization is one-sided, favouring (usually) sellers over buyers. But collusion becomes more difficult when the number of participants increases and the organization includes representatives of all sides of the transaction, i.e. both

121 See <www.gafta.com>.

122 See also Hadfield 2009, p. 246 who refers to a publicly provided infrastructure for private provision of law.

123 See, for instance, Ogus 1995, p. 98; Ogus 2000, p. 587; Pirrong 1998; Hadfield 2009.

124 McMillan & Woodruff 2000, p. 2454-2458; Richman 2004, p. 2346-2347; Hadfield 2009. Also see Posner 1996, who doubts whether private group norms are efficient due to externalities, strategic behaviour, information asymmetries, human nature and appeal to other moral values and Katz 1996, p. 1749.

buyers and sellers at various levels of the supply chain as members.[125] If there are competing organizations performing similar functions, collusion will also be reduced.[126] These concerns indicate where the role of the public legislator is to be positioned; in particular this will require measures to be undertaken to address concerted practices and anti-competitive behaviour and to promote competition between contracting communities. In this way, there is an important role for public regulation, in the form of competition law (such as Arts. 101 and 102 TFEU), to establish the boundaries of private regulation.

4.3. *Corporate Social Responsibility in Global Supply-Chains: Regulating Adverse Human Rights Impact of Commercial Parties*

The last case study to discuss our proposal for an appropriate regulation of commercial relations concerns the constellation of regulation that aims at preventing negative impact of commercial relations on fundamental interests of society. The example to illustrate this constellation is, for this purpose, the infringement of fundamental human rights in the execution of transnational commercial contracts. The following section seeks to take this constellation and the vivid debate on the appropriate regulation as a starting point to show how the normative framework developed above can be applied and result in specific recommendations for the legal policy debate.

Under the current conditions of globalization, large companies have begun to disperse their production patterns globally. This can take the form of foreign direct investment, in which a dependent office or a legally separated subsidiary is established, but it appears frequently also in the form of outsourcing production to independent contractors, which are mostly located in developing countries. It is the latter constellation in which commercial law comes into play. One can observe this development towards outsourcing in many sectors, such as apparel, electronics, food or light manufacturing. Very recently, however, it was one particular sector that was specifically under scrutiny with respect to its fundamental human rights violations, which should accordingly serve in this case study as a concrete example. After a building collapsed in Bangladesh killing over 1000 workers in April 2013, the legal debate concerned in particular the potential regulation of the textile industry and their global contracting networks.[127] What can be observed here are cross-border commercial relations that have a negative impact on fundamental societal values, in particular the human right to life and health as laid down in the International Bill of Human Rights[128] and the core labour right of providing a safe

125 Richman 2004, p. 2347; McMillan & Woodruff 2000, p. 2456; Epstein 1999, p. 829.

126 McMillan & Woodruff 2000, p. 2456.

127 For the facts of this disaster, see the material collected on the Business and Human Rights Resource Center: <http://business-humanrights.org/en/rana-plaza-building-collapse-april-2013>.

128 Art. 3, 25 Universal Declaration of Human Rights, General Assembly resolution 217 A (III) of 10 December 1948, Art. 12 International Covenant on Economic, Social and Cultural Rights, General Assembly resolution 2200A (XXI) of 16 December 1966.

and health workplace as laid down in the International Covenant on Economic, Social and Cultural Rights and the conventions of the International Labor Organisation.[129]

In the debate on how to regulate commercial relations in order to prevent similar human rights violations from occurring and to safeguard the global contracting networks' respect for human rights, several proposals have already been made. On the one hand, one can find manifold suggestions that aim to regulate such constellations by enacting mandatory laws that restrict commercial relations and oblige them directly to respect such rights. Proposals range from urging the national or European politics to develop mandatory laws in European contract law that render such contracts void and thus deprive commercial parties from the possibility of legally enforcing contracts that infringe upon the rights of others or to restrict the import of goods if these have been produced under violation of fundamental rights[130] to mandatory laws for international trade that should be developed by the WTO to prevent or hinder the import of such ethically-contaminated products[131] or to strengthen efforts by the UN to develop a treaty for companies to oblige them to respect human rights, including obligations towards their contractual partners up the supply chain, the violation of which could result in liability.[132] In short, these suggestions seek to make the argument that it is the national, European or the international political legislator that is called upon to take over and should impose constraints on commercial relations to the extent they violate human rights. On the other hand, one can equally find positions in the literature that seem to favour a stronger role for the rules developed by private actors as an effective form of regulating commercial parties to that respect. The focus is set here on the value of the agreements of commercial actors themselves to prevent labour exploitation,[133] multi-stakeholder initiatives and certification programmes[134] or the mere social pressure by consumers, with supportive regulation in consumer law[135] or by civil society with the support of new rules on collective enforcement of unilateral declarations[136] or, finally, self-regulation by civil society and companies in the form of legally binding agreements that are enforceable by contract law.[137] Given these

129 See Art. 7 International Covenant on Economic, Social and Cultural Rights and ILO Occupational Safety and Health Convention 1981 (Convention No. 155); Occupational Health Services Convention 1985 (Convention No. 161); Promotional Framework for Occupational Safety and Health Conventions 2006 (No. 187).

130 Tjon Soei Len 2013. See also on this point already Study Group on Social Justice in European Contract Law 2004, p. 668.

131 Although this is due to the restrictions in WTO law on trade barriers difficult to realize, cf. Collins 2014, p. 627 *et seq.*

132 Prominently the contributions in Deva & Bilchitz 2013.

133 For empirical evidence on the use of such mechanisms of contractual control, see e.g. McBarnet & Kurkchiyan 2007; Vytopil 2012.

134 Cafaggi 2013, p. 1603 *et seq.*

135 Recently Collins 2014.

136 On this possibilities with further references to the debate Beckers 2015, MS, p. 304 *et seq.*

137 The most prominent example for this type of 'civil society regulation through contract' is probably the recent agreement between Companies and International Trade Unions on Accord on Fire and Building Safety in Bangladesh (<http://www.bangladeshaccord.org/>).

manifold suggestions, what can our normative framework on 'who should regulate on what level' add to this debate? What answer could it provide for the question of an appropriate solution for regulating the constellation in which commercial relations breach fundamental human rights? To remain for the purpose of finding an answer, in the two categories that we have previously used to determine the appropriate form of regulation in commercial law: Firstly, what would be the appropriate level of adopting regulation for this constellation and, secondly, who is the appropriate regulatory authority, namely public or private?

Focussing, at first, on the level of regulation concerned, our main normative frame of reference was the presumed preference for local regulation, which appeared in different variations. Firstly, we argued that the level of regulation would need to depend on the sector and trade concerned and pay due respect to its specifics.[138] For the level of adopting regulation on the detrimental effects of commercial relations on fundamental societal values, this consequently means that the appropriate level of regulation needs to be determined with a view to the sector and the trade under scrutiny. Pursuant to our framework, it is thus important not to develop general rules on respect for human rights in the performance of commercial transactions, but to develop specific rules that match the characteristics of the sector or trade. In the concrete example of the textile industry with globally dispersed production patterns, this suggests a trade-specific regulation that takes into consideration the specific organization of a sector and focuses on those human rights that the sector is prone to have negative impact on. Next to the suggestion of developing sector-specific regulation, the argument for local preferences was considered also to play a role when it comes to determining the level of regulation according to the interest that is affected.[139] Provided that the interests of local societies require local regulation and global interests require regulation on a global level, the question of the appropriate level depends here on the interest affected. For the specific example of regulating human rights impact of the contracting networks in the textile industry, this suggests regulation on a global level due to the global interest of respect for fundamental human rights.[140] A different perspective would, however, be necessary insofar as the human rights impact concerns specific social rights for which differences on a national level remain. To be more precise, in the general debate on preventing negative human rights impact of global contracting networks, one additional claim is the commercial parties' respect for the employees' rights to collective bargaining and freedom of association. For this social interest, which is highly influenced by each country's national organization of industrial relations and still differs significantly,[141] regulation on the level of the affected society, namely national or even local, would be suggested. Consequently, with a

138 See *supra* section 3.4.1.

139 See *supra* section 3.4.2.

140 For the understanding of severe human rights violations as a genuine problem, see Michaels 2011, p. 170 *et seq.* ('Global Problem by Definition').

141 For the fundamental differences of organizing industrial relations already Western cultures, see Hall & Soskice 2001. For related cultural problems between Western and non-Western countries, in particular China, see Lin 2007, p. 336 *et seq.*

view to the level of regulation, there is no overall decision for one most appropriate level of regulation; instead, a decision is required that takes account of the specifics of the regulated object (the commercial relation) and the objective of regulation.

The second component for an appropriate regulation of the particular constellation under scrutiny is to determine who should be the actor enacting regulation on this point. Given that the case of adverse human rights impact of commercial relations is eventually oriented on the objective to safeguard the interests and expectations of society, it is, as established above, public actors that should take over the regulation of such constellations and, as argued above, this would need to take the form of an interaction between the political legislator and the politicized private sphere. How can this be organized in this particular case? In the previous part, we have indicated that regulation with a view to the societal interest can be taken over by the institutionalized political sphere of society, namely the political legislator in the form of mandatory laws. In the realm of a globalized and fragmented society, the political lead role can, however, partly also be taken over by private actors to the extent they embrace matters of public interest.[142] In the specific example of human rights violations by private actors, one can indeed find regulatory attempts by international politics as well as regulatory attempts by private actors. As to the relation between the two actors, it was argued that the level of regulation would need to be taken into consideration. Due to the global nature of this form of regulation, our normative framework would here indeed suggest viewing the self-regulatory attempts of private actors as the primary applicable actors to develop regulation with a supportive and corrective function of the political legislator. Therefore, it would in the first place be the contracting on human rights in the form of supplier codes of conduct, multi-stakeholder initiatives and agreements between civil society groups and companies that should take over the role of regulating human rights compliance in the performance of commercial contracting with a view to the affected sector and the specific human rights that are affected. However, in order to prevent a too strong influence of private interests in this regulatory undertaking, the political legislator may still have a role to play. It would need to shape the content of such private regulatory initiatives in order for them to be oriented on the social interest and provide means for their enforcement in case self-regulatory initiatives fail. This can, firstly, take the form of providing private self-regulation with authoritative frameworks that specify what regulation serving the social interest entails, as is currently attempted on an international level by 'soft law' instruments of international organizations, notably by the OECD[143] and the UN[144] and, on a European level by the recent strategy of the European Commission.[145]

142 See *supra* section 3.4.2.

143 OECD Guidelines for Multinational Corporations, last update 2011. The provision relevant for commercial contracting are in particular Chapter II, No. 10,12, 13, Chapter IV, No. 3.

144 UN Guiding Principles on Business and Human Rights. The provisions relevant for human rights respect in commercial contracting are in particular Principles 12, 13 (b), 19.

145 On this point, one can refer to the recent strategy of the European Commission to view specific international frameworks enacted by international organizations as providing 'authoritative guidance' on what corporate social responsibility should entail, see in detail Communication from the European Commission, A Renewed EU Strategy 2011-14 for Corporate Social →

These guidelines by international politics can serve as benchmarks that specify what respect for fundamental rights would entail and thus influence private actors in their regulatory attempt, i.e. civil society when putting pressure on commercial actors and companies when initiating self-regulation. Secondly, the public actor can here again serve as the authority that enforces the developed self-regulation as legally binding and, in so doing, is able to interpret this form of legal regulation with a view to it being in accordance with the interest of society and not biased by private interests.[146] Although an international enforcement authority might be desirable, in the absence of a 'world court for multinationals', this enforcement role would need, for the time being, be realized on a national level.[147]

A different perspective on the actors that regulate would need to be taken with respect to the social interests that are perceived as interests of a national community. In this respect, it is the national legislator that would again take the lead role in the form of specifying factors under which private self-regulation would be recognized. To remain with the example of industrial relations and freedom of association, it would for these cases be a decision within national private law how far private self-regulation in commercial contracts or self-regulatory initiatives would be accepted and for which cases national specifics of organizing industrial relations would prevent the enforcement. One can even go further to the regional level and discuss the interaction between the interests of local communities and commercial parties by claiming that, for such specific cases, prior consent of the community to the private regulatory initiative would need to be present.[148]

5. Conclusion

In this contribution, we sought to develop a normative approach to determine what regulation in the field of commercial law should look like. In this context, our starting point was the observation that commercial law is a broad field that has evolved along two core themes. Firstly, commercial law is characterized by the simultaneous competence of public and private actors and thus characterized by the regulatory undertakings of private actors and the intervention of the political actor in the form of commercial law, which rendered it necessary to develop criteria on the distribution of competences between these two spheres. Secondly, commercial law is a complex field, in which, in contrast to consumer law, no dominant regulatory level can be identified. Instead, commercial relations are regulated in some aspects on a national, in others at a European and even a global level. In order to be capable of developing criteria on the actor ('who') and the level ('where') for commercial law, we then introduced the idea that in order to further the core function of commercial relations, namely to perform the exchange on goods and

Responsibility, COM(2011) 681, p. 6. Suggestions in a similar direction have been provided already by Murphy 2005, p. 425 *et seq*.

146 On this suggestion with further references Beckers 2015, MS p. 299 *et seq*., 327.

147 Michaels 2011.

148 On successful examples of this interaction between private contracting and the right to informed consent of local communities, see Cafaggi 2013, p. 1568, note 27.

services on a competitive market, commercial law would need to be oriented on three objectives: The interests of the commercial parties to enter into a transaction that is beneficial for them, the interest of the competitive market as the immediate context providing the basis for such beneficial exchange, and the expectations of society that legitimize the competitive market as a social system fulfilling the function to further exchange to improve overall welfare. On this basis, we made an inquiry for each of these interests who is best capable of protecting the interest and on which level, and suggested a multi-level and a multi-actor approach.

With this proposal on what a desirable system of commercial law could look like, we seek to contribute, in the first place, to the debate on how to enact regulation that should govern commercial relations. We sought to show that appropriate regulation supporting the core function and the potential of the commercial relation can be understood only when taking a multi-disciplinary perspective. To combine insights from economics and sociology, as we suggest, can provide a wider perspective on the functions and the impact of commercial relations in the context of the market and society and a historical approach can place suggestions in a wider context. With the help of these different perspectives and the related case studies, we also sought to link the so far unrelated debate on how to develop regulation that suits the characteristics of the commercial relation, but also takes account of the recent debate on corporate social responsibility in supply-chains and the recent claims for commercial relations to respect fundamental interests of society.

Our contribution can, secondly, also shed light into the debate on the distribution of competences in European private law in general, which is the overall aim of this book. On this point, we attempted to emphasize that private (in our case commercial) relations are not only governed by the regulatory frameworks of public actors, but also, and on a global level in fact to a major extent, by the regulatory framework of private actors. Accordingly, any debate on the distribution of competences would need to take into consideration such contributions by private actors and their potential to govern private relations and the relation to the contribution of public regulators. In addition, our contribution sought to underline that regulation in European private law is not only about the distribution of competences between the national and European legislator, but remains incomplete if two other regulatory levels, the broader global regulatory perspective on private relations as well as the specific locally-shaped practices of sectors and trades, are not taken into consideration.

Bibliography

Abbott & Snidal 2009
Abbott, K. & Snidal, D., 'Strengthening International Regulation through Transnational New Governance: Overcoming the Orchestration Deficit', 42 *Vanderbilt Journal of Transnational Law*, 2009, p. 501-578.

Aldcroft 1992
Aldcroft, D., 'The Railway Age', in: A. Digby, C.H. Feinstein & D. Jenkin (eds.), *New Directions in Economic and Social History* (volume II), Basingstoke: MacMillan 1992, p. 64-80.

Anderson 2013
Anderson, G.W., 'Societal Constitutionalism, Social Movements, and Constitutionalism from Below', 20 *Indiana Journal of Global Legal Studies*, 2013, p. 881-906.

Asser 1987
Asser, W.D.H., 'Bills of Exchange and Agency in the 18th Century Law of Holland and Zeeland. Decisions of the Supreme Court of Holland and Zeeland', in: V. Piergiovanni (ed.), *The Courts and the Development of Commercial Law* (Comparative Studies in Continental and Anglo-American Legal History, 2), Berlin: Duncker & Humblot 1987, p. 101-130.

Backer 2011
Backer, L.C., 'Governance without Government: An Overview', in: G. Handl, J. Zekoll & P. Zumbansen (ed.), *Beyond Territoriality: Transnational Legal Authority in an Age of Globalization*, Frankfurt/Tulane: Martinus Nijhoff Publishers 2011, p. 87-123.

Bairoch 1989
Bairoch, P., 'European Trade Policy, 1815-1914', in: M. Peter *et al.* (eds.), *The Cambridge Economic History of Europe: from the Decline of the Roman Empire* (volume VIII: The Industrial Economies: the Development of Economic and Social Policies), Cambridge: Cambridge University Press 1989, p. 1-160.

Baker 1979
Baker, J.H., 'The Law Merchant and the Common Law Before 1700', 38 *The Cambridge Law Journal*, 1979, p. 295-322.

Baker 1999
Baker, J.H., 'The Law Merchant as a Source of English Law', in: W. Swadling & G. Jones (eds.), *The Search for Principle: Essays in Honour of Lord Goff of Chieveley*, New York, NY [etc.]: Oxford University Press, 1999, p. 79-96.

Beckers 2015
Beckers, A., *Enforcing Corporate Social Responsibility Codes: On Global Self-Regulation and National Private Law*, Oxford: Hart Publishing 2015.

Beckert 2012
Beckert, J., 'Die sittliche Einbettung der Wirtschaft. Von der Effizienz- und Differenzierungstheorie zu einer Theorie wirtschaftlicher Felder', 22 *Berliner Journal für Soziologie*, 2012, p. 247-266.

Bergfeld 1987
Bergfeld, C., 'Preußen und das Allgemeine Deutsche Handelsgesetzbuch', *Zeitschrift für Europäische Rechtsgeschichte*, Ius Commune XIV, Veröffentlichungen des Max-Planck-Instituts für Europäische Rechtsgeschichte, Frankfurt am Main 1987, p. 101–114.

Bernstein 1996
Bernstein, L., 'Merchant Law in a Merchant Court: Rethinking the Code's Search for Immanent Business Norms', 144 *University of Pennsylvania Law Review*, 1996, p. 1765-1821.

Bernstein 1998
Bernstein, L., 'Private Commercial Law', in: P. Newman (ed), *The New Palgrave Dictionary of Economics and the Law*, London, New York: MacMillan 1998, p. 108-114.

Bernstein 1999
Bernstein, L., 'The Questionable Empirical Basis of Article 2's Incorporation Strategy: A Preliminary Study', 66 *University of Chicago Law Review*, 1999, p. 710-780.

Bernstein 2001
Bernstein, L., 'Private Commercial Law in the Cotton Industry: Creating Cooperation through Rules, Norms, and Institutions', 99 *Michigan Law Review*, 2001, p. 1724-1790.

Böhm 1966
Böhm, F., 'Privatrechtsgesellschaft und Marktwirtschaft', in: F. Böhm (ed.), *Freiheit und Ordnung in der Marktwirtschaft*, Baden-Baden: Nomos 1966, p. 105-168.

Bouvier 1997
Bouvier, J., 'Le mouvement d'une civilisation nouvelle 1852–1914', in: G. Duby (ed.), *Histoire de la France des origines à nos jours*, Paris: Larousse 1997, p. 645-690.

Braithwaite 1982
Braithwaite, J., 'Enforced Self-Regulation: A New Strategy for Corporate Crime Control', 80 *Michigan Law Review*, 1982, p. 1466-1507.

Brox 2005
Brox, H., *Handels- und Wertpapierrecht*, München: C.H. Beck 2005.

Cafaggi 2013
Cafaggi, F., 'The Regulatory Functions of Transnational Commercial Contracts: New Architectures', 36 *Fordham International Law Journal*, 2013, p. 1557-1618.

Campbell, Collins & Wightman 2003
Campbell, D., Collins, H. & Wightman, J. (eds.), *Implicit Dimensions of Contract. Discrete, Relational and Network Contracts*, Oxford: Hart Publishing 2003.

Christodoulidis 2013
Christodoulidis, E., 'On the politics of Societal Constitutionalism', 20 *Indiana Journal of Global Legal Studies*, 2013, p. 629-663.

Collins 2003
Collins, H., *The Law of Contract* (4th edition), Cambridge: Cambridge University Press 2003.

Collins 2014
Collins, H, 'Conformity of Goods, the Network Society, and the Ethical Consumer', 22 *European Review of Private Law*, 2014, p. 619-640.

Cutler, Haufler & Porter 1999
Cutler, A.C., Haufler, V. & Porter, T., 'Private Authority and International Affairs', in: A.C. Culter, V. Haufler & T. Porter (eds.), *Private Authority and International Affairs*, Albany: State University of New York Press 1999, p. 3-28.

Deane 1973
Deane, Ph., 'The Industrial Revolution in Great Britain', in: C.M. Cipola (ed.), *Fontana Economic History of Europe 4.1*, London: Collins 1973, p. 161-227.

Deane & Cole 1969
Deane, Ph. & Cole, W.A., *British Economic Growth 1688-1959*, Cambridge: Cambridge University Press 1969.

De Roover 1953
De Roover, R., *L'évolution de la lettre de change XIVe-XVIIIe siècles*, Paris: Armand Collin 1953.

De ruysscher 2009a
De ruysscher, D., 'Antwerp Commercial Legislation in Amsterdam in the 17th Century: Legal Transplant or Jumping Board?', 77 *Tijdschrift voor Rechtsgeschiedenis*, 2009, p. 459-479.

De ruysscher 2009b
De ruysscher, D., *'Naer het Romeins recht alsmede den stiel mercantiel'. Handel en recht in de Antwerpse rechtbank (16de-17de eeuw)*, Kortrijk-Heule: UGA 2009.

Deva & Bilchitz 2013
Deva, S. & Bilchitz, D. (eds.), *Human Rights Obligations for Business. Beyond the Corporate Responsibility to Respect?*, Cambridge: Cambridge University Press 2013.

DiMatteo 2014
DiMatteo, L.A. (ed), *International Sales Law. A Global Challenge*, New York: Cambridge University Press 2014.

Donahue 2004
Donahue, C., 'Medieval and Early Modern Lex Mercatoria: an Attempt at the Probatio Diabolica', 5 *Chicago Journal of International Law*, 2004, p. 21-37.

Epstein 1999
Epstein, R.A., 'Confusion about Custom: Disentangling Informal Customs from Standard Contractual Provisions', 66 *University of Chicago Law Review*, 1999, p. 821-835.

Epstein 2004
Epstein, R.A., 'Reflections on the Historical Origins and Economic Structure of the Law Merchant', 5 *Chicago Journal of International Law*, 2004, p. 1-20.

Etzioni 1988
Etzioni, A., *The Moral Dimension. Toward a New Economics*, New York/London: The Free Press/ Collier Macmillan Publishers 1988.

Ewart 1903
Ewart, J.S., 'What is the Law Merchant?', 3 *Columbia Law Review*, 1903, p. 135-154.

Fischer-Lescano & Teubner 2008
Fischer-Lescano, A. & Teubner, G., 'Cannibalizing Epistemes: will Modern Law protect Traditional Cultural Expressions?', in: C.B. Graber & M. Burri-Nenova (eds.), *Intellectual Property and Traditional Cultural Expressions in a Digital Environment*, Cheltenham: Edward Elgar 2008, p. 17- 45.

Flohr et al. 2010
Flohr, A., Rieth, L., Schwindenhammer, S. & Wolf, K.D., *The Role of Business in Global Governance. Corporations as Norm-Entreprenuers*, London: Palgrave MacMillan 2010.

Flume 2014
Flume, J.W., 'Law and Commerce: The Evolution of Codified Business Law in Europe', 2 *Comparative Legal History*, 2014, p. 45-83.

Gelderblom 2013
Gelderblom, O., Cities of Commerce: *The Institutional Foundation of International Trade in the Low Countries, 1250-1650*, Princeton & Oxford: Princeton University Press 2013.

Gereffi, Humphrey & Sturgeon 2005
Gereffi, G., Humphrey, J. & Sturgeon, T., 'The Governance of Global Value Chains', 12 *Review of International Political Economy*, 2005, p. 78-104.

Goode 2010
Goode, R.M., & McKendrick, E., *Goode on Commercial Law*, London: Penguin 2010.

Granovetter 1985
Granovetter, M., 'Economic Action and Social Structure: The Problem of Embeddedness', 91 *American Journal of Sociology*, 1985, p. 481-510.

Greif 2004
Greif, A., 'Impersonal Exchange without Impartial Law: the Community Responsibility System', 5 *Chicago Journal of International Law*, 2004, p. 109-138.

Gunningham 2007
Gunningham, N., 'Corporate Environmental Responsibility: Law and the Limits of Voluntarism', in: D. McBarnet, A. Voiculescu & T. Campbell (eds.), *The New Corporate Accountability: Corporate Responsiblity and the Law*, Cambridge: Cambridge University Press 2007, p. 476-500.

Gunningham & Rees 1997
Gunningham, N. & Rees, J., 'Industry Self-Regulation: An Institutional Perspective', 19 *Law & Policy*, 1997, p. 363-414.

Habermas 1989
Habermas, J., *The Structural Transformation of the Public Sphere: an Inquiry into a Category of Bourgeois Society*, Cambridge: Polity Press 1989.

Hadfield 2009
Hadfield, G., 'The Public and the Private in the Provision of Law for Global Transactions', in: V. Gessner (ed), *Contractual Certainty in International Trade. Empirical Studies and Theoretical Debates on Institutional Support for Global Economic Exchanges*, Oxford: Hart Publishing 2009, p. 239-256.

Hall & Soskice 2001
Hall, P. & Soskice, D., 'An Introduction to Varieties of Capitalism', in: P. Hall & D. Soskice (eds.), *Varieties of Capitalism: The Institutional Foundations of Comparative Advantage*, Oxford: Oxford University Press 2001, p. 1-68.

Hartkamp 2011
Hartkamp, A.S., 'Principles of Contract Law', in: A.S. Hartkamp *et al.* (eds.), *Towards a European Civil Code*, Arnhem: Ars Aequi 2011, p. 239-259.

Haufler 2001
Haufler, V., *A Public Role for the Private Sector. Industry Self-Regulation in a Global Economy*, Washington D.C.: Carnegie Endowement for International Peace 2001.

Henderson 1975
Henderson, W.O., *The Rise of German Industrial Power 1834-1914*, London: Temple Smith 1975.

Hoffmann 1963
Hoffmann, W.G., 'The Take-Off in Germany', in: W.W. Rostow (ed.), *The Economics of Take-Off in to Self-sustained Growth*, London: MacMillan 1963, p. 95-118.

Irvine 2001
Lord Irvine, 'The Law: An Engine for Trade', 64 *Modern Law Review*, 2001, p. 333-349.

Jansen & Rademacher 2012
Jansen, N. & Rademacher, J., 'European Civil Code', in: J.M. Smits (ed.), *Elgar Encyclopedia of Comparative Law*, Cheltenham: Edward Elgar Publishing Ltd 2012, p. 299-313.

Joerges 2011
Joerges, C., 'A new Type of Conflicts Law as the Legal Paradigm of the Postnational Constellation', in: J. Falke & C. Joerges (eds.), *Karl Polanyi, Globalisation and the Potential of Law in Transnational Markets*, Oxford: Hart Publishing 2011, p. 465-501.

Kadens 2004
Kadens, E., 'Order within Law, Variety within Custom: the Character of the Medieval Merchant Law', 5 *Chicago Journal of International Law*, 2004, p. 39-65.

Kadens 2012
Kadens, E., 'The Myth of the Customary Law Merchant', 90 *Texas Law Review*, 2012, p. 1153-1206.

Kanning 2003
Kanning, A.J., *Unifying Commercial Laws of Nation-States: Coordination of Legal Systems and Economic Growth*, Maastricht: University Library 2003.

Katz 1996
Katz, Av., 'Taking Private Ordering Seriously', 144 *University of Pennsylvania Law Review*, 1996, p. 1745-1763.

Kenny, Gillies & Devenney 2011
Kenny, M., Gillies, L & Devenney, J., 'The EU Optional Instrument: Absorbing the Private International Law Implications of a Common European Sales Law', 13 *Yearbook of Private International Law*, 2011, p. 315-344.

Klomp 1998
Klomp, R.J.Q., *Opkomst en ondergang van het handelsrecht : over de aard en de positie van het handelsrecht, in het bijzonder in verhouding tot het burgerlijk recht, in Nederland in de negentiende en twintigste eeuw*, Nijmegen: Ars Aequi Libri 1998.

Koehler & Yujun 2008
Koehler, M.F. & Yujun, G., 'The Acceptance of the Unified Sales Law (CISG) in Different Legal Systems', 20 *Pace International Law Review*, 2008, p. 45-60.

Kornet 2006
Kornet, N., *Contract Interpretation and Gap Filling: Comparative and Theoretical Perspectives*, Antwerpen: Intersentia 2006.

Kornet 2012
Kornet, N., 'The Common European Sales Law and the CISG - Complicating or Simplifying the Legal Environment?' 19 *Maastricht Journal of European and Comparative Law*, 2012, p. 164-179.

Kornet 2013
Kornet, N., 'The Interpretation and Fairness of Standardized Terms: Certainty and Predictability under the CESL and CISG Compared', 24 *European Business Law Review*, 2013, p. 319-339

Kötz & Flessner 1998
Kötz, H. & Flessner, A., *European Contract Law. Volume 1: Formation, Validity, and Content of Contract; Contract and Third Parties*, Oxford: Oxford University Press 1998.

Labrousse 1954
Labrousse, E., *Aspects de l'évolution économique et sociale de la France et du Royaume-Uni de 1815 à 1880: d'après les notes du cours*, Paris: Centre de Documentation Universitaire 1954.

Levy & Kaplan 2008
Levy, D.L. & Kaplan, R., 'Corporate Social Responsibility and Theories of Global Governance: Strategic Contestation in Global Issue Arenas', in: A. Crane, A. McWilliams, D. Matten, J. Moon & D.S. Siegel (eds.), *The Oxford Handbook of Corporate Social Responsibility*, Oxford: Oxford University Press 2008, p. 432-451.

Lichtenauer 1956
Lichtenauer, W.F., *Geschiedenis van de wetenschap van het handelsrecht in Nederland tot 1809* (Geschiedenis der Nederlandsche rechtswetenschap; dl. 5, afl. 1), Amsterdam: Noord-Hollandsche Uitgevers Maatschappij 1956.

Lin 2007
Lin, L.-W., 'Corporate Social Accountability Standards in the Global Supply Chain: Resistance, Reconsideration and Resolution in China', 15 *Cardozo Journal of International and Comparative Law*, 2007, p. 321-370.

Loos & Samoy 2014
Loos, M. & Samoy, I. (eds.), *The Position of Small and Medium-Sized Enterprises in European Contract Law*, Antwerp: Intersentia 2014.

Magnus 2012
Magnus, U. (ed.), *CISG vs Regional Sales Law Unification. With a Focus on the New Common European Sales Law*, Munich: Sellier 2012.

McBarnet & Kurkchiyan 2007
McBarnet, D. & Kurkchiyan, M., 'Corporate Social Responsibility through Contractual Control? Global Supply Chains and 'other Regulation', in: D. McBarnet, A. Vioiculescu & T. Campbell (eds.), *The New Corporate Accountability. Corporate Social Responsibility and the Law*, Cambridge/Mass.: Cambridge University Press 2007, p. 59-92.

Mathias 1983
Mathias, P., *The First Industrial Nation: An Economic History of Britain 1700-1914*, London: Routledge 1983.

McMillan & Woodruff 2000
McMillan, J. & Woodruff, Ch., 'Private Order under Dysfunctional Public Order', 98 *Michigan Law Review*, 2000, p. 2421-2458.

Michaels 2005
Michaels, R., 'The Re-State-Ment of Non-State Law: The State, the Choice of Law, and the Challenge from Global Legal Pluralism', 51 *Wayne Law Review*, 2005, p. 1209-1259.

Michaels 2011
Michaels, R., 'Global Problems in Domestic Courts', in: S. Muller, S. Zouridis, M. Frishman & L. Kistemaker (eds.), *The Law of the Future and the Future of Law*, Oslo: Torkel Opsahl Academic EPublisher 2011, p. 165-175.

Michaels & Jansen 2006
Michaels, R. & Jansen, N., 'Private Law beyond the State? Europeanization, Globalization, Privatization', 54 *American Journal of Comparative Law*, 2006, p. 843-890.

Micheletti 2003
Micheletti, M., *Political Virtue and Shopping: Individuals, Consumerism, and Collective Action*, New York/Basingstoke: Palgrave MacMillan 2003.

Murphy 2005
Murphy, S.D., 'Taking Multinational Corporate Codes of Conduct to the next Level', 43 *Columbia Journal of Transnational Law*, 2005.

Nonet & Selznick 1978
Nonet, P. & Selznick, P., *Law and Society in Transition: Toward Responsive Law*, New York/Hagerstown/San Francisco/London: Harper Torchbooks 1978.

North 1991
North, D.C., 'Institutions', 5 *The Journal of Economic Perspectives*, 1991, p. 97-112.

Ogus 1995
Ogus, A., 'Rethinking Self-Regulation', 15 *Oxford Journal of Legal Studies*, 1995, p. 97-108.

Ogus 2000
Ogus, A., 'Self-Regulation', in B. Bouckaert & G. De Geest (eds.), *Encyclopedia of Law and Economics*, Cheltenham: Edward Elgar (University of Ghent) 2000, p. 587-602.

Parker 2007
Parker, C., 'Meta-Regulation: Legal Accountability for Corporate Social Responsibility', in: D. McBarnet, A. Voiculescu & T. Campbell (eds.), *The New Corporate Accountability: Corporate Social Responsibility and the Law*, Cambridge: Cambridge University Press 2007, p. 207-237.

Pierenkemper & Tilly 2004
Pierenkemper, T. & Tilly, R., *The German Economy during the Nineteenth Century*, New York/Oxford: Berghahn Books 2004.

Pirrong 1998
Pirrong, S.C., 'Self-Regulation of Private Organized Markets', in: P. Newman (ed.), *The New Palgrave Dictionary of Economics and the Law*, London/New York: MacMillan/Stockton Press 1998, p. 433-438.

Philippopoulos 2008
Philippopoulos, G.V., 'Awareness of the CISG among American Attorneys', 40 *UCC Law Journal*, 2008, p. 357-371.

Polanyi 2001 [1944]
Polanyi, K., *The Great Transformation. The Political and Economic Origins of Our Time*, Boston: Beacon Press 2001 [1944].

Posner 1996
Posner, E.A., 'The Regulation of Groups: The Influence of Legal and Nonlegal Sanctions on Collective Action', 63 *University of Chicago Law Review*, 1996, p. 133-197.

Posner 2003
Posner, R., *Economic Analysis of Law*, New York: Aspen 2003.

Price 1981
Price, R., *An Economic History of Modern France, 1730–1914*, London: MacMillan 1981.

Richman 2004
Richman, B.D., 'Firms, Courts and Reputation Mechanisms: Towards a Positive Theory of Private Ordering', 104 *Columbia Law Review*, 2004, p. 2328-2367.

Richman 2009
Richman, B.D., 'Ethnic Networks, Extra-legal Certainty and Globalisation: Peering into the Diamond Industry', in: V. Gessner (ed), *Contractual Certainty in International Trade. Empirical Studies and Theoretical Debates on Institutional Support for Global Economic Exchanges*, Oxford: Hart Publishing 2009, p. 31-47.

Rodrik 2011
Rodrik, D., *The Gobalization Paradox. Democracy and the Future of the World Economy*, New York/London: W.W. Norton & Company 2011.

Rogers 1995
Rogers, J.S., *The Early History of the Law of Bills and Notes: a Study of the Origins of Anglo-American Commercial Law*, Cambridge: Cambridge University Press 1995.

Rückert 1993
Rückert, J., 'Handelsrechtsbildung und Modernisierung des Handelsrechts durch Wissenschaft zwischen ca. 1800 und 1900', in: K.O. Scherner (ed.), *Modernisierung des Handelsrechts im 19. Jahrhundert*, Heidelberg: Verlag Recht und Wirtschaft 1993, p. 19-66.

Sandel 2012
Sandel, M.J., *What Money can't Buy: The Moral Limits of Markets*, London: Penguin Books 2012.

Schäfer & Ott 2004
Schäfer, H.-B. & Ott, C., *The Economic Analysis of Civil Law*, Cheltenham: Edward Elgar 2004.

Schlechtriem 2007
Schlechtriem, P. 'Non-Material Damages - Recovery under the CISG', 89 *Pace International Law Review*, 2007, p. 89-102.

Schmitthoff 1981
Schmitthoff, C.M., *Commercial Law in a Changing Economic Climate*, London: Sweet & Maxwell 1981.

Schwenzer 2012
Schwenzer, I., 'The Proposed Common European Sales Law and the Convention on the International Sale of Goods', 44 *Uniform Commercial Code Law Journal*, 2012, p. 457-481.

Schwenzer & Leisinger 2007
Schwenzer, I. & Leisinger, B., 'Ethical Values and International Sales Contracts', in: R. Cranston, J. Ramberg & J. Ziegel (eds.), *Commercial Law Challenges in the 21st century: Jan Hellner in memorium*, Stockholm: Stockholm Centre for Commercial Law Juridiska Institutionen 2007, p. 249-275.

Scott 2000
Scott, R.E., 'The Uniformity Norm in Commercial Law: a Comparative Analysis of Common Law and Code Methodologies', in: J.S. Kraus & S.D. Walt (eds.), *The Jurisprudential Foundations of Corporate and Commercial Law*, Cambridge: Cambridge University Press 2000, p. 149-192.

Screpanti & Zamagni 1993
Screpanti, E. & Zamagni, S., *An Outline of the History of Economic Thought*, Oxford: Clarendon Press 1993.

Shleifer 2004
Shleifer, A., 'Does Competition Destroy Ethical Behaviour', 94 *The American Economic Review*, 2004, p. 414-418.

Simmonds 1984
Simmonds, N., *The Decline of Juridical Reason. Doctrine and Theory in the Legal Order*, Manchester: Manchester University Press 1984.

Sjåfjell 2011
Sjåfjell, B., 'Regulating Companies as if the World Matters: Reflections on the Ongoing Sustainable Companies Project', 47 *Wake Forest Law Review*, 2011, p. 113-134.

Smits 2010
Smits, J.M., 'The Complexity of Transnational Law: Coherence and Fragmentation of Private Law,' 14(3) *Electronic Journal of Comparative Law*, <http://www.ejcl.org/143/art143-14.pdf>.

Smits 2014
Smits, J.M., *Contract Law. A Comparative Introduction*, Cheltenham: Edward Elgar 2014.

Spagnolo 2010
Spagnolo, L., 'Green Eggs and Ham: The CISG, Path Dependence, and the Behavioural Economics of Lawyer's Choices of Law in International Sales Contracts', 6(2) *Journal of Private International Law*, 2010, p. 417-464.

Spufford 1987
Spufford, P., 'Coinage and Currency', in: M.M., Postan *et al.* (eds.), *The Cambridge Economic History of Europe: from the Decline of the Roman Empire; Vol. II: Trade and industry in the Middle Ages*, Cambridge [etc.]: Cambridge University Press 1987, p. 788-863.

Stehr, Henning & Weiler 2006
Stehr, N., Henning, C. & Weiler, B. (eds.), *The Moralization of Markets*, New Brunswick: Transaction Publishers 2006.

Streeck 1997
Streeck, W., 'Beneficial Constraints: on the Economic Limits of Rational Voluntarism', in: R. Hollingsworth & R. Boyer (eds.), *Contemporary Capitalism. The Embeddedness of Institutions*, Cambridge: Cambridge University Press 1997, p. 197-219.

Study Group on Social Justice in European Contract Law 2004
Study Group on Social Justice in European Contract Law, 'Social Justice in European Contract Law: a Manifesto', 10 *European Law Journal*, 2004, p. 653-674.

Taggert 2005
Taggert, M. 'From "Parliamentary Powers" to Privatization: the Chequered History of Delegated Legislation in the Twentieth Century', 55 *University of Toronto Law Journal*, 2005, p. 575-627.

Tiebout 1956
Tiebout, C., 'A Pure Theory of Local Expenditures', 64 *Journal of Political Economy*, 1956, p. 416-424.

Teubner 1983
Teubner, G., 'Substantive and Reflexive Elements in Modern Law', 17 *Law and Society Review*, 1983, p. 239-285.

Teubner 2012
Teubner, G., *Constitutional Fragments. Societal Constitutionalism in the Globalization*, Oxford: Oxford University Press 2012.

Tjon Soei Len 2013
Tjon Soei Len, L.K.L., *The Effects of Contracts beyond Frontiers: a Capabilities Perspective on Externalities and Contract Law in Europe* (PhD Dissertation, Universiteit van Amsterdam), Amsterdam: University of Amsterdam 2013.

Twigg-Flesner & Villalta Puig 2011
Twigg-Flesner, C. & Villalta Puig G., (eds.), *The Boundaries of Commercial and Trade Law*, Sellier: Munich 2011.

Van der Wee 1977
Van der Wee, H., 'Monetary, Credit and Banking Systems', in: J.H. Clapham *et al.* (eds), *The Cambridge Economic History of Europe: from the Decline of the Roman Empire; Vol. V: The Economic Organization of Early Modern Europe*, Cambridge: Cambridge University Press 1977, p. 290-392.

Van Hofstraeten
Van Hofstraeten, B., 'Jurisdictional Complexity in Antwerp Company Law (1480-1620)', in: S. P. Donlan & D. Heirbaut (eds.) *Jurisdictional Complexity in Western Legal History (ca.1600-1900)*, Berlin: Duncker & Humblot, forthcoming.

Van Zanden & Van Riel 2004
Van Zanden, J.L. & Van Riel, A., *The Strictures of Inheritance: the Dutch Economy in the Nineteenth Century*, Princeton, N.J.: Princeton University Press 2004.

Von Savigny 1840
Von Savigny, F.C., *System des heutigen römischen Rechts*, Berlin: Bei Veit und Comp. 1840.

Vytopil 2012
Vytopil, L., 'Contractual Control and Labour-Related CSR Norms in the Supply Chain: Dutch Best Practices', 8 *Utrecht Law Review*, 2012, p. 155-169.

Wagner 2005
Wagner, G., 'The Virtues of Diversity in European Private Law', in J.M. Smits (ed.) *The Need for a European Contract Law*, Groningen: Europa Law Publishing 2005, p. 1-24

Weber 2002 [1920]
Weber, M., *The Protestant Ethic and the Spirit of Capitalism. Translation by Stephen Kalberg* (3rd edition), Los Angeles: Roxbury Publishing Company 2002 [1920].

Weinrib 1995
Weinrib, E.J., *The Idea of Private Law*, Cambridge/Mass: Harvard University Press 1995.

Wielsch 2013
Wielsch, D., 'Global Law's Toolbox: How Standards Form Contracts', in: H. Eidenmüller (ed.), *Regulatory Competition in Contract Law and Dispute Resolution*, Munich/Oxford: C.H. Beck/Hart/Nomos, p. 71-111.

Wightman 2003
Wightman, J., 'Beyond Custom: Contracts, Contexts, and the Recognition of Implicit Understandings', in: D. Campbell, H Collins & J Wightman (eds), *Implicit Dimensions of Contract. Discrete, Relational and Network Contracts*, Oxford: Hart Publishing 2003, p. 143-186.

Wilhelmsson 1998
Wilhelmsson, T., 'Consumer Law and the Environment: From Consumer to Citizen', 21 *Journal of Consumer Policy*, 1998, p. 45-70.

Wilhelmsson 2002/2003
Wilhelmsson, T., 'A Green Sales Law?', 6 *Yearbook of New Zealand Jurisprudence*, 2002/2003, p. 83-102.

Wilhelmsson 2004
Wilhelmsson, T., 'Varieties of Welfarism in European Contract Law', 10 *European Law Journal*, 2004, p. 712-733.

Wintle 2000
Wintle, M.J., *An Economic and Social History of the Netherlands, 1800-1920: Demographic, Economic, and Social Transition*, Cambridge: Cambridge University Press 2000.

Ziegel 2005
Ziegel, J. 'The Scope of the Convention: Reaching out to Article One and Beyond', 25 *Journal of Law and Commerce*, 2005, p. 59-73.

Bram Akkermans

EUROPEAN UNION CONSTITUTIONAL PROPERTY LAW: SEARCHING FOR FOUNDATIONS FOR THE ALLOCATION OF REGULATORY COMPETENCES*

1. Introduction

For lawyers in Europe, property law is the law of things, with 'things' used in the widest sense of the word.[1] It concerns relations of individuals or groups to each other in respect to an object, or more in a traditional sense, relations between individuals or groups of individuals and a thing.[2] A thing can be a tangible object, such as land or a movable object, but also an intangible object, such as a claim or another right.[3] In fact, although the law of property originally developed around land, intangible objects have become the most valuable subject matter in property law.[4] Some modern property lawyers therefore exclusively focus on intangibles, whereas other property lawyers have remained with land as the subject matter of their study. This is especially so in common law systems where land law, personal property law, and commercial law are distinct disciplines.[5]

For centuries, the law of things has been the primary focus of property lawyers, but in recent decades some property lawyers have started to concern themselves with property as part of constitutional law.[6] This approach focuses on the protection of individuals and individual property rights against the state, but

* I owe special thanks for dr. Eveline Ramaekers of Wadham College, University of Oxford, for her value remarks on an earlier version of this paper. Any mistakes, as usual, are fully my own.

1 There are other approaches to property law, especially those that take a constitutional viewpoint. Such approaches are more advocated in the United States. For a different US perspective see Smith 2012, p. 1691 *et seq*.

2 See, on the different approaches, Sagaert 2005, p 983-1086; Akkermans 2008, p 456-457.

3 See, on objects of property law, Gretton 2007, p. 802-851; Van Erp 2011, p. 227-248.

4 See, on the dematerialization of property law, Libchaber 2004, p. 297-372.

5 Even the law of trusts, which reaches far into each of these three areas is considered, taught and practiced as a separate subject. This is, however, not exclusive to the common law systems. Also in German law the term *Liegenschafsrecht* denotes land law, see Baur, Baur & Stürner 2009, Part III.

6 Most notably in the United States, but also in South Africa and Australia. See, on this, Van der Walt 1999, p. 39 *et seq*. (Australia), p. 121 *et seq*. (Germany), p. 389 *et seq*. (United States).

also concerns the organization of property law and the effect of constitutional law on the more traditional private-law property law, i.e. property law as the law of things.[7] Constitutional property law is sometimes met with skepticism by the private-law property lawyer, but greatly enriches the understanding of the superstructure as well as the underlying thought-patterns of property law.[8]

In the context of the European Union (EU), property law has an additional, i.e. third, dimension. In the EU there is an internal market in which there is freedom of movement of goods, persons, services and capital. European Citizens enjoy freedom to reside wherever they want, including the right to acquire property elsewhere.[9] Moreover, also the other freedoms, especially the free movement of goods and capital rely on property law to a considerable extent. The EU internal market is a social market economy, as provided by Article 3 of the Treaty on European Union:

> '(...) 3. The Union shall establish an internal market. It shall work for the sustainable development of Europe based on balanced economic growth and price stability, a highly competitive *social market economy*, aiming at full employment and social progress, and a high level of protection and improvement of the quality of the environment. It shall promote scientific and technological advance.'[10]

The term ‚social market economy' derives from the German model for the economy and refers to the idea of a free market where government interference is accepted to promote the best possible outcome, contrary to a free market economy where a race for the lowest level of protection can occur. For example, in case of consumer protection, interference with the market is justified to achieve the best - or otherwise desired - standard of consumer protection. The way in which this market functions is not always considered by private lawyers although private law, and especially property law, has an important part to play in its functioning.[11]

At the foundation of any functioning market economy are three very important - fundamental - principles of private law: (i) freedom of ownership (individual property rights), (ii) free circulation of goods, and (iii) the freedom of contract.[12] Each of these is essential for the functioning of a market economy. Individuals, i.e. citizens and companies, need to be able to hold an individual entitlement to property. These property entitlements - or better, property rights - must be transferable to other individuals, either for value or gratuitously. In order to do so, finally, these individuals must have the right to enter into binding agreements with each other to

7 Most notably Van der Walt 2012.

8 The famous German handbook on property law by Baur, Baur & Stürner, for example, pays attention to the constitutional dimension of property law for about one and half page, before devoting 900 pages to private-law property law. French handbooks on private-law property generally do not even mention the constitutional dimension. On the importance of an overarching analysis see Van Erp 2006, p. 16 *et seq.*; Van Erp 2009, p. 1517 *et seq.*

9 See, on the observation that the freedom of establishment includes the acquisition of property Ramaekers 2013, p. 82-83.

10 Art. 3 TEU, emphasis made by author.

11 See Micklitz 2008.

12 On freedom of contract and, in relation to that, the other two -property related- freedoms, see Reich 2014, p 19.

realize these fundamental underlying principles.[13] In such a market system therefore, trade naturally occurs when individuals value property rights (assets) at a higher value than those who currently hold these and are willing to pay for their acquisition.[14]

The understanding of property and its function in this way sheds new light on the question of allocation of regulatory competences. In the EU these fundamental principles are generally provided by the law of the Member States, as shown, *inter alia*, by the Copenhagen criteria for accession of new Member States that require an aspiring Member State to have a functioning market economy.[15] In order to have a functioning market economy these systems must provide freedom of ownership, free circulation of goods and freedom of contract before they can become an EU Member State.[16] That this is not self-evident is shown by former socialist republics, that have had to introduce these when they transitioned to a market economy.[17]

In the first decades of the EU internal market, these fundamental freedoms were ‚uploaded' from the national level to the EU level in order to ensure its functioning.[18] Since 2000, however, Article 17 of the Charter of Fundamental Rights of the European Union, with binding force since the entry into force of the Treaty of Lisbon in 2009, deals with the right to property. It states:

> 'Right to property
> 1. Everyone has the right to own, use, dispose of and bequeath his or her lawfully acquired possessions. No one may be deprived of his or her possessions, except in the public interest and in the cases and under the conditions provided for by law, subject to fair compensation being paid in good time for their loss. The use of property may be regulated by law in so far as is necessary for the general interest.
> 2. Intellectual property shall be protected.'

With Article 17 of the EU Charter, both a positive and a negative element of constitutional property law has been brought to the EU level. The positive element is included in the first sentence and states that everyone has the right to hold and exercise property rights: freedom of ownership in other words. The negative element is included in the second sentence, which states that no one may be deprived of his or her property rights. This last sentence is in line with traditional constitutional property provisions such as the 5th Amendment to the US Constitution, Article 1 First Protocol to the European Convention on Human Rights and Section 25 of the South African Constitution.[19]

With that, property law in the EU has now become a complex multi-level system in which fundamental principles of national property law and of EU internal

13 See, on these principles, also Akkermans 2014.

14 See Posner 1973, p. 10 *et seq.*

15 On the 'Copenhagen criteria' see European Council in Copenhagen - Conclusions of the Presidency - European Council Doc/93/3 22/06/1993.

16 See on the same argument of underlying values for the internal market Reich 2014, p. 18-19.

17 Reich 1972, p. 275 *et seq.*; Collins 1982, p. 77-93; Reich 2004.

18 Uploading, meaning that the laws of the Member States supply the concept or concepts to the EU level. On uploading see Börzel 2002, p. 193-214.

19 See Van der Walt 1999, p. 69 *et seq.* (ECHR) and p. 320 *et seq.* (South Africa).

market law supplement each other, with most 'regular' (private-law) property rules remaining at national level. Although it has not yet proven to be problematic, this is an unstable situation. If one of the Member States would change its system from a market economy to a planned economy, or - somewhat less extreme - seek to nationalize an entire part of its national industry - such as the banking or financial industry, the EU internal market would be in great difficulties. In fact, I submit, EU internal market law, especially in the form of economic constitutional law resists such a development. Those restrictions are not simply measures of general EU law, but actually part of the constitutional system of EU property law. We can therefore reconsider the allocation of competences in property law to create a system that fits the 21st century reality.

In this contribution I will explore the current and future state of EU property law. I will start with European Economic Constitutional Law (section 2) and property law in the internal market (section 3), before I will move to the future of property law in the EU and especially the allocation of regulatory powers. I will do this by exploring the foundations of property law in the EU internal market, by reference to socialist systems (section 4). This will provide a better understanding of the current organization of property law in the European Union (section 5). I will then turn to the future and will draw inspiration from the current development of South African property law (section 6) and I will broaden my look to other functions property fulfils besides the economic aspects (section 7). I will then argue how EU (property) law and national (property) law are actually part of a single legal order in which European Economic Constitutional Law is guiding future development (section 8).

2. European Economic Constitutional Law

It is sometimes argued that the Treaties governing the European Union, i.e. the Treaty on European Union (TEU) and the Treaty on the Functioning of the European Union (TFEU) provide the constitutional order of the European Union (EU).[20] This includes the EU institutions and the rules governing EU decision making.[21] Following this theory it is argued by some that also the EU Internal Market is governed by constitutional rules.[22] These economic rules, the argument entails, give shape to the functioning of the EU internal market by guaranteeing free movement of goods, persons, services and capital as well as ensuring free competition wherever possible. They provide, in other words, the economic constitution of the Internal Market. However, speaking of an economic constitution creates confusion, as there is not one single document or even section of a document that would

20 Joerges 1997; Joerges 2004.

21 Lenaerts & Van Nuffel 2011; Dinnage & Laffineur 2010; Schieck 2012, p. 64 *et seq.*

22 Joergest 1997; Joerges 2004; Bacquero Cruz 2002, p. 25 *et seq.*; Collins 2009, p. 71-94, a similar argument is also made by Dagmar Schieck in respect to social justice, Schieck 2012, p. 30 *et seq.*

be such an economic constitution.[23] Moreover, an economic constitution is both an economic, political as well as a legal term and as such is difficult to describe. A concept of economic constitution generally presupposes the existence of a single piece of legislation, whereas in reality a wide variety of rules - such as rules on free movement and on competition law - belong to the economic constitution. An alternative term - economic constitutional law - is better suited to describe what we are dealing with. The use of the term economic constitutional law brings the discussion into the legal domain, as well as provides for the inclusion of a multitude of rules at various levels that all fall under the same part of constitutional law.[24]

The European Union is a unique international organization. It provides a legal order with an internal market, comprising the national markets of the Member States. At the foundation of this legal order is the *Schuman*-declaration of 9 May 1950 in which French minister Robert Schuman gave shape to the foundations of what is now the European Union. At a central point in his declaration, Schuman states:

> 'By pooling basic production and by instituting a new High Authority, whose decisions will bind France, Germany and other member countries, this proposal will lead to the realization of the first concrete foundation of a European federation indispensable to the preservation of peace.'

The union that has followed from this, was built incrementally, and not without controversy, in the past 60 years. The foundations built by Schuman, particularly the creation of an internal market with a 'High Authority' overlooking its functioning, have found their way into the Treaty of Rome and all subsequent Treaties. The current Treaty on European Union and Treaty on Functioning of the Internal Market still follow the same underlying idea of a joint effort to combine markets, based on solidarity between countries, to increase welfare.[25]

The constitution of the European Union therefore also embodies these values. In fact the Court of Justice stated in its *Les Verts* judgment that the Treaty establishing the European Community (The EC Treaty) is 'the constitutional charter of a Community based on the rules of law'.[26] The institutional rules of the EU in the Treaty are therefore part of EU constitutional law. The internal market rules in the Treaty are therefore also part of EU constitutional law, but of its economic constitution. These are rules establishing the internal market and its principles, as well as the rules governing the functioning of the internal market, such as rules on freedom of movement of goods, persons, services, and capital, as well as competition law.

23 The Economic Constitution has exactly been criticized on this basis. See Bacquero Cruz 2002, p. 26-27.

24 Bacquero Cruz 2002, p. 27.

25 Schuman stated in this respect: 'Europe will not be made all at once, or according to a single plan. It will be built through concrete achievements which first create a de facto solidarity. The coming together of the nations of Europe requires the elimination of the age-old opposition of France and Germany. Any action taken must in the first place concern these two countries.'

26 Case 294/83 *Les Verts* [1986] ECR 1330, para 23.

These rules are rules of European economic constitutional law. These are the rules of the treaty itself, but also the case law of the European Court of Justice interpreting these rules, and adding a framework of general principles of EU law.

The rules of economic constitutional law function in the framework of EU law as it was established by the 1957 Treaty of Rome and the case law of the Court of Justice that builds on this Treaty. This means that EU law goes before national law (doctrine of supremacy) and that rules in the Treaties that are clearly and precisely formulated can directly create rights and obligations for individuals (doctrine of direct effect).[27] Member States have loyalty towards the Union and towards each other (doctrine of sincere cooperation), can be brought to court for non-conformity, and can be held liable for the incorrect or non-implementation of EU law.[28]

3. Property Law and the EU Internal Market

It is no longer contested that EU law has an effect on property law.[29] In fact, the effect of EU law on the law of property seems to be increasing in the last decade.[30] From the very beginning of the Treaty, deriving directly from the Schuman declaration, the Treaty has stated that it 'shall in no way prejudice the rules of property ownership'.[31] This rule, research shows, does not relate to the law of property as such, but rather to the way in which undertakings are managed. It refers to the principle of neutrality of the EU Treaties in relation to state- or private ownership of enterprises.[32] The law of property, in other words, has been subject to the influence of EU law from the very beginning. There is legislation in this area and the ECJ has made judgements that affect the law of property on many occasions.

In terms of EU legislation, there is legislation relating to stolen cultural objects, retention of title in late payment and insolvency situations, financial collateral arrangements and succession.[33] There is also a lot of legislation that indirectly affects property law, such as legislation relating to greenhouse gas emission rights, maintenance obligations and environmental legislation, as well as future legislation in the area of consumer contract law, marital property regimes and property regimes between registered partners, as well as possible mortgage legislation.[34]

In terms of the effect of EU Economic Constitutional Law on property law, there are cases in relation to the free movement of goods and to the free movement of services and capital that consider national property legislation that hinders access

27 Craig & De Burca 2011, p. 180 *et seq.*

28 Art. 4(3) TEU (principle of sincere cooperation) and Joined Cases 6/90 and 9/90 *Andrea Francovich and Danila Bonifaci* v *Italy* [1991] ECR I-5357, Craig & De Burca 2011, p. 241-243.

29 See, for example, Kieninger 1996, p. 251 *et seq.*; Rutgers 1999, p. 195 *et seq.*; Israël 2005, p. 110-111; Akkermans 2008, p. 482-494; Akkermans 2012a, p. 201-206; Ramaekers 2013, p. 137-156.

30 Eveline Ramaekers provides an elaborate overview in her book Ramaekers 2013, p. 233-238.

31 Akkermans & Ramaekers 2011, p. 300.

32 See on this article also, Losada *et al.* 2012, p. 203-224. Akkermans 2008, p. 508-509; Ramaekers 2013, p. 97-120.

33 For an overview see Van Erp & Akkermans 2012a, p. 173 *et seq.*; Ramaekers 2013, p. 137-156.

34 On indict effect of EU legislation on property law see Akkermans 2013, p. 47-60. For an overview of future property law, Akkermans 2012b, p. 280-283.

to the market of another Member State incompatible with the TFEU. As a result, such national legislation cannot apply in such and like situations.[35] Examples are the consideration of a special right of seizure of goods by national tax authorities and the effect of that right on foreign holders of property security rights, and restrictions on the acquisition of ownership by buyers from another Member State.[36] Especially the latter series of cases, i.e. those that deal with the acquisition of land by EU citizens from another Member State, has a much more controversial dimension to it. In many countries for many centuries the ownership of land has been restricted to nationals of that same country. Although western European countries have not used such a restriction for a long duration of time, in many central and eastern - now member - states, such a restriction was commonplace until recently.[37] In fact, as a part of the accession agreements reached with new Member States there is usually a clause that deals with the acquisition of land, with only Malta having obtained a restriction to the free movement of capital in this respect, due to its unique geographical situation.[38]

The existence of EU law in these areas of property law shows how dealing with property is inevitable when dealing with a market economy. When a *single* market exists, there cannot be boundaries within that market that cause distortions to its functioning. Within a single country, therefore, there are generally no barriers to trade. Within an international single market, such as the EU internal market, these barriers do exist, but must be overcome if the functioning of the market economy is at stake. Property law therefore plays a central role in this, even when this does not always come to the surface. The relationship between markets and property law is, exactly because of this invisibility, complex.

A market economy functions on the basis of three general principles: (i) there is freedom of ownership, so that every market participant is entitled to the goods that exist on the market, (ii) free circulation of goods, so that every market partici-

35 Akkermans 2012a, p. 201 *et seq.*; Ramaekers 2013, p. 91-96.

36 Case C-69/88, *H. Krantz GmbH & Co* v *Ontvanger der Directe Belastingen en de Staat der Nederlanden* [1990] ECR I-583 (right of seizure, free movement of goods), and Case C-302/97, *Klaus Konle* v *Republic of Austria* [1999] ECR I-3099, and Joined Cases C-515/99, C-519/99 to C-524/99 and C-526/99 to C-540/99, *Hans Reisch and others* v *Bürgermeister des Landeshauptstadt Salzburg und Grundverkehrsbeauftragter des Landes Salzburg* and *Anton Lassacher and Others* v *Grundverkehrsbeauftragter des Landes Salzburg and Grundverkehrslandeskommission des Landes Salzburg* [2002] ECR I-2157 (acquisition of ownership of land, free movement of capital).

37 For example, in Poland Act of 24 March 1920 on the acquisition of immovable property by foreign persons, and Art. 44 of the Polish Civil Code, in Bulgaria Art. 22 of the Bulgarian Constitution of 1991, Wording of Art. 22, Bulgarian Constitution, Amended State Gazette no 85, 26.09.2003, as well as Art. 29 of the Bulgarian Constitution, as amended by Amended State Gazette no 24, 2007. See, Swinnen & Vranken 2006.

38 Documents concerning the accession of the Czech Republic, the Republic of Estonia, the Republic of Cyprus, the Republic of Latvia, the Republic of Lithuania, the Republic of Hungary, the Republic of Malta, the Republic of Poland, the Republic of Slovenia and the Slovak Republic to the European Union, Protocol No 6 on the acquisition of secondary residences in Malta, 23 September 2003, [2003] OJ 947. The rationale behind this exception is that Malta is so small and there is so little land available that foreign buyers might push out a very large part of the local population.

pant can transfer his or her goods to another without restrictions, and (iii) freedom of contract, so that market participants can actually trade.[39] These three fundamental principles form the foundation of a market economy, but that does not mean that they are always visible. In some countries, such as Germany, they have been the subject of the discussion leading to the civil code, but in most countries these principles are almost self-evident. In Germany Von Savigny wrote in his treatise on *heutiges römisches Recht* in his famous paragraph 52 and onwards about legal relations (*Rechsverhältnisse*) about men's dominion over nature in the form of property rights and the need to create an effective system of private law.[40] In the *Motive*, the explanations to the first draft of a Civil Code for the Germanic countries, uniting them into a single country with a single private law, Reinhold Johow writes about *Verkehrsrecht*.[41] In its first design of the German Civil Code §137 stated: 'Die verträgsmaßiche Verpflichtung des Eigenthümers, die Sache nicht zu veräußern oder zu belasten, ist gegen Dritte wirkungslos.'[42]

The German experience shows the interrelatedness of market economy and private law. From this perspective private law becomes an instrument to enable trade. However, this crucial dimension of private law is often overlooked or taken for granted, especially as it is not necessarily entrenched in a specific legal provision. Still, each country with its own market must abide by these rules. The EU internal market, which is also a market economy, must therefore also comprise these fundamental principles.[43] In fact, due to its limited legal basis, mainly provided by Article 114 TFEU, to provide for this by itself, the existence of these fundamental principles is even more crucial.

The European Union's Internal Market is not a mere sum of the national markets of the Member States, but is a single market. The constitutional order of the European Union provides for a single legal order, in which the legal systems of the Member States and that of the European Union work together. The constitutional law of the EU provides some 'federal' rules when there is a conflict between these two levels. Generally speaking, (i) EU law has preference over national law and, unless justified and deemed proportional, will therefore set aside national law, and (ii) the EU will not concern itself with matters that have no Union-dimension. This second requirement is of crucial importance to the Member States that often seek to invoke that there is no Union-dimension to a case. The most often heard example is when a Member State argues there is no cross-border dimension to a certain case. However, this second requirement goes well beyond the aspect of a cross-border element. Especially since the introduction of EU citizenship by the Treaty of

39 See, Reich 2014, p. 18-21.

40 Von Savigny 1982, paras. 52 *et seq*.

41 Wiegand 1990, p. 118; Wiegand 1984, p. 109 *et seq*.

42 The final version of the paragraph states: 'Die Befugnis zur Verfügung über ein veräußerliches Recht kann nicht durch Rechtsgeschäft ausgeschlossen oder beschränkt werden. Die Wirksamkeit einer Verpflichtung, über ein solches Recht nicht zu verfügen, wird durch diese Vorschrift nicht berührt.' See Schubert 1982, para. 91, see for parallel development in Switzerland, Wiegand 1984, p. 107-137.

43 Art. 3(3) TEU.

Maastricht in 1993, a Union-dimension can also be found in cases that were considered as purely domestic before that.[44]

From the very beginning the EU has recognized and regulated the free circulation of goods under what is now Article 34 TFEU. Since the Treaty of Nice (2001) and with the force of law since the Treaty of Lisbon (2009) the EU also regulates ownership in Article 17 of the Fundamental Rights Charter. Article 17, different from its counterpart in the First Protocol to the European Convention on Human Rights, provides both a positive and a negative guarantee of ownership.[45]

In terms of freedom of contract the EU does not directly regulate this aspect of the market economy.[46] The laws of the Member States must thus provide - i.e. upload - the principle to the EU level. However, the Court of Justice is sensitive to this and will refer to freedom of contract and its effects as general principles of EU law when it can to provide EU states to national principles. Therefore in *Société thermale* the Court referred to the idea that promises should be kept, i.e. *pacta sunt servanda*, as a general principle of EU law.[47] In relation to the freedom to exercise an economic or commercial activity under Article 16 of the EU Charter on Fundamental Rights, the Court even explicitly referred to freedom of contract.[48] However, in EU law, the freedom of contract is always framed in the light of the legislative competencies, which focus on regulating the market by, for example, competition law or consumer protection.[49] It could be held that therefore a limited freedom of contract is recognized by the EU legal order.

The European Union thus regulates the essentials of the EU market economy at the EU level. However, at the same time it also heavily relies on the functioning of the systems of the Member States. A very interesting scenario therefore arises when one of the Member States would decide to leave the market economy system in favour of either a return to socialism or a new type of planned economy.[50]

44 See Case C-34/09 *Gerardo Ruiz Zambrano* v *Office national de l'emploi (ONEm)* [2011] ECR I-01177, but also Case C-434/09 *Shirley McCarthy* v *Secretary of State for the Home Department* [2011] ECR I-3375, and Case C-256/11 *Murat Dereci and Others* v *Bundesministerium für Inneres* [2011] ECR I-11315.

45 On Art. 17 of the EU Charter on Fundamental Rights see above in section 1.

46 Rather, it is presumes. See Müller-Graff 2001, p. 135-150; Reich 2013, p. 18.

47 Case C-277/05 *Société thermale d'Eugénie-les-Bains* v *Ministère de l'Économie, des Finances et de l'Industrie* [2007] ECR I-6428, para 24.

48 Case C-283/11 *Sky Österreich* v *Österreichischer Rundfunk* [2013] ECR I-(22.01.2013), paras. 42-43.

49 See, extensively, Reich 2014, p. 28-36.

50 Not at stake here is the question whether or not this would actually be possible, but rather a theoretical exercise what would happen if one of the Member States would start supplying the necessary elements to the EU internal market. A second aspect of this exercise is also to provide evidence of how the fundamental principles presented above relate to the market economy, as these are the distinguishing characteristics between a socialist economy and a (free) market economy.

4. Scenario: Return to Socialism or a New Type of Planned Economy

Imagine the following scenario: after the financial crisis one of the Member States of the EU comes to the conclusion that the (free) market economy system is no longer of use and that a return to, or introduction of, socialism is a much better way to deal with the economy. Suppose that a democratically elected government manages to amend that Member State's constitution and all other relevant legislation, and that the EU is indecisive on what to do and has not (yet) taken action against this Member State.[51]

Socialism offers a social and economic system that is organized significantly differently from a market economy. A socialist economy, in whatever form, means a significant change in the way in which a country is organized.[52] A socialist system is organized around the idea of social ownership, meaning that the significant assets, e.g. land, and means of production, in such a country are collectively owned and managed.[53] More technical rules, such as property relations and contracts, function at the 'base level' providing input for the ,superstructure' level in which the political ideology and the organization of the state find their place.[54] At this base level, rules of private law play a supporting role, as in the ideology of socialism law is there to support the general functioning of society. This society is a collective society, in which the ,means of production', i.e. those assets needed to manufacture, produce or process, are jointly held and jointly managed.[55] This applies both to land as well as to movable and even intangible objects.[56]

Like in a market economy property law plays a crucial role in socialist systems. This role, however, is very different, and in many ways the opposite of market-economy property law. In a socialist system there are generally four types of ownership available: (i) state ownership, (ii) collective ownership, (iii) personal ownership, and (iv) private ownership.[57] The most important forms are state and collective ownership, with personal ownership only available for private assets, such as clothing, furniture and - sometimes - housing.[58] Private ownership in this approach is almost non-existent, and usually a remainder from times past, and cannot interfere with the socialist economy. Hence, private ownership of ,means of production', that are collectively owned, is impossible. Both state and collective

51 At some stage, as will be demonstrated below, the EU must take action, because the functioning of its internal market comes is in danger.

52 There have been many socialist systems in the past 100 years, with important differences between them varying form a centralist communist system in the former Soviet Union to more decentralized systems in, for instance, Poland. For a comparative overview of some of these systems see Petev 1975.

53 Petev 1975, p. 17-21.

54 See Collins 1982, p. 77.

55 Petev 1975, p. 76 *et seq.*

56 Petev 1975, p. 82-85.

57 Petev 1975, p. 77-85.

58 But all of these four types of ownership, even private ownership, are protected by the state. See Petev 1975, p. 77-85.

ownership are types of ownership by everyone, where the state is considered the 'embodiment' of the collective and manages the most important assets.

In a socialist economy the market is organized different from a market economy. The state and not the market decides on production and allocation of resources. A planned economy generally results from this and in such a system there is no room for trade for profit, but rather an equal allocation of resources. Trade, in other words, generally takes the form of simple contracts of sale or simple service contracts. These contracts for the sale of goods will transfer personal ownership from one owner to the other, not necessarily for value in money.[59]

Much more can be stated about socialist systems and socialist property and contract law, but for this scenario, the above description should provide enough information.[60] When the system of the economy changes, fundamental principles of private law must change with it. In a socialist economy there is no place for freedom of ownership, free circulation of goods and freedom of contract. Instead, there is collective (or socialist) ownership, organized distribution of resources, and a supporting contract law with a limited freedom.

In a market economy, in many ways the system to which socialist systems have reacted in the past century, these fundamental principles are therefore central to its functioning. Evidence of this is provided when we consider changing the system of the economy, where consequently these general principles must change to make such an alternative economy function.

When we return to the scenario at hand and consider a Member State changing its economy from a market economy to a socialist economy, problems arise at many levels. Of course the democratically elected government of a Member State is sovereign on its own territory and following the appropriate procedures such a government may amend the Member State's constitution and private law legislation. Such a change, however, will bring immediate problems for the EU internal market, where one part of the market now no longer fulfils the requirement of a market economy of Article 3(3) TEU. Although a socialist-Member State can still trade with its trade partners, and its law can apply to contracts through choice of law or through default rules in the Rome-I Regulation, the freedom of movement of goods, persons, services and capital, as well as EU competition law, will be substantially hindered.[61] A justification of such hindrances on the basis of a different system of economy is, because of its impreciseness in relation to the issue at hand, not likely to be accepted as a valid ground for justification.

In fact, the question arises whether such a scenario is actually possible, considering the existence of European economic constitutional law. The market

59 A trade for a service instead of a good is not uncommon. See Reich 1972, p. 63 *et seq.*; Petev 1975, p. 105-112, 122-124.

60 For an overview see Petev 1975, Reich 1972; Collins 1982; Jakobs 1965.

61 Regulation 593/2008 of the European Parliament and of the Council of 17 June 2008 on the law applicable to contractual obligations (Rome I). The addition of the term substantial here refers to the famous *Dassonville* formula of the European Court of Justice in which it stated that all measures of national law that directly or indirectly, actually or potentially hinder intra-Union trade fall within the ambit of the freedom of movement of goods. See, Craig & De Burca 2011, p. 638-640.

economy and its economic constitutional rules have the potential power to prevent such a change from occurring in favour of maintaining the functioning of the EU's internal market and the fundamental principles of property law play a crucial role in this.

Without express intention, therefore, the European Union has given shape to a framework to organize its market economy and to oversee its functioning but also to protect the market from influences that are contrary to its core values. That framework can now be considered.

5. Who does What?

This excursion brings us back to the question at hand, namely how to regulate property law in the European Union. It is clear that the law of property should take a central place, much more central than it currently does, in the multi-level legal order of the EU, in the legal systems of its member States and between private parties. It is also clear that there is great complexity between the EU and the Member States and that there are many explicit, but also implicit, links that determine the functioning of the EU legal order.[62] The link between the market and fundamental principles of private law, mostly property law, concerns very general 'organizational' rules of private law, but does not concern transactional rules. Transactional rules are rules and regulations that deal with the actual functioning of private law. These concern principles, ground rules and technical rules of property law.[63] By principles, we mean the principles of *numerus clausus*, transparency and accessority.[64] By ground rules we mean the rules of *nemo dat*, *prior tempore*, priority of limited rights over their mother right, and special protection rules for property rights.[65] Other rules of private law are interface or operating rules, such as rules dealing with the creation, transfer and termination of property rights, or rules of third party protection.[66]

As a final level of transactional rules, we can add a fourth level of to this distinction. Private parties are increasingly able to frame their own legal relations by making creative use of the technical rules of property and contract law. By making use of their freedom of contract, parties combine contractual and proprietary arrangements to innovate the way in which they do business.[67] Examples are the creation of positive duties by creative use of rights of real servitudes, the introduc-

62 Complexity occurs when there are many interdependencies. In relation to property law see Smith 2011, p. 152.

63 Van Erp 2006, p. 13 *et seq*.

64 On these principles see Van Erp 2006, p. 14-17; Akkermans 2013b, p. 109-110.

65 On these ground rules see Van Erp 2006, p. 16-17; Akkermans 2013b, p 109.

66 On the term interface rules see Smith 2011, p. 151-153. On the term operating rules (operating system), see Ramaekers 2013, p. 236.

67 On these developments see Akkermans 2008, p. 142-154, 226-234, 289-309; Libchaber 2004, p. 305 *et seq*.

tion of trust-like devices to create syndicate security rights, and the slow rise of community housing projects throughout Europe.[68]

These two aspects of property regulation, i.e. constitutional property law and private-law property law, fulfil a different purpose. The first category are rules of constitutional law, as they deal with the *organization* and *embedding* of property in society, the second are rules of transactional private law, as they deal with the *functioning* of property.[69] Within that second group there is also a hierarchy of rules where the principles of property deal with the functional organization of property law, and the other rules frame the functioning of property itself.

Within any legal order, there is a need to establish the hierarchy between these levels of regulation. Especially within a multi-level legal order, such as the European Union, there is a need to allocate regulatory competences to the different levels - i.e. the who does what question. Some of these property regulations cannot be dealt with at a national level, as the differences between the various solutions chosen in the Member States can be very disadvantageous to the legal order the national systems form together. After all, there is an EU *single* market, and not a mere collection of national single markets.

The way in which the EU internal market has developed has led to the current division of powers, in which organizational rules are mainly unregulated or dealt with at the national (constitutional) level, and all transactional rules are (almost) exclusively dealt with at the national level. However, as our understanding of the EU and of the role of property increases, this system can certainly be reconsidered. The effective functioning of the EU internal market will continue to become more and more important as both the Member States and the EU reconsider the division of competences.[70]

The situation we are currently in is an internal market that is a social market economy (Art. 3(3) TEU), in which the right to property is protected as a part of the EU charter on fundamental rights (Art. 17 of the Charter), and in which there is a freedom of movement of goods, persons, services and capital (Arts. 34, 45, 56 and 63 TFEU respectively). Within the EU legal order, Member State law determines which property rights are available and how these are created, transferred and will terminate.[71] The available property rights, as well as the rules governing their creation, transfer and termination, therefore differ widely within the European Union.[72] When these private-law property rules lead to a hindrance to the access of the market of a Member State, the rules governing free movement may prevent the application of a national rule in such a situation. This is a working system, but not an optimal balance between the national and EU level and there are certainly high transaction costs involved in dealing with another Member State law and high

68 Akkermans & Swadling 2012, p. 265 *et seq.*; Wibier 2007, an example of social housing projects is offered by the, community land trust', see, e.g., <http://www.communitylandtrusts.org.uk/home>.

69 Another way to express this is to state that these are rules of private-law property law.

70 See, for example, the speech delivered by UK PM David Cameron on 22 January 2013.

71 See Van Erp & Akkermans 2012, p. viii.

72 Akkermans 2008, p. 396-422.

externalities, such as increased information costs and higher risk for the parties involved, because of the increasing danger a national rule of private-law property law may be inapplicable because it is incompatible with EU economic constitutional law.

There is therefore some need to rethink this division of competences in the light of the case law of the CJEU as well as of current EU legislative developments.[73] The effect of the case law of the CJEU on the law of property of the Member States has been dealt with before.[74] The free movement of goods, persons, services and capital have both an actual as well as a potential effect on national private-law property law. Hindrance to market access leads to the inapplicability of these rules with the - for now - potential effect of opening up national systems of property to recognize property rights created and regulated by another Member State's law.[75] This last argument - that of potentially breaking open national systems of property law - is undesirable as it is deemed to decrease legal certainty and therefore hinder the functioning of the market. Moreover, such a situation would almost inevitably lead to a proposal for EU legislation from the European Commission.[76] This potential danger is further increased by the legislative developments in the EU. In the past years legislation has been proposed and partially already adopted to regulate cross-border property succession and martial property law.[77] Following these Regulations it is not unthinkable that Member States will be forced by the EU doctrine of effectiveness (*effet utile*) to apply a foreign property law and with that accept a foreign property rights in their domestic legal order.[78]

The current state of EU integration therefore brings tension to the Member State level and EU economic constitutional law brings limitations to the national legislative powers. A Member State can no longer legislate completely free in any area, as EU economic constitutional law may resist the application of such legislation in certain circumstances. In such an event the ‚method' of EU law will mean

73 Especially also in the light of the CJEU's recent decision in Case C-390/12 *Rober Pfleger, Autoart as, Mladen Vucicevic, Maroxx Software GmbH, and Hans-Jörg Zehetner* [2014] not yet reported (30 April 2014), in which the CJEU held that the EU Charter on Fundamental Rights applies to national law in any context where EU law in involved. For a first analysis, see <http://www.mepli.eu/2014/05/the-net-of-eu-law-tightens-on-the-member-states-case-c-39012-pfleger-on-the-application-of-the-eu-charter-on-fundamental-rights/>.

74 See Kieninger 1996, p. 251 *et seq.*; Rutgers 1999, p. 195 *et seq.*; Akkermans 2008, p. 518-520; Akkermans 2012a, p. 246-248; Akkermans & Ramaekers 2013, p. 262-266; Ramaekers 2013, p. 91-93.

75 See on this Kieninger 1996, p. 251 *et seq.*, Rutgers 1999, p. 195 *et seq.*, Ramaekers 2013, p. 91-95.

76 On the role between internal market law and the EU's competence to act see Weatherill 2011, p. 827–864.

77 Regulation 650/2012 of the European Parliament and of the Council of 4 July 2012 on jurisdiction, applicable law, recognition and enforcement of decisions and acceptance and enforcement of authentic instruments in matters of succession and on the creation of a European Certificate of Succession, Council Regulation 1259/2010 of 20 December 2010 implementing enhanced cooperation in the area of the law applicable to divorce and legal separation and Proposal for a Council Regulation on jurisdiction, applicable law and the recognition and enforcement of decisions in matters of matrimonial property regimes (Rome IV) COM(2011) 126 final.

78 See on this Akkermans 2013a, p. 50-56.

that all similar cases are to be treated alike (the *acte claire* doctrine), and that EU law will have precedence over national law.[79]

But where does the primacy of legislative power over property lie in the EU internal market? The Member States have, of course, created the EU, but the EU as a supranational organization has legislative powers of its own. The internal market is a shared competence between the EU and the Member States, but when should the EU and when should the Member States act? Moreover, when should both these levels leave the market free for the market participants and party autonomy? When we rethink the allocation of power to regulate property in the EU internal market, some further guidance is therefore needed. Inspiration for this can be drawn from other complex legal orders, such as the United States of America, but also - and perhaps more surprisingly - South Africa. South Africa, although not a federation, has many levels of government as well as many sources of law to deal with. In that respect, it resembles the EU context to some extent.[80] I will therefore turn to South Africa as a second intermezzo, before I return to the question of the role of property law in the European Union (section 7) and the need for a re-allocation of regulatory competences in this area (section 8).

6. Scenario: South African Law

After the fall of the *apartheid* regime in the early 1990s, South Africa is an openly pluralist society with many levels of governance. Moreover, South Africa is facing major challenges in social change and further development. At the centre of the political and social reforms taking place is the question of land and land-use.[81] The country and therefore also its legal system must move from an institutionalized race-based inequality, to an open, democratic, and equal system of land holding. To this effect the South African Constitution provides guarantees of equality, the protection of property and the right to housing.[82]

In this reform process there is a tension between the existing arrangements and property rights, usually governed by the South African common law - comprising of rules of unwritten Roman-Dutch law - and pre-constitutional (i.e. pre 1994) legislation on the one side, and the new Constitutional order and newly adopted legislation seeking change on the other side.[83] Each of these sources of law can theoretically apply to a single case and lead to different results. The South African Constitutional Court has given guidance on how to do this. In its *Ex Parte President of the Republic of South Africa: In re Pharmaceutical Manufacturers Association of South*

79 On this analysis in respect to property law see Akkermans 2013b, p. 95 *et seq.*

80 Of course, this comparison does not apply for the societal challenges South Africa faces in overcoming its history of *apartheid*. My argument for comparison sees more to the levels of government - state, regional and local - and the plurality of sources of law - such constitutional law, national law, common law, and indigenous law. See Van der Walt 2012, p. 19 *et seq.*

81 Van der Walt 2012, p. 1.

82 Sections 9, 25 and 26 South African Constitution of 1996 respectively. Van der Walt 2012, p. 1-2.

83 Van der Walt 2012, p. 1-18.

Afrtica decision the Court held: 'There is only one system of law. It is shaped by the Constitution which is the supreme law, and all law, including the common law, derives its force from the Constitution and is subject to constitutional control.'[84]

Supported by the text of Section 39 of the Constitution, which holds that when interpreting any legislation and when developing the common law, every court, tribunal and forum must promote the spirit, purport and object of the Bill of Rights in the Constitution, a new way of dealing with property law is arising. In *Port Elizabeth Municipality* v *Various Occupiers*, the Constitutional Court stated:

> 'In sum, the Constitution imposes new obligations on the courts concerning right relating to property not previously recognized by the common law. It counterposes to the normal ownership rights of possession, use and occupation, a new and equally relevant right not arbitrarily to be deprived of a home. The expectations that ordinarily go with title could clash head-on with the genuine despair of people in dire need of accommodation. The judicial function in those circumstances is not to establish a hierarchical arrangement between the different interests involved, privileging in an abstract and mechanical way the rights of ownership over the right to to be dispossessed of a home, or vice versa. Rather it is to balance out and reconcile the opposed claimed in as just a manner as possible taking account of all the interests involved and the specific factors relevant in each particular case.'

The South African situation is unique in the world, both from the perspective of the complexity of the legal system and its sources, and from the perspective of the societal challenges this country faces. However, notwithstanding the special situation South Africa is in, there are lessons to be learned from the South African experience. Especially the technique used by the South African Constitutional Court to approach change and further development of the law can be a source of inspiration to other legal orders that seek change and especially further development of the law. This South African ,method' becomes more clear when it is abstracted from specific cases. Van der Walt summarizes this development in what he names ,the algorithm of post-apartheid South African Law' as:

> '(a) There is just one system of law. (b) It is shaped by the Constitution, which is the supreme law. (c) All law, including the common law and legislation, derives its force from the Constitution and is subject to constitutional control via the courts. (d) Rights or freedoms that are recognized or conferred by common law, customary law or legislation are protected to the extent that they are consistent with the Constitution and in so far as they promote the spirit, purport and objects of the Bill of Rights. (e) The function of the legislature is to enact laws that give effect to the provisions of the Constitution, especially the rights in the Bill of Rights (f) The job of the executive and administration is to formulate policy and implement programs to promote the constitutional goals. (g) The task of the courts is to interpret legislation and, in the absence of legislation, to develop the common law and customary law, so as to promote the spirit, purport and objects of the Bill of Rights. (h) If possible, existing law should be brought into line with the spirit, purport and objects of the Bill of Rights through either interpretation of legislation or development of the common law and customary law. (i) In so far as existing law, whether legislation or common law or

84 *Ex Parte President of the Republic of South Africa: In re Pharmaceutical Manufacturers Association of South Africa* 2000 2 SA 647 (CC) para 44.

customary law, is in conflict with and cannot be interpreted or developed to bring it in line with the Constitution, it is invalid or can be invalidated. (j) In this context, the job of academic lawyers is to help figure out how legislation could be introduced, amended and interpreted and how the common law or customary law could be developed so as to promote the spirit, purport and objects of the Bill of Rights.'[85]

The single-system approach of course also creates problems, especially in respect to existing case law, i.e. the South African common law, and legislation.[86] Although there is a generally recognized need to change these, change is not automatic. Citizens and other parties need to claim that a certain right or rule is in violation of the Constitution so that a court can consider the case and balance the rights and interests involved. Van der Walt emphasizes that the courts exercise restriction in these cases, not in denying the rights of the parties, but by forcing parties to rely on legislation that gives effect to the rights protected by the Constitution, or on the common law, wherever possible.[87] Only in attacking the constitutionality of legislation or the common law, parties may rely directly on the Constitution.[88] These South African principles of subsidiarity ensure that the lowest level of regulation, be it legislation, common law, or customary law, is used to deal with the case at hand and that only when necessary in the light of the spirit, purport and objects of the Bill of Rights in the Constitution higher sources of law can be applied. Even in a single system, therefore, there is not necessarily central regulation on every matter. But when the parties need to rely on a constitutional right, such as the principle of equality or the protection of property, the Constitutional rights are open to them.

The effects, finally, can be very far reaching, from annulling legislation and changing legislation and common law by interpretation to interference into private party agreements.[89] On example of the latter may illustrate the reach of this approach. In *Minister of Education* v *Syfrets Trust* the Western Cape High Court considered a (charitable) trust set up by a doctor in his last will in 1921, in which he gave money to the University of Cape Town for scholarships.[90] The terms of the trust stipulated that the money was to go to 'persons of "European decent", not of Jewish decent, and *not* female'.[91] The High Court considers/ed this provision in violation of the principle of equality, in particular section 9 of the Bill of Rights, and contrary to both public interest and public policy.[92] As the provisions of the principle of equality have horizontal effect, to give rise to an effective system of

85 Van der Walt 2012, p. 23-24.

86 See Van der Walt 2012, p. 35-112 for a detailed description of situations when problems of conflict between sources of law occur.

87 Van der Walt 2012, p. 35-36.

88 Van der Walt 2012, p. 36.

89 See, *inter alia*, *South African National Defence Union* v *Minister of Defence* 2007 SA 400 (CC), *MEC for Education: KwaZulu-Natal* v *Pillay* 2008 1 SA 474 (CC), *Walewe* v *City of Cape Town and Others* 2008 6 SA 129 (CC), *Bato Star Fishing (Pty) Ltd* v *Minister of Environmental Affairs* 2004 4 SA 490 (CC), Van der Walt 2012, p. 36-37.

90 *Minister of Education* v *Syfrets Trust* 2006 SA 205 (C).

91 *Minister of Education* v *Syfrets Trust* 2006 SA 205 (C), para. 1.

92 *Minister of Education* v *Syfrets Trust* 2006 SA 205 (C), para. 34 per Griesel J.

protection, but with respect to the freedom of testation, the Court adapted the terms of the trust to exclude the reference to 'European decent'.[93]

The European context is, of course, very different from South Africa. Social change, although perhaps much needed, is not a primary objective of the European integration project.[94] Instead, the EU is a project traditionally focused on economic change and market building. For the moment therefore, the framework governing the EU is still very much a matter of economic constitutional law. However, there are also social challenges in the EU, especially in terms of equality and non-discrimination. These are increasingly becoming more important and some therefore argue that there is also EU social constitutional law.[95] Such arguments are convincing as they show that although market building may usually be at the centre of activities, there is an equally large need for the advancement and protection of principles such as equality, human dignity, family life and (EU) citizenship.[96] The South African experience learns us that property law plays a crucial role the development of any society and that societal change usually fundamentally affects property rights. It is therefore worth considering if the current private-law approach of considering property is sufficient to understand the meaning and role of property in society.

7. Beyond the Economic Framework: Property as Democracy (or in Constitutional Context)

In the United States there is a highly important debate on the role of property that has not completely made its way to Europe. Henry Smith has advocated a new-private law approach, whereby he stresses the importance of private-law doctrinal analysis.[97] Property is, Smith argues, a relation between a person and object that can be explained and clarified using transaction-cost analysis.[98] In Smith's view, property law deals with coordination problems and in discussing this Smith reacts to the realist approach to law, that considers property as a relationship between persons in respect to things, especially as a bundle of rights. Smith's argument is that such realist analysis eventually is more limiting and restrictive than a new-private law approach, that may give room for formalism that the realist school reacted against, but which provides more flexibility in the end.[99]

In response to this Joseph Singer proposes another understanding of property.[100] In this contribution Singer adds to Smith's analysis that not all aspects of property can be understood from an economic – transaction-costs – analysis. Prop-

93 *Minister of Education* v *Syfrets Trust* 2006 SA 205 (C), paras. 47-49 per Griesel J.

94 On social change perhaps needed to overcome great differences between income and capital in the 21st century see Pickety 2014, p. 480 *et seq.*

95 On social challenges and the EU's Social Constitution see Schieck 2012, p. 1-5.

96 See also Reich 2014, p. 37 *et seq.* and 59 *et seq.*

97 Smith 2012.

98 Smith 2012, p. 1693.

99 Smith 2012, p. 1691-1694.

100 Singer 2014.

erty, in this view, is more than the law that solves coordination problems. Singer focuses the attention on the context in which private-law property rules function. By providing examples of situations where economic analysis does not provide a clarification for a certain situation, Singer demonstrates that property law also has a constitutional dimension. That constitutional context, Singer argues, must be examined and be made explicit because it reflects fundamental value choices. A strong illustration of his point is offered by the consideration not to foreclose sub-prime mortgages of those who cannot pay their mortgage instalments anymore. From an economic private-law point of view, there is no reason to delay foreclosure in these cases, as this is the primary reason the property security right (i.e. the mortgage) was created in the first place. However, from a societal point of view, there may be good reasons to prevent foreclosure or to prohibit sub-prime mortgages all together.[101] The decision to do so and therefore to regulate property law is not one of transaction costs analysis, but a fundamental ethical and political question.[102] In this respect, property reflects not only our choices regarding the functioning of our market economy, but also our conceptions on the treatment of others with respect and human dignity.

Gregory Alexander has very recently also brought attention to these aspects.[103] Alexander argues that the objective of property law is to facilitate human flourishing. Values such as autonomy, self-realization, personhood, community and equality, all influence the way in which we understand and use property.[104] Understanding property in this perspective enables, so Alexander argues in line with Singer, a much deeper understanding of the way in which property law works and provides for the possibility to solve public-law questions in a private law setting.[105] For example, in a situation where a home owner is not allowed by the rules of his home owner's situation to display the Nation's flag on his balcony, and where thus autonomy and self-expression are in conflict with each other. The home owner has contracted away his right to display a flag, but the (public) value of self-expression may in a certain situation be of a higher value. Balancing the values of human flourishing involved, sometimes private-law property law rules make way for 'constitutional' values.[106]

There is more to property law than economic theory. Although the functioning of the market economy and property law are inextricably linked, this is only one of the contexts in which private-law property law functions. The economic constitutional approach is part of a larger constitutional framework, in which also other values such as democracy, equality and human dignity play a very important role.

101 Singer 2014, p. 1331-1334.
102 Singer 2014, p. 1334.
103 Alexander 2014.
104 Alexander 2014, p. 5-22.
105 Alexander 2014, p. 22-32.
106 I add the term 'constitutional' to the value of self-expression to bring Alexander's argumentation in parallel to the discussion in this paper. It is not a term expressed by Alexander himself, but by all means his public value can be understood in the same manner as my property constitutional values as developed at the beginning of this contribution. Alexanders 2014, p. 29.

We can understand, I submit, this further extension of the context from economic to social constitutional law on the same basis as I developed the economic context in this paper: property rules are transactional rules that facilitate the functioning of society; in a market context this means rules that ensure freedom of ownership, free circulation of goods and party autonomy, but also rules that reflect our democratically determined values, equality, and human dignity. On occasion therefore, the application of private-law rules will be amended to give way to a certain contextual - i.e. constitutional - value: the functioning of the market economy, ensuring equality, or creating room for the right to self-expression. Economic constitutional law - or better, economic constitutional rights - will therefore conflict with social constitutional law - or social constitutional rights and a balancing of rights, like in any other instance of conflict between fundamental rights, will be necessary to resolve any particular case.[107]

I offer three examples to illustrate that this is more commonplace than private-law property lawyers may think. First, in order to preserve the functioning of the economy, many legal systems create special rules for the enforcement of security rights. Out of fear for disturbing the circulation of the economy, for example, the Dutch Supreme Court allowed the priority position connected to holding a right to of pledge on a claim to continue to exist even when the claim exited through payment. Following the strict private-law property law rules the right of pledge expired through payment of the underlying claim. However, such a situation would create a threat to the functioning of the economy, as business may not choose this method of financing anymore.[108] Second, on the basis of equality many private agreements cannot continue to exist or have to be amended. The best example is offered by Section 9 of the Bill of Rights to the South African Constitution. On the basis of this Section courts can interfere into private arrangements, such as last wills and contracts.[109] Similarly, equality as a general principle of EU law has enabled the European Court of Justice to interfere into contracts concluded by private parties in, for example, labour law.[110] Finally, the case about the displaying of a Nation's flag is a clear example where the right to autonomy makes way for the right to self-expression.[111] Other examples include considerations to prevent a bank from realizing - or foreclosing - a right of mortgage when this concerns a sub-prime mortgage loan and protective legislation (temporarily) prevents such realization to protect those living in the house from personal bankruptcy and poverty.[112]

107 On balancing of rights see Goldsworthy 2012, p. 693; Reich 2014, p. 89 *et seq.*

108 HR 17 February 1995, *NJ* 1996/471 (*Mulder q.q./CLBN*), see on this case (in English) Akkermans 2008, p. 283-284.

109 See *Minister of Education* v *Syfrets Trust* 2006 SA 205 (C).

110 See C-144/04 *Werner Mangold* v *Rüdinger Helm* [2005] ECR I-9981, Devroe 2007, p. 161-169; Reich 2014, p. 74.

111 Alexander 2014, p. 29.

112 See Singer 2014, p. 1332-1334.

8. Multi-Dimensional and Multi-level Property Law

There are two axes along the lines of which we must thus consider property: (i) property is of constitutional value as well as a system of transactional rules (multi-dimensional), and (ii) different aspects of property should be dealt with at a different level. The first axis has been the topic of discussion in section 7, and the focus will now be on allocation of powers along the second axis.

The framework for the multi-level legal order is mostly already in place. The European Union is a single legal order with a single market in which there is freedom of movement of goods, persons, services and capital, and in which there is free competition wherever possible.[113] EU law takes precedence over national law (principle of supremacy) and both treaty provisions and secondary legislation that are sufficiently clear and precise will have direct effect in the laws of the Member States.[114] Member States are bound to sincere cooperation towards the European Union and each other in the implementation of EU law.[115] The Court of Justice of the European Union is entrusted with the task to ensure that in the interoperation and application of the Treaties the law is observed.[116] At the same time, the EU will only have competences where the EU Treaties provide this, and in the absence of that, legislative power rests with the Member States.[117] The principle of conferral determines that only when there is a specific legislative competence in the Treaty the EU can take action, in accordance with the principles of subsidiarity and proportionality, and that this competence is shared with the Member States.[118]

The EU legal order is therefore characterized by a constant tension between the national and EU level. To state that the Member States are supreme and therefore all primacy of legislative power rests at this level is a misunderstanding of the nature of EU law. Because of the special nature of the EU as a supranational legal order, and the special tasks entrusted to it in respect to the internal market and the promotion of human dignity, freedom, democracy, equality, the rule of law and respect for human rights, there is by all means an EU legal order that is not a mere collection of national legal orders.[119] After all, even in the exercise of purely national legislative competences, national law that restricts the access to the market of another Member State is still caught by European economic constitutional law. In this respect, the European Commission and the European Court of Justice serve as watchdogs of the functioning of the single market.[120]

Without the need for the EU to be declared the United States of Europe, the EU legal order answers to many federal dynamics. Not by way of a central authority from which all law and decision making power is derived, but from the fact that the

113 Art. 3 TEU.

114 Craig & De Burca 2011, p. 180 *et seq.*

115 Art. 4(3) TEU.

116 Art. 19(1) TEU.

117 Art. 4(1) and 5 TEU.

118 Art. 5 TEU; Art. 4(1) TFEU. Art. 4(2)(a) TFEU mentions the internal market as one of the principal areas in which there is a shared competence.

119 Arts. 2 and 17 TEU.

120 Art. 17 and 19 TEU.

Member States have inextricably bound each other to a social market building exercise. Following the principles of subsidiarity and proportionality, matters are to be dealt with at the Member State level first. Even more so, the market is there for market participants and private law regulation is there to facilitate their actions. Here the decentralization theorem, as developed and used by law and economic scholars in the context of the economics of federalism, is of assistance.[121] It finds, in a simple form 'that, in the absence of spillovers, local provision of public goods will be Pareto superior to centralized provision of public goods, given that centralized provision is presumed to be synonymous to a uniform level of output across jurisdictions'.[122]

Only when an EU effort can lead to a uniform level of output across jurisdictions which would be more beneficial to the EU legal order than national solutions, the EU should act. Pluralism of rules in this respect is therefore not a negative aspect. To the contrary, the EU is based on respect for the

> 'rich cultural and linguistic diversity' and the ensuring of Europe's cultural heritage.[123] The EU level must respect the ,national identities, inherent in [the Member States', BA] fundamental structures, political and constitutional, inclusive or regional and local self-government',

and

> 'the essential State functions, including ensuring the territorial integrity of the State, maintaining law and order and safeguarding national security'.[124]

The tension, in other words, is between the EU social and economic constitutional law and the laws of the Member States, with a system of checks and balances in place: where the EU level takes precedence over Member State law it can only do so in accordance with the principle of subsidiarity and proportionality. Member States can defend themselves against the effect of EU law by relying on these principles as well as on the various grounds for justification the Treaties provide, of which national public policy is perhaps the most well-known.[125] The effect of EU law on the national level is clear, and where there is horizontal direct effect, such as in case of EU competition law, or the freedom of movement of persons, services and capital, the effect of EU law also extends to private party arrangements, including

121 A critical reflection on this approach, which certainly also has its merit, falls outside the scope of this contribution. See, on the economics of federalism in general, the contributions of Jan Smits and of Caroline Cauffman and Niels Philipsen in this volume.

122 Oates 1972. See, on this and further clarification of the terminology used Oates 2006, and Van Zeben 2012, p. 6, note 19.

123 Art. 3(3) TEU.

124 Art. 4(2) TEU.

125 For example, Member States may justify the hindrance to the access of their national market in violation of one of the four freedoms with public policy under Arts. 34 (goods), 45 (persons), 56, (services) and 63 (capital) TFEU.

contracts.[126] In combination with the existing framework of EU law, i.e. supremacy, direct effect and *effet utile,* this European constitutional law is a normative framework according to which national systems of law can be further developed and altered when necessary, and according to which private parties can and must shape their legal relations.

In terms of property law an incomplete picture thus arises. Property law is almost exclusively dealt with at the national level, which focuses almost exclusively on private-law property law. Some Member States, such as Germany, also offer national constitutional protection of property and therefore also ensure constitutional protection of property rights.[127] At the EU level, only recently Article 17 of the Charter on Fundamental Rights has begun to provide protection of property at the EU level. However, fundamental aspects of property law, such as the constitutional framework, not only for its protection, but also for its functioning, has been left unregulated at the EU level. Whether or not there is sufficient protection, not even to speak of legislation, in this area remains dependent on the Member States themselves. The scenario of a return to a socialist economy by one of the Member States, although extreme, shows the danger of this approach. Analogous to this scenario the same could of course apply in case of a grand nationalization effort by a Member State in an attempt to retain grip on the national economy in times of crisis. The nationalization of banks and other financial institutions in the last years is only an example of that.[128]

Without (much) change to the existing legal order, it is possible to redesign the system of EU property law. At the EU level, in correlation to the EU's internal market and the EU's social objectives, we can safeguard the three fundamental principles of property law (freedom of ownership, free circulation of goods and freedom of contract), and clarify the relationship between these elements of European economic constitutional law and the principles of European social constitutional law.[129] This normative framework provides guidance, and therefore a necessary context, to the Member State and private party levels on how to develop and possibly alter legislation, how to apply property law in case law, and how to give shape to horizontal legal relations.

There is - analogous to Van der Walt's South African version - therefore also an 'algorithm' for the development in EU property law, which can be summarized as the following: (i) there is a single EU legal order. (ii) It is shaped by the TEU and TFEU treaties, which form the supreme law, but on the basis of the national legal systems of the Member States that remain sovereign to a considerable extent. (iii) Although legislation in this multi-level order derives its force from different

126 The free movement of goods is generally deemed not to have horizontal direct effect, because in the system of EU law this function is taken care of by EU competition law. See, p. 144-145. On the effect of EU law on private law and private parties see Reich 2014; Devroe 2007, p. 133-189.

127 Art. 14 *Grundgesetz,* see Wolff 1923, p. 1-30; Van der Walt 1999, p. 121 *et seq.*

128 Some concerns can be raised on the effect of nationalization of industries in the light of the EU Treaties, most notably Article 345 TFEU. See on this Akkermans & Ramaekers 2011, p. 293, 314.

129 Schieck 2012, p. 13-52.

sources, each of these must be in line with the spirit and objectives (*effet utile*) of EU economic and social constitutional law. (iv) National law is valid and applicable to the extent that such legislation is consistent with EU economic and social constitutional law. (v) Legislatures are therefore bound by the spirit and objectives of EU constitutional law, their task is to govern their own system, but always with the functioning of the EU internal market in mind. (vi) The job of the executive and administration is to formulate policy and implement programs to promote the EU constitutional goals. (vii) The task of the courts is to interpret legislation and to develop the law in line with the content and effectiveness of EU law. This includes examining national legislation as well as private party arrangements in the light of existing and future EU economic and social constitutional law. (viii) If possible, existing law, legislation and case law, should be brought in line to EU economic and social constitutional law, including the Charter on Fundamental Rights, through interpretation or legislation, or by starting infringement procedures against Member States that do not or cannot do this. (ix) Private parties must equally follow the framework set forth by EU social and economic constitutional law; their agreements cannot infringe on the fundamental freedoms guaranteed in the EU, and will be void, partially void or amended to remain in conformity with this framework. (x) In this context, it is the job of academic lawyers to figure out how legislation can be introduced, amended and interpreted and how transactional rules can best be applied to promote the spirit and objectives of EU economic and social constitutional law.[130]

9. Conclusion

The algorithm for the development of European Property Law brings us back to property law as the law of things. For centuries this has been the focus of property lawyers in Europe. These property lawyers have always given effect to a wider framework of values, to a constitutional framework, perhaps without knowing it. Uncovering the constitutional framework that provides private-law property law its necessary context may seem obvious, but it has not been in the attention of mainstream private-law property law thus far. Moreover, in so far as some of the constitutional context has been discovered and discussed, this has always taken place at the national level.[131]

When, in 1957, six countries embarked on a market-building exercise, they did not necessarily consider all the implications this would have for a market-wide constitutional framework. With help by the European Court of Justice in its *Van Gend en Loos* and *Costa* v *E.N.E.L.* cases, the EU became a supranational legal order in which EU law takes precedence over national law and clear and precisely

130 This algorithm is heavily based on the work of André van der Walt, see Van der Walt 2012, p. 23-24.

131 The best example is perhaps offered by German law, where Art. 14 *Grundgesetz* has given rise to an extensive field of German constitutional property law. See Van der Walt 1999, p. 121 *et seq*.

formulated articles in the EU Treaties and secondary legislation have direct effect.[132] Over the years a constitutional framework resulted that does not only see to the organization of the EU level, but also to the economic and social constitution of the EU legal order.

Without explicit reference, property law has taken a central place in this process. First of all, without freedom of property, free circulation of goods and freedom of contract, there cannot be a market economy. Second, the EU forms not a free market, but a social market economy. Social values, such as democracy and equality, are also of great importance. Also in this respect property law, as a vehicle for the promotion of democracy and human flourishing, plays an important role.

At the same time, however, the EU has not sought to legislate private-law property law at an EU level. Only specific aspects of property law, for example concerning stolen cultural objects, specific property security rights, and some specific financial arrangements have been dealt with. In those cases, it has - in short - proven worthwhile to deal with this at a central rather than at a decentralized level. In all other cases, property law remains to be dealt with at the national level. This is good, because that is where transactional rules belong. In the EU legal order, primacy of regulation lies with the lowest possible level. Therefore party autonomy is first, following the transactional rules set forth by national law, that in its turn must fit and remain to fit within the context of EU law. This has been the situation until now.

However, increasingly there is more intra-Union trade and movement of persons. As internet sales increase, partly stimulated by the European Commission's proposal on a Common European Sales Law (CESL), more and more goods will circulate on the internal market.[133] More citizens move to another Member State, partly stimulated by the European Commission's Rome III Regulation, Succession Regulation, and proposed Rome IV and V Regulations.[134] The problems that both traders and EU citizens experience, especially because of the divergences of national rules and complicated rules of private international law that point to the application of a foreign law for most of the parties involved, create problems with the functioning of the EU internal market.[135] When this is the case, either the European Court of Justice declares national law inapplicable, as it infringes EU economic constitutional law, or the European Commission will use its legislative

132 Proposal for a Regulation of the European Parliament and of the Council on a Common European Sales Law (CESL) COM(2011) 635 final.

133 Commission Staff Working Paper, *Impact Assessment Accompanying the Document: Proposal for a Regulation of the European Parliament and of the Council on a Common European Sales Law* SEC(2011) 1165 final, p. 95 *et seq*.

134 Proposal for a Council Regulation on jurisdiction, applicable law and the recognition and enforcement of decisions in matters of matrimonial property regimes (Rome IV) COM(2011) 126 final, Proposal for a Council Regulation on jurisdiction, applicable law and the recognition and enforcement of decisions regarding the property consequences of registered partnerships (Rome V) COM(2011) 127 final.

135 See on this Akkermans & Ramaekers 2013, p. 262-265; Akkermans 2013a, p. 58-60; Akkermans 2013b, p. 116-118. For a property law perspective see Akkermans & Ramaekers 2012, p. 123 *et seq*.

powers under Article 114 TFEU to propose legislation to remedy the functioning of the EU internal market.[136]

The increasing tension between the European and the Member State level therefore calls for a reconsideration of the allocation of regulatory competences. There is an algorithm for the development of EU property law that can be followed to give shape to this, and plenty of research by academics pointing out potential failures of the EU internal market and possible solutions for that.[137] The algorithm connects to an understanding of the EU legal order and the EU internal market as a uniform order or market. It then derives criteria from existing EU principles and EU law (in that order) to provide arguments when property law should be regulated at the EU level. In the absence of that, however, 'the local provision of public goods will be Pareto superior to the centralized provision of public goods', and therefore to be left as much as possible to the private parties.[138]

For the moment Member States should regulate the transactional rules of property law, but where the EU can offer additional value by reducing transaction costs and other externalities by providing uniform transactional rules, for example, to stimulate cross border acquisition of land, the EU should not hesitate or be restricted to act. When the diversity of transactional rules becomes a real hindrance to trade or when transactional rules restrict the free movement on the internal market, there is no reason why the EU should not have the competence to act. For example, Member States that only accept a notarial deed made by a national officer from that Member State – such as a notary or a court – for registration in the land registry should rethink the compatibility of such a rule with the freedom to provide services.[139] Similarly, there are good arguments for the creation of a European security right on both intangibles as well as land in the form of a Eurohypothec.[140]

In time, therefore, the algorithm for the development of EU property law will enable us to take these building blocks of EU property law and construct a EU multi-level property law in which fundamental principles of property law are guaranteed and explicitly regulated at the EU constitutional level, where there are EU transactional rules of property law to enable private parties to act on the EU internal market and where Member States supplement these rules, which will then diverge locally from each other, but will all be in conformity with the EU constitu-

136 There is a link between the Court of Justice establishing infringement of one of the four freedoms and the use of Art. 114 TFEU as a suitable legal basis. See, on this, Low 2012; Weatherill 2011.

137 See, for example, Van Erp & Akkermans 2012; Von Bar & Clive 2010, Books 7, 8 and 9; Lurger & Faber 2011; Van Vliet 2000; Van Erp 2003; Akkermans 2008, p. 523-548; Van Erp & Akkermans 2013; Ramaekers 2013, p. 239-276.

138 Referring to the *Decentralisation Theorem*, see above note 121.

139 Since Cases C-47/08 *Commission* v *Belgium* [2011] ECR I-04105, Case C-50/08 *Commission* v *France* [2011] ECR I-4195, Case C-51/08 *Commission* v *Luxembourg* [2011] ECR I-04231, Case C-52/08, *Commission* v *Portugal* [2011] ECR I-4275, Case C-53/08 *Commission* v *Austria* [2011] ECR I-04309, Case C-54/08 *Commission* v *Germany* [2011] ECR I-044355, C-61/08 *Commission* v *Greece* [2011] ECR I-04399, notaries are not considered as public authorities in the sense of a public service exception from EU law and hence are - to a certain extent and until perhaps further cases are decided - to be considered as providers of services.

140 Ramaekers 2013, p. 259-268.

tional framework, allowing private parties to make optimal use of diversity in the market.

Bibliography

Akkermans 2008
Akkermans, B., *The Principle of Numerus Clausus in European Property Law*, Cambridge-Antwerp-Portland: Intersentia 2008.

Akkermans 2012a
Akkermans, B., 'Property Law and the Internal Market', in: S. van Erp, A. Salomons & B. Akkermans (eds.), *The Future of European Property Law*, München: Sellier European Law Publishers 2012, p. 199-246.

Akkermans 2012b
Akkermans, B., 'The role of the (D)CFR in the Making of European Property Law', in: V. Sagaert, E. Terryn & M. Storme (eds.), *The Draft Common Frame of Reference (DCFR): a national and comparative perspective*, Cambridge-Antwerp-Portland: Intersentia 2012, p. 263-286.

Akkermans 2013a
Akkermans, B., The EU Development of European Property Law', in: C. Godt (ed.), *Hanse Law School in Perspective. Legal teaching and cross-border research after Lisbon*, Kluwer: Deventer 2013, p. 39-60.

Akkermans 2013b
Akkermans, B., 'The Use of the Functional Method European Union Property Law', 2(1) *European Property Law Journal*, 2013, p. 95-118.

Akkermans 2014
Akkermans, B., 'The Comparative Method', *Property Law Review*, 2014, p. 203-211.

Akkermans & Ramaekers 2011
Akkermans, B. & Ramaekers, E., 'Article 345 TFEU (Ex. Article 295 EC Treaty). It's meanings and interpretations', *European Law Journal*, 2011, p. 292-314.

Akkermans & Ramaekers 2012
Akkermans, B. & Ramaekers, E., '*Lex Rei Sitae* in Perspective: National Developments of a Common Rule', in: B. Akkermans & E. Ramaekers (eds.), *Property Law Perspective I*, Cambridge-Antwerp-Portland: Intersentia 2012, p. 123-149

Akkermans & Ramaekers 2013
Akkermans, B. & Ramaekers, E., 'Free Movement of Goods and Property Law', *European Law Journal*, 2013, p. 237-266.

Akkermans & Swadling 2012
AkkermansB. & Swadling, W., 'Chapter 3 - Types of Property Rights on Immovables and Movables (Goods)', in: S. van Erp & B. Akkermans (eds.), *Text, Cases and Materials on Property Law* (Ius Commune Casebooks for the Common Law of Europe - Volume 8), Oxford: Hart Publishing 2012, p. 211-364.

Alexander 2014
Alexander, G., *Property's Ends: The Publicness of Private Values*, Cornell Law School 2014, research paper No 14-13.

Baur, Baur & Stürner 2009
Baur, T., Baur, J.F., Stürner, R., *Sachenrecht* (18th edition), München: C.H. Beck'sche Verlagsbuchhandlung 2009.

Bacquero Cruz 2002
Bacquero Cruz, J., *Between Competition and Free Movement: the economic constitutional law of the European Community*, Oxford: Hart Publishing 2002.

Börzel 2002
Börzel, T., 'Pace-Setting, Foot-Dragging, and Fence-Sitting: Member State Responses to Europeanization', 40(2) *Journal of Common Market Studies*, 2002, p. 193-214.

Collins 1982
Collins, H., *Marxism and Law*, Oxford: Clarendon Press 1982.

Collins 2009
Collins, H., 'The European Economic Constitution and the Constitutional Dimension of Private Law', 5(2) *European Review of Contract Law*, 2009, p. 71-94.

Craig & De Burca 2011
Craig, P. & De Burca, G., EU Law. *Text, Cases and Materials* (5th edition), Oxford: Oxford University Press 2011.

Devroe 2007
Devroe, W., 'Impact van door het Europees hof van justitie ontwikkelde algemene beginselen op privaatrechtelijke verhoudingen', in: A.S. Hartkamp, C.H. Sieburgh & L.A.D. Keus (eds.), *De invloed van het Europese recht op het Nederlandse privaatrecht – Part I*, Deventer: Kluwer 2007, p. 133-189.

Dinnage & Laffineur 2010
Dinnage, J. & Laffineur, J.-L., *The Constitutional Law of the European Union* (2nd edition), San Francisco: Lexis-Nexis 2010.

Goldsworthy 2012
Goldsworthy, J., 'Constitutional Interpretation', in: M. Rosenfeld & A. Sajo (eds.), *Oxford Handbook of Comparative Constitutional Law*, Oxford: Oxford University Press 2012, p. 689-716.

Gretton 2007
Gretton, G., 'Ownership and its Objects', *Rabels Zeitschrift*, 2007, p. 802-851.

Israël 2005
Israel, J., *European Cross-Border Insolvency Regulation*, Antwerp-Oxford: Intersentia 2005.

Jakobs 1965
Jakobs, O.-W., *Eigentumsbegriff und Eigentumssystem des sowjetischen Rechts*, Köln-Graz: Böhlau Verlag 1965.

Joerges 1997
Joerges, C., *The Market without a State? The 'Economic Constitution' of the European Community and the Rebirth of Regulatory Politics*, European Integration Online Papers (EIoP), Volume 1, No. 019, 1997.

Joerges 2004
Joerges, C., *What is Left of the European Economic Constitution*, EUI Working Paper LAW, No. 13, 2004.

Kieninger 1996
Kieninger, E.-M., *Mobiliarsicherheiten im Europäischen Binnenmarkt. Zum Einfluß der Warenverkehrsfreiheit auf das nationale und internationale Sachenrecht der Mitglied-Staaten*, Baden-Baden: Nomos Verlagsgesellschaft 1996.

Lenaers & Van Nuffel 2011
Lenaerts, K. & Van Nuffel, P., *European Union Law* (3rd edition), London: Sweet & Maxwell 2011.

Libchaber 2004
Libchaber, R., 'La recodification du droit des biens', in: *Le Code civil 1804-2004* (Livre du Bicentenaire), Paris: Dalloz/Lexis Nexis Litec 2004.

Losada et al. 2012
Losada, F., Juutilainen, T., 'Havu, K. & Vesala, J., Property and European Integration: Dimensions of Article 345 TFEU', *Tidskrift utgiven av Juridiska föreningen i Finland*, 2012, p. 203-224.

Low 2012
Low, G., *Unitas via Diversitas: Can the Common European Sales Law Harmonize Through Diversity?*, Maastricht Faculty of Law Working Paper No. 2, 2012.

Lurger & Faber 2011
Lurger, B. & Faber, W. (eds.), *Principles of European Law (PEL) – Volume Ten: Transfer of Titles in Movables*, München: Sellier European Law Publishers 2011.

Micklitz 2008
Micklitz, H., *The Visible Hand of Regulatory Private Law. The Transformation of European Private Law from Autonomy to Functionalism in Competition and Regulation*, EUI Working Paper LAW, No. 14, 2008.

Müller-Graff 2001
Müller-Graff, P.-C., Basic Freedoms - Extending Party Autonomy across Borders, in: S. Grundmann, W. Kerber & S. Weatherill (eds.), *Party Autonomy and the Role of Information in the Internal Market*, Berlin: Walter de Gruyter 2001, p. 133-150.

Oates 1972
Oates, W., *Fiscal Federalism*, New York: Harcourt Brace Jovanovich 1972.

Oates 2006
Oates, W., *On the Theory and Practice of Fiscal Decentralisation*, IFIR Working Paper No 2006-05, available at: <http://www.ifigr.org/publication/ifir_working_papers /IFIR-WP-2006-05.pdf>.

Petev 1975
Petev, V., *Sozialistisches Zivilrecht*, Berlin/New York: Walter de Gruyter 1975.

Pickety 2014
Pickety, T., *Capital in the 21st Century* (Translated by Arthur Goldhammer), Cambridge MA: The Belknap Press of Harvard University Press 2014.

Posner 1973
Posner, R., *Economic Analysis of Law*, Boston: Little Brown 1973.

Ramaekers 2013
Ramaekers, E., *European Union Property Law. From Fragments to a System*, Cambridge-Antwerp-Portland: Intersentia 2013.

Reich 1972
Reich, N., *Sozialismus und Zivilrecht. Eine rechtstheoritisch-rechtshistorische Studie zur Zivilrechtstheorie und Kodifikationspraxis im sowjetirischen Gesellschafts- und Rechts-system*, Mannheim: Antenäum Verlag 1972.

Reich 2004
Reich, N., *Transformation of Contract Law and Civil Justice in New EU Member Countries. The example of the Baltic States, Hungary and Poland*, RGSL Working Paper No 21 (Riga 2004), available at: <http://www.rgsl.edu.lv/images/stories/publicati ons/RWP21Reich.pdf>.

Reich 2014
Reich, N., *General Principles of EU Civil Law*, Cambridge-Antwerp-Portland: Intersentia 2014.

Rutgers 1999
Rutgers, J., *International Reservation of Title Clauses. A study of Dutch, French and German Private International Law in the Light of European Law*, The Hague: T.M.C. Asser Press 1999.

Sagaert 2005
Sagaert, V., 'Het goederenrecht als open systeem van verbintenissen? Poging tot een nieuwe kwalificatie van de vermogensrechten', *Tijdschrift voor Privaatrecht*, 2005, p 983-1086.

Schieck 2012
Schieck, D., *Economic and Social Integration*, Northampton: Edward Elgar 2012.

Schubert 1982
Schubert, W., *Die Vorlagen der Redaktoren für die erste Kommission zur Ausarbeitung des Entwurfs eines Bürgerlichen Gesetzbuches, Sachenrecht, verfaßt von Reinhold Johow, Teil 1*, Berlin: De Gruyter 1982.

Singer 2014
Singer, J., 'Property as the Law of Democracy', 63 *Duke Law Journal*, 2014, p. 1287-1335.

Smith 2011
Smith, H., 'Standardization in Property Law', in: K. Ayotte & H. Smith (eds.), *Research Handbook on the Economics of Property Law*, Northampton: Edward Elgar 2011.

Smith 2012
Smith, H.E., 'Property as the Law of Things', 125 *Harvard Law Review*, 2012, p. 1691-1726.

Swinnen & Vranken 2006
Swinnen, J. & Vranken, L., *Review of Transitional Restrictions Maintained by New Member States on the Acquisition of Agricultural Real Estate*, final report, study for the European Commission, No ETD/2006/IM/F1/47, available at <http://ec.europa.eu/internal_market/capital/docs/study_en.pdf>.

Van den Bogaert 2002
Van den Bogaert, S., 'Horizontality: the Court Attacks?', in: C. Barnard & J. Schott (eds.), *The law of the Single European Market: Unpacking the Premises*, Oxford: Hart Publishing 2002.

Van der Walt 1999
Van der Walt, A., *Constitutional Property Clauses*, Cape Town-Dordrecht: Juta-Kluwer Law International 1999.

Van der Walt 2012
Van der Walt, A., *Property and Constitution*, Pretoria: Pretoria University Law Press 2012.

Van Erp 2003
Van Erp, S., 'A Numerus Quasi-Clausus of Property Rights as a Constitutive Element of a Future European Property Law', 7 *Electronic Journal of Comparative Law*, 2003.

Van Erp 2006
Van Erp, S., *European and National Property Law: Osmosis or Growing Antagonism?* (Walter van Gerven Lectures, 6) Groningen: Europa Law Publishing 2006.

Van Erp 2009
Van Erp, S., From 'Classical' to Modern European Property Law', in: *Essays in Honour of Konstantinos D. Kerameus/Festschrift für Konstantinos D. Kerameus, Vol. I*, Athens/Brussels: Ant. A. Sakkoulas/Bruylant 2009, p. 1517-1533.

Van Erp 2011
Van Erp, S., 'European Property Law: a Methodology for the Future', in: R. Schulze & H. Schulte-Nölke (eds.), *European Private Law – Current Status and Perspectives*, München: Sellier European Law Publishers 2011, p. 227-248.

Van Erp & Akkermans 2011
Van Erp, S. & Akkermans, B., 'European Union Property Law', in: C. Twigg-Flessner, *The Cambridge Companion to European Union Property Law*, Cambridge: Cambridge University Press 2011, p. 173-186.

Van Erp & Akkermans 2012
Van Erp, S. & Akkermans B. (eds.), *Text, Cases and Materials on Property Law* (Ius Commune Casebooks for the Common Law of Europe, Volume 8), Oxford: Hart Publishing 2012.

Van Erp & Akkermans 2013
Van Erp, S. & Akkermans, B., 'Public or Private Harmonisation of the EU Mortgage Market?', *Zeitschrift für Europäisches Privatrecht*, 2013, p. 43-59.

Van Vliet 2000
Van Vliet, L., *Transfer of Movables in German, French, English and Dutch Law*, Nijmegen: Ars Aequi Libri 2000.

Van Zeben 2012
Van Zeben, J., *Regulatory Competence Allocation. The Missing Link in Theories if Federalism*, paper presented at the Law, Institutions and Economics Nanterre Workshop, Paris, France 2012, available at: <http://economix.fr/pdf/seminaires/lien/Van-Zeben.pdf>.

Von Bar & Clive 2010
Von Bar, Chr. & Clive, E. (Eds.), *Principles, Definitions and Model Rules of European Private Law. Draft Common Frame of Reference, Full Edition*, Oxford: Oxford University Press 2010.

Von Savigny 1981
Von Savigny, F.K., *System des Heutigen römischen Rechts*, Aalen: Scienta Verlag 1981.

Wiegand 1984
Wiegand, W. 'Sachenrecht im Obligationenrecht', in: *Das Obligationenrecht 1883-1983, Berner Ringvorlesung zum Jubiläum des schweizerischen Obligationenrechts*, Bern: Pio Caroni 1984, p. 107-137.

Wiegand 1990
Wiegand, W., Die Entwicklung des Sachenrechts im Verhältnis zum Schuldrecht, *Archiv für die civilistische Praxis*, 1990, p. 112-138.

Weatherill 2011
Weatherill, S., 'The Limits of Legislative Harmonisation Ten Years after Tobacco Advertising: How the Court's Case Law has become a "Drafting Guide"', 12 *German Law Journal*, 2011, p. 827-864.

Wibier 2007
Wibier, R., *Alternatieven voor zekerheid op bankrekeningen*, Den Haag: Kluwer 2007.

Wolff 1923
Wolff, M., 'Reichsverfassung und Eigentum', in: *Festgabe der Berliner Juristischen Fakultät für Wilhelm Kahl zum Doktorjubiläum am 19. April 1923*, Tübingen: Verlag von J.C.B. Mohr 1923, p. 1-30.

Willem Loof
Anna Berlee

CASE STUDY: HARMONIZING SECURITY RIGHTS

1. Introduction

An undertaking is financed primarily by two groups: the financiers, generally banks, and the suppliers of the undertaking. The law gives both financiers and suppliers certain options to secure their claims. Generally the financiers take security on most existing and future assets of an undertaking, while suppliers will try to retain their rights in the supplied goods and their proceeds until the claim has been discharged. The extent to which these separate groups can take security is a policy choice made by the lawgiver; this choice affects the position of each group of creditors in the event of insolvency of the undertaking.

Currently these policy choices are made on a national level. Should that remain so, or should the choices be made on a different level? We aim to provide an answer to that question not by formulating criteria to determine on which level the best rules could be made. Rather, we concentrate on the substantive legal political choices that are currently made by the national legislators, and assess whether harmonization, either by a top-down or bottom-up approach, would provide at least a minimal efficiency gain (similar to a *Pareto*-improvement) relative to the current situation.

On that test, harmonization *would* be desirable if the policy choices in the national legal systems are similar but the technical rules are different.[1] Harmonization would *not* be desirable, at least from a *Pareto*-improvement point of view, where the policy choices, as well as the technical rules, differ. Where policy choices are the same, the balance of interests would not be changed post-harmonization. Where they differ, harmonization would disturb this balance. In the former situation, creditors could expect to be in roughly the same position in an insolvency, whereas in the latter situation, at least certain creditors, as a result of harmonization, can no longer have the same expectations. Therefore, if harmonization results in certain increases in efficiency (lower costs of legal advice, contractual costs, risk assessments etc.), then harmonization is certainly desirable in the former situation,

1 Technical rules provide in more detail how property rights function and are of a more specific nature (e.g. whether or not the creation of a pledge require only a private deed or an authenticated deed). Cf. Van Erp 2006, p. 14.

given that these gains then lead to a 'Pareto-improvement' in which some gains are had, while no party would have to expect to be worse of.

We will assess the policy choices made by the Dutch, English, and Belgian legislatures and courts. These jurisdictions were chosen because the law of secured transactions has recently either been subject to extensive reform or scholarly debate on the extent of both the rights of financiers and the rights of suppliers. In particular, our focus will be on the ability of the financier to obtain security on *all* assets of the undertaking. This may depend largely on the financiers' ability to include future assets into the scope of their security right(s). With regard to the suppliers, the focus will be on the suppliers' ability to 'compete' with the financiers for collateral. Apart from the national jurisdictions, we will also take into account various model laws aimed at the harmonization of this area of the law, such as Book IX DCFR and Article 9 UCC. These model laws provide an example of how harmonization can be done in a cost effective and efficient way, without upsetting the balance of interests achieved by the various legislatures involved.

2. The Netherlands

2.1. *Security on Future Assets?*

Pursuant to Article 3:98 and 97 of the Dutch Civil Code (DCC) future assets can be burdened with a right of security in advance. It is possible to grant a pledge in advance with regard to a car that has not yet been built and it is possible to grant a pledge in advance on a claim that has not yet 'materialized'. To be clear, though the pledge can be granted *in advance*, the pledge itself arises as soon as the object materializes and comes into the patrimony of the grantor.[2] It is not possible to grant a general right of security over one's patrimony, so as to include, automatically, any future object once it materializes. Only specific and ascertained objects can be burdened with a right of pledge. Recent developments, specifically with regard to the pledging of claims, have, however, undermined this principle and have enabled creditors to obtain what amounts effectively to a general right of security over all the existing and future assets of debtors.

2.2. *Pledging Claims*

In The Netherlands, the appropriate way to vest security on claims is by way of a so-called silent pledge (*stil pandrecht*) or public pledge (*openbaar pandrecht*). Pursuant to Article 3:236 (2) and 3:94 (1) DCC, claims can be pledged publicly by way of a deed and notification to the debtor. Pursuant to Article 3:239 DCC, claims can be pledged silently by way of an authentic or registered private deed (the deed is registered with the tax authorities, which is not a public register and the registration is only meant to prevent antedating). As long as the silent pledge has not been notified to the debtor, it is the creditor who is entitled to demand performance and

2 See also Janssen 2006.

receive payment. After the pledge has been notified to the debtor, only the pledgee is entitled to claim - and receive - performance.

Future claims can be pledged publicly, but as a matter of course such a pledge is limited to future claims the debtor of which is already known (as the pledge must be notified to the debtor). The more popular alternative is, therefore, the silent pledge, which does not require an existing debtor. There is one important restriction to the silent pledging of future claims: the future claim must be acquired - directly - from a legal relationship that already exists at the moment the pledge is vested.[3] This restriction was included in the law so as to make sure unsecured creditors would have at least some recourse to the assets of their debtor; any claim arising from new legal relationships that would accrue to the debtor, would be available to the unsecured creditors. Furthermore, when introducing the silent pledge,[4] the legislator wished to continue existing models of finance which were based on the fiduciary assignment for security purposes (thenceforth to be invalidated) and which had been subject to the same restriction.[5]

Evidently, this restriction is a significant hindrance to banks which finance undertakings on a continuous basis: because of the accessory nature of the right of pledge,[6] every time the bank's debtor receives payment of a claim, the pledge resting on the claim will disappear with it. Any claims that arise out of a new legal relationship are not automatically included under the scope of the right of pledge, which leads to a gradual 'atrophication' of the security over time. To counter that 'atrophication' it is necessary that claims arising from new legal relationships are pledged to the bank from time to time.

3 The criterion is inherently vague. For one example of a discussion of the criterion, see Hof 's-Hertogenbosch, 16 August 2011, *JOR* 2012/25. By joining a cooperation tomato grower Y obliged himself to supply the cooperation with all his produce, which the cooperation would then sell on. The cooperation would then pay the proceeds to the grower after deduction of costs. Y pledged all his existing and future claims relating to the proceeds of the sale of his produce to the Rabobank. At some point the Rabobank notified this pledge to the cooperation, but the cooperation contested the validity of the pledge, saying that the claim that Y had on the cooperation had not directly arisen from an existing legal relation at the time of the vesting of the pledge (at which time the claim was still a future claim). The court, however, held that the claim that Y had on the cooperation had *directly* arisen from him being a member of the cooperation and, consequently, there had been a valid pledge. The annotator Schuijling disagreed with this assessment. In his opinion the claim had not arisen from membership of the cooperation, but, rather, directly from payment, by the buyer to the cooperation, of the purchase price of the tomatoes.
The criterion is also applied with regard to the question which future claims can be assigned (Art. 3:94 (3) CC); which claims, arisen after insolvency of the debtor, can be set off against debts owed to the insolvent debtor (Art. 53 FW); and which future claims can be arrested (Art. 475 (1) RV). From case law on these provisions it can be said that, in general, claims do not directly arise from an existing legal relation if the claims have arisen as a result of arbitrary acts by third parties (for instance, payments made by a third party to a bank account). Cf. HR 27 January 1989, *NJ* 1989/422 (Otex/Steenbergen); HR 15 April 1994, *NJ* 1994/607 (Verhagen q.q./INB); HR 17 February 2012, *NJ* 2012/605 (Rabobank/Kézér).

4 By way of the New Civil Code of 1992, replacing the old Civil Code of 1838.

5 Parl. Gesch. Boek 3 (Inv. 3, 5 and 6), p. 1337.

6 Cf. Arts. 3:7 and 3:82 CC.

It is in relation to this practice that the Supreme Court has had to issue a number of judgments, clarifying, *inter alia,* the validity of the practice of consecutive pledging and the degree of specificity with which claims have to be pledged. We will first to look at the requirement of specificity.

2.2.1. Specificity

Pursuant to Article 3:82 DCC, the agreement on the basis of which certain claims are pledged, must indicate with a sufficient degree of specificity which claims are pledged to the creditor. Because of administrative burdens it is often impossible to adequately indicate every individual claim that the debtor pledges to the bank. The banks have therefore sought to achieve an adequate degree of specificity by way of more generic descriptions of the claims in the deed of pledge. The Supreme Court first dealt with such a generic description in the case of *Spaarbank Rivierenland* v *Gispen q.q.*[7] In casu, Litho House BV regularly pledged their claims to the Bank by way of a deed that referred to a computer list containing the specifics of all the pledged claims. In the deed itself, only the specifics of the first and last claims of a specified computer list were mentioned. When Litho House went into insolvency, the bankruptcy trustee contested the validity of the pledge, *inter alia,* on the basis that the deed did not specify with a sufficient degree of specificity the claims that were pledged. The Supreme Court held that it was not necessary for the pledged claim itself to be specified in the deed: 'It is sufficient for the deed to contain such information as to be able to determine, possibly later on, which claims are pledged.'[8]

In the case of *Mulder q.q.* v *Rabobank,*[9] the deed simply stated that all existing and all future claims arising from existing legal relationships were pledged to the bank.[10] According to the court, the claims were thereby specified to an adequate degree, as it is sufficient for the deed to contain such information as to be able to determine, later on, which claims were in fact pledged. This was possible by consulting debtors records, contracts, order sheets etcetera.

Interestingly, Rabobank pledged the claims to itself on the basis of an irrevocable power of attorney that was granted by the debtor to the bank. The validity of that power of attorney was contested by the bankruptcy trustee at the district court, which found the power of attorney to be valid. That finding was not challenged in cassation. Only several years later, in the case of *Dix q.q.* v *ING,*[11] did the practice and validity of pledging by way of irrevocable power of attorney become the focal point of litigation.[12]

7 HR 14 October 1994, *NJ* 1995/447.

8 At 4.2.

9 HR 20 September 2002, *NJ* 2004/182.

10 Cf. Verstijlen 2011; Strucyken 2010 and literature mentioned in footnote 11 of that contribution.

11 HR 3 February 2012, *NJ* 2012/261. See also, Hof Arnhem 4 May 2010 and 28 December 2010, *JOR* 2011/160 (Wiegerink/IFN).

12 The case has provoked a lot of scholarly attention, see, *inter alia,* Wibier 2012; Kaptein 2012; Orval 2012; Veder 2012; Van Buchem & De Man 2012.

2.2.2. Pledging by Power of Attorney

In *Dix q.q.* v *ING*, the Bank concluded a credit agreement with JHSM on the basis of a credit offer that was signed by JHSM and registered by the Bank with the tax authorities. The offer contained the following clause:

> 'Collateral to be vested: Pledging of assets:
> To provide security for all that is owed or shall be owed by the debtor to the creditor, the debtor hereby pledges, as far as necessary in advance, to the creditor, who accepts said pledge, all existing and future assets as described in the General Conditions of Pledge, in as far as these were not pledged to the creditor before; these assets comprise company equipment, credit balance, claims and supplies that belong to the debtor. The debtor also undertakes to pledge to the creditor all future claims arising out of legal relations non-existing at the time of this pledge, obtained by the debtor - in whichever capacity - against third parties.'

In Article 7 of the General Conditions of Pledge, which were applicable to the credit agreement, JHSM granted an irrevocable power of attorney to the Bank to pledge claims to itself in order to provide security for what was owed by the debtor to the Bank. These general conditions were included in the registered credit documentation.

This procedure had become standard practice for some time already. On the basis of the power of attorney, a bank is able to pledge all claims that accrue to its debtor to itself on a weekly, or even daily, basis. As all debtors are normally bound by the General Conditions, the bank can do this for every single one of its debtors at once. By registering one deed with the tax authorities, banks are thus able to pledge to themselves all claims belonging to every debtor of the bank.

ING pledged the claims of all of its debtors, including JHSM, by way of consecutive pledge deeds, which described the pledgors and the claims to be pledged in a very generic way. Article 1 of the deed defined debtor as: 'every natural person, legal person or other juridical entity, which owes the Bank any amount, on account of a credit facility, or on any other account'. Pledgor was defined as: 'any natural person, legal person or other juridical entity, be it in the capacity of debtor or not, who has given the Bank a power of attorney to pledge claims ...'. The claims to be pledged were then defined as: 'all existing and future claims from a pledgor ... of which the Bank has the power to pledge to themselves on the basis of a power of attorney'. In Article 2 the bank then pledges to itself - and accepts in pledge - all existing and future claims.

After insolvency of JHSM, the bankruptcy trustee contested the validity of the pledge, *inter alia*, on the basis that the pledge deed did not indicate with a sufficient degree of specificity which claims were pledged, because the pledgors themselves were not named in the deeds of pledge. The Supreme Court dismissed those claims, repeating the earlier established norm that it is sufficient for the deed to contain such information as to be able to determine, possibly later on, which claims are pledged. That norm does not require the pledgor to be specifically named.

The Court also addressed the bankruptcy trustee's complaint that the practice of pledging by power of attorney would completely undermine Article 3:239 (1), as it would rob the ordinary creditors of any effective redress. The Court acknowledges the truth of that concern:

> 'The present construction makes pledging considerably more simple and allows for *all* [emphasis by the authors] new future claims to be pledged almost immediately after they arise and without intervention of the pledgor. This entails that unpaid and unsecured creditors of companies that are financed by banks, cannot - or only scarcely - take redress as against the claims that these companies have on third parties. This is why the present construction cannot easily be reconciled with the remark, made in parliamentary history, that art. 3:239 leaves some room for ordinary creditors, who have to rely to an important extent on the possibility of garnishment orders. Considering that all other assets of the company, such as buildings and trade supplies, will normally also be burdened with security rights in favor of financiers or suppliers, the present construction entails an effective erosion of the principles of articles 3:276 and 3:277 (1) DCC[13] with regard to ordinary creditors.'[14]

2.2.3. The Silent Pledge on Balance

By consistently interpreting the law in favour of the pledgee, the Supreme Court has introduced something that amounts to a right of security over the entirety of a debtor's patrimony into Dutch law. The Court's most important justification to do so is that it is in the interest of a well-functioning credit market and a low price of credit that the creditor has ample possibility to obtain security on the assets of its debtor.[15] Naturally, it is not only banks that finance undertakings. Certainly after the financial crisis, companies increasingly depend on supplier credit to finance their business. The Supreme Court considers that for suppliers there is the possibility to retain ownership of the supplied goods until the purchase price is paid or demand security in return for any goods or services supplied. Of course, if - which will mostly be the case - a bank is able to vest security on all the assets of its debtor in an earlier stage, the supplier will rank below the bank in a possible insolvency of the debtor. Hence, in most cases only reservation of ownership is a viable alternative for suppliers and then only for suppliers of goods.[16] In the following, then, this possibility will be briefly discussed in order to assess the position of a supplier of goods, relative to that of a bank.

13 Art. 3:276 establishes the principle that, unless provided otherwise by law or contract, a creditor has redress to all the assets of a debtor. Art. 3:277 (1) establishes the principle that creditors have an equal right to redress in proportion to their claims, subject to those reasons of preference recognized by law.

14 At 4.8.2-3.

15 At 4.9.3. That rationale is criticized by different authors on different grounds. Van den Heuvel concludes that the economic efficiency argument cannot justify the scope of the silent pledge. Others argue that it is questionable whether the strength of security rights actually influences the price of security. Cf. Van den Heuvel 2004, p. 131; Kaptein 2012, para. 4.2. It seems safe to say, however, that the less money is lost on any given credit, the less interest a bank will be able to charge to its customers.

16 For the supplier of services there is very little hope of vesting any meaningful security on the assets of their debtors.

2.3. *Retention of Ownership in Dutch Law*

2.3.1. The Limitations of Retention of Ownership under Dutch Law

Article 3:92 DCC allows creditors to retain ownership of a good that is transferred to the debtor until the debtor performs an obligation that is owed to the creditor. That the Civil Code allows for reservation of ownership seems to be in conflict with Article 3:84 DCC, which invalidates transfers of ownership for security purposes. After all, all the policy reasons for invalidating transfers of ownership for security purposes apply equally to reservation of ownership.[17] For this reason, the legislator has limited the claims that can be secured by way of retention of ownership to (i) claims concerning the counter performance for delivery of goods and connected services and (ii) claims that have arisen out of non-performance of these obligations.

More importantly perhaps, the provisions on original acquisition of ownership by processing the original goods are considered to be provisions of mandatory law.[18] When the debtor, therefore, produces a new object out of the material supplied to him by the creditor, the debtor will normally become owner of that new object.[19] That is so, even if the debtor and creditor have agreed on a so-called extended retention of ownership encompassing also objects produced out of the supplied materials. The rules on acquisition of ownership will prevent such a clause from having any effect. Obviously, in many cases where materials are supplied under retention of ownership, such materials will be used in order to produce new objects. In those cases, retention of ownership does not provide the creditor with an effective security. Apart from the risk of losing his ownership in the way described above, the supplier's security will 'atrophy' over time, as the debtor resells the supplied goods. He will typically be allowed to do so in the normal exercise of his business. The supplier used to have some possibilities to counter this 'atrophication' but these possibilities have been limited after the introduction of the new Civil Code and the subsequent development of the silent pledge and its use by banks.

A big disadvantage for suppliers in The Netherlands is the possibility of the Tax Authority to seize any movable that is durably present on the premises of the tax debtor, regardless of any rights that third parties may have on those assets.[20] The Tax Authority only makes an exception for beneficial owners of those assets; of course, security ownership does not qualify as beneficial ownership. When a seller supplies the debtor with machinery or other inventory under a reservation of ownership clause or on a sale-and-lease-back transaction, he or she runs a big risk

17 Those reasons were, *inter alia*, the existence of a 'surplus of security' on the side of the creditor and the fact that it is not a public type of security right.

18 Spath 2012 and literature mentioned under footnote 9 of that contribution. For a recent case applying the provisions to a German extended retention of ownership, see Gerechtshof Leeuwarden, 3 March 2009, LJN: BH5277.

19 For example: Art. 5:16 (2) CC: 'If someone forms – for himself – a new object out of one or multiple corporeal movables which do not belong to him, he becomes the owner of the new object, unless the costs of forming the new object, because of their minor size, do not justify that result.'

20 For instance, company cars or supplies don't classify as durably present on the premises.

that the Tax Authority will seize those assets when the debtor his in arrears on his taxes.

Finally, unlike the provisions for pledge and hypothec, the provisions for reservation of ownership do not provide for real subrogation in case the object of security is destroyed or rendered worthless.[21]

2.3.2. Alternatives

In order to work around the rules on original acquisition of ownership, some authors have suggested to insert a clause into the agreement designating the supplier to be the one for whom the new objects are produced or 'formed'.[22] The buyer would then be some kind of agent for the supplier, who becomes owner of the newly formed goods immediately upon their formation. Of course, in most cases such a clause would be entirely fictional given that the buyer will usually produce for himself (i.e. not as an agent) and not for the supplier. In such cases, the rules on original acquisition of ownership will inevitably mean that the buyer becomes owner of the newly formed good, in spite of any contractual agreement to the contrary.[23]

Apart from this, it is always possible to include a clause into the agreement by which the buyer pledges in advance (i) any objects produced out of the goods supplied or (ii) any claims for the payment of the purchase price when the buyer resells to third parties. However, this requires the agreement to be registered, which is an additional administrative burden. More importantly, it will leave the supplier with a right of security that ranks below that of any creditor who has previously obtained security on any future asset of the debtor – i.e. the bank.

Spath advocates for the option of reconveyance of any new object that is formed out of the goods supplied, *inter alia*, because such a reconveyance could be done without the administrative burdens imposed by a pledge.[24] Another option might be to insert an obligation for the buyer to assign his claims against sub-purchasers to the supplier. Both would however, be in conflict with the ban on transfers of ownership for security purposes. Though the Supreme Court has allowed certain such transfers in the context of sale-and-lease-back transactions, it is not likely that the exception would apply also to a reconveyance of a newly formed object or to a fiduciary assignation.[25] In any case, the supplier would again be confronted with security rights previously vested in favour of other creditors of the buyer, whom would be ranked above him in case of insolvency of the debtor. Spath, under the slogan 'nothing ventured, nothing gained', speculates that the Supreme Court might be willing to 'lend a hand' and favour the supplier above other credi-

21 Jansen 2012.

22 Van Maanen 1998. Cf. Spath 2012.

23 Fikkers 1998; Spath 2012. For an answer to the question when someone forms a good for himself, so as to become the owner of the good, see HR 5 October 1990, *NJ* 1992/226 (Breda/Antonius).

24 It must be noted that the administrative burdens are minimal.

25 Given that such a reconveyance would be solely for security purposes and not a type of sale-and-lease-back transaction.

tors with a higher ranking security right.[26] This suggestion is not as extraordinary as it sounds. In Germany the so-called *Globalzession* (fiduciary assignment) of all claims on sub-purchasers to the bank, may clash with the right of a supplier who has included an extended reservation of ownership into his contracts, as such an extended reservation of ownership can include fiduciary assignment of claims on sub-purchasers to the supplier as well. Given that the bank will usually have priority over the suppliers, the debtor is forced to commit a breach of his obligations towards his supplier. The *Bundersgerichtshof* decided that, therefore, the *Globalzession* may be void as in conflict with the law (§ 134 BGB) and good custom (§ 138 BGB).[27] The bank has to take the interests of the supplier into account.[28] It is not inconceivable that a similar result could be reached by the Dutch Supreme Court. At the moment, however, there is nothing indicating such a shift.

Verstijlen, finally, proposes for the supplier to make use of the option of daily pledging by way of the irrevocable power of attorney, discussed above.[29] In case of insolvency of the buyer, both the bank, who pledges daily to itself, and all suppliers, who pledge daily to themselves, then have an equally ranking right of security on the claims of their debtor.[30] It must be noted that such is true only with regard to claims arising out of new legal relations. On claims arising out of legal relations existing at, for instance, the time when the bank started pledging to itself, the bank should have a higher ranking right, given that it is possible to validly pledge these claims in advance (on the basis of the aforementioned Art. 3:239 DCC). Nonetheless, the fact remains that suppliers are capable, in this way, of obtaining very effective security for their claims.

Some caveats should be made: Certain suppliers will not be in a position to demand this type of security from their buyers. Suppliers, contrary to banks, must sell their goods to make money and are, therefore, not always in a position to make demands. Banks, on the other hand, normally require their debtors to refrain from vesting any security rights on their assets in favour of third parties. Hence, if that condition of the contract is breached and *if* the bank finds out about it (which will be very difficult seeing that the pledge is not publicized) banks might threaten to withdraw the credit facility. If suppliers indeed pick up on the idea of Verstijlen, it remains to be seen in what way banks will react.

2.4. *The Balance of Powers*

The balance has shifted decisively in favour of banks and financiers in Dutch law. This, in spite of the expressed desire of the legislator to create a system in which at

26 Spath 2012.
27 BGH 30 April 1959, NJW 1959/1533.
28 Verheul 2014, para. 5.1.
29 Verstijlen 2013. For individual suppliers the administrative burden of doing this might be a bit too much. Associations of suppliers could, however, do this on their behalf. It is then the association who is empowered to pledge to all its individual members.
30 When pledges are registered only the day and not the time is registered. When multiple parties register a pledge on the same day, they all have an equal ranking.

least some future assets would remain available to other classes of creditors, specifically suppliers. Some authors have lamented this development, others have argued in favour of making it complete by eliminating the existing - now superfluous - limitations on pledging future assets.[31] Here it may be remarked that the existence of a general right of security over the totality of the debtor's (future) assets may very well be justified for reasons of economic expediency. However, if there are such reasons to allow a bank to have a most effective right of security on the assets of its debtor, those reasons equally apply to any other party that, in some way, finances the debtor's undertaking, most prominently, of course, the supplier of the debtor.

3. English Law

Vesting security rights in English law is not confined to current assets, but may extend to after-acquired property, i.e. future assets. These are generally restricted to *equitable* securities. The common law does allow a transfer of, and security right over, future corporeals, but such a transfer requires *a new act* for every new asset that came into existence.[32] Furthermore, a transfer or vesting of a security right over an incorporeal such as a claim is not possible at common law.[33] There are no such limitations in the law of equity. In equity, the encumbrance or transfer takes place once the asset, be it corporeal or incorporeal, comes into existence in the patrimony of the debtor without requiring any additional action.[34] This meant that the impracticability of the common law, which did not meet the needs of undertakings,[35] led to equity being leading in the development of security rights and especially security rights over future assets.[36]

The pledge is therefore left out of this analysis as it is a common law security. Its equitable equivalent is, however, discussed. Equity developed the charge, which is a non-possessory security right.[37] Two different types of charge developed, both are discussed below.

31 Cf. Verstijlen's annotation on *Dix q.q.* v *ING*; Kaptein 2012; Wibier 2012; Van Buchem & De Man 2012.

32 This reasoning is based on Bacon's *Maxims* of common law, stated in regula 14 that: 'Licet dispositio de interessefuturo sit inutilis, tamen potest fieri declaratio praecedens quae sortiatur effectum interveniente novo actu' which was translated by Hogan and Schwartz as 'Although the disposition of a future interest is pointless, a preceding declaration may be made, to take effect once a new event has occurred.' Hogan & Schwartz 1985, p. 717. See also *Lunn* v *Thorton* (1845) 1 Common Bench Reports 379.

33 Beale *et al.* 2012, para 1.13.

34 Provided the grant of an interest in future property is one made with valuable consideration. *Edward Tailby* v *The Official Receiver (Trustee of the Property of H G Izon, a Bankrupt)* (1888) XIII App Cas 523 which makes reference to the below *Holroyd* v *Marshall* case citing Lord Chemsford's view.

35 Pennington 1960, p. 631-632.

36 See extensively Pennington 1960, p. 630-634.

37 Justice Peter Gibson in *Carreras Rothmans Ltd* v *Freeman Mathews Treasure Ltd and Another* [1984] Ch 207, 227.

3.1. *Charges*

3.1.1. Fixed Charges

The equitable non-possessory equivalent of a pledge is a fixed charge. The advantage of a fixed charge over a pledge is that it is a non-possessory security, meaning, the chargor is still able to use the object for its business.[38] Furthermore, it is possible to create such a charge over future assets. Disposal of a good subject to a fixed charge, however, requires the consent of the chargee. Therefore, subjecting all the property of a business to fixed charges would in fact paralyze the undertaking's dealings.[39] This commercially uninteresting feature of the fixed charge lay at the heart of the development of the floating charge. As becomes clear from the case law discussed below, the issue of characterizing a charge as either fixed or floating, in particular relating to charges over claims, has given rise to extensive litigation and was not truly settled until 2005, when the House of Lords ruled in *Spectrum Plus*.

3.1.2. Floating Charges

For the origins of the floating charge, one need not dig deep into the history books.[40] It was only in 1861 that *Holroyd* v *Marshall* signalled the entrance of the floating charge in English law.[41] Though the case concerned a mortgage, it would later be identified as one of the first floating charges. On the question whether the charge could be on a future asset Lord Chelmsford observed that: 'in equity it is not disputed that the moment the property comes into existence the agreement operates upon it'. This means that a charge is created upon the moment the asset comes into existence and into the patrimony of the debtor, without requiring any additional action.[42]

38 Moreover, claims can be the object of security, whereas such is not possible with a pledge, which is restricted to tangible property.

39 Worthington 2006, p. 27.

40 Though one could, as there are indications that the floating charge has a precursor in Roman law, Pennington 1960, p. 634; Milo 2010; Zwalve 2006.

41 *Holroyd* v *Marshall* (1861) 11 ER 999. This did not mean that the floating charge was instantly recognized by the judiciary, cases such as *King, on behalf , & c* v *Marshall* (1864) 55 ER 488; *In the Matter of The Joint Stock Companies Winding-up Acts*, 1848, 1849 *In the Matter of The Joint Stock Companies Winding-up Amendment Act*, 1857 *In the Matter of The British Provident Life and Fire Assurance Society, Stanley's Case* [1864] ER 976 show that even two years after *Holroyd* v *Marshall* certain provisions were not considered floating charges, whereas, in hindsight, they should have been.

42 'The judgment of Lord Campbell resting, as he states, upon Lord Bacon's maxim, determines that some subsequent act is necessary to enable "the equitable interest to prevail against a legal interest subsequently bona fide acquired". It is agreed that this maxim relates only to the acquisition of a legal title to future property. It can be extended to equitable rights and interests (if at all) merely by analogy; but in thus proposing to enlarge the sphere of the rule, it appears to me that sufficient attention has not been paid to the different effect and operation of agreements relating to future property at law and in equity. At law property, non-existing, but to be acquired at a future time, is not assignable; in equity it is so. At law (as we have →

It would be some eight years later with *In re Panama New Zealand and Australian Royal Mail* that the practice of a company charging its 'undertaking and all sums of money arising therefrom' would be judicially recognized.[43] Lord Gifford stated here that 'undertaking' meant 'all the property of the company, not only which existed at the date of the debenture, but which might afterwards become the property of the company'. He also stated that the word undertaking 'necessarily infers that the company will go on, and that the debenture holder could not interfere until either the interest which was due was unpaid, or until the period had arrived for the payment of his principal, and that principal was unpaid'.[44] And with that latter consideration, the necessary distinction with a fixed charge is made. Thus, all property[45] current and future could be subject to a charge that would not hinder the use of these objects for the business. No consent by the chargee was required for any disposition of the assets.

The foregoing case law set up the parameters for a floating charge, but not yet coined the term. In *In Re Colonial Trusts Corporation* in 1879, this form of charge would be called for the first time a 'floating security' by Jessel MR, and by the applicants 'a floating charge'.[46] In 1903 Romer LJ summarized the previous case law and gave one of the most widely cited definitions of a floating charge:[47]

> 'I certainly think that if a charge has the three characteristics that I am about to mention it is a floating charge. (1.) If it is a charge on a class of assets of a company present and future; (2.) if that class is one which, in the ordinary course of the business of the company, would be changing from time to time; and (3.) if you find that by the charge it is contemplated that, until some future step is taken by or on behalf of those interested in the charge, the company may carry on its business in the ordinary way as far as concerns the particular class of assets I am dealing with.'

seen), although a power is given in the deed of assignment to take possession of after-acquired property, no interest is transferred, even as between the parties themselves, unless possession is actually taken; in equity it is not disputed that the moment the property comes into existence the agreement operates upon it.'

43 *In re Panama, New Zealand, and Australian Royal Mail Company* [1870] LR 5 Ch App 318.

44 See also *In re Florence Land and Public Works Company Ex parte Moor* [1878] Ch D 530. This also means that the chargor is free to create a fixed charge or mortgage upon the assets whilst they are also subjected to a floating charge. Moreover, the fixed charge will be considered to be the older right, which has its consequences in insolvency.

45 In *Edward Tailby* the formulation was 'all the book debts due and owing or which may during the continuance of this security become due and owing to the said mortgagor, which fixtures, stock-in-trade, machinery, furniture, chattels, goods, effects and debts are for the most part and as near as may be mentioned in the respective schedules hereunder written'.

46 *In re Colonial Trusts Corporation Ex parte Bradshaw* (1879) XV Ch D 465.

47 Until *Spectrum,* in which the Lord Justices considered the third characteristic was the decisive factor. Lord Justice Romer in *In re Yorkshire Woolcombers Association, Limited Houldsworth* v *Yorkshire Woolcombers Association, Limited* (1903) 2 Ch D 284, 295.

3.1.3. Judicial Inception, Legislative Dismantling

In its earliest forms the floating charge was a very extensive security right, and seemingly unlimited.[48] The floating chargee could, upon insolvency, appropriate all the assets of a business that were not subject to specific mortgages or charges.[49] Especially the fact that unsecured creditors, which included employees, were virtually left with nothing in a winding-up procedure was criticized.

Lord Macnagthen in *Salomon* v *Salomon* in 1896: 'Everybody knows that when there is a winding-up debenture-holders [*in casu* a floating charge holder] generally step in and sweep off everything; and a great scandal it is.'[50] Parliament shared the sentiment[51] and in 1897 enacted the Preferential Payments in Bankruptcy Amendment Act, which gave preferential creditors priority over a floating charge, including the aforementioned employees.[52] This would be the first of many statutory limitations placed on the floating charge. In 1900 the mandatory registration of floating charges followed.[53] Then in 1986 the floating charge was left especially vulnerable by The Insolvency Act of 1986. Section 245 of that Act dictated that the floating charge was subject to the claw-back provisions. Only the floating charge was subject to such vulnerability, it was not extended to fixed charges or the like.[54]

The biggest legislative blow, however, came with the Enterprise Act 2002.[55] The possibility of the floating chargee to appoint an administrative receiver was replaced with the power to appoint an administrator out of court. The primary task of the administrator out of court would be to ensure the business would remain going

48 It was however, settled that fixed charges would take preference over floating charges, as the latter would not hinder the debtor's ability to establish a fixed charge on assets already subject to a floating charge. See, for example, *Moor* v *Anglo-Italian Bank* (1879) 10 Ch D 681 (1879) 10 Ch D 681.

49 Called by Gullifer the 'draconian nature of the floating charge'. Gullifer 2009, p. 18.

50 *Salomon* v *Salomon and Co. Ltd* [1897] AC 22, 53.

51 An audible 'hear, hear' was recorded when the prioritizing of these preferential creditors over floating charges was discussed, in 1888 in the Preferential Payments in Bankruptcy Act (1888) Amendment Bill, HC Deb 10 February 1897 vol. 46 cc 72-73. In Richard Calnan even goes so far as to say: 'On the other [side, of the judges who created the floating charge, AB] stands the legislature which set its face against the floating charge almost from the outset, and whose hostility to it continues unabated.' Calnan 2010, para. 1.139.

52 Currently in Companies Act 2006 c. 46 s. 754 jo. Schedule 6 Insolvency Act 1986 c. 45. It used to include Debts due to Inland Revenue, debts due to Customs and Excise, social security contributions but with the Enterprise Act 2002 this class of creditors (Crown Creditors) was no longer considered preferential. NB. The preferential creditors would not have priority over the fixed charges.

53 Companies Act 1900 s. 14. (1)(d): '(1)Every mortgage or charge created by a company after the commencement of this Act and being either (d) a floating charge on the undertaking or property of the company, shall so far as any security on the company's property or undertaking is thereby conferred, be void as against the liquidator and any creditor of the company, unless filed with the registrar for registration in manner required by this Act within twenty-one days after the date of its creation, but without prejudice to any contract or obligation for repayment of the money thereby secured.' Currently to be found Companies Act 2006 c. A1 859A jo. 859D(2)(b) jo. 859H.

54 See also Beale *et al.* 2012, para. 1.14.

55 See extensively Gullifer 2009.

concern, rather than to realize assets which would be distributed to the secured creditors as was previously the case.[56]

Prior to the Enterprise Act 2002, the Crown Creditors (i.e. Inland revenue, Customs and Excise and social security contributions) had preference over the floating charge. This preference of the Crown creditors was abolished with the Enterprise Act 2002.[57] In turn, the accrued benefit of the abolition was from then on to be ring-fenced for the unsecured creditors. This 'prescribed part' determines that where a company's net value exceeds £10,000 it would have to set aside for the satisfaction of unsecured debts of the company; 50% of the first £ 10,000 and 20% of the rest of the company's net property value, a combined total of which shall not exceed £600,000.[58] And thus, some 107 years later, Lord Macnaughten's dissatisfaction with the position of the floating chargee vis-à-vis the unsecured creditor resonated in legislation.[59] The overall practical effect of the ring-fenced fund, however, has been modest at most.[60]

Since its acceptance by the judiciary the floating charge has gone from a very extensive security right, to one that slowly but surely lost its strength, and is considered to be more of a backup that 'sweeps up all assets that escape the row of fixed charges' rather than an strong security right.[61] Fixed charges were therefore preferred security, for those assets not already financed by asset-based financing, i.e. receivables.[62]

3.1.4. Charges over Book Debts: Fixed or Floating?

Fixed charges were also subject to legislative initiatives, however, these were not as stringent as those imposed on the floating charge. The popularity of fixed charges hence increased in light of the demise of the floating charge.

For a long time it was thought that *an unrestricted right* to draw on the proceeds of debts paid to the chargor which were the subject of the charge would make a charge floating. Any type of restriction would make a charge over book

56 Insolvency Act 1986 Sch. B1 para 14 jo. Sch. B1 para 3(1), see Gullifer 2009, p. 21-27.

57 Particular reference was made to Germany and Australia, which had just before restricted or abolished the Crown or State preference.

58 The Insolvency Act 1986 (Prescribed Part) Order 2003(3).

59 *Supra* note 50.

60 According to Louise Gullifer: 'At best, and on the Government's own figures, it will yield about £100m extra for unsecured creditors each year. Unsecured creditors, before the change comes into effect, recover about £2.1 bn each year (about 7 pence in the pound). Adding an extra £100m will increase this to 7.4 pence, an increase of less than 1 per cent.' Gullifer 2009, p. 28. In particular, this references Mokal 2005, p. 129-130, in relation to the abolition of tax preference.

61 Beale *et al.* 2012, para. 1.13. Gullifer calls it a combination of the weak priority position of the floating charge in combination with the fact that the administrator, in administration, could transfer only those assets which were subjected to a floating charge without leave of the court (Insolvency Act 1986, Sch. B1, Para. 70), and the fact that the administrator's costs are to be paid out of the floating charge assets. Gullifer 2009, p. 37-38.

62 Gullifer 2009, p. 38.

debts a fixed one.[63] A restriction such as not being able to freely draft from the proceeds of the book debts would already be sufficient to create a fixed charge. This type of fixed charge, however, would not be very burdensome to the chargor, as he was still able to make use of the proceeds in the course of his business. As such the fixed charge was an attractive security.

The decision in 2005 in *Spectrum Plus* changed the direction of the Supreme Court[64] who changed the way in which fixed and floating charges would be characterized.[65]

3.1.5. Spectrum Plus Ltd

The facts of the case are as follows.[66] Spectrum carried on the business of a manufacturer of dyes, paints, pigments and other chemical products for the paint industry. In the autumn of 1997 Spectrum changed banks. It opened an account with the new bank, obtained an overdraft facility of £250,000 and, on 30 September 1997, executed the debenture to secure its indebtedness to the bank. The security created by the debenture was expressed to include:

> '... [a] specific charge [of] all book debts and other debts ... now and from time to time due or owing to [Spectrum]' (para. 2(v))

and (...)

> '[a] floating security [of] its undertaking and all its property assets and rights whatsoever and wheresoever present and/or future including those for the time being charged by way of specific charge pursuant to the foregoing paragraphs if and to the extent that such charges as aforesaid shall fail as specific charges but without prejudice to any such specific charges as shall continue to be effective.' (para. 2(vii))

Paragraph 5 of the debenture supported the grant of the charge over books debts:

> '5. With reference to the book debts and other debts hereby specifically charged [Spectrum] shall pay into [Spectrum's] account with the Bank all moneys which it may receive in respect of such debts and shall not without the prior consent in writing of the Bank sell factor discount or otherwise charge or assign the same in favour of any other person or purport to do so and [Spectrum] shall if called upon to do so by the Bank from time to time execute legal assignments of such book debts and other debts to the Bank.'

63 Following the ruling in *Siebe Gorman & Co Ltd* v *Barclays Bank Ltd* [1979] 2 Lloyd's Rep. 142.

64 Then still called the 'House of Lords'

65 The case had been criticized in scholarly writing and Supreme Courts from Ireland and New Zealand took a different view from the one advanced in *Siebe Gorman*, similar to what would be decided later in *Spectrum Plus*, see Addy 2010, p. 12 *et seq*.

66 Largely taken from the presentation of the facts by Lord Scott of Foscote in *In re Spectrum Plus Ltd (in liquidation)* (2005) 3 WLR 58.

This provision barred Spectrum from dealing with its book debts in any of the ways specified but left Spectrum free to deal with the debtors who owed the debts and, in particular, to collect the debts in the normal course of business. Upon collection, however, they had to be paid into Spectrum's account with the bank that had the overdraft facility. Provided the limit was not reached, Spectrum was free to make use of the overdraft facility. Thus, the proceeds of the debt collection would go on the account that Spectrum was free to draw on. The question therefore was, is this 'specific charge' a floating or a fixed one?

Before the Supreme Court decided on the case, the Court of Appeals had, stating it was a fixed charge. This lead to a critical article published by Worthington, which later had a noticeable effect on the Supreme Court ruling. Worthington stated that while Lord Philips MR (Appeals Court) rightly surmised that 'the critical issue of principle [is] whether the restrictions imposed … on the use that the charger can make of the proceeds of the book debts charged are sufficient in law to create a fixed charge on those debts', he was wrong in his conclusion that the charge in *Spectrum* was fixed.[67]

Worthington asserts a different starting point, specifically that

> 'any definition should start at the fixed charge end of the continuum. In other words, a charge is either "fixed" or "not-fixed": if it is not fixed, then it is floating. A charge is fixed, and only if, it imposes restrictions on the activities of the charger that are sufficient to ensure that the charged assets are preserved for the benefit of the security holder'.[68]

In *Spectrum* the charge was therefore not fixed, as the imposed restrictions were not sufficient enough to have such effect, rather the charged assets upon payment were preserved not for the benefit of the chargee but rather the chargor. The undertaking was free to draw on the account, (and hence to decrease the value of the security). It was a floating charge therefore.

Worthington then gave three ways by which to ensure that a charge over book debts is fixed:

> 'The first is to prevent all dealings with the book debts so that they are preserved for the benefit of the chargee's security. (…) The second method is to prevent all dealings other than collection, and to require the collected proceeds to be paid to the chargee in reduction of the chargor's outstanding debt. (..) The third method is again to prevent all dealings other than collection, and to require the collected proceeds to be paid into a bank account with the chargee bank. This account must then be *blocked*.'[69]

The Supreme Court agreed.[70] Worthington's opinion that the Court of Appeals was incorrect in its opinion that the charge in casu was a fixed one, was followed by the Supreme Court. In the words of Lord Scott:

67 Worthington 2010, p. 2.
68 Worthington 2010, p. 4.
69 Worthington 2010, p. 8-9.
70 *In re Spectrum Plus Ltd (in liquidation)* [54].

> 'If a book debt were to be charged as security but with an accompanying provision that any money received from the debtor in payment of the debt would belong to the chargor, the so-called "charge", whether expressed to be a fixed charge or a floating charge, would not be a security at all. It would not constitute a possible source for the repayment of the allegedly secured debt. As Lord Millett said, it would be worthless. (...) And if the charge were to be expressed to be a fixed charge as respects the receivable debt but a floating charge as respects the money received from the debtor there would be an internal contradiction in the formulation of the charge. Since the essential value of a book debt as a security lies in the money that can be obtained from the debtor in payment it seems to me that Lord Millett was right in concluding that such a security should be categorised as a floating security and that New Bullas [1994] 1 BCLC 485 was wrongly decided.'

Thus, the internal conflict as displayed here, is untenable. It cannot be so that the control over the book debts lies with the chargee, whereas the proceeds of these book debts are at the free disposal of the chargor. That would indeed make the security worthless by way of atrophication. Even if the proceeds were paid into an account that was permanently in overdraft (either partially or up to the limit). The decrease of the overdraft by virtue of payment says nothing about the control of the chargor/chargee.[71]

The bank asserted that it was chargee of a fixed charge, one created closest to the third type of method as described by Worthington above. Having to assess this particular point Lord Scott stated that:

> '(...) *Spectrum was free to draw on the account. Its right to do so was inconsistent with the charge being a fixed charge* and the label placed on the charge by the debenture cannot, in my opinion, be prayed-in-aid to detract from that right.'[72]

Thus, the Supreme Court, characterized the charge as floating. This caused quite a stir as the formulations used were common in debenture agreements used by many banks. This ruling meant that the paralyzing effect that the fixed charge had in relation to movables, was now extended to intangibles. In order to effectively create a fixed charge, one would have to set aside the proceeds of the debts in a blocked account that could only be controlled by the chargor with specific permission of the chargee.[73] This made the fixed charge again very unattractive. Nevertheless, the combination of several fixed and a floating charge on the assets of the undertaking that is financed is still largely used by the financers.[74]

3.2. *Reservation of Title*

In order to bypass the vesting of any fixed charge on movables and retain some form of security for themselves, suppliers frequently include a clause in their supply

71 See more eloquently phrased Worthington 2010, p. 7-8.

72 *In re Spectrum Plus Ltd (in liquidation)* [119] emphasis added by authors.

73 A general permission would not be enough.

74 They of course make use of hire-purchase and factoring agreements extensively as well, however, that is outside the scope of this particular piece. Beale *et al.* 2012, para. 1.33.

contract, by which they retain the title to the goods until the full purchase price has been paid. The (simple) reservation of title is available to creditors by virtue of S. 19 of the Sale of Goods Act 1979.[75] Such a reservation of title clause is not a charge, provided it remains confined to the particular goods supplied, and does not extend to produced or commingled goods.

In practice, these types of reservation clauses take various shapes and sizes. A reservation of title clause may be restricted to the goods supplied, but can also extend to the end product processed from the raw materials supplied. Moreover, it may even cover the proceeds of sale of the goods prior to satisfaction of the supplier creditor. Extending the reservation of title clause beyond the original goods supplied may, however, result in the clause being characterized as a charge, which means that it should be registered. This is not a requirement for a simple retention of title clause.

The simple retention of title clause to the original goods is unappealing as these will be extinguished by *specificatio*, mixing of goods either resulting in a new good or the inability to ascertain the goods, sale of the goods subject to the clause by the buyer to another in the course of the business (which often releases the object of the clause) or *accessio* of the goods, either to other goods or as fixtures to land.[76]

3.2.1. Romalpa Aluminium Ltd.

Some of these different types of retention of title clauses were tested in the *Romalpa* Case.[77] This was the first case in which the Supreme Court had to assess the validity of these clauses, later aptly referred to as *Romalpa*-clauses.[78] The facts of the case are as follows. A Dutch company, Aluminium Industrie Vaassen B.V. (AIV), sold aluminium foil to an English company, Romalpa Aluminium Ltd., some of which was re-sold to third parties. In the contract between the two companies there was a clause that stipulated that: 'The ownership of the material to be delivered by [the supplier] will only be transferred to the purchaser when he has met all that is owing to [the supplier], no matter on what grounds ...'[79] Should the foil be used to create

75 This section reads: 'Where there is a contract for the sale of specific goods or where goods are subsequently appropriated to the contract, the seller may, by the terms of the contract or appropriation, reserve the right of disposal of the goods until certain conditions are fulfilled; and in such a case, notwithstanding the delivery of the goods to the buyer, or to a carrier or other bailee or custodier for the purpose of transmission to the buyer, the property in the goods does not pass to the buyer until the conditions imposed by the seller are fulfilled.'

76 See more extensively Beale *et al.* 2012, para. 7.11 *et seq*. Note, it does not follow, however, from there mere occurrence of *specificatio* or *accessio* that the clause will extinguish. It might very well be that the objects are still identifiable which in turn might lead to the clause extending over the transformed but still identifiable object. Only upon loss of identity also the reservation of title will disappear. See further below.

77 *Aluminium Industrie Vaassen BV* v *Romalpa Aluminium Ltd* [1976] WLR 676.

78 Now also simply referred to as retention of title clauses.

79 The full clause read: 'Until the date of payment, purchaser, if A.I.V. so desires, is required to store this material in such a way that it is clearly the property of A.T.V. A.I.V. and purchaser agree that, if purchaser should make (a) new object(s) from the material, mix this material with (an)other object(s) or if this material in any way whatsoever becomes a constituent of →

another object AIV would also become the owner of said object until Romalpa was discharged of all debts to AIV. Also, should any foil be transferred in the normal course of carrying out of business, AIV would 'be handed' all claims for the purchase price against this third party purchaser.

After several deliveries of aluminium foil had been made from the supplier to the purchaser, the latter went into liquidation, still owing the supplier an amount exceeding £122,239.74. The receiver certified that £35,152.66 was held in an account in his name with the purchaser's bankers, representing the proceeds of sale of aluminium foil supplied which the purchaser had sold to sub-purchasers. Furthermore, the receiver had certified that aluminium foil to a value alleged to be £50,235 was held by him, having originated in deliveries to the purchaser by the supplier.

The House of Lords, had no difficulty in holding that the foil that was held by the purchaser, having originated from the supplier, belonged to the latter, based on a simple retention of title clause. The main question of the case was whether the Romalpa clause which extended the retention of title to monies received from the sale of the foil to sub-purchasers, would be able to be traced by the supplier into the patrimony of the purchaser.

Romalpa argued that once the foil had been sold to bona fide purchasers, the relationship between AIV and Romalpa was one of debtor/creditor. As such, the monies paid by the sub-purchasers would not be available to AIV but was for Romalpa to do with at it saw fit. AIV on the other hand argued that a fiduciary relationship stemming from the bailment continued after sales to third parties, and that in consequence they could trace the proceeds to discharge the debts Romalpa had outstanding with them.[80] The court agreed with the latter contention. Romalpa had the (implied) consent to use the delivered materials to sell on, and was able to do so as 'principal' in his relationship towards the sub-purchaser. Romalpa should not be construed as 'principal' in its legal relationship with supplier AIV. Romalpa in that situation acted as an agent of AIV. This fiduciary relationship created was intended by the parties[81] according to the Court.[82]

(an)other object(s) A.I.V. will be given the ownership of this (these) new objects(s) as surety of the full payment of what purchaser owes A.I.V. To this end A.I.V. and purchaser now agree that the ownership of the article(s) in question, whether finished or not, are to be transferred to A.I.V. and that this transfer of ownership will be considered to have taken place through and at the moment of the single operation or event by which the material is converted into (a) new object(s), or is mixed with or becomes a constituent of (an)other object(s). Until the moment of full payment of what purchaser owes A.I.V. purchaser shall keep the object(s) in question for A.I.V. in his capacity of fiduciary owner and, if required, shall store this (these) object(s) in such a way that it (they) can be recognized as such. Nevertheless, purchaser will be entitled to sell these objects to a third party within the framework of the normal carrying on of his business and to deliver them on condition that - if A.I.V. so requires - purchaser, as long as he has not fully discharged his debt to A.I.V. shall hand over to A.I.V. the claims he has against his buyer emanating from this transaction.'

80 *Ibidem* 680.

81 Here clearly the party intentions, or their expression thereof was leading. Roskill L.J. noted: '(...) This is a formidable argument if one looks at the matter solely from the point of view of the defendants. But this matter has to be regarded in the light of the contractual provisions agreed upon by both parties, and the question of business efficacy, in relation to which there →

Roskill L.J.:

> '[i]f an agent lawfully sells his principal's goods, he stands in a fiduciary relationship to his principal and remains accountable to his principal for those goods and their proceeds. [...] What, then, is there here to relieve [Romalpa] from their obligation to account to [AIV] for those goods of [AIV] which they lawfully sell to sub-purchasers? The fact that they so sold them as principals does not, as I think, affect their relationship with [AIV]'.[83]

Therefore, AIV could trace the proceeds of sale of the foil to sub-purchasers whilst the debt owed to them had not been fully discharged. Subsequent cases have, however, distinguished *Romalpa* as a peculiarity.[84] Currently, one would not so easily establish a fiduciary relationship as was done in *Romalpa*, nor would it suffice if one has established such a relationship, as there are different sorts of fiduciary type relationships with their own traits.[85]

What happens to the retention of title upon processing of the goods, is not entirely settled yet.[86] It appears that if goods 'lose their identity' the supplier's retention of title is lost as well, and he cannot trace.[87] However, if the goods have been processed but retain their identity, then the right also remains.[88] As the tracing right is lost upon the creation of a new good where the identity is lost, suppliers tend to include provisions stating a right in the new products as well. The construction of such a clause: is it a retransfer; an immediate vesting once the new product is created;[89] or a granting of a new interest to the supplier, has been the subject of many cases.[90] The most prevalent suggestion is that a new interest granted to the supplier means that a charge has been created. As charges require registration to be valid, this means all these extended retention of title clauses fail to deliver the security sought.

3.2.2. Balance of Interests in English Law

In English law, the balance of interests between financiers and suppliers, has developed rather sketchy over the years. Around the late 1800's the balance seemed

are here obvious competing business considerations, must be answered in the light of what both parties expressly agreed upon and therefore must be taken also impliedly to have agreed upon, and not unilateraly from the point of view of one party only.' *Ibidem* 689. This is outcome of what Michael Bridge calls '[t]he basic idea that drives forward the English law of security is that of freedom of contract'. Bridge 2004, p. 85.

82 Roskill L.J. *Aluminium Industrie Vaassen B.V.* v *Romalpa Aluminium Ltd.*

83 *Ibidem* 690.

84 Kieninger *et al.* 2004, p. 330; Beale *et al.* 2012, para. 7.19.

85 Kieninger *et al.* 2004, p. 330.

86 See case law cited in: Beale *et al.* 2012, para. 7.13.

87 For tracing the leading case here still is *In re Hallett's Estate* (1880) XIII Ch D 696. Note that if a claim is construed as a charge, there can be no tracing. See Beale *et al.* 2012, para. 7.22.

88 The tipping point of when a good has lost its identity in the processing is not at all clear. Beale *et al.* 2012, para. 7.15.

89 As Goff LJ was sympathetic to in his *obiter dicta* in *Clough Mill Ltd* v *Martin* [1985] WLR 111.

90 See extensively Beale *et al.* 2012, para. 7.19.

to be clearly in favour of the banks, with the single most important security of a floating charge available to them. This uneven spread of security was deemed undesirable and over the next century, the legislature and the courts have curtailed its effect. The floating charge fell out of grace and the focus was put on using a combination of fixed and floating charges. The *Spectrum*-case in 2005 ended speculation on what makes a charge fixed or floating in relation to book debts. This seminal judgment had a great impact on financing, as the charges that were deemed fixed all these years, were characterized into the, by now crippled, floating charge. This brief overview shows that the strength of the security rights held by banks has been mitigated over the years.

On the other hand, the strong position suppliers' had after *Romalpa*, where their retention of title also extends to monies received after sale to third parties, has also been mitigated over the years. The strong simple retention of title loses much of its strength upon sale of the goods to a third party, furthermore if the goods are processed and used to make a new product the supplier no longer has a right. The possibility to contractually alter this outcome has limited effect. Yes, the supplier will have a charge in the new product or the proceeds of the sale, but this is a floating charge that requires registration. The supplier still misses out. The balance of interests in English law therefore still leans towards the financiers such as banks, rather than the suppliers.

4. Belgian Reform of Security Rights in Relation to Movables

In 2013, the Belgian legislator adopted[91] a significant reform of its security rights on movables that changes the rights of pledge, reservation of ownership, transfer of ownership for security purposes and the right of retention.[92] In their proposal for the reform, the drafters of the legislation have looked beyond the Belgian borders for inspiration, not only to neighbouring legal systems,[93] but also at supranational initiatives. They specifically refer to the efforts of the UNCITRAL Legislative Guide & DCFR, and looked at Article 9 UCC of the United States.[94] The drafters have even stated that the reform is largely based on these foreign examples and international

91 It should enter into force before the end of 2014.

92 The right of retention is left out of this overview.

93 The French, German and Dutch laws have all been featured in the explanatory memorandum. *Wetsontwerp tot wijziging van het Burgerlijk Wetboek wat de zakelijke zekerheden op roerende goederen betreft en tot opheffing van diverse bepalingen ter zake*, wetsontwerp Kamer 2012-13, No. 2463/001.

94 See reference to these in: *Wetsontwerp tot wijziging van het Burgerlijk Wetboek wat de zakelijke zekerheden op roerende goederen betreft en tot opheffing van diverse bepalingen ter zake*, wetsontwerp Kamer 2012-13, No. 2463/001, p. 16-17 where the UCC approach and DCFR functional approach as well as the EBRD and the Cape Town Convention on International Interests in Mobile Equipment were taken as examples.

models.[95] With this international flavour to their reform, the code can contribute to the harmonization of this matter within Europe.[96]

4.1. *Background to the Reform*

The recovery from the aftermath of the credit crisis that hit Belgium as well, has been one of the reasons for the reform. The reform is intended to give new impetus to the Belgian economy by facilitating credit. The alterations proposed in the reform however, go further than that. The reform should, according to the drafters, alter the current property security right system into a system that is (i) *efficient, flexible and predictable,* which would promote credit facilitation. The new system should be (ii) *well-balanced.* Taking into account not only the interests of the debtor or the creditor, but also of third parties. The penultimate goal of the new legislation is that it should (iii) *make use of the functional approach,*[97] whereby similar arrangements, irrespective of their conceptual differences, should have the same legal effect, such as the almost equal treatment of the reservation of ownership provisions with those of the right of pledge.[98] The last goal of the reform is to (iv) *rehabilitate (the structure of) the Civil Code.* Under the old law, in order to gain a full overview of security rights system, one had to look at many different laws, and the reform would want to bring continuity and structure back to Belgian property (security) law. These goals are clearly reflected in the new law, of which its most significant changes are recapitulated. The focus will be on the right of pledge and the reservation of ownership. The complex arrangement of the privileges (*voorrechten*) remains largely untouched, in particular also the fiscal privileges,[99] which the drafting committee suggested should be abolished.[100]

4.2. *Pledge*

The right of pledge is subject to a great deal of attention in the reform. Under the old regime a right of pledge required dispossession of the good. This possessory pledge[101] has now been supplemented with a non-possessory variety, which

95 *Wetsontwerp tot wijziging van het Burgerlijk Wetboek wat de zakelijke zekerheden op roerende goederen betreft en tot opheffing van diverse bepalingen ter zake,* wetsontwerp Kamer 2012-13, No. 2463/001, p. 11-12. Dirix 2013, p. 4.

96 Dirix 2013, p. 4 . *Wetsontwerp tot wijziging van het Burgerlijk Wetboek wat de zakelijke zekerheden op roerende goederen betreft en tot opheffing van diverse bepalingen ter zake,* wetsontwerp Kamer 2012-13, No. 2463/001, p. 10-12.

97 The judges are also encouraged to make use of this functional approach in their interpretation of the law. Dirix 2013, p. 11. This was even considered a fifth goal (see para. 4.1) of the draft law. *Wetsontwerp tot wijziging van het Burgerlijk Wetboek wat de zakelijke zekerheden op roerende goederen betreft en tot opheffing van diverse bepalingen ter zake,* wetsontwerp Kamer 2012-13, No. 2463/001, p. 10-11.

98 See in particular Art. 70 Reform law.

99 Art. 422 Wetboek inkomstenbelastingen 1992.

100 Dirix 2013, p. 7.

101 Can be found in Art. 39 Reform Law.

requires registration. The registration, however, is not mandatory for the validity of the pledge itself, it is needed for third-party effect of the pledge.[102] Thus, the registered pledge here follows the French example.[103] According to the drafters, having only a right of pledge that requires dispossession for movables or 'control' for claims,[104] was no longer up to date. They looked at the legal systems around them and found discord in the approaches taken, though a general trend towards registered pledges that carry some form of publicity.[105] They followed suit in the reform and proposed a right of pledge that can be created with registration without having to dispossess. The register, in which the pledge is registered, would be semi-public, and open (via online-access) to at least the pledgor and pledgee. Other groups may have access too, but this is to be determined by Royal Decree later on.[106] Different from the current registration systems in Belgium, access to this register will be without the intervention from a registrar who keeps the register.[107] The aforementioned foreign influence is clearly noticeable here, as the register is heavily based on the Article 9 UCC notice-filing system and the DCFR notice-filing suggestion.[108]

This new registered pledge brought about the demise of the transfer of ownership for security purposes.[109] According to the drafters there would be no need to have both instruments exist at the same time, and with the introduction of the registered pledge, the transfer of ownership will be replaced/re-characterized as a right of pledge.[110] The re-characterized right of pledge, however, is not registered

102 The Explanatory Memorandum refers to the 'internal and external' effect of the pledge. *Wetsontwerp tot wijziging van het Burgerlijk Wetboek wat de zakelijke zekerheden op roerende goederen betreft en tot opheffing van diverse bepalingen ter zake,* wetsontwerp Kamer 2012-13, No. 2463/001, p. 15.

103 As also mentioned in the Explanatory Memorandum. *Wetsontwerp tot wijziging van het Burgerlijk Wetboek wat de zakelijke zekerheden op roerende goederen betreft en tot opheffing van diverse bepalingen ter zake,* wetsontwerp Kamer 2012-13, No. 2463/001, p. 15.

104 Which could be achieved by mere agreement under the old law: Art. 2074 BW and under the new law, if in this agreement it is stipulated that the pledgee has the power to inform the debtor of the right of pledge (Art. 60 Reform Law). The Reform law thus added a requirement, as was necessitated according to the drafters. *Wetsontwerp tot wijziging van het Burgerlijk Wetboek wat de zakelijke zekerheden op roerende goederen betreft en tot opheffing van diverse bepalingen ter zake,* wetsontwerp Kamer 2012-13, No. 2463/001, p. 28-29.

105 Introducing publicity by way of registration as opposed to only publicity via dispossession fits in with the fundamental standpoint of the Belgian legal tradition in which there is strong hesitation against security rights without publicity. Dirix 2013, p. 5.

106 Art. 34 Reform Law. The Royal Decree has not been issued at the time of writing, but is expected before December 2014.

107 *Wetsontwerp tot wijziging van het Burgerlijk Wetboek wat de zakelijke zekerheden op roerende goederen betreft en tot opheffing van diverse bepalingen ter zake,* wetsontwerp Kamer 2012-13, No. 2463/001, p. 22.

108 *Wetsontwerp tot wijziging van het Burgerlijk Wetboek wat de zakelijke zekerheden op roerende goederen betreft en tot opheffing van diverse bepalingen ter zake,* wetsontwerp Kamer 2012-13, No. 2463/001, p. 22-23.

109 The Explanatory Memorandum of the Reform was critical towards this device. *Wetsontwerp tot wijziging van het Burgerlijk Wetboek wat de zakelijke zekerheden op roerende goederen betreft en tot opheffing van diverse bepalingen ter zake,* wetsontwerp Kamer 2012-13, No. 2463/001, p. 8.

110 Art. 62 Reform Law.

nor has the object been dispossessed. Hence, it does not (yet) carry with it third party effect. Either registering the pledge after the re-characterization or dispossessing of the object in favour of the pledgee can resolve this situation.

The right of pledge under the new law extends to both current and future objects,[111] be it material or immaterial,[112] on a specified object or a generality of goods.[113] The reason for this wide scope was the idea that in principle, the debtor should be able to use any and all of his assets for security purposes.[114] The reform law provides for such a possibility. The new law also produced an option for everyone to create a pledge on the entirety of a business (*handelszaak*).[115] Under the old law such a pledge was available only to financial institutions and was limited to the business *without* its stock.[116] These limitations are foregone in the reform.

Taking the above into account, the right of pledge has become a very extensive security right under the new Belgian law.[117] In order to preserve the balance between security right holders the reservation of ownership has also been updated and extended in the reform.

4.3. *Reservation of Ownership*

In the new law, the reservation of ownership incorporated into to the Civil Code, which ends the discussions on its scope of application.[118] In the old law the reservation of ownership was deemed to be only effective (against third parties)[119] during insolvency proceedings, as the provisions on the reservation of ownership were in the insolvency code.[120] By limiting its scope, the Belgian Civil Law was lacking internal consistency,[121] which had to be remedied. Furthermore, it was

111 Art. 13 Reform Law states: 'The right of pledge can have future assets as its subject.' (*Het pand kan toekomstige goederen tot voorwerp hebben*).

112 Art. 12 Reform Law.

113 Art. 12 Reform law. With a generality one should think of a pledge on a business as a whole (*handelszaak*). Though the applicability is very general, whenever there are more specific regulations, these will take precedence. Such as the law on financial collateral arrangements, sale and lease back, intellectual property law and insolvency law. See also Dirix 2013, p. 11.

114 *Wetsontwerp tot wijziging van het Burgerlijk Wetboek wat de zakelijke zekerheden op roerende goederen betreft en tot opheffing van diverse bepalingen ter zake*, wetsontwerp Kamer 2012-13, No. 2463/001, p. 37. Commentary to Art. 11. Referencing to the modern day view as expressed in the UNCITRAL Legislative Guide, recommendation no. 17.

115 Art. 12 Reform Law.

116 See Dirix 2013, p. 17.

117 The problem of *Übersicherung*, the situation in which the security granted excessively exceeds the claim it is securing, has been dealt with for consumers, for whom the security cannot exceed 200% of the value of the claim. See Art. 12 Reform Law. There is no such provision for businesses.

118 Arts. 80 *et seq.* Reform Law.

119 Art. 20 Reform Law. See Dirix 2013, p. 39. *Wetsontwerp tot wijziging van het Burgerlijk Wetboek wat de zakelijke zekerheden op roerende goederen betreft en tot opheffing van diverse bepalingen ter zake*, wetsontwerp Kamer 2012-13, No. 2463/001, p. 19.

120 Art. 101 Insolvency Code.

121 It scattered the provisions of providing security for claims into the different codes, and the treatment of these similar instruments was not equal. See also the remarks in the Explanatory →

putting Belgium in an *isolated position within Europe* as it was the only legal system that approached the reservation of ownership in this manner.[122] With the reform, the reservation of ownership is placed firmly in the Civil Code and the third party effect has been extended to any situation of concurrence (not just insolvency) or any form of attachment, be it sequestration or garnishment order etc. (*beslag*). By doing so it is regaining coherency within Belgian private law and its place within Europe.

The functional approach equates the right of pledge with that of reservation of ownership. According to the draftsmen, the fact that these two security instruments are very different in their method does not mean they do not both fulfil the same function, specifically to secure a creditor's claim. Their treatment should therefore be similar as well.[123] From this viewpoint stems Article 70 of the Reform law, which refers to certain provisions of the pledge and applies these to the reservation of ownership.[124]

One of these provisions that are applicable to both the right of pledge and a reservation of ownership is the new Article 18[125] that deals with the pledge in the event of *specificatio*. It states:

> 'Unless otherwise agreed, the pledgor is entitled to processing of goods intended for processing (verwerking). Is a new good created by such authorized processing, then the pledge encumbers this new good, unless otherwise agreed. In the event of unauthorized processing, Articles 570 and following apply. Were goods of third parties used for the processing and the separation of these goods is impossible or economically unwarranted, then the pledge encumbrances the newly created good if the good is principal (het voornaamste) within the meaning of Article 567 or, if need be, this good has the highest value. In that case, the third has a claim on the pledgee for enrichment without cause.'[126]

The right of pledge and the reservation of ownership are subrogated into the newly created goods in the event of *specificatio*, an extended pledge/reservation of ownership if you will.[127] In particular for suppliers, this provision is important, as most suppliers of base materials lose their security in the event of *specificatio* should such

Memorandum, *Wetsontwerp tot wijziging van het Burgerlijk Wetboek wat de zakelijke zekerheden op roerende goederen betreft en tot opheffing van diverse bepalingen ter zake*, wetsontwerp Kamer 2012-13, No. 2463/001, p. 30-31.

122 Dirix 2013, p. 39.

123 Dirix 2013, p. 9.

124 See, for instance, Art. 70 Reform Law.

125 Art. 23 Reform Law.

126 Translation by the authors. Original: *Behoudens anders overeengekomen, is de pandgever gerechtigd tot verwerking van goederen die bestemd zijn voor verwerking. Ontstaat door die toegestane verwerking een nieuw goed, dan bezwaart het pandrecht dit nieuw tot stand gekomen goed, behoudens anders overeengekomen. In geval van niet toegestane verwerking zijn de artikelen 570 en volgende van toepassing. Werden voor de verwerking goederen van derden aangewend en is de afscheiding van deze goederen onmogelijk of economisch niet verantwoord, dan bezwaart het pandrecht het nieuw totstandgekomen goed indien dit goed het voornaamste is in de zin van artikel 567 of, desgevallend, indien dit goed de grootste waarde heeft. In dat geval heeft de derde op de pandhouder een vordering wegens verrijking zonder oorzaak.*

127 Extensive reading of subrogation of property rights in Belgium, see Sagaert 2003.

a provision be missing. Furthermore, the rights of the supplier who retained ownership are also subrogated into the proceeds of the sale to sub-purchasers.[128]

The functional approach has its limitations. One of the differences with the right of pledge is that the reservation of ownership need not be registered to have third party effect. The drafters found that registration is not required in any other Member State and consequently did not favour its introduction in Belgian law.[129] Moreover, the rather high burden it would place on smaller enterprises to register this right for each delivery was not deemed desirable.[130]

4.4. *The Balance of Interest in Belgian Law*

The foregoing description of the Belgian reform of security interest, in particular in relation to movables, shows a search for balance between creditor and debtor and the creditors amongst themselves. The need for a proper balance was highlighted in the draft law, its Explanatory Memorandum,[131] and the commentary on the draft law by the consumer authority (*Raad voor het Verbruik*).[132]

The Explanatory Memorandum stated that it

> '[w]ould be a misconception to think that a modern and effective system of security rights solely serves the interests of the credit facilitators (in particular the banks). The lack of credit available after the recent credit crisis shows the detrimental consequences of a bad functioning credit system for our economy and employment rate. Moreover, a modern and effective credit system is not only there to serve the interests of the creditors, but first and foremost to serve the interest of the numerous small and medium size enterprises and of the families that are dependent on external financing. Of course one could imagine a system of complete equality of creditors and credit facilitation without property security. The question however is, against what cost would such credit facilitation take place.'[133]

128 Dirix 2013, p. 40.

129 See also Inge Faes en Yoeri Vasterssavendts, *Verslag namens de commissie voor de Justitie*. Ps, Senaat, 5-1992/4, Paragraph C. *Wetsontwerp tot wijziging van het Burgerlijk Wetboek wat de zakelijke zekerheden op roerende goederen betreft en tot opheffing van diverse bepalingen ter zake*, wetsontwerp Kamer 2012-13, No. 2463/001, p. 30. This is a deviation from the suggestions in the UCC and DCFR where such publicity is mandated.

130 Dirix 2013, p. 38-39.

131 *Wetsontwerp tot wijziging van het Burgerlijk Wetboek wat de zakelijke zekerheden op roerende goederen betreft en tot opheffing van diverse bepalingen ter zake*, wetsontwerp Kamer 2012-13, No. 2463/001.

132 Raad voor het Verbruik. *Advies Over een voorontwerp van wet tot wijziging van het Burgerlijk Wetboek wat de zakelijke zekerheden op roerende goederen betreft*, RvV-450, 2012, p. 4.

133 *Wetsontwerp tot wijziging van het Burgerlijk Wetboek wat de zakelijke zekerheden op roerende goederen betreft en tot opheffing van diverse bepalingen ter zake*, wetsontwerp Kamer 2012-13, No. 2463/001. p. 6-7. Translation by the Authors. In relation to the *paritas creditorum* principle, which Belgian law adheres to, such adherence is more theoretical than practical. The tremendous number of exceptions by virtue of statutory privileges, security rights and deviation by way of contract has made the *paritas creditorum* largely a theoretical principle rather than one that has any practical effect. *Wetsontwerp tot wijziging van het Burgerlijk Wetboek wat de zakelijke* →

The reform opted for a functional approach of security rights, which treats the rights of pledge and the reservation of ownership as equal. These rights are traditionally the most important instruments[134] utilized by banks and suppliers respectively to secure the repayment of their credit granted to the debtor, i.e. the undertaking. By adhering to this functional approach, the trade creditors (suppliers) and the banks have been made to stand on a somewhat equal footing. Furthermore, the risk that the suppliers would lose their security by way of *specificiatio* has been limited, as their rights would subrogate into the newly formed good. The very extensive right of pledge is therefore counterbalanced. The functional method applied in the reform law means that a strong right of pledge, also means a strong reservation of ownership. A balance between secured creditors is thereby found.

5. Harmonization of Security Rights; Article 9 UCC and Book IX DCFR

5.1. *The Functional Approach*

There are and have been a number of initiatives to come to harmonization of security rights. A successful method has been to approach the concept of security rights only functionally. That is to say, any arrangement that serves to give security to a creditor - in whatever shape or form - is treated as a security rights for the purposes of the application of the harmonized rules. The EBRD Model Law on Secured Transactions and the Cape Town Convention employ such a method. Book 9 of the DCFR, though originally intended as an integral part of a sort of European Civil Code, also approaches the concept of security rights in a functional way: the term can encompass retention of ownership and liens. All of the abovementioned treaties and model laws were heavily influenced by the most successful of all: Article 9 UCC, which is the model we shall focus on first.

5.2. *Article 9 UCC*

§ 9-109 (a) UCC (2010) gives the scope of the article: '(…) this article applies to (…) a transaction regardless of its form, that creates a security interest in personal property or fixtures by contract (…).' The article applies to virtually every form of security in property. Article 9 distinguishes between two phases in the creation of an Article 9 security interest; *attachment* and *perfection*. A security interest attaches to the collateral when it becomes enforceable against the debtor (§ 9-203). The interest becomes enforceable if value (a loan) has been given, if the debtor was capable of vesting the security, and if there is a valid agreement that specifies the collateral and/or the collateral is in the possession of the creditor. Of course, Article 9 also allows for the creation of security interest in future assets (§ 9-204 (a)). The collateral

zekerheden op roerende goederen betreft en tot opheffing van diverse bepalingen ter zake, wetsontwerp Kamer 2012-13, No. 2463/001, p. 12 and 18.

134 Where the objects concerned are future goods, such as movables and claims.

must, however, be 'reasonably identified' in the agreement. § 9-108 (c) makes it clear that it is not enough to include a generic description such as 'all the debtor's assets'.

For the security interest to be enforceable *erga omnes* it must be perfected. Perfection can take place by transferring possession or, in some case, upon attachment (§ 9-309, 312-314). More importantly, however, it takes place by filing a so-called financing statement (§ 9-310-312) at a filing office. Such a filing notice must at least contain the names of the creditor and the debtor and a description of the collateral. The filing notice is generally indexed according to the name of the debtor (§ 9-519 (c)). All subsequent documents related to the security interest must also be filed on the name of the debtor. The idea is that creditors can do a search at the filing office, which may reveal other security interests. The creditor can then ask his debtor to provide information on those specific security interests, but is also able to request information from the person who is entitled to that security (§ 9-210).[135]

The moment of perfection establishes the rank of the creditor. A perfected security interest ranks higher than an unperfected security interest even if the perfected interest is from a later date. Certain exceptions to this rule are provided for, the most important of which, for the purposes of this article, is the interest of the supplier of goods or software. Pursuant to § 9-324, the so-called purchase money security interest has priority over all other security interest, provided it is perfected. This priority also extends to the proceeds of the collateral. § 9-102 (64) defines 'proceeds' as, *inter alia*, 'whatever is acquired upon the sale, lease, license, exchange, or other disposition of collateral'. Moreover, if the collateral becomes commingled goods, a security interest attaches to the product or mass. If that security interest is perfected before the collateral becomes commingled it will be a perfected security interest afterwards as well. If therefore a supplier supplies goods which are subsequently processed, the supplier will retain his priority with regards to the processed goods, as long as it remains traceable.

6. Book IX DCFR

Book IX makes an explicit distinction between security rights and retention of ownership devices. Pursuant to Article 1:102 (1), '[a] security right in a movable asset is any limited proprietary right in the asset which entitles the secured creditor to preferential satisfaction of the secured right from the encumbered asset'. A retention of ownership devices is any arrangement in which 'ownership is retained by the owner of supplied assets in order to secure a right to performance of an obligation (art. 1:103 (1))'.

Like Article 9 UCC, book IX distinguishes between the creation of a security right and its effectiveness against third parties. Such effectiveness can be obtained by either registration of the security right or retention of ownership, or by possession of, or control over the asset by the creditor (Art. 3:102). Book IX provides for an electronic European register of proprietary security, which would function parallel to the national registration systems. Like Article 9 UCC, book IX only requires a

135 Struycken 2009.

notice filing, indexed on the name of the debtor, which indicates that there is a security right in relation to certain assets. For more information on the security right itself, third parties must request information about the extent of the security right from the creditor.

Again, the moment of perfection determines the rank of the creditors. Pursuant to Article 4:101, an acquisition finance device, such as retention of ownership, takes priority over any other security right or limited proprietary right created by the security provider. If encumbered materials are used for the production of new goods, the security right may be extended by party agreement to the products (Art. 2:307 jo. 4:103). The drafters of Book IX have chosen not to extend the security right to cover also a right of payment of the sales price of the asset, though the security right does extend to rights to payment due to a defect in, damage to, or loss of the originally encumbered asset (Art. 2:306 (1) jo. 4:104). In this respect, suppliers have a less strong position as they would have under, for instance, current German law or Article 9 UCC.

6.1. *Key Elements of Harmonization of Security Rights*

Article 9 UCC is an example of bottom-up harmonization. It is a model law that the different states of the US were able to adopt wholesale or in an amended version, as they saw fit. Book IX of the DCFR, on the other hand, is part of a civil code that is supposed to be a unitary set of rules. Book IX is, however, not a substantive body of law that distinguishes between different security rights and the rules applicable to those rights. Like Article 9 UCC, it is much more a model law than an integral part of a civil code. Book IX could, therefore, serve a similar function as Article 9 UCC.

Both Article 9 UCC and book IX have in common that they approach security interests in a functional way. They provide for a common conceptual basis for the creation and perfection of secured transactions, the registration of such transactions and the rules on priority of different security interests. In this way they provide a relatively cheap, yet effective, method of law reform for the different jurisdictions. These can simply sign up to the model law, but adapt it in any way they see fit.

Both model laws provide for a security right the priority of which is determined on the basis of the moment of its perfection. The bank or financier that finances an undertaking would in most instances be the creditor with the highest ranking. Both also provide for a type of 'superpriority' for purchase money security interest, though book IX DCFR limits this superpriority in an important way; it does not extend to claims on sub-buyers of the assets. In practice, this would make a big difference with respect to the amount of collateral a supplier will have recourse to, as the bank will then typically have the highest ranking security right on such claims. Finally, both model laws also provide for a public registry of security interests. Such a registry is necessary not only to determine the priority of the security interest but also to enable a financier to determine relatively quickly what kind of security interest are already vested in the assets of a debtor, especially if such a debtor is from another state or Member State than the state where the financier is situated.

7. Conclusion

Possibly the most extensive security right for financiers is the Dutch silent pledge. It can be vested on basically all current and future assets of an undertaking and it does not have much competition from other creditors of an undertaking such as suppliers. In comparison to suppliers elsewhere, the Dutch supplier is rather handicapped in his options to secure his claim for the payment of the supplied goods. The supplier can only reserve ownership of the supplied goods as long as they remain identifiable and the buyer does not process them into new goods or sells them to sub-purchasers. The supplier cannot be granted a silent pledge on the supplied goods that would outrank the silent pledge of the financiers. Unless the financiers give permission for such a change in rank, which is unlikely.

The Dutch silent pledge resembles the 'old' floating charge in English law. The judiciary and legislator, however, deemed this old floating charge to be too extensive and therefore heavily curtailed it to its current form, the lowest ranking security right. The decline of the floating charge caused an increase in the use of the fixed charge. This use of fixed charges, however, took a nose-dive after the ruling in *Spectrum Plus*, re-characterizing the common use of the fixed charge on book debts as a floating one. Currently, a combination of fixed and floating charges is commonly used to secure a financiers claim for repayment. The supplier's recourse to retention of title appears stronger than the Dutch reservation of ownership. The supplier may have recourse to the proceeds of the sale of the supplied goods to sub-purchasers. However, this right is vulnerable to characterization as a floating charge, which, if registered, ranks below that of the financier. Where the supplied goods are processed, the supplier may: retain title, have the goods retransferred to them, or obtain a new interest in the processed goods. Again, the supplier runs the risk of ranking below the financier.

The new Belgian registered pledge is equally as extensive as the Dutch silent pledge. It extends to current and future goods, can be on the entire undertaking and its assets, and has third party effect upon registration. Contrary to the Dutch pledgee, the Belgian pledgee faces stronger competition from the suppliers. A supplier may reserve the ownership of the goods and even retains this security in the event of processing of the goods or sale to a sub-purchaser. The position of the supplier therefore is stronger than in England and the Netherlands.

In many respects, the Belgian policy choices have been the same as those of the drafters of Article 9 UCC. Certainly the position of the financier and supplier are the same. Book IX DCFR is only different, in that it limits the reservation of ownership of the supplier to the goods supplied, or the newly created goods. It does not extend the right to the proceeds of sale of the supplied goods to sub-purchasers.

On analysis, it appears that all jurisdictions, including the model laws, enable the financier to (effectively) take a general security on the assets of the undertaking. Moreover, they also all allow suppliers to take a 'super priority', at least on the supplied goods. The biggest discrepancy among the jurisdiction appears to in relation to the extent of the security taken by the supplier. Does it extent to newly formed goods and even to proceeds of the sale to sub-purchasers? Belgian law and its inspiration Article 9 UCC answer both questions in the affirmative. The Dutch answer is a resounding 'no' to both. English law is ambivalent and can go both ways.

It may be relatively easy to come to an agreement on the extent of a harmonized security right for financiers. The policy choices that are made by the various legislators and drafters are roughly the same. A functional approach, on the basis of a model law, would provide a relatively cheap method of harmonization. The Member States should then implement the model law, containing the harmonized security right, which is in conformity with their national policy choices. This can be done without upsetting their national system of 'superpriorities', which they will be able to retain. Should they want to, the Member States might opt to adapt their national systems to the choices made in the model law with regards to 'superpriorities' as well. Such a step-by-step process of harmonization could result in '*pareto* improvements'; the cost of harmonization is low, certain efficiency gains may be had, while the expectations of everyone involved remain the same.

The model law-approach requires a designer who can approach the topic from a transnational or supranational angle. This designer can be the EU, but it may also be an entity like the European Law Institute, or UNCITRAL. The success of the model law will, in the end, depends on the number of Member States actually adopting it. But this reflects one of the strengths of the model law-approach, unlike a top-down approach, it allows for the harmonization of the law in an incremental way.

Bibliography

Addy 2010
Addy, C., 'Fixed and Floating Charges over Book Debts – the Implications of the House of Lords' Decision in Re Spectrum Plus Limited [2005] UKHL 41, Part I', *International Corporate Rescue*, 2010, p. 11-18.

Beale et al. 2012
Beale, H. *et al.*, *The Law of Security and Title-Based Financing*, Oxford: Oxford University Press 2012.

Bridge 2004
Bridge, M., 'The English Law of Security: Creditor-Friendly but Unreformed', in: E.M. Kieninger *et al.* (eds.), *Security Rights in Movable Property in European Private Law*, Cambridge: Cambridge University Press 2004, p. 81-97.

Calnan 2010
Calnan, R., *Proprietary Rights and Insolvency*, Oxford: Oxford University Press 2010.

Dirix 2013
Dirix, E., *De Hervorming van de Roerende Zakelijke Zekerheden*, Mechelen: Kluwer 2013.

Fikkers 1998
Fikkers, H.A.G., 'Varkens zonder verlengd eigendomsvoorbehoud', 6321 *Weekblad voor Privaatrecht, Notariaat en Registratie*, 1998, p. 465-469.

Gullifer 2009
Gullifer, L., 'The Reforms of the Enterprise Act 2002 and the Floating Charge as a Security Device', in: W.-G. Ringe, L. Gullifer & Ph. Théry (eds.), *Current Issues in European Financial and Insolvency Law. Perspectives from France and the UK*, Oxford: Hart Publishing 2009, p. 17-44.

Hogan & Schwartz 1985
Hogan, J.C. & Schwartz, M.D., 'A Translation of Bacon's Maxims of the Common Law', 77 *Law Library Journal*, 1985, p. 707-717.

Jansen 2012
Jansen, J.E., 'Het eigendomsvoorbehoud en artikel 3:229 BW', *Tijdschrift voor Insolventierecht*, 2012, p. 134-139.

Janssen 2006
Janssen, J.F.M., 'De levering bij voorbaat van toekomstige goederen', 6685 *Weekblad voor Privaatrecht, Notariaat en Registratie*, 2006, p. 745-755.

Kaptein 2012
Kaptein, F.J.L., 'Een failliet pandrecht', *Nederlands Tijdschrift voor Burgerlijk Recht*, 2012, p. 214-220.

Kieninger et al. 2004
Kieninger, E-M. *et al.* (eds.), *Security Rights in Movable Property in European Private Law*, Cambridge: Cambridge University Press 2004.

Milo 2010
Milo, J.M., 'Floating Charge in Civiele Traditie. Het Wetboek Napoleon Ingerigt Voor Het Koningrijk Holland Als Venster Op Verleden En Heden van Generale Zakelijke Zekerheidsrechten', in: J.H.A. Lokin, J.M. Milo & C.H. van Rhee (eds.), *Tweehonderd jaren codificatie van het privaatrecht in Nederland*, Groningen: Chimaira 2010, p. 73-96.

Mokal 2005
Mokal, R.J., *Corporate Insolvency Law: Theory and Application*, Oxford: Oxford University Press 2005.

Orval 2012
Orval, M.J.H., 'Rechtsgeldigheid van de 'verzamelpandakte'-constructie', *Bedrijfsjuridische berichten*, 2012, p. 100-104.

Pennington 1960
Pennington, R.R., 'The Genesis of the Floating Charge', 23 *The Modern Law Review*, p. 630-646.

Sagaert 2003
Sagaert, V., *Zakelijke Subrogatie*, Antwerpen: Intersentia 2003.

Spath 2012
Spath, J.B., 'Verlengd eigendomsvoorbehoud in strijd met artikel 3:84 lid 3 BW?', *Nederlands Tijdschrift voor Burgerlijk Recht*, 2012, p. 329-334.

Struycken 2009
Struycken, T.H.D., 'Zekerheidsrechten en registratie', in: *Zekerhedenrecht in Ontwikkeling. Preadvies KNB 2009*, Den Haag: SDU Uitgevers 2009, p. 115-186.

Struycken 2010
Struycken, T.H.D., 'Dagelijkse bulkverpanding door middel van een verzamelpandakte', in: N.E.D. Faber (ed.), *Bancaire Zekerheid. Liber Amicorum mr. J.H.S.G.K. Timmermans*, Deventer: Kluwer 2010, p. 305-328.

Van Buchem & De Man 2012
Van Buchem, F. & De Man, B., 'De verpanding van absoluut toekomstige vorderingen', 2 *Onderneming en Financiering*, 2012, p. 5-15.

Van den Heuvel 2004
Van den Heuvel, N.W.M, *Zekerheid en Voorrang*, Den Haag: Boom Juridische uitgevers 2004.

Van Erp 2006
Van Erp, S., *European and National Property Law: Osmosis or Growing Antagonism?*, Groningen: Europa Law Publishing 2006.

Van Maanen 1998
Van Maanen, G.E., 'Varkens met verlengd eigendomsvoorbehoud', 6309 *Weekblad voor Privaatrecht, Notariaat en Registratie*, 1998, p. 237-238.

Verheul 2014
Verheul, E.F., 'De wedloop tussen leverancierskrediet en geldkrediet', *Nederlands Tijdschrift voor Burgerlijk Recht*, 2014, p. 136-144.

Verstijlen 2011
Verstijlen, F.M.J., 'Het pandrecht op de schop', *Nederlands Tijdschrift voor Burgerlijk Recht*, 2011, p. 272-275.

Verstijlen 2013
Verstijlen, F.M.J., 'Iedereen pandhouder: door de 'verzamelpandakte' naar paritas creditorum', 6983 *Weekblad voor Privaatrecht, Notariaat en Registratie*, 2013, p. 563-564.

Veder 2012
Veder, P.M., 'Verpanding made easy: verpanding van vorderingen door middel van een verzamelpandakte', *Ars Aequi*, 2012, p. 455-460.

Wibier 2012
Wibier, R.M., 'Twintig jaar stil pandrecht op vorderingen in Nedeland', 6931 *Weekblad voor Privaatrecht, Notariaat en Registratie*, 2012, p. 381-388.

Worthington 2006
Worthington, S., 'Floating Charges: Use and Abuse of Doctrinal Analysis', in: J. Getzler & J. Payne (eds.), *Company Charges: Spectrum and Beyond*, Oxford: Oxford University Press 2006, p. 25-50.

Worthington 2010
Worthington S, 'An "Unsatisfactory Area of the Law" – Fixed and Floating Charges Yet Again', *International Corporate Rescue*, 2010, p. 1-10.

Zwalve 2006
Zwalve W.J., 'Too Convenient a Form of Security to Be Lightly Abolished', *Weekblad voor Privaatrecht, Notariaat en Registratie*, 2006, p. 349-358.

Caroline Cauffman
Niels Philipsen

WHO DOES WHAT IN COMPETITION LAW: HARMONIZING THE RULES ON DAMAGES FOR INFRINGEMENTS OF THE EU COMPETITION RULES?

1. Introduction

In the previous century, the enforcement of EU competition law was mainly a matter left to the European Commission. This was partly due to the unfamiliarity of national lawyers, national courts and (where they existed) national competition authorities with EU competition law. To a large extent it was also due to the fact that the first regulation implementing the provisions of the Treaty of Rome on competition law (Regulation 17/62) reserved to the Commission the exclusive competence to decide whether an agreement or decision satisfied the requirements of Article 85(3) of the Treaty so that it was not prohibited under Article 85(1) of the Treaty. In order to obtain an exemption under Article 85(3) of the Treaty, the agreement or decision in question had to be notified to the Commission. By the end of the previous century the Commission realized that, given the ever extending European Union, it was no longer capable of dealing with all the requests for exemptions and of ensuring compliance with the EU competition rules throughout the EU. It therefore proposed the adoption of a new implementation regulation, abolishing the notification system and making Article 85(3), which had in the meantime become Article 81(3) of the Treaty, directly applicable by national courts and national competition authorities (NCAs). This implied that national courts and NCAs would need to play a larger role in the enforcement of the EU competition rules. The new Regulation (No. 1/2003) entered into force on 1 May 2004. Against this background, the Commission started to show a special interest in the so-called private enforcement of EU competition law, i.e. the application of EU competition rules in disputes between private parties before national courts. Especially national actions for damages were at the centre of the Commission's interests. The Commission started to actively promote such actions and it investigated the need for harmonizing the relevant national rules on damages actions, *inter alia*, by having studies carried out on the state of play regarding such damages actions in the EU Member States and by publishing green and white papers on the need for harmonization.

In the meantime, the Court of Justice had recognized in *Courage* the right of any individual to claim damages caused by an infringement of the competition rules.[1] This right to damages seems to be a matter of EU law itself. However, in the absence of Union rules governing the matter, the Courts having jurisdiction and the detailed procedural rules governing actions for safeguarding rights which individuals derive directly from Union law, are to be determined by the national legal systems, provided that such rules are not less favourable than those governing similar domestic actions (principle of equivalence) and that they do not render practically impossible or excessively difficult the exercise of rights conferred by Union law (principle of effectiveness).

In later case law, the Court gave further indications about the national rules which would and those which would not satisfy the requirements of the principle of effectiveness.[2] In two of those cases, the Court of Justice adopted a position on access to documents held by (national) competition authorities by alleged victims of an infringement of the antitrust rules that ran counter to the Commission's practices.[3] This seems to have triggered the submission of the proposal for a Directive on antitrust damages actions, on which after amendments, an agreement has been reached by the European Parliament and the Council.[4] While this Directive is aimed at the compensation of a specific type of damages and it aims to improve the interaction between public and private enforcement (which is a competition law specific aim), it touches upon one of the most typical private law actions: the action for damages for an infringement of a statutory duty. Should this harmonization initiative be applauded? That is precisely the central question of this chapter. To answer it, we will start by describing the aims and content of the Directive (section 2). This will be followed by an evaluation of the Directive in section 3, whereby we will not only address the question whether harmonization as such is desirable (3.1), but also the question to what extent other aims of the Directive are likely to be achieved (3.2 and 3.3). Section 4 concludes.

This chapter hence provides some insights to the 'Who Does What' question in relation to competition law, as it, *inter alia*, discusses the allocation of competences between national and European actors in the enforcement of competition law, as well as the interaction between public and private enforcement. Rather than looking at the whole area of competition law, however, we have chosen to focus on one

1 Case C-453/99, *Courage* v *Crehan* [2001] ECR I-6297.

2 Joined cases C-295/04 to C-298/04, *Vincenzo Manfredi* v *Lloyd Adriatico Assicurazioni SpA* (C-295/04), *Antonio Cannito* v *Fondiaria Sai SpA* (C-296/04) and *Nicolò Tricarico* (C-297/04) and *Pasqualina Murgolo* (C-298/04) v *Assitalia SpA* [2006] ECR I-06619; Case C-360/09, *Pfleiderer AG* v *Bundeskartellamt*, [2011] ECR I-5161; Case C-536/11, *Bundeswettbewerbsbehörde* v *Donau Chemie AG et al.*, <www.eurlex.eu>, Nos. 34 *et seq.* and 51; Case C-557/12, *Kone AG, Otis GmbH, Schindler Aufzüge und Fahrtreppen GmbH, Schindler Liegenschaftsverwaltung GmbH, ThyssenKrupp Aufzüge GmbH* v *ÖBB-Infrastruktur AG*, <www.eurlex.eu>, Nos. 33 *et seq.*

3 Case C-360/09, *Pfleiderer AG* v *Bundeskartellamt*, [2011] ECR I-5161; Case C–536/11, *Bundeswettbewerbsbehörde* v *Donau Chemie AG et al.*, <www.eurlex.eu>.

4 Directive 2014/104/EU of the European Parliament and of the Council of 26 November 2014 on certain rules governing actions for damages under national law for infringements of the competition law provisions of the Member States and of the European Union Text with EEA relevance, OJ L 349, 5 December 2014, 1.

specific and recent legal document, being the Directive on antitrust damages actions.

2. Aims and Content of the Directive

2.1. *Aims of the Directive*

According to Recitals 6 and 9 of the Directive the main aims of the Directive on antitrust damages actions are the following:

- to improve the interaction between public and private enforcement of the competition rules;
- to ensure a more level playing field for undertakings operating on the internal market;
- to improve the conditions for consumers to exercise the rights they derive from the internal market;
- to increase legal certainty;
- to reduce the differences between the Member States as to the national rules governing actions for damages for infringements of Union competition law and, when applied in parallel to the latter, national competition law. An approximation of these rules would also help to prevent the increase of differences between the Member States' rules governing actions for damages in competition cases.

In section 3 we will evaluate the Directive in the light of these aims, focusing on the aims that are closest to the topic of this book. We will therefore focus in particular on the need to create a level playing field, by applying the economics of federalism (3.1), as well as on the aim of improving the interaction between public and private enforcement (3.3). We also provide a more detailed assessment of the aim to increase the possibilities for victims of antitrust infringements to obtain compensation (3.2). The aim to increase legal certainty will not be addressed in detail, but will be referred to in section 3.1, as it can be related to the transaction costs argument discussed there.[5] The aim of reducing differences between EU Member States can be assumed to be reached if the Directive is correctly implemented by the Member States. We will not further discuss this specific aim in this chapter.

2.2. *Content of the Directive*

The Directive consists of 8 chapters: (i) Subject matter, scope and definitions, (ii) Disclosure of evidence, (iii) Effect of national decisions, limitation periods, joint and several liability, (iv) The passing-on of overcharges, (v) Quantification of harm, (vi)

5 See also Visscher 2010, p. 15, stating that 'the transaction cost argument is closely related to the traditional legal argument of reducing legal uncertainty and reducing costs of international transactions, although that traditional legal argument is often set in the context of hindering cross-border trade'.

Consensual dispute resolution and (vii) Final provisions. They will be discussed in turn below.

2.2.1. Scope and Definitions

In order to achieve the above mentioned aims, the Directive reaffirms in its first chapter that 'any natural or legal person who has suffered harm caused by an infringement of competition law is able to claim and to obtain full compensation for that harm' (Art. 3(1). See also Art. 1(1)).

The Directive specifies that full compensation means that a person who has suffered harm shall be put in the position in which he would have been had the infringement not been committed. Full compensation shall therefore cover the right to compensation for actual loss and for loss of profit, plus payment of interest (Art. 3(2)). The Directive further provides that full compensation shall not lead to overcompensation, whether by means of punitive, multiple or other types of damages (Art. 1(3)). This provision seems to restrict the rights of claimants compared to the status quo ante. Indeed in *Manfredi*, the Court of Justice held that there was no EU requirement to award extra-compensatory damages, but that 'where special forms of damages can be awarded under national competition law, they must also be available if the claims concerned are based on an infringement of Community competition law'. Where national law provided for extra-compensatory damages in cases of infringements of national competition law, the principle of equivalence thus required them to be also available in cases of infringements of EU competition law. After the entry into force of the Directive on antitrust damages, however, the award of extra-compensatory damages seems to be irreconcilable with this Article 3(3).

In general, however, the Directive confirms the application of the principles of equivalence (national rules and procedures relating to actions for damages resulting from infringements of Article 101 or 102 TFEU shall not be less favourable to the alleged injured parties than those governing similar actions for damages resulting from infringements of national law) and effectiveness (national rules and procedures may not render practically impossible or excessively difficult the exercise of the Union right to full compensation for harm caused by an infringement of competition law) (Art. 4).

The list of definitions in Article 2 contains 24 entries which cannot all be repeated here. It can be noted that the concept 'infringement of competition law' only refers to an infringement of Articles 101 or 102 TFEU or of national competition law[6] and that 'national competition law' refers to the provisions of national law that predominantly pursue the same objective as Articles 101 and 102 TFEU and that are applied to the same case and in parallel to Union competition law pursuant to Article 3(1) of Regulation (EC) No. 1/2003. It does not include national laws which impose criminal penalties on natural persons, except to the extent that such penalties are the means whereby competition rules applying to undertakings are enforced.[7]

6 Art. 2(1) Directive.
7 Art. 2(3) Directive.

Surprisingly, the Chapter on the scope of the Directive does not explicitly mention that it applies to actions for damages for infringements of EU competition and insofar as they are applied in parallel with the rules of EU competition law, the rules of national competition law. This is to be derived from the definitions of 'competition law' and 'national competition law' read against the background of recital 10.

2.2.2. Disclosure of Evidence

The rules on disclosure of evidence are of central importance, since the right to disclosure of evidence, and especially the limits to this right, was one of the main concerns of the Commission when drafting the proposal for the Directive (cf. *supra*, Introduction (1) and *infra*, Improving the interaction between public and private enforcement of the competition rules (3.3)).

The drafters of the Directive recognize that litigation on antitrust damages is characterized by an information asymmetry to the detriment of the claimant. The Directive therefore provides that upon request of a claimant, national courts must be able to order the defendant or a third party to disclose relevant evidence which lies in their control. In order to ensure equality of arms,[8] national courts shall also be able to order the claimant or third party to disclose evidence upon the request of the defendant (Art. 5(1)).[9]

In order to prevent 'fishing expeditions', the claimant's request will, however, only be taken into account where it presents 'a reasoned justification containing reasonably available facts and evidence sufficient to support the plausibility of its claim for damages' (Art. 5(1)). In the same vein it is provided that disclosure may be ordered of 'specified items of evidence or relevant categories of evidence circumscribed as precisely and as narrowly as possible on the basis of reasonably available facts in the reasoned justification' (Art. 5(2)). Furthermore, national courts must limit disclosure of evidence to that which is proportionate, taking into account the legitimate interests of all parties and third parties concerned (Art. 5(3)). The interest of undertakings to avoid damages actions following an infringement of the competition rules does not constitute an interest that warrants protection (Art. 5(5)). Subject to the proportionality requirement, disclosure of confidential information may be ordered where national courts consider it relevant for the action for damages. However, in such cases, they need to have at their disposal effective measures to protect the confidential information (Art. 5(4)). The applicable legal professional privilege under Union or national law must be respected (Art. 5(6)). Undertakings from which disclosure is sought have the right to be heard before disclosure is ordered (Art. 5(7)). Without prejudice to paragraphs 4 and 7 and Article 6, Member States may maintain or introduce rules leading to wider disclosure of evidence.

8 See recital 14.

9 This provision does not affect the rights and obligations of national courts under Regulation (EC) No. 1206/2001 of 28 May 2001 on cooperation between the courts of the Member States in the taking of evidence in civil or commercial matters, OJ L 174, 27 June 2001, p. 1.

When assessing the proportionality of disclosure of evidence included in the file of a competition authority, additional rules apply. In this case national courts must take special care and in particular they need to consider the need to safeguard the effectiveness of the public enforcement of competition law (Art. 6(4)). Also, a competition authority acting on its own initiative may submit observations on the proportionality of a disclosure request to the national court before which a disclosure order is sought (Art. 6(11)). It must be noted, however, that the rules of Article 6 do not affect the rules and practices on public access to documents under the Transparency Regulation. Neither do they affect the rules and practices under Union or national law on the protection of internal documents of competition authorities and of correspondence between competition authorities (Arts. 6(2) and (3)).

Certain categories of evidence are subject to even more special rules. With regard to a first category of evidence disclosure may only be ordered only after a competition authority has closed its proceedings. This category includes: (i) information that was prepared by a natural or legal person specifically for the proceedings of a competition authority; (ii) information that the competition authority has drawn up and sent to the parties in the course of its proceedings; and (iii) settlement submissions that have been withdrawn (Art. 6(5)). Evidence falling into this category and which is obtained by a natural or legal person solely through access to the file of a competition authority is either deemed to be inadmissible in actions for damages or otherwise protected under the applicable national rules to ensure full effect of the limits on the use of evidence pursuant to Article 6(5) until that competition authority has closed its proceedings by adopting a decision or otherwise (Art. 7(2)).

With regard to a second category of evidence, national courts cannot at any time order disclosure from a party or a third party. This category includes leniency statements and settlement submissions (Art. 6(6)). Evidence falling into this category and which is obtained by a natural or legal person solely through access to the file of a competition authority is either deemed inadmissible in actions for damages or otherwise protected under the applicable national rules to ensure full effect of the limits on the use of evidence pursuant to Article 6(6) (Art. 7(1)).

Evidence which is obtained by a natural or legal person solely through access to the file of a competition authority and which does not fall into either of the two just mentioned categories, can only be used in an action for damages by that person or by the natural or legal person that succeeded in his rights, including the person that acquired his claim (Art. 7(3)). This rule is intended to prevent the trading of such evidence. It does not, however, prevent a national court from ordering the disclosure of that evidence under the conditions provided for in the Directive (Recital 32).

Where a party or a third party is unable to or cannot reasonably provide the evidence requested, national courts must be able to order disclosure of the evidence from the competition authority. The same limitations on disclosure apply as where disclosure is requested from a party or a third party (Art. 6(10)).

Article 8 of the Directive provides that Member States shall ensure that national courts are able effectively to impose penalties on parties, third parties and their legal representatives in the event of (i) failure or refusal to comply with any national court's disclosure order; (ii) the destruction of relevant evidence; (iii) failure or refusal to comply with the obligations imposed by a national court order protecting confidential information; or (iv) breach of limits on the use of evidence.

The penalties shall be effective, proportionate and dissuasive and shall include, insofar as the behaviour of a party to damages action proceedings is concerned, the possibility to draw adverse inferences, such as presuming the relevant issue to be proven or dismissing claims and defences in whole or in part, and the possibility to order the payment of costs (Art. 8(2)).

2.2.3. Effect of National Decisions, Limitation Periods, Joint and Several Liability

Final decisions of the public enforcement authorities of the own Member State finding an infringement of competition law are binding on the national courts of that Member State deciding on actions for damages caused by that infringement. Final decisions of the public enforcement authorities of other Member States can, in accordance with the respective national laws, be presented before national courts as at least *prima facie* evidence that an infringement of competition law has occurred and, as appropriate, may be assessed along with any other material brought by the parties (Art. 9).

Limitation periods shall not begin to run before the infringement has ceased and the claimant knows, or can reasonably be expected to know: (i) the behaviour and the fact that it constitutes an infringement of competition law; (ii) the fact that the infringement of competition law caused harm to him; and (iii) the identity of the infringing undertaking. The minimum duration of limitation periods is five years. Action taken by a competition authority for the purpose of the investigation or proceedings in respect of an infringement of competition law to which the damages action relates lead to suspension or, depending on national law, interruption of the limitation period for the damages action. The suspension shall end at the earliest one year after the infringement decision has become final or the proceedings are otherwise terminated (Art. 10).

The Directive provides for the joint and several liability of undertakings which have infringed competition law through joint behaviour. This means that, in the relationship to the victims, each of those undertakings is bound to compensate for the harm in full, and the injured party has the right to require full compensation from any of them until it has been fully compensated (Art. 11(1)). This rule is subject to two exceptions: one for small or medium sized enterprises (SMEs) pursuant to the definition in Commission Recommendation C (2003) 1422[10] and one for immunity recipients.

According to Article 2(1) of the Annex to the said Recommendation, the category of micro, small and medium-sized enterprises (SMEs) is made up of enterprises which employ fewer than 250 persons and which have an annual turnover

10 Commission Recommendation 2003/361/EC of 6 May 2003 concerning the definition of micro, small and medium-sized enterprises, OJ L 124, 20 May 2003, p. 36.

not exceeding EUR 50 million, and/or an annual balance sheet total not exceeding EUR 43 million. Such enterprise shall only be liable to their own direct and indirect purchasers where their market share remained below 5% at any time during the infringement and the application of the normal rules on joint and several liability would irretrievably jeopardize their economic viability and cause their assets to lose all their value. However, this exception is 'without prejudice to the right of full compensation'. Where victims, other than the small and medium sized undertaking's direct and indirect purchasers have no other opportunity to obtain full compensation, they may therefore address themselves to the small and medium sized undertaking. Moreover, the exception to the joint and several liability shall not apply if the SME was the ringleader or if it coerced other undertakings to participate in the infringement or in case of recidivism, i.e. in case it has previously been found to have infringed competition law (Arts. 11(2) and 11(3)).

Similarly, immunity recipients shall in principle only be liable to their direct or indirect purchasers or providers. They will be liable to other victims only where full compensation cannot be obtained from other undertakings taking part in the same infringement. Member States need to determine the limitation period for this type of cases in such a way that it is reasonable and sufficient to allow victims to bring such actions (Art. 12(4)).

The amount of contribution an infringing undertaking may recover from other infringing undertakings is to be determined in the light of their relative responsibility for the harm caused. In principle such contribution shall not exceed the amount of the harm it caused to its own direct or indirect purchasers or providers (Art. 11(4)). However, to the extent the infringement caused harm to others than the direct or indirect purchasers of the infringing undertakings (i.e. in the case of umbrella pricing),[11] the amount of the contribution by the immunity recipient is to be determined in the light of its relative responsibility for that harm (Art. 11(5)).

2.2.4. Passing-on of Overcharges

Where an undertaking pays a higher than the competitive price due to an infringement of the competition rules, it is likely to pass on at least part of the overcharge to its own buyers. It has long been disputed – and national rules diverged as to – whether the infringer against whom a claim for damages is brought may invoke this passing-on as a defence, arguing in essence that it should not compensate the undertaking for the part of the overcharge it has passed on to a further level in the supply chain.[12] The Directive provides clarity. It orders Member States to make the passing-on defence available. The burden of proving that the overcharge was passed on shall rest with the defendant who may reasonably require disclosure from the claimant and from third parties (Art. 13).

11 Umbrella pricing occurs where non-cartelist are able to raise their prices above the competitive level as a consequence of the cartel, see Case C-557/12, *Kone AG and Others* v *ÖBB Infrastruktur AG*, <www.eurlex.eu>, not yet published.

12 See, *inter alia*, Andrelang 2007; Bulst 2006; Dubow 2003; Parlak 2010; Petrucci 2008.

The Directive takes into account that where an undertaking passes on at least part of the overcharge it has paid itself, it is likely that it will sell less. The passing-on defence does not hamper the right of an injured party to claim and obtain compensation for loss of profits due to a full or partial passing-on of the overcharge (Art. 12(3)).

Where an indirect purchaser claims to have suffered loss as result of an infringement of the competition rules, it will normally have to prove that the overcharge was passed on to it. Because overcharges are generally passed on down the supply chain, the Directive, however, provides that the indirect purchaser will be deemed to have proven that the overcharge was passed on to him where he proves that (i) the defendant has committed an infringement of competition law; (ii) the infringement of competition law resulted in an overcharge for the direct purchaser of the defendant; and (iii) he purchased the goods or services that were the subject of the infringement of competition law, or purchased goods or services derived from or containing the goods or services that were the subject of the infringement. This presumption will, however, not apply where the defendant can demonstrate credibly to the satisfaction of the court that the overcharge was not, or not entirely, passed on to the indirect purchaser (Art. 14).

National courts must be given the power to estimate which share of the overcharge was passed on, in accordance with national procedures (Art. 12(5)). The Commission will issue guidelines to facilitate this (Art. 16).

The rules on passing on apply accordingly where the infringement of competition law relates to supply to the infringer (Art. 12(4)). In that case, the purchasing cartel will force the supplier to charge less, and as a consequence he will put pressure on his suppliers to charge less too.

To avoid that actions for damages by claimants from different levels in the supply chain lead to a multiple liability or to an absence of liability of the infringer, Member States need to ensure that in assessing whether the burden of proof relating to the passing on of overcharges is satisfied, national courts seized of an action for damages are able, by means available under Union and national law, to take due account of: (i) actions for damages that are related to the same infringement of competition law, but are brought by claimants from other levels in the supply chain; or (ii) judgments resulting from such actions; (iii) relevant information in the public domain resulting from public enforcement cases (Art. 15). This rule does not prejudice the application of Article 30 Brussels I Regulation dealing with related actions pending in the courts of different Member States.[13]

[13] Art. 30 Brussels I Regulation reads: '1. Where related actions are pending in the courts of different Member States, any court other than the court first seised may stay its proceedings.
2. Where the action in the court first seised is pending at first instance, any other court may also, on the application of one of the parties, decline jurisdiction if the court first seised has jurisdiction over the actions in question and its law permits the consolidation thereof.
3. For the purposes of this Article, actions are deemed to be related where they are so closely connected that it is expedient to hear and determine them together to avoid the risk of irreconcilable judgments resulting from separate proceedings.'

2.2.5. Quantification of Harm

With regard to the quantification of harm, Member States shall ensure that the burden and the standard of proof required do not render the exercise of the right to damages practically impossible or excessively difficult. They need to ensure that the national courts have the power, in accordance with national procedures, to estimate the amount of harm if it is established that a claimant suffered harm but it is practically impossible or excessively difficult to precisely quantify the harm suffered on the basis of the available evidence (Art. 16(1)). Moreover, the Directive establishes a rebuttable presumption that cartel infringements cause harm (Art. 16(2)). It also provides that if an NCA deems it appropriate, it must be able to assist on the determination of the quantum of damages upon request of a national court (Art. 16(3)). Furthermore, the Commission published non-binding guidance on the quantification of harm.[14]

2.2.6. Consensual Dispute Resolution

Where an infringer and a victim reach a settlement, the victim's claim is reduced by the settling co-infringer's share of the harm that the infringement caused to the victim. Its remaining claim can only be exercised against non-settling co-infringers, and the non-settling co-infringers cannot recover contribution for it from the settling co-infringer. However, where the non-settling co-infringers cannot pay the damages corresponding to the victim's remaining claim, the latter can exercise its remaining claim against the settling co-infringer unless this is expressly excluded under the terms of the consensual settlement (Art. 19).

The Directive also contains rules dealing with the interaction of settlements, actions for damages before the national courts and public enforcement by competition authorities.

Where parties involved in consensual dispute resolution bring an action before the national courts concerning the same claim, national courts may suspend proceedings for a maximum duration of two years. This provision does not, however, prejudice the provisions of national law in matters of arbitration (Art. 18(2) and (3)).

In order to prevent claims from becoming time-barred during processes of consensual dispute resolution and to avoid the filing of claims during such processes, the Directive provides for the suspension of the limitation period for bringing a court action for the duration of the consensual dispute resolution process. Note, however, that the suspension only applies to those parties that are or were involved or represented in consensual dispute resolution (Art. 18(1)).

[14] Commission Staff Working Document of 11 June 2013 – Practical Guide on Quantifying Harm in Actions for damages based on breaches of Art. 101 or 102 of the Treaty on the Functioning of the European Union accompanying the Communication from the Commission on quantifying harm in actions for damages based on breaches of Art. 101 or 102 of the Treaty on the Functioning of the European Union, SWD(2013) 205.

Where compensation is paid as a result of a consensual settlement and prior to competition authority's decision imposing a fine, the consensual settlement may be considered to be a mitigating factor in the setting of the fine (Art. 18(4)).

2.2.7. Final Provisions

The Directive must be implemented by 27 December 2016 (Art. 21). The implementation measures shall not apply to actions for damages brought before a national court before the entry into force of this Directive (Art. 22). The Directive entered into force on 25 December 2014 (i.e. the twentieth day following that of its publication in the Official Journal of the European Union, Art. 23).

3. Evaluation of the Directive

In this section we will provide an evaluation of the Directive on antitrust damages actions, in relation to the main aims defined in the Directive (see *supra* section 2.1) and in relation to the central theme of this book, i.e. the question whether a higher level of regulation (European rather than national) is needed. The latter question will be addressed from a law and economics perspective in section 3.1, which provides arguments in favour and against harmonization,[15] based on the economic theory of federalism. Section 3.2 will focus on the question whether the Directive can fulfil its aim of increasing the possibilities for victims of antitrust infringements to obtain compensation. Section 3.3, subsequently, addresses the important issue of the interaction between public and private enforcement of EU competition law, notably in the light of the Leniency program.

3.1. *Creating a Level Playing Field: was Harmonization as such Desirable?*

The Directive is based on the assumption that '(t)here exist marked differences between the rules in the Member States governing actions for damages for infringements of national or Union competition law'. This was indeed the conclusion reached by Ashurst which conducted in 2004 a study for the Commission on the state of play of antitrust damages actions in the EU Member States.[16] Although the case law of the Court of Justice has in the meantime provided more details about the conditions under which victims of antitrust infringements must be able to claim damages before the national Courts, and certain Member States have made amendments to their legislation, it is true that marked differences still exist.[17]

15 Whereby it should be pointed out that, contrary to a Regulation, a Directive will not always lead to a full harmonization of law.

16 Ashurst 2004.

17 Compare, for example, the application of the *Pfleiderer* rule made by the Amtsgericht Bonn 18 January 2012, case 51 Gs 53/09, <http://www.bundeskartellamt.de/wDeutsch/download/pdf/Presse/2012/Urteil_des_AG_Bonn_vom_18.01.2012_-_Az._51_GS_53-09.pdf> and by the →

Recital 7 states that:

> 'As injured parties often choose the forum of their Member State of establishment to claim damages, the discrepancies between the national rules lead to an uneven playing field as regards actions for damages and may affect competition on the markets on which these injured parties, as well as the infringing undertakings, operate.'

Recital 8 adds:

> 'Undertakings established and operating in different Member States are subject to procedural rules that significantly affect the extent to which they can be held liable for infringements of competition law. This uneven enforcement of the right to compensation in Union law may result in a competitive advantage for some undertakings which have infringed Articles 101 or 102 TFEU, and a disincentive to the exercise of the rights of establishment and provision of goods or services in those Member States where the right to compensation is more effectively enforced. (...) the differences in the liability regimes applicable in the Member States may negatively affect both competition and the proper functioning of the internal market.'

> 'Bearing in mind that large-scale infringements of competition law often have a cross-border element,'

it would therefore be necessary

> 'to ensure a more level playing field for undertakings operating in the internal market. It is also appropriate to increase legal certainty and to reduce the differences between the Member States as to the national rules governing actions for damages for infringements of Union competition law and, when applied in parallel to the latter, national competition law. An approximation of these rules will also help to prevent the emergence of wider differences between the Member States' rules governing actions for damages in competition cases' (Recital 9).

Do these considerations justify a harmonization of the national rules applicable to actions for antitrust damages?

From a law and economics perspective reducing the differences between the legal systems of the Member States (harmonization) and the creation of a level playing field is not per se good.[18] According to the economics of federalism decentralized, local decision making, decentralization is to be preferred. A good reason is required to shift competences to a higher level.[19]

UK High Court in *National Grid Electricity Transmission Plc* v *ABB Ltd & Ors* [2012] EWHC 869 (Ch) (04 April 2012).

18 Faure 2001, p. 343-345.

19 See generally Van den Bergh 1996; Revesz 2000a; Revesz 2000b; Faure 2003; Van Boom 2011. See also the work by Bruno Frey on functionally overlapping and competing jurisdictions (FOCJ): e.g. Frey (2009). Such a 'bottom-up approach' to harmonization also follows from the legal principle of subsidiarity.

3.1.1. Arguments against Harmonization

3.1.1.1. Economics of Federalism

According to the economics of federalism, national legislators should be allowed to offer their citizens rules that best fit their preferences. Individuals that are not satisfied with the choices made by their legislator may try to change the applicable rules (vote), or move to the jurisdiction that best suits their preferences (exit or vote with their feet). As such, Member States and their legislators will compete and a competitive equilibrium will be reached provided that imperfections on the market for legal rules do not prevent efficient outcomes.[20] Market imperfections can result from the fact that individuals do not have sufficient knowledge of the applicable rules, or from the fact that an individual's power to change specific rules through voting are limited and that moving to another legal system (either physically or through choice of law mechanisms under international private law) is not always possible or would entail significant costs.[21]

3.1.1.2. Experimentation

A further advantage of national, non-harmonized rules is that it allows for experimentation. Different choices will be made in different Member States and the effects of these different legislative choices can be observed. Subsequently, national legislators may copy the system that leads to results they consider the most desirable. In this way too, there will be a competition between legal rules and the most efficient rules will win the competition.[22] Especially in an area such as private enforcement of competition law, where opinions vary about the desirability of certain legislative options (e.g. the recognition of the passing on defence), experimentation could have been useful. It must be admitted though that the Commission has brought private enforcement to the agenda since its White Paper on Modernization published in 1999 and that it has made quite some efforts to increase the level of private actions for damages ever since. As a consequence, there has been quite some time for the Member States to experiment with different options in order to facilitate the bringing of such actions. Nevertheless, in many Member States little was done in this regard.

20 With regard to the optimal provision of local public goods (by means of competition between local authorities), see Tiebout 1956. The model has later been applied to decision making in federal states and decision-making in the EU, see e.g. Ogus 1999; Van den Bergh 2000; Faure 2003.

21 See e.g. Van den Bergh 1996, p. 365-366.

22 Van den Bergh 2000, p. 437-439. See also Smits 1998; Ogus 1999.

3.1.2. Arguments in Favour of Harmonization

3.1.2.1. Economic Arguments

There are situations where harmonization can be justified from an economic perspective. Harmonization may be justified when (i) it can be established that Member States attract industry by having low regulatory standards (race to the bottom), (ii) inefficiencies are created under national law that cause damage to be externalized to other Member States, (iii) harmonization would create economies of scale or (iv) reduce transaction costs.[23]

Below we will consider whether any of the four criteria mentioned above are fulfilled in the area of damages actions for infringements of the EU competition rules and that of damages actions for infringements of the national competition rules when applied in parallel with the EU rules.

Race to the bottom

The EU's desire to create a level playing field is closely related to the desire to prevent a race to the bottom. The idea of a race to the bottom relies on the fact that different legislation imposes different costs on industry, leading to different conditions of competition within the common market. Not only would this as such hamper the functioning of the internal market, it would also constitute an incentive to national legislators to try to attract industry by adopting industry-friendly rules (such as low corporate taxes, relaxed rules on workplace safety, and low environmental standards) which minimize costs for industry, even if this would lead to a reduction of social welfare.[24] If there is a genuine race to the bottom, which is also empirically proven to lead to such reduction of social welfare, only then there is an economic justification for moving legislation (e.g. on workplace safety, consumer protection or environmental standards) to the EU level rather than leaving it at Member State level.[25]

As we already pointed out above, law and economics scholars reject the idea that differences in legislation would as such hamper the internal market.[26] The conditions of competition vary for many other reasons than the applicable legal rules, for example because of transportation facilities (low areas vs mountain areas, closeness to important waterways etc.), costs of labour, political stability, access to raw materials, etc.). Harmonizing the rules relating to private enforcement of com-

23 See generally Faure 2003; Van Den Bergh; Camesasca 2006, p. 132.

24 Van den Bergh 2000, p. 445; Enriques 2005, p. 5-7; Faure 2012, p. 208.

25 Faure 2003, p. 47. The author stresses that in some cases there has been a race to the top rather than a race to the bottom. This is often referred to as the 'California effect', which has been defined by Vogel as a 'shift of consumer, environmental and other regulations in the direction of political jurisdictions with stricter regulatory standards' (Vogel 1995, p. 259). In the context of (private enforcement of) competition law, this would mean that Member States aim for more victim-friendly rules.

26 See in addition to the sources mentioned in the preceding footnotes also Cauffman, Faure & Hartlief 2009, p. 201, 205 and 214-216; Visscher 2010, p. 11-13.

petition law will therefore not in itself lead to equal market conditions.[27] It must be admitted, however, that it would remove one element that contributes to unequal market conditions.

Would there be a genuine risk for a race to the bottom in the field of private enforcement of EU competition law? In other words, would it be possible that Member States introduce (or maintain) rules on private enforcement which are industry-friendly, at the expense of potential victims of infringements of competition law or society at large? And if so, is there empirical evidence of this actually occurring? Let's consider this question more closely.

An element for an answer to the question whether a race to the bottom may occur in the field of private enforcement of EU competition law can be found in the rules of international private law. It must be noted that only the procedural rules in the sense of the rules of civil procedure will be determined by the law of the forum.[28] To the extent that the damages action is subject to national rules,[29] the national law governing the material rules for obtaining damages will be determined by the Rome I Regulation if the action is of a contractual nature,[30] and by the Rome II Regulation if the action is of non-contractual nature.[31] As actions for damages for infringements of the EU competition rules will often be of a non-contractual nature, the applicable law will be usually determined by Article 6 Rome II Regulation, which determines the law applicable to non contractual obligations arising out of restrictions of competition. According to this provision, the applicable law is in principle that of the country where the market is, or is likely to be, affected. When the market is, or is likely to be affected in more than one country, the person seeking compensation for damage who sues in the court of the domicile of the defendant, may instead choose to base his or her claim on the law of the court seized, provided that the market in that Member State is amongst those directly and substantially affected by the restriction of competition out of which the non-contractual obligation on which the claim is based arises. Where the claimant sues, in accordance with the applicable rules on jurisdiction, more than one defendant in that court, he or she can only choose to base his or her claim on the law of that court if the restriction of competition on which the claim against each of these defendants relies directly and substantially affects also the market in the Member State of that court. Article 6

27 Faure 2003, p. 51-53. Law and economics generally considers the argument of 'harmonizing market conditions' (sometimes simply labelled 'levelling the playing field') a political rather than an economic goal, to the extent that it goes beyond taking away artificial trade barriers. As explained in this section, the main economic arguments for harmonization relate to race to the bottom, transboundary externalities, economies of scale and transaction costs.

28 See, for example, Idot 2012, p. 263.

29 Cf. *supra*, section 1 (Introduction).

30 Regulation 593/2008/EC of the European Parliament and of the Council of 17 June 2008 on the law applicable to contractual obligations (Rome I), [2008] OJ L 177/6.

31 Regulation 864/2007/EC of the European Parliament and of the Council of 11 July 2007 on the law applicable to non-contractual obligations (Rome II), [2007] OJ L 199/40. See on the problems this distinction raises: Poillot-Peruzetto & Lawnicka 2012, p. 131-157. On private international law issues relating to private enforcement generally, see Basedow, Francq & Idot 2012.

Rome-II Regulation is mandatory. Parties may not derogate from the law applicable under Article 6 by agreement.

For an infringer of the EU competition rules, this means that he needs to consider the possibility of being held liable according to the rules of each Member State where it causes loss. As soon as his illegal behaviour also affects the market of the Member State where he is domiciled, he needs to take into account the possibility that losses caused on the markets of other Member States are compensated according to the rules of its own Member State. This could indeed be a reason for would-be infringers to establish themselves in a Member State whose national rules offer potential victims low chances of obtaining full compensation. Consequently, by adopting, within the boundaries permitted by the Court of Justice, rules that are disadvantageous for victims of an infringement of the EU competition rules, a Member State could attempt to attract industry. It would, however, also make it difficult for its own citizens to obtain damages for loss caused by anticompetitive conduct, except where this would be caused by undertakings established in another Member State having more victim friendly rules and whose market would also be directly and substantially affected. Could the Member State seeking to attract industry by victim unfriendly rules of private enforcement mitigate the impact thereof for its own citizens by investing in strong public enforcement by its national competition authority, deterring anticompetitive behaviour within its own borders? Doing this would undermine its aim to attract business since it is only those undertakings who are planning to resort to anticompetitive behaviour on the market where they are established which have to fear for the application of the rules of private enforcement of that Member State to losses caused in other Member States.

We cannot give a full answer to these questions without empirical evidence. It is beyond the scope of this paper to investigate whether Member States in fact have attempted to attract industry in this manner. We may conclude that this is unlikely, though not impossible. Nevertheless, many Member States have not done much to facilitate antitrust damages actions either.

Transboundary externalities

A second potential justification for moving legislation to a higher (than the national) level is the presence of transboundary externalities. A prime example is environmental pollution that crosses the borders of two or more Member States, e.g. air pollution or water pollution (when a river passes a country border). Economic theory suggests that the social costs of environmental pollution (the so-called 'negative externalities') imposed on other countries, will not (fully) be taken into account by the country that caused them. This leads to overproduction and a reduction of social welfare.[32]

32 Revesz 1996; Faure 2003, p. 38-40; Van Boom 2011, p. 444-445. Van Boom (p. 444) notes in relation to torts that, as a result of the Rome II regulation (EC Regulation 864/2007), the law applies of the country in which the damage occurs. Therefore, 'domestic law itself may deal adequately with cross-border externalities', which reduces the relevance of the 'cross border externalities' argument in those markets where this is the case.

In relation to substantive competition law, i.e. the rules on cartels, abuse of dominance and mergers, transboundary externalities provide a key argument for transnational regulation. If e.g. a cartel or merger results in substantial externalities, this 'must be supervised by supranational competition authorities in order to prevent a bias in favour of national interests'.[33] However, this does not necessarily imply that also all procedural rules need to be harmonized. After all, many differences continue to exist between procedural and other laws in the EU Member States, and only harmonizing procedural rules in one domain of law - without taking into account the specifics of each national legal system, nor the differences between social security systems, health insurance, and so on[34] - is not likely to be efficient. Nevertheless, the transboundary externalities argument is related to another possible justification for harmonization, which we will address now.

Economies of scale

Will harmonization of the rules of private enforcement produce economies of scale? The enforcement of the rules will in any case be left to the national courts. The Commission is probably in a better position than the Member States to carry out research on difficult questions relating to private enforcement, such as the quantification of damages. However, it would suffice to make the results of this study available to the Member States without making them binding. This is actually exactly what it did with the results of the study on the quantification of damages.

However, the economies of scale criterion has also been used to argue that when the conduct to be regulated has cross-border effects, it should be regulated by an authority which has jurisdiction over the entire area where the effects can be felt.[35] As the application of the EU competition rules implies that the conduct in question has an appreciable effect on trade between the Member States,[36] this would mean that regulation of the consequences of infringing the competition rules should indeed take place at EU level.[37]

It must be noted that the scope of the Directive on antirust damages actions is not limited to damages actions for infringements of EU competition law, but also extends to damages actions for infringements of national competition law, when

33 Van den Bergh 1996, p. 372. See further Van den Bergh 1996, p. 372-374.

34 These indicators are more relevant than they seem at first sight. After all, how much money is needed to compensate a victim does not only depend on what he or she can obtain via private law (e.g. damages actions), but also depends on a country's social security system, the availability of (e.g. health or corporate) insurance, tax law, and even a country's GDP in comparison to other countries, etc. These differences between Member States are exactly the reason why a bottom-up approach is called for, as we argued above.

35 Faure 2003, p. 40. In that respect the argument is related to the transboundary externalities argument, discussed in the previous subsection.

36 Art. 101 TFEU, Whish & Baily 2012, p. 140 *et seq.*; Jones & Sufrin 2014, p. 181 *et seq.*

37 But for a more critical (i.e. narrow) perspective on the argument of scale economies in law production, see Enriques 2005, p. 13-14. He states that harmonization measures in the form of directives leave plenty of space for Member States' choices at the implementation stage. This implies that 'the costs related to the search for the best rules by national regulators at the implementation stage will be at best reduced'.

applied in parallel with EU competition law. As a justification, the preamble of the Directive refers here too to the interest of the proper functioning of the internal market, the creation of greater legal certainty and a more level playing field for undertakings and consumers. Was this extension of the scope of the Directive to purely national rules necessary? Could the same result not be achieved without this extension? Where compensation would not be available based on the fact that a certain act constitutes an infringement of national competition law, but the same act constituted an infringement of EU competition law compensation would nevertheless be available under the rules applicable to infringements of EU competition law since national rules cannot deprive an individual from the rights it derives from EU law. The extension, however, prevents the existence of national rules that would be 'overruled' by provisions founded on EU law as well as discussions about this principle before the national courts. The Directive does not affect damages actions for infringements of national competition law which do not affect trade between Member States within the meaning of Article 101 or 102 TFEU. Uncertainty could, for example, arise where a cartel existed over a longer period of time but only affected trade between the Member States as of a certain date. Strictly speaking, there is no parallel application of EU and national competition rules with regard to the period before trade between the Member States was affected, so that the harmonized rules would not need to be applied with regard to that period. However, in practice, applying national rules that would e.g. provide victims with wider rights of access to leniency documents might be difficult to reconcile with the aim of the Directive, when this could possibly affect the position of the undertakings with regard to its liability incurred in the period where there was an impact on trade between the Member States. However, it is likely that many Member States will extend the scope of their implementation legislation to also include damages actions for infringements of the national competition rules only.

Reducing transaction costs

An argument for harmonization that can count on support from law and economics scholars is that harmonization can lead to a reduction of transaction costs.[38] The economic concept of transaction costs generally refers to the costs of using the market, and consists of three categories: the costs of (obtaining) information, the costs of bargaining (contracting), and the costs of enforcement and compliance.[39] In the more specific context of this chapter, the transaction costs refer to the costs for businesses of finding out which rules (on private enforcement; or competition law more broadly) apply in which Member State and how to adapt their behaviour in order to comply with the rules that are in force in each Member State. These costs may be reduced if there are less differences between the rules in EU Member States

38 Van den Bergh 1996, p. 374-375; Faure 2003, p. 59-62; Van Boom 2011, p. 446-447.

39 For more information, see e.g. Shavell 2004, p. 84 *et seq.*; Cooter & Ulen 2012, p. 88-91, referring to the seminal work conducted by Ronald Coase. See for a classification of costs in relation to having national laws rather than EU law also Visscher 2010, p. 15-16, who adds that the potential of uniform law to save on transaction costs should, however, not be overestimated.

(as in case of a directive that is implemented correctly by all Member States) and will even be reduced to zero in case of a full harmonization of rules (as in the case of a Regulation).[40]

However, harmonization will also entail costs in itself, which according to some authors can be very high.[41] Consequently, the reduction in (transaction) costs that follows from harmonization has to be balanced against the costs of harmonization itself. The costs of harmonization include not only the costs of adopting harmonized rules at EU level, but also – where directives are used – of implementing them at national level, the costs for individuals, businesses, legal practitioners, courts and legal education to adapt to the new rules and the costs of the application of harmonized rules in the future. While the first mentioned costs are short-term costs, the cost of the application of harmonized rules in the future is a long-term cost. It refers, *inter alia,* to the fact that national courts, when in doubt about the meaning of a harmonized rule, will have to make a preliminary referral to the Court of Justice, which will increase the costs of the procedure and extend its duration. Also, it may be harder to change harmonized rules when they are no longer considered suitable to apply in a changed social and economic environment. Furthermore, it must be noted that the material rules of EU competition law already are uniform as they are included in the TFEU. Therefore, when operating on the markets of other Member States, undertakings do not suffer from uncertainty about the rules that determine what they may and must not do in the light of the EU competition rules. There is only uncertainty about the private law consequences of infringing these rules and as a consequence of potentially different rules about access to leniency documents and potential criminal sanctions that may be incurred by undertakings and/or individuals. Reduced uncertainty about the sanctions applicable in other Member States might increase calculated wrongs. When the costs of infringing a rule can be determined more easily and with more certainty, better predictions can be made about the potential benefits of infringing a rule.[42]

Apart from these considerations relating to the costs and benefits of harmonization in general, the costs and benefits resulting from the adoption and implementation of the Directive on antitrust damages actions will of course also depend on the actual content of the rules contained therein, compared to the rules that existed

40 Note that when transaction costs are zero, this would also imply that there is an increase in legal certainty. In that respect, the discussion in this section can be linked to the fourth aim of the Directive, discussed above in section 2.1.

41 See notably Enriques 2005, p. 12, stating in relation to the area of company law that 'harmonization [...] has made the company law framework across the EU highly complex and uncertain, perhaps even more than it would have been if left to itself' and that 'the general aim of reducing transaction costs stemming from differences in national company laws is unattainable through top-down harmonization'.

42 This argument, however, can also work in the other direction. Generally, the more information parties have at their disposal, e.g. about possible sanctions and the possibility of being caught and punished, the better they can make the trade-off between expected costs and expected benefits of antitrust violations. Uncertainty may either lead to under-deterrence or to over-deterrence, depending on whether a person is risk neutral, risk loving, or risk averse. For an introduction to the analysis of risk and uncertainty and further references, see Cooter & Ulen 2012, p. 43-45.

before. In that respect, it must also be taken into account that the Directive will not remove all uncertainty about the rules on antitrust damages applying in other Member States. Important elements for determining liability such as the causal link are not harmonized.[43] The further existence of uncertainty entails that the EU legislator will not entirely achieve his aim of levelling the playing field, but this may also deter calculated wrongdoing. In any case, it can be stated that the argument that harmonization can be justified if it reduces transaction costs, is valid only when the marginal benefits of harmonizing outweigh the marginal costs thereof.[44]

3.1.2.2. Non-Economic Arguments in Favour of Harmonization

In addition to the economic arguments for harmonizing law that we presented in the previous subsection, several non-economic arguments may be advanced. Most prominent among those arguments, in the sense that it has received attention also in the 'economics of federalism' literature, is the (supposed) need for a minimum level of protection.

Minimum level of protection

With regard to the harmonization of tort law in general it has been argued that the desire to create a minimum level of harmonization is not necessarily a good reason for harmonization because the desired minimum level of protection may differ between Member States. With regard to minimum levels of protection in the field of for example environmental legislation and medical malpractice it has been argued that raising the existing level of protection is likely to lead to an increase of prices is some Member States (more particularly, those Member States where currently e.g. environmental protection or prices for medical services are low), which citizens of these Member States may not be willing to pay.[45]

In the field of private enforcement of competition law too there may be national differences about whether or not victims of such infringements need to be compensated and about the material and procedural rules according to which such compensation is to be determined. Is it likely that an increase of the level of protection of victims of anticompetitive infringements will lead to an increase in price? It seems that a difference is to be made between the situation before and after an undertaking has been held liable for an infringement of the competition rules. Once an undertaking has been held liable for an infringement of the competition rules, it will have to compensate the victims and most likely (unless it obtained leniency) it will also have to pay fines. It is likely indeed that the undertaking in question will try to pass on some of the resulting costs to its customers in the form

43 Recital 11 of the Preamble to the Directive on antitrust damages actions. This recital further mentions that: 'Where Member States provide other conditions for compensation under national law, such as imputability, adequacy or culpability, they should be able to maintain such conditions in so far as they comply with the case-law of the Court of Justice, the principles of effectiveness and equivalence, and this Directive.'

44 Faure 2012, p. 215; Van den Bergh 1998, p. 146-148.

45 Faure 2003, p. 67-72.

of an increase of price (as far as market conditions make this possible). Will an increase of the level of protection of victims of anticompetitive infringements lead to an increase of prices before an undertaking has committed an infringement of the competition rules? At this point, there seems to be a difference between the rules of private enforcement of competition law on the one hand, and rules of environmental protection and medical malpractice on the other hand. Indeed, to the extent that private enforcement contributes to deterring anticompetitive behaviour, it may prevent anticompetitive increases in princes. Moreover, there seems to be a higher risk of infringements of environmental rules or medical malpractice rules to occur by accident, out of negligence, while infringements of the competition rules often take place intentionally (especially in cartel cases). An undertaking could therefore be less likely to increase prices as a result of stricter rules of private enforcement when it knows that it has not engaged in anticompetitive conduct. However, intention is not required for an infringement of the competition rules to be found to have taken place.[46] Although intentional anticompetitive behaviour is more common, non-intentional infringements of the competition rules are not unthinkable. The EU competition rules are only defined in vague terms. In some cases, it is not clear whether certain conduct is permitted or not. Since the abolition of the notification system, it is hardly impossible for firms to obtain *ex ante* certainty about the compatibility of certain conduct with the competition rules. Regulation 1/2003 provides the possibility for the Commission to issue guidance where novel questions arise,[47] but up until present the Commission has not yet used this possibility. Where uncertainty exists, the possibility of not only having to pay fines, but also damages, may indeed lead to an increase of prices. Moreover, even the fear for being held liable for intentional infringements of the competition rules may lead to an increase in prices. Indeed, an undertaking may be held to have committed an intentional infringement of the competition rules, where only sales staff has infringed the competition rules without the management being aware of this. Fear for anticompetitive behaviour of the own staff of an undertaking may therefore be a reason to increase prices when more stringent rules of private enforcement enter into force. It must be noted however, that the Directive in principle allows Member States to maintain conditions such as culpability 'in so far as they comply with the case-law of the Court of Justice, the principles of effectiveness and equivalence, and this Directive'.[48] In our opinion, however, a condition of culpability is difficult to reconcile with the CJEU's consistent case law that

> '(t)he full effectiveness of Article 85 of the Treaty and, in particular, the practical effect of the prohibition laid down in Article 85(1) would be put at risk if it were not open to

46 See, for example, Whish & Bailey 2012, p. 119; Jones & Sufrin 2014, p. 215 (both with a few nuances).

47 Regulation 1/2003/EC of the Council of 16 December 2002 on the implementation of the rules on competition laid down in Articles 81 and 82 of the Treaty, [2003] OJ L 1.

48 Recital 11.

any individual to claim damages for loss caused to him by a contract or by conduct liable to restrict or distort competition'.[49]

In the case of private enforcement of the competition rules, the institution of a minimum level of protection of victims might be justified by the fact that the amount of damages to be paid will have an impact on deterring infringements of the competition rules. When the Commission wants to determine the 'optimal' level of fines in order to deter infringements of the EU competition rules, it is useful to have at least an indication about the circumstances where damages will have to be paid and about the level of those damages. In fact, in order to determine the optimal level of fines and to also prevent overdeterrence, the Commission would need to have certainty about these elements, which would plead in favour of full harmonization. On the other hand, it must be observed that in the current system of parallel enforcement of the EU competition rules by the Commission and the NCAs, there is no harmonization of the sanctions to be imposed within the framework of public enforcement. Where NCAs enforce the EU competition rules, they act in accordance with their own procedural rules and, within the limits of Article 5 Regulation 1/2003, they impose the sanctions provided for under their own legal system.[50] The level of fines imposed may therefore differ according to the authority which enforces the competition rules. If the EU wants to harmonize the rules having an effect on deterrence of infringements of the EU competition rules, harmonizing the sanctions within the system of public enforcement would seem to be at least equally urgent as harmonizing the rules of private enforcement. Moreover, certain Member States impose criminal sanctions not only on undertakings but also on individuals who are responsible for infringing the competition rules.[51] Divergences relating to criminal enforcement of the competition rules also have an impact on deterrence of infringements of the competition rules in the various EU Member States.

Other non-economic arguments

Further non-economic arguments for harmonizing law (besides minimum protection) that have been advanced in the literature include corrective justice, equal treatment, access to justice, and the right to an effective judicial protection. Although all of these arguments cannot be directly linked to the 'economics of federalism' literature, we briefly discuss each of these arguments below.

- Corrective justice:

The concept of 'corrective justice' has been discussed notably in relation to tort law. In the classic book 'Exploring the Domain of Accident Law', Dewees, Duff and Trebilcock (1996) discuss the various goals underlying tort law. These goals, according to the authors, include not only deterrence and compensation,[52] but also

49 Courage, point 26. See also Manfredi, point 60; Pfleiderer, point 28; Kone, point 33.
50 See, for example, Mikroulea 2010, p. 64.
51 For example, Denmark, the UK and Ireland, see Jones & Harrison 2014, p. 3-4, 10.
52 For a discussion, see Philipsen 2007, p. 198-202.

corrective justice. Following the corrective justice perspective, 'the purpose of tort law is to correct past injustices, not to deter future behaviour of other potential wrongdoers or to compensate victims of misfortune whose misfortune is not directly caused by the morally culpable conduct of another'.[53] Corrective justice hence is a normative term - after all, one needs to agree on the types of conduct that fall short of acceptable community standards - and in that respect it is difficult to make general statements about the desirability of striving for corrective justice at the EU level, at least from an economic (efficiency) perspective.

It is precisely for this reason that, following the bottom-up approach to harmonization discussed in the previous section, the argument of corrective justice seems not very strong here. Moreover, Member States are in principle able to deal adequately with issues of corrective justice themselves.

- Equal treatment:

Equal treatment of victims of competition law infringements across the EU may be another argument for harmonizing laws across Member States, if it is held that victims are entitled to similar levels of compensation across the EU, regardless of the Member State they are residing in. To the extent that differences among Member States currently exist in this respect, the EU legislator could indeed try to reduce these differences. Again, this is a non-economic argument, and it goes beyond the scope of this paper to present a full-fledged analysis of equal treatment in relation to EU law.

- Access to justice:

Access to justice generally refers to the concept of *locus standi* (standing) for victims of e.g. torts, environmental pollution, or antitrust infringements. Widening access to justice for victims can be a goal that politicians try to achieve for distributional reasons (shifting welfare from potential injurers to potential victims) or for reasons of e.g. fairness. Also from an economic (i.e. efficiency) perspective, a widened access to justice may be called for, namely if private law remedies to be used by individual victims in classic tort or nuisance cases do not work well. Shavell (1984) offers many reasons why private enforcement may not work: the damage may be too widespread, resulting in low damage amounts to individual victims even if total damages are high, there may be problems of causation or latency, etc.[54] These may indeed constitute arguments for allowing a lower threshold for legal standing, or for other solutions such as allowing collective litigation or public interest litigation.[55] However, they may also be reasons for stronger public enforcement of regulation, rather than relying on tort law.[56] In its essence, the question whether access to justice at EU level needs to be harmonized in relation to (antitrust) damages actions is also a political question. Since, moreover, the access to justice argument is

53 Dewees, Duff & Trebilcock 1996, p. 8.
54 Shavell 1984.
55 Faure, Mühl & Philipsen 2014, p. 49.
56 Shavell 1984.

related to the other arguments we discussed in this section, and to the discussion on the possibilities for victims to obtain compensation at other places in this chapter (see section 3.2 below) we will not address it any further here.

- The right to an effective judicial protection:

The Preamble to the Directive points out that '(t)he need for effective procedural remedies' also follows from Article 47, first paragraph, of the Charter of Fundamental Rights of the European Union (the Charter) and Article 19(1), second subparagraph, of the Treaty on European Union'. This in itself is an argument for legal intervention, albeit not necessarily at EU level, to the extent that Member States themselves make sure that procedural remedies are effective. Again, this argument seems to be related to those we discussed above, notably those on equal treatment and access to justice.

3.1.3. Concluding Remarks

In this section we addressed the question whether, from an economic perspective, the aim of creating a level playing field in the EU can be supported in relation to damages actions for infringements of competition law. We started by explaining that law and economics scholars take a bottom-up approach to harmonization , which implies that there needs to be a good reason to harmonize laws. It should be kept in mind, furthermore, that the Directive (different from a regulation) does not result in a full harmonization of national laws, but rather in 'more' harmonization.

When applying the potential economic justifications for harmonization to the domain of antitrust damages actions, we concluded that most of these justifications do not directly seem to apply. It is unlikely, for example, that the 'race to the bottom' argument applies in this context, as that would mean that Member States actively try to attract industry by maintaining victim unfriendly rules of private enforcement. Moreover, it will be difficult for Member States to do this also in the light of existing private international law (notably Art. 6 of the Rome II Regulation).

With respect to the transboundary externalities argument, which is an important argument to harmonize e.g. environmental law (as well as substantive competition rules), we concluded that it is difficult to argue that this provides sufficient justification to harmonize all procedural rules in relation to competition law, as long as differences in many other areas (general procedural rules, social security, tax, private law, etc.) remain to exist between EU Member States. However, the related argument of economies of scale is more likely to apply here, to the extent that infringements of competition law have cross-border effects, and considering that the European Commission is already responsible for enforcing the substantive rules on cartels, abuse of dominance, and mergers. Having different procedural rules may after all lead to additional costs.

The argument of a possible reduction of transaction costs is not very strong in this context, although it cannot be excluded. First, differences between procedural rules in the different Member States will remain also after the implementation of the Directive on antitrust damages claims. Second, one should also take into account that harmonizing laws, through formulating a directive and implementing it in the various Member States, itself entails costs. What we can expect, however, is that the Directive will result in reduced uncertainty about the (levels of) sanctions that apply in other Member States in case of competition law infringements. Whether this leads to under-deterrence of undertakings or entrepreneurs (e.g. if it increases calculated wrongs) or over-deterrence (meaning that undertakings do not engage in particular risky conduct that may in fact increase social welfare), depends, *inter alia*, on the risk type of the potential infringer.

We also provided a number of non-economic arguments for harmonization: minimum level of protection, corrective justice, equal treatment, access to justice, and the right to an effective protection. These all have in common that they are not (necessarily) supported by economists.[57] All of these arguments, however, may still provide justifications for politicians to harmonize laws, but these are not related to efficiency goals, but to goals such as fairness, distribution, non-discrimination, etc.[58]

3.2. *Increasing the Possibilities for Victims of Antitrust Infringements to Obtain Compensation*

The Ashurst study of 2004 found only 28 cases where damages actions for infringement of the EU and/or national competition rules had been successful throughout the Member States since the adoption of EU and national competition laws.[59] More recent studies show that currently in some Member States damages actions are flourishing, where in other Member States there are very few successful cases. In some Member States hardly any claims are brought at all.[60]

The Commission's Staff Working Paper accompanying its Green Paper derived from the Ashurst Study eleven principle obstacles to antitrust damages actions. These obstacles relate to (i) the absence of collective action mechanisms, (ii) fault requirements, (iii) burden and standard of proof, (iv) collection and presentation of evidence, (v) evidential value of national competition authorities and national court decisions, (vi) quantification of damages, (vii) the passing-on defence and indirect purchaser claims, (viii) amount of damages, (ix) time limitations, (x) costs, (xi) applicable law.[61]

57 With the possible exception of the access to justice argument, in cases where a broader access to justice is needed to solve the so-called 'rational apathy problem', i.e. to prevent under-deterrence of liability rules.

58 Another explanation for harmonization may lie in the fact that political and legislative bodies, including notably the European Commission, have a tendency to try to increase the size of their bureaucracy. Also, the lack of transparency at the European level may be a useful cover for lobbying activities. This 'private interest (or public choice) perspective to regulation' always needs to be kept in mind, in order to critically assess any proposals for harmonization. See e.g. Vaubel 1994, p. 153-158; Faure 2003, p. 73; Philipsen 2010, p. 207-208.

59 Ashurst 2004, p. 1.

60 Rodger 2014, chapters 3 and 4. In the UK, for example, there were 57 cases ere damages were claimed during the period between May 1999 and May 2012. In Bulgaria, by contrast, there were no private enforcement cases during that period.

61 Green Paper on Damages Actions 2005, p. 12-14.

It can indeed be argued that this situation is difficult to reconcile with '(t)he need for effective procedural remedies' which follows from Article 47, first paragraph, of the Charter of Fundamental Rights of the European Union (the Charter) and Article 19(1), second subparagraph of the Treaty on European Union, so that measures are required to facilitate the victim's access to justice. On the other hand, it must be mentioned that certain scholars have also expressed the fear that increased private enforcement would lead to overdeterrence, overburdening infringers,[62] provoking unmeritorious suits and even suits aimed at harming certain undertakings which are competing on the merits.[63] However, especially in the case of cartels, the fear for overdeterrence must not be exaggerated given the low detection rate. Moreover, the Directive provides for the possibility to take settlements into account when determining fines (Art. 18(3)), which can be seen as an incentive to early settlement which at the same time prevents overdeterrence. The risk of unmeritorious suits must not be exaggerated either. Firstly, an undertaking who wants to harm another undertaking by bringing an unmeritorious suit will also harm itself as it will also incur litigation costs. Secondly, to the extent that unmeritorious suits are brought this must be handled by specific sanctions, other than decreasing the opportunities for claiming damages in all cases, meritorious or not.

Anyway, the decision to improve the conditions for claiming antitrust damages has been taken. The question is now whether the Directive will be effective in removing the existing obstacles for such claims.

3.2.1. Collective Action Mechanisms?

Competition law infringements and in particular cartel infringements give rise to scattered, low value damages claims for indirect purchasers. If they can only bring suits individually, the costs and efforts of filing a claim do not outweigh the benefits they can receive in case their claim is successful. Consequently, they do not claim compensation for their losses. In order to increase damages claims by indirect purchasers, some mechanism of collective action is required so that costs and risks can be shared. However, the Preamble to the Directive provides explicitly that it 'should not require Member States to introduce collective redress mechanisms for the enforcement of Articles 101 and 102 TFEU'.[64] Yet, the Commission's White Paper on Damages Claims for Infringements of Competition Law provided for two types of collective action: opt-in collective actions and representative actions.[65] In the meantime it has been decided that collective action should not be dealt with in a competition specific instrument, but should be dealt with horizontally. This approach is to be applauded. However, the measure that has in the meantime been taken with regard to collective action is only a recommendation, a soft law instrument that is not binding on the Member States.[66] It remains to be seen how Member

62 See also Pardolesi 2012, p. 294-297 (critically) referring to Prosperetti *et al.* 2009.

63 In this sense: Pardolesi 2012, p. 293-294. See also McAfee *et al.* 2005.

64 Recital 13.

65 White Paper, p. 4.

66 Communication on Collective Redress 2013.

States will respond. In the absence of some form of collective action, indirect purchasers' claims are unlikely to increase.

3.2.2. Fault Requirements

The fact that in some Member States proof of negligence or intent is required, in addition to proof of the infringement was regarded as an obstacle to private actions by the Ashurst Study since it constitutes an additional hurdle to be overcome by the claimant.[67] Yet, the Directive allows Member States to maintain conditions such as culpability 'in so far as they comply with the case-law of the Court of Justice, the principles of effectiveness and equivalence, and this Directive'.[68]

3.2.3. Burden and Standard of Proof

The Ashurst Study pointed out that the fact that the burden of proof of causation and damage is on the claimant, which is the case in all Member States, is an obstacle to private actions. Also the high standard of proof required in some Member States constitutes an obstacle, particularly where the available evidence may not be very complete.[69] The Directive improves the position of indirect claimants by providing for a rebuttable presumption that a cartel causes harm (Art. 17(2)). It also provides a rebuttable presumption that the overcharge was passed on to an indirect purchaser where he proofs that (i) the defendant has committed an infringement of competition law; (ii) the infringement of competition law resulted in an overcharge for the direct purchaser of the defendant; and (iii) he purchased the goods or services that were the subject of the infringement of competition law, or purchased goods or services derived from or containing the goods or services that were the subject of the infringement (Art. 14(2)).

In addition, damages claimants will generally benefit from the fact that final decisions of the public enforcement authorities of a Member State are binding for the courts of that Member State and that final decisions of the public enforcement authorities of other Member States can, in accordance with the respective national laws, be presented before national courts as at least, *prima facie*, evidence that an infringement of competition law has occurred (Art. 9). Furthermore, claimants will benefit from the fact that with regard to the quantification of harm, Member States must ensure that the burden and the standard of proof required does not render the exercise of the right to damages practically impossible or excessively difficult and that courts must have the power to estimate the amount of harm if it is established that a claimant suffered harm but it is practically impossible or excessively difficult to precisely quantify the harm suffered on the basis of the available evidence (Art. 17(1)).

67 Ashurst 2004, p. 2-3, 42-47, 119 and 123; Commission Staff Working Paper, Annex to the Green Paper on Damages Actions 2005, p. 12.

68 Recital 11.

69 Ashurst 2004, p. 3-4, 11, 55-56 and 107; Commission Staff Working Paper, Annex to the Green Paper on Damages Actions 2005, p. 12.

3.2.4. Collection and Presentation of Evidence

The relevant evidence for proving infringements of the competition rules and the loss they caused is not easily available and is generally held by the party committing the anti-competitive behaviour. The Ashurst Study established that in most Member States, the powers of national courts to order production of documents are very limited and very few Member States have mandatory pre-trial disclosure requirements. Parties are thus not obliged to produce relevant documents unless the requesting party can expressly identify the individual document he seeks, which makes it more difficult to obtain the evidence necessary to support a claim. The Study furthermore considered that the fact that in some Member States only the judge can question witnesses constitutes an obstacle to private actions because this would be a less effective way of obtaining information than direct questioning by the parties.[70]

The Directive on antitrust damages actions requires Member States to ensure that national courts can order the defendant or a third party to disclose evidence, where a claimant has presented a reasoned justification containing reasonably available facts and evidence sufficient to support the plausibility of its claim for damages and were the evidence is both relevant and sufficiently specified (Art. 5(1) and (2)). It follows that requests for disclosure still need to satisfy quite some requirements, which are only vaguely described: 'reasonably available facts', 'sufficient to support the plausibility of the claim'. In addition national courts are ordered to subject the request for disclosure to a proportionality test (Art. 5(3)). It remains to be seen how these concepts will be interpreted and applied. While it is understandable that a case by case assessment is required, the use of these open concepts reduces legal certainty for the victim. Moreover, access to the most useful pieces of evidence is limited. The rule that information prepared specifically for the proceedings of a competition authority and information drawn up by a competition authority can only be disclosed after the competition authority has closed its proceedings[71] does not seem to cause too much harm to damages claimants, as most claims for damages will only be brought after an infringement decision was taken (follow-on actions). More detrimental, however, is the absolute protection of leniency corporate statements and settlement submissions (Art. 6(6)). The absolute protection of these documents is given in by the fear to discourage undertakings from coming forward to the competition authorities confessing their participation in a cartel and claiming leniency and from agreeing to a settlement instead of long proceedings. Both instruments facilitate the burden of the competition authorities to detect and punish anticompetitive behaviour. It can be argued that such more effective public enforcement is also in the interest of victims as future anticompetitive behaviour is more effectively deterred preventing future harm and current anticompetitive behaviour is quicker punished which facilitates the bringing of follow-on claims for antitrust damages. The question arises, however, whether the absolute protection of corpo-

70 Ashurst 2004, p. 11, 61-65 and 124-125; Commission Staff Working Paper, Annex to the Green Paper on Damages Actions 2005, p. 12.

71 Art. 6(5) Directive.

rate statements and settlement procedures is the most efficient tool to limit the fear of undertakings to cooperate with the Commission through leniency corporate statements and settlement submissions.[72]

While the rules on disclosure are not as victim friendly as they could have been, it must be admitted that the Directive contains other elements that relieve his need for evidence (see *supra* 3.2.3: Burden and Standard of Proof).

3.2.5. Evidential Value of National Competition Authorities and National Court Decisions

The Ashurst study considered that the fact that decisions of NCAs (the home NCA and those of other Member States) and courts' decisions of other Member States do not have binding effect on the courts in most Member States constitutes an obstacle to private actions.[73] This issue is addressed by the Directive, although only decisions of the NCA of the Member State where the Court is established are binding on the Court. Decisions of other NCAs count as at least, *prima facie,* evidence that an infringement of competition law has occurred (Art. 9).

3.2.6. Quantification of Damages

The Ashurst Study indicated that proof and quantification of damages is complex and difficult, that generally recognized models for qualification are lacking, that differences in approach in relation to lost profits can result in diverging awards and that restrictions on claiming lost profits could operate as a disincentive for private enforcement.[74]

The right to compensation of lost profits has been recognized by the Court of Justice in *Manfredi*[75] and is confirmed by Art. 3(2) of the Directive.[76] As mentioned above in 3.2.3, the Directive contains measures to alleviate the burden and standard of proof with regard to the existence and the quantification of harm, *inter alia,* by requiring that courts must have the power to estimate the amount of harm if it is established that a claimant suffered harm but it is practically impossible or excessively difficult to precisely quantify the harm suffered. The Commission also provided non-binding guidance on the methods to quantify harm.[77]

3.2.7. The Passing-on Defence and Indirect Purchaser Claims

The Ashurst Study found that the lack of clarity as regards the possibility for indirect purchasers to bring a claim, combined with difficulties of proof (in particular

72 See Cauffman 2013 and *infra,* section 3.3 (Improving the interaction between public and private enforcement of the competition rules).

73 Ashurst 2004, p. 5, 69-70, 109 and 126.

74 Ashurst 2004, p. 6-7, 70-72, 106-107, 112 and 125. Commission Staff Working Paper, Annex to the Green Paper on Damages Actions 2005, p. 13.

75 Point 100.

76 See also Art. 12(3) and recitals 12 and 40.

77 Commission Practical Guide on Quantifying Harm.

as regards establishing causation and damages), constitute serious obstacles to claims by indirect purchasers. The existence of the passing-on defence would further complicate actions brought by direct purchasers and constitute a disincentive for bringing such actions.[78]

The Directive, however, orders Member States to recognize the existence of the passing-on defence. The burden of proving that passing-on occurred lies with the defendant, but this is only a confirmation of the widely recognized principle that the party who invokes a defence bears the burden of proof thereof. The recognition of the passing-on defence is in conformity with the principle that compensation should not exceed the harm suffered. It will, however, indeed complicate actions brought by direct purchasers while a refusal of the passing-on defence would have constituted an additional incentive for direct purchasers to bring actions for (extra-compensatory) damages. The Directive tries to compensate for this, fully in line with the principle of full compensation and the case law of the Court of Justice by facilitating actions by indirect purchasers (see section 2.2.4). However, where indirect purchasers are consumers and/or small undertakings suffering scattered losses, the measures taken by the Directive will probably not suffice to induce them to bring actions for damages. Some kind of collective redress mechanism will be required.

3.2.8. Amount of Damages

The Ashurst Study found that disincentives to damages actions were created by restrictions on the amounts that could be awarded, such as the unavailability of punitive damages and restrictions on the availability of interest.[79]

In line with the case law of the Court of Justice, the Directive confirms the victim's right to interest.[80] In line with the principle that compensation should not exceed the loss suffered, the award of punitive or other types of extra-compensatory damages is prohibited (Art. 3(3)), although the Court of Justice did not consider them irreconcilable with EU law before.[81]

3.2.9. Time Limitations

The Ashurst Study pointed out that short limitation periods constituted obstacles to private actions, by for example time barring follow-on actions or parallel actions brought after an original successful test case.[82]

The Directive tries to remedy this by imposing a minimum duration of five years on limitation periods, which shall not begin to run before the infringement

78 Ashurst 2004, p. 6, 110-111 and 126-127; Commission Staff Working Paper, Annex to the Green Paper on Damages Actions, p. 13.
79 Ashurst 2004, p. 7-8, 12 and 129-130; Commission Staff Working Paper, Annex to the Green Paper on Damages Actions 2005, p. 14.
80 Art. 2(2) and recital 12.
81 Manfredi, point 99 and dispositive part point 5.
82 Ashurst 2004, p. 8 and 114; Commission Staff Working Paper, Annex to the Green Paper on Damages Actions 2005, p. 14.

has ceased and the claimant knows, or can reasonably be expected to know of the behaviour and the fact that it constitutes an infringement of competition law, the fact that the infringement caused harm to him and the identity of the infringer who caused such harm. Furthermore, it provides that limitation periods shall not run from the moment action is taken by a competition authority for the purpose of the investigation or proceedings in respect of the infringement of competition law to which the damages action relates until at the earliest one year after the infringement decision has become final or the proceedings are otherwise terminated (Art. 10). This will remedy the problem with regard to follow-on actions. Whether it will remedy the problem regarding parallel actions after test cases will depend on whether a victim will be expected to reasonably have known that certain conduct constituted an infringement of competition law before the test case was decided. This will in turn depend on whether the test case followed on to an infringement decision by the public enforcement authorities.

3.2.10. Costs

The Ashurst Study observed that notwithstanding the general application of the loser pays rule, court and attorney fees are usually not fully recoverable. While this can be an advantage for unsuccessful claimants, it is also a disincentive for meritorious claims. In general, the high costs and risks involved in competition actions, as well as the length of proceedings, would operate as a disincentive to bringing private actions.[83]

Although the Commission considered changes to the loser pays rule in its Green Paper,[84] the Directive does not directly touch upon the issue of costs. Some of the rules in the Directive, such as the rules relating to the effect of the decisions of competition authorities and the rules on the quantification of damages may, however, reduce the length and costs of antitrust damages cases. A significant reduction of claimants' costs and risks could have been achieved by introducing collective redress mechanisms, but as mentioned before the Directive does not include these (cf. *supra* 3.2.1, Collective Action Mechanisms?).

3.2.11. Applicable Law

The Ashurst study was written before the adoption of the Rome II regulation. It noted that issues relating to the applicable law can constitute an obstacle to private enforcement.[85] The Green Paper supported the rule in the proposal for the Rome II regulation according to which the place where the damage occurs is determining the law applicable to the rules on non-contractual damages actions and suggested to

83 Ashurst 2004, p. 10-12, 115-117, 119-123 and 128-129; Green Paper on Damages Actions 2005, 9; Commission Staff Working Paper, Annex to the Green Paper on Damages Actions 2005, p. 14.

84 See also Commission Staff Working Paper, Annex to the Green Paper on Damages Actions 2005, p. 57-63.

85 Ashurst 2004, p. 98-99.

make a proposal for a specific rule for the law applicable to damage claims for breach of Community antitrust law.[86] At the initiative of the Presidency a specific rule on antitrust damages actions has been introduced in Article 6(3) of the Rome II regulation.

3.2.12. Other Obstacles?

The Directive does not define the causal relationship that needs to exist between the infringement and the damage. This is to be determined by the national law of the Member States which must, however, respect the principles of effectiveness and equivalence.[87] This was also the position taken by the Court of Justice in *Manfredi*[88] and confirmed in *Kone*.[89] However, in this last case the Court specified that

> '33. The full effectiveness of Article 101 TFEU would be put at risk if the right of any individual to claim compensation for harm suffered were subjected by national law, categorically and regardless of the particular circumstances of the case, to the existence of a direct causal link while excluding that right because the individual concerned had no contractual links with a member of the cartel, but with an undertaking not party thereto, whose pricing policy, however, is a result of the cartel that contributed to the distortion of price formation mechanisms governing competitive markets.
>
> 34. Consequently, the victim of umbrella pricing may obtain compensation for the loss caused by the members of a cartel, even if it did not have contractual links with them, where it is established that the cartel at issue was, in the circumstances of the case and, in particular, the specific aspects of the relevant market, liable to have the effect of umbrella pricing being applied by third parties acting independently, and that those circumstances and specific aspects could not be ignored by the members of that cartel. It is for the referring court to determine whether those conditions are satisfied.'

The Court thus seems to hold that the principle of effectiveness requires a rather broad interpretation of the causal link. Nevertheless it is to be expected that the requirement of a causal link will give rise to extensive litigation both as regards the question whether the national rules comply with the principle of effectiveness and as regards proof of the existence of a causal link.

3.3. *Improving the Interaction between Public and Private Enforcement of the Competition Rules*

Public enforcement concerns the enforcement of competition law in the general interest by public authorities. Its main concern is the punishment of current or past infringements and the deterrence of future infringements. Private enforcement, and in particular damages actions for infringements of the competition rules, takes place at the initiative of private parties who in their own interest seek compensation of the

[86] Commission Staff Working Paper, Annex to the Green Paper on Damages Actions 2005, p. 14.
[87] Recital 11.
[88] Point 64.
[89] *Kone*, point 24.

loss they suffered as a result of an infringement of the competition rules.[90] However, these damages actions also have a deterrent effect and as such they contribute to a higher compliance with the competition rules, which serves the general interest.[91] This effect is recognized by the Court of Justice.[92] To a certain extent, public and private enforcement therefore serve the same aim. Yet, from the time when it drafted its Green Paper, the Commission was alert for the risk that private enforcement would undermine one of the central elements of its public enforcement strategy: its leniency programme.[93] By coming forward to the Commission, confessing its participation in a cartel and supplying the Commission with information it can use to bring proceedings against its co-cartelists, an undertaking can obtain immunity (if it is the first) or a reduction (if it's the second or a later leniency applicant) of fines. However, leniency does not alleviate a cartelist from its obligation to compensate those who suffered loss as a result of the cartel. Therefore, it has been argued that an increase of private damages claims would discourage potential leniency applicants from coming forward.[94] Potential leniency applicants could in particular be deterred from coming forward by the fact that victims would already be able to bring claims against it as soon as its leniency application becomes public (which occurs at the latest at the moment of the publication of the Commission's infringement decision), while other cartelists' infringements would often only be established much later as they will generally appeal the Commission's decision.[95]

The challenge for the drafters of the Directive was to find a balance between guaranteeing the victim's opportunities to obtain compensation for the harm suffered, and preventing damages claims from undermining its leniency program. The Directive uses two techniques in order to prevent the right to damages from undermining its leniency program. On the one hand, it provides that disclosure of leniency applications (and settlement submissions) may not be ordered at any time; on the other hand, it limits the liability of immunity recipients.

90 See, for example, Case T-24/90 *Automec Srl* v *Commission of the European Communities*, Jur. 1992 II-02223, point 85; Notice on cooperation between national courts and the Commission in applying Articles 85 and 86 of the EEC Treaty, OJ C 039, 13 February 1993, 6 point 4.

91 See Crane 2010 on public vs private enforcement of competition law. On the deterrent effect of liability rules vs regulation more generally, see Shavell 1984.

92 See Case C-453/99, *Courage Ltd* v *Bernard Crehan* and *Bernard Crehan* v *Courage Ltd and Others*, [2001] ECR I-6297: 'the existence of (a right to damages) strengthens the working of the Community competition rules and discourages agreements or practices, which are frequently covert, which are liable to restrict or distort competition. From that point of view, actions for damages before the national courts can make a significant contribution to the maintenance of effective competition in the Community'. See also Manfredi, point 60; Pfleiderer, point 29; Donau Chemie point 46; Kone, point 33. See also the Commission's Green and White Paper, although it must be noted that the deterrent function of damages action played a more prominent role in the Green Paper than in the White Paper. See further Cauffman 2011, p. 182-183.

93 Green Paper on Damages Actions 2005, p. 9-10.

94 Hodges 2006, p. 1390.

95 See, for example, Explanatory Memorandum Damages Directive, p. 16; Cauffman 2011, p. 215; Jones & Sufrin 2014, p. 1116; Ottervanger 2014, p. 21.

The absolute non-discoverability of leniency applications may be a good marketing instrument for the Commission's leniency program as it creates the impression of a safe environment for leniency applicants who as a result may be more willing to cooperate with the Commission than in the absence of such a rule. Whether the non-discoverability of leniency documents will effectively protect infringers remains to be seen. If the information contained in the leniency application may also be derived from other documents, it may end up in the hands of damages claimants anyway. The rule only makes it more difficult and/or more costly for victims to obtain the information they need to prove the existence and quantification of their claim. From the perspective of morality and legislative techniques, it seems questionable to first recognize the right of victims to full compensation of the harm suffered as a result of competition law infringements and then establish hurdles to the exercise of this right.

Admittedly, there is a public order justification available: the protection of the leniency program, which is considered to be a useful tool for discovering cartels within the framework of the public enforcement of the competition rules. However, the usefulness of the leniency program to achieving the end of a more effective public enforcement has been questioned in legal scholarship.[96] Moreover, even if the value of the leniency program is recognized, the question arises whether its effectiveness could not be guaranteed in another, more suitable way. This is all the more so because depriving victims of access to corporate statements or settlement submissions does not only benefit the leniency recipient but also the co-cartelists who are jointly and severally liable for the entire damage caused by the cartel. If the aim of non-disclosure of the corporate statements is to prevent undertakings from not coming forward and cooperating with the competition authorities out of fear for being held liable for cartel damages, it may have been better to further limit the leniency applicant's liability while granting the victim access to all the information it needs to obtain full compensation from the other cartelists.

The Directive already contains certain measures to limit the immunity recipients' liability. The immunity recipient is normally only jointly and severally liable to its direct or indirect purchasers or providers. It will be only jointly and severally liable to other injured parties where full compensation cannot be obtained from the other undertakings that were involved in the same infringement of competition law. Furthermore, it is provided that, as regards direct or indirect purchasers or providers of the infringing undertakings, the amount of contribution of an undertaking which has been granted immunity from fines by a competition authority under a leniency program shall not exceed the amount of the harm it caused to its own direct or indirect purchasers or providers.[97] The Directive adds that to the extent the infringement of competition law caused harm to injured parties other than the direct or indirect purchasers or providers of the infringing undertakings, the amount of contribution of the immunity recipient shall be determined in the light of its relative responsibility for that harm.[98]

96 See Stephan 2008.

97 Art. 11(4).

98 Art. 11(5).

To the extent these rules alone are considered insufficient to prevent potential leniency applicants from coming forward and cooperating with the competition authorities when there is no guarantee that corporate statements remain absolutely confidential, the rules could have been extended to all leniency applicants and it could have been provided that the leniency recipients' liability is limited to cases where victims, including the leniency applicants' (in)direct purchasers, show to be unable to obtain compensation from the other cartelists. The extension of this proposal to (public law) settlements is a bit more difficult. Regarding settlements there is no race to be the first or to adduce sufficient additional information as with leniency applications. Every infringer may settle. Limiting the liability of the settling parties to cases where no full compensation can be obtained from non-settling parties, may therefore significantly reduce the cartelists to whom the claimants may primarily turn in order to obtain full compensation. Moreover, if all cartelists would settle, there would not be other cartelists to turn to in order to obtain full compensation and the claimants could immediately turn to the settling parties anyway.

4. Conclusion

After a long preparatory process, a Directive harmonizing certain national rules on private enforcement of competition law has been adopted. In this contribution we investigated whether harmonization of these rules was desirable and whether the other main objectives of the Directive, the improvement of the possibilities for victims to obtain damages and of the interaction between public and private enforcement, are likely to be achieved.

According to the economics of federalism, decentralized rulemaking is to be preferred. Furthermore, in a field where questions are still unsettled, experimentation with different national rules may be beneficial. Therefore, a good reason is required to justify obligatory harmonization. Two traditional grounds of justification, namely the need to prevent a race to the bottom as well as the existence of transboundary externalities do not seem to play a significant role in the field of private enforcement of competition law (although the latter argument provides the main rationale for harmonizing substantive competition law, i.e. the rules on cartels, abuse of dominance and mergers). Harmonization of the rules of private enforcement of EU competition law may, however, be justified by the fact that the rules of EU competition law apply in cases which have an appreciable effect on competition on the internal market and on trade between the Member States, so that the competence to regulate the enforcement of these rules should move to the authority who has jurisdiction over the entire internal market and all the EU Member States. This is the 'economies of scale' argument for moving to a higher (transnational) level of regulation. It could also be argued that the EU has more means to invest in research aimed at designing the best rules to regulate the complex issues at stake. Furthermore, one could argue that harmonization leads to a reduction of transaction costs, but in this case we are dealing with a Directive (which does not result in full harmonization) rather than a Regulation.[99] Finally, there are non-economic arguments for harmonization, including minimum level of protection, corrective justice, equal treatment, access to justice, and the right to an effective protection. Although these arguments are not related to efficiency goals, they may provide justifications for politicians to harmonize laws, for reasons of fairness, income distribution, non-discrimination, paternalism, and the like.

With regard to the aim of increasing the possibilities for victims of antitrust infringements to obtain compensation, we can conclude that the Directive indeed increases this possibility, although various obstacles to private action are likely to remain. This includes obstacles in relation to (lacking) possibilities for collective action, the requirement to prove negligence or intent, and rules on disclosure of evidence, just to mention a few.[100]

The Directive also aims at improving the interaction between public and private enforcement of the competition rules. Although both public and private enforcement aim at preventing infringements of competition law (while private enforcement of course also aims at compensation, as we showed above), the different types of enforcement not only add to each other but may also clash. A crucial issue in relation to enforcement of competition law is finding the right balance between using the leniency program (which the European Commission needs in order to be able to effectively trace cartels) in the public enforcement of competition law and compensating victims via private enforcement. Whether the Directive has chosen the most desirable option to achieve this balance is debatable.

99 See on these economic arguments *supra*, section 3.1.3.

100 See further *supra*, section 3.2.

Bibliography

Andrelang 2007
Andrelang, C., 'Damages for the Infringement of Art. 81 EC by Cartel Agreements According to sec. 33(3) GWB: The Changes of Law Concerning "Protective Law" Requirement and the "Passing-On" Defence', 30(4) *World Competition*, 2007, p. 573-593.

Ashurst 2004
Waelbroeck, D., Slater, N. & Even-Shoshan, G., *Study on the Conditions of Claims for Damages in Case of Claims for Damages of EC Competition Rules. Comparative Report*, Ashurst, 31 August 2004, available at: <http://ec.europa.eu/comm/competition/antitrust/actionsdamages/comparative_report_clean_en.pdf>.

Basedow, Francq & Idot 2012
Basedow, J., Francq, S. & Idot, L. (eds.), *International Antitrust Litigation: Conflict of Laws and Coordination* (Studies in Private International Law, 8), Oxford: Hart Publishing Limited 2012.

Bulst 2006
Bulst, F.W., *Schadensersatzansprüche der Marktgegenseite im Kartellrecht: zur Schadensabwälzung nach deutschem, europäischem und US-amerikanischem Recht*, Baden-Baden: Nomos 2006.

Cauffman 2011
Cauffman, C., The Interaction of Leniency Programmes and Actions for Damages, 7(2) *Competition Law Review*, 2011, p. 181-220.

Cauffman 2013
Cauffman, C., The European Commission Proposal for a Directive on Antitrust Damages: A First Assessment, 20(4) *Maastricht Journal of European and Comparative Law*, 2013, p. 623-634

Cauffman, Faure & Hartlief 2009
Cauffman, C., Faure, M.G. & Hartlief, T., *Harmonisatie van het consumentencontractenrecht in Europa. Consequenties voor Nederland*, Den Haag: Boom Juridische uitgevers 2009.

Commission Practical Guide on Quantifying Harm
Commission Staff Working Document of 11 June 2013 - *Practical Guide on Quantifying Harm in Actions for damages based on breaches of Article 101 or 102 of the Treaty on the Functioning of the European Union accompanying the Communication from the Commission on quantifying harm in actions for damages based on breaches of Article 101 or 102 of the Treaty on the Functioning of the European Union*, SWD(2013) 205.

Communication on Collective Redress 2013
Towards a European Horizontal Framework for Collective Redress. [Communication from the Commission to the European Parliament, the Council, the European Economic and Social Committee and the Committee of the Regions on 11.06.2013], COM 401/2; also available at: <http://ec.europa.eu/justice/civil/files/com_2013_401_en.pdf> (last visited 27.09.2013).

Communication on Quantifying Harm 2013
Communication from the Commission on *Quantifying Harm in Actions for Damages based on Breaches of Article 101 or 102 of the Treaty on the Functioning of the European Union.* [C167/19, 2013]; also available at: <http://eur-lex.europa.eu/LexUriServ/LexUriServ.do?uri=OJ:C:2013:167:0019:0021:EN:PDF> (last visited 27.09.2013).

Cooter & Ulen 2012
Cooter, R. & Ulen, T., *Law and Economics* (6th edition), Boston, MA: Pearson Addison-Wesley 2012.

Crane 2010
Crane, D.A., 'The Economics of Antitrust Enforcement', in: K.N. Hylton (ed.), *Antitrust Law and Economics*, Cheltenham, UK and Northampton, US: Edward Elgar 2010, p. 1-22.

Dewees, Duff & Trebilcock 1996
Dewees, D., Duff, D. & Trebilcock, M., *Exploring the Domain of Accident Law: Taking the Facts Seriously*, Oxford: Oxford University Press 1996.

Dubow 2003
Dubow, B., 'The Passing On Defence: An Economists Perspective – Should a Down-Stream Firm, which has paid Excessive Charges to an Upstream Supplier, be able to sue that Supplier for Antitrust Damages when the Downstream Firm may have "passed on" the Higher Charges to its Own Customers? This article reviews the economic theory which indicates to what extent downstream firms will be able to pass on excess charges to their customers', 24(6) *European Competition Law Review*, 2003, p. 238-240.

ECN Model Leniency Programme
ECN Model Leniency Programme [as revised in November 2012], available at: <http://ec.europa.eu/competition/ecn/mlp_revised_2012_en.pdf> (last visited 27.09.2013).

Enriques 2005
Enriques, L., *Company Law Harmonization Reconsidered: what Role for the EC?*, Law Working Paper No. 53/2005, University of Bologna and ECGI. Available at <http://ssrn.com/abstract=850005>.

Executive Summary Impact Assessment Report 2013
Executive Summary of the Impact Assessment Report; *Damages Actions for Breach of the EU Antitrust Rules – Accompanying the Proposal for a Directive of the European Parliament and of the Council on Certain Rules Governing Actions for Damages under National Law for Infringements of the Competition Law Provisions of the Member States and of the European Union*. [COM Staff Working Document (2013) 204 final, 11.6.2013]; also available at: <http://ec.europa.eu/governance/impact/ia_carried_out/docs/ia_2013/swd_2013_0204_en.pdf> (last visited 27.09.2013).

Faure 2001
Faure, M., 'Toward a Harmonized Tort Law in Europe? An Economic Perspective (Editorial)', 8(4) *Maastricht Journal of European and Comparative Law*, 2001, p. 339-350.

Faure 2003
Faure, M. (2003), 'How Law and Economics may Contribute to the Harmonisation of Tort Law in Europe', in: R. Zimmerman (ed.), *Grundstrukturen des Europäischen Deliktsrechts*, Baden-Baden: Nomos 2003, p. 31-82.

Faure 2012
Faure, M., 'Private Law I: Tort', in: Th. Eger & H.-B. Schäfer (eds.), *Research Handbook on the Economics of European Union Law*, Cheltenham, UK and Northampton, US: Edward Elgar 2012, p. 201-228.

Faure, Mühl & Philipsen 2014
Faure, M., Mühl, M. & Philipsen, N.J., 'Incentives, Costs and Benefits: A Law and Economics Analysis', in: M. Faure & N.J. Philipsen (eds.), *Access to Justice in Environmental Matters*, The Hague: Eleven International Publishing 2014, p. 23-74.

Frey 2009
Frey, B.S. (2009), *A New Concept of European Federalism, LSE 'Europe in Question'* Discussion Paper Series, LEQS Paper No. 03/2009, London: London School of Economics and Political Science 2009.

General Secretariat of the Council Analysis
General Secretariat of the Council *analysis of the final compromise text with a view to agreement of 24 March 2014 on the Proposal for a Directive of the European Parliament and of the Council on certain rules governing actions for damages under national law for infringements of the competition law provisions of the Member States and of the European Union*, Interinstitutional File 2013/0185 (COD), 11381/13 RC 29 JUSTCIV 177 CODEC 1566.

Green Paper on Damages Actions 2005
Green Paper on *Damages Actions for Breach of the EC Antitrust Rules*. [COM/2005/0672 final]; also available at: <http://eur-lex.europa.eu/LexUriServ/LexUri Serv.do?uri=COM:2005:0672:FIN:EN:HTML> (last visited 27.09.2013).

Hodges 2006
Hodges, C., 'Competition Enforcement, Regulation and Civil Justice: What is the Case?', 43(5) *Common Market Law Review*, 2006, p. 1381-1407.

Idot 2012
Idot, L., 'Access to Evidence and Files of Competition Authorities', in: J. Basedow, S. Francq, & L. Idot (eds.), *International Antitrust Litigation. Conflicts of Laws and Coordination*, Oxford: Hart Publishing 2012, p. 259-287.

Impact Assessment Report on Damages Actions 2013
Impact Assessment Report on *Damages Actions for Breach of the EU Antitrust rules – Accompanying the Proposal for a Directive of the European Parliament and of the Council on Certain Rules Governing Actions for Damages under National Law for Infringements of the Competition Law Provisions of the Member States and of the European Union.* [COM (2013) 404 final, 11.6.2013]; also available at: <http://ec.europa.eu/competition/antitrust/actionsdamages/impact_assessment_en.pdf> (last visited 27.09.2013).

Jones & Sufrin 2014
Jones, A. & Sufrin, B., *EU Competition Law: Text, Cases, and Materials*, Oxford: Oxford University Press 2014.

Jones & Harrison 2014
Jones, K. & Harrison, F, Criminal Sanctions: An overview of EU and National Case Law, *Bulletin e-Competitions Criminal sanctions*, 25 mars 2014, Art. No. 64713, available at < http://www.bakermckenzie.com/files/Publication/1b980bad-7c98-4d38-8019-5dd9f9b2bde2/Presentation/PublicationAttachment/855e3c1d-99fc-4685-be 15-5f88edc5b046/AR_AP_CriminalSanctions_Mar14.pdf>.

McAfee, Mialon & Mialon 2008
McAfee, R.P., Mialon, H.M. & Mialon, S.H., 'Private v. Public Antitrust Enforcement: A strategic Analysis', 92 *Journal of Public Economics*, 2008, p. 1863-1875.

Mikroulea 2010
Mikrouea, A., Case Allocation in Antitrust and Collaboration between the National Competition Authorities and the European Commission, in: I. Kokkoris & I. Lianos (eds.), *The Reform of EC Competition Law: New Challenges*, Alphen aan den Rijn: Kluwer Law International 2010, p. 55-73.

Ogus 1999
Ogus, A., 'Competition between National Legal Systems. A Contribution of Economic Analysis to Comparative Law', 48 *International and Comparative Law Quarterly*, 1999, p. 405-418.

Ottervanger 2014
Ottervanger, T., 'Designing a Balanced System: Damages, Deterrence, Leniency and Litigants' Rights, in: Ph. Lowe & M. Marquis (eds.), *European Competition Law Annual 2011, Integrating Public and Private Enforcement of Competition Law – Implications for Courts and Agencies*, Oxford: Hart Publishing 2014, p. 17-25.

Parlak 2010
Parlak, S., 'Passing-on Defence and Indirect Purchaser Standing: Should the Passing-on Defence Be Rejected Now the Indirect Purchaser Has Standing after Manfredi and the White Paper of the European Commission?', 33(1) *World Competition*, 2010, p. 31-53.

Petrucci 2008
Petrucci, C., 2008, 'The Issues of the Passing-on Defence and Indirect Purchasers' Standing in European Competition Law', 29(1) *European Competition Law Review*, p. 33-42.

Philipsen 2007
Philipsen, N.J., 'Prevention and Compensation of Work Injury in the United States: An Overview of Existing Empirical Evidence', in: S. Klosse & T. Hartlief (eds.), *Shifts in Compensating Work-Related Injuries and Diseases*, Wien/New York: Springer 2007, p. 197-220.

Philipsen 2010
Philipsen, N.J., 'Regulation and Competition in the Legal Profession: Developments in the EU and China', 6(2) *Journal of Competition Law and Economics*, 2010, p. 203-231. (Advance access published on 21 April 2009, doi:10.1093/joclec/nhp009).

Poillot-Peruzetto & Lawnicka 2012
Poillot-Peruzetto, S. & Lawnicka, D., 'Relevance of the Distinction between the Contractual and Non-Contractual Spheres (Jurisdiction and Applicable Law)', in: J. Basedow, J. *et al.* (eds.), *International Antitrust Litigation: Conflict of Laws and Coordination* (Studies in Private International Law, 8), Oxford: Hart Publishing Limited 2012, p. 132-157.

Properetti, Paini & Tomasi 2009
Prosperetti, L, Paini, E. & Tomasi, I., *Il danno antitrust*, Bologna: Il Malino 2009.

Recommendation on collective redress
Commission Recommendation on common principles for injunctive and compensatory collective redress mechanisms in the Member States concerning violations of rights granted under Union Law, [2013] OJ L 201, 11 June 2013.

Revesz 1996
Revesz, R., 'Federalism and Interstate Environmental Externalities', 144(6) *University of Pennsylvania Law Review*, 1996, p. 2341-2416.

Revesz 2000a
Revesz, R., 'Federalism and Regulation: Extrapolating from the Analysis of Environmental Regulation in the United States', 3 *Journal of International Economic Law*, 2000, p. 219-233.

Revesz 2000b
Revesz, R., 'Federalism and Environmental Regulation: An Overview', in: R. Revesz, Ph. Sands & R. Stewart (eds.), *Environmental Law: The Economy and Sustainable Development*, Cambridge: Cambridge University Press 2000, p. 37-79.

Rodger 2014
Rodger, B. (ed.), *Competition Law – Comparative Private Enforcement and Collective Redress across the EU*, The Hague: Kluwer 2014.

Shavell 1984
Shavell, S., 'Liability for Harm versus Regulation of Safety', 13 *Journal of Legal Studies*, 1984, p. 357-374.

Shavell 2004
Shavell, S., *Foundations of Economic Analysis of Law*, Cambridge: Belknap 2004.

Smits 1998
Smits, J., 'A European Private Law as a Mixed Legal System: Towards a Ius Commune Through the Free Movement of Legal Rules', 5 *Maastricht Journal of European and Comparative Law*, 1998, p. 328-340.

Stephan 2008
Stephan, A., An Empirical Assessment of the European Leniency Notice, 5(3) *Journal of Competition Law & Economics*, 2008, p. 537-561.

Tiebout 1956
Tiebout, C., 'A Pure Theory of Local Expenditures', 64 *Journal of Political Economy*, 1956, p. 416-424.

Van Boom 2011
Van Boom, W., 'Harmonizing Tort Law: A Comparative Tort Law and Economics Analysis', in: M. Faure (ed.), *Tort Law and Economics, Encyclopedia of Law and Economics* (2nd edition), Cheltenham, UK and Northampton, MA, USA: Edward Elgar Publishing 2011, p. 435-449.

Van den Bergh 1996
Van den Bergh, R., 'Economic Criteria for Applying the Subsidiarity Principle in the European Community: The Case of Competition Policy', 16 *International Review of Law and Economics*, 1996, p. 363-383.

Van den Bergh 1998
Van den Bergh, R., 'Subsidiarity as an Economic Demarcation Principle and the Emergence of European Private Law', 5 *Maastricht Journal of European and Comparative Law*, 1998, p. 129-152.

Van den Bergh 2000
Van den Bergh, R., 'Towards an Institutional Legal Framework for Regulatory Competition in Europe', 53(4), *Kyklos*, 2000, p. 435-466.

Van den Bergh & Camesasca 2006
Van den Bergh, R.J. & Camesasca, P.D, *European Competition Law and Economics: A Comparative Perspective*, Stamford, Connecticut, USA: Thomson 2006.

Vaubel 1994
Vaubel, R., 'The Political Economy of Centralization and the European Community', 81(1) *Public Choice*, 1994, p. 151-190.

Visscher 2010
Visscher, L., *A Law and Economics View on Harmonization of Procedural Law*, Rotterdam Institute of Law and Economics (RILE) Working Paper Series, No. 2010/09, Erasmus University Rotterdam, 2010.

Vogel 1995
Vogel, D., *Trading Up: Consumer and Environmental Regulation in a Global Economy*, Cambridge, MA: Harvard University Press 1995.

Whish & Bailey 2012
Whish, R. & Baily, D., *Competition Law*, Oxford: Oxford University Press 2012.

Kristel De Smedt
Michael Faure

WHO DOES WHAT? ENVIRONMENTAL LIABILITY IN THE EU

1. Introduction

There are several ways in which one could discuss environmental law generally or environmental law specifically within the European Union. In order to focus our contribution to the allocation of competences in European Private Law, we have decided to narrow down this contribution to a discussion of the Environmental Liability Directive. The reason is that with the Environmental Liability Directive of 21 April 2004 (hereafter Directive or ELD), the Community aims to establish a framework of environmental liability based on the 'polluter-pays' principle, to prevent and remedy environmental damage.[1] The Directive covers water pollution, damage to biodiversity and land contamination.[2]

The development process of the ELD gave rise to significant controversy and conflict. Much of the conflict precisely addressed the allocation of competences with respect to environmental liability and especially the question whether the European Union should have a European environmental liability regime at all. Furthermore, the final text of the ELD also was heavily criticized, as being too limited in scope and as having little real significance or added value. Hence, we will use this specific instrument of the ELD to provide a more indepth and theoretical discussion of the desirability of harmonization of environmental liability at EU level. The ELD to some extent nicely shows many of the difficulties in harmonizing private law at EU level.

Indeed, it is striking that the final decision on crucial elements of the liability regime, such as the scope of the regime, the insertion of a permit or a state-of-the-art defence, causation issues, or the decision on compulsory financial guarantees, has been passed on to the Member States. Member States may also adopt or maintain

1 Directive 2004/35/CE of the European Parliament and of the Council of 21 April 2004 on Environmental Liability with regard to the Prevention and Remedying of Environmental Damage, OJ L 143/56, 30 April 2004, Art. 1, hereafter ELD.

2 This is made clear from a combination of the rather complicated definitional Arts. 2 and 3, which deals with the scope of the Directive.

more stringent provisions in relation to the prevention and remedying of environmental damage.[3]

Hence, the Directive gives a significant degree of latitude to the Member States on how they transpose the Directive's provisions. Yet, this also means that the transposition in the Member States can differ. On the one hand, Member States might take the opportunity to go further than what the Directive requires, but on the other hand Member States could take advantage of the discretionary provisions to minimize the Directive's impact.[4]

Under the Commission's 'smart regulation' policy, *ex-post* evaluation of regulations has now been formally adopted as part of the Commission's approach to law making and implementation. This kind of evaluation is intended to assess whether EU legislation is achieving its objectives, whether the benefits of the legislation exceed the costs, and what changes can be made to increase its efficiency.[5] The ELD is no exception. Based on Article 18 § 1 ELD, Member States have to report to the Commission on the experience gained in the application of the Directive. On that basis, the Commission shall submit a report to the European Parliament and the Council which will evaluate the Directive and include a review of it, in principle by 30 April 2014. At this moment, all Member States have submitted their national reports but with delays. Yet, due to the delayed Member States' reports and the Commission's own evaluation studies, it has been decided to postpone the adoption of the ELD report until after the European Parliament elections and the establishment of the new Commission. The adoption of the ELD report is therefore planned for the first quarter of 2015. Based on the reactions from the European Parliament, the Council and the ELD stakeholder communities, the new Commission will consider appropriate amendments. At this moment, however, it is difficult to anticipate what these amendments will be.[6]

This contribution first analyses the reasons for an environmental liability regime at European level from a law and economics perspective. Second, it provides an insight in how the Directive was implemented in the Member States. As it is not possible to do a complete analysis of all Member States, we focus on the implementation of the ELD in three Member States, combined with a general evaluation. Finally, this chapter attempts to evaluate the ELD a decade after its adoption and discusses whether the ELD is achieving its objectives and what the effects of the ELD have been or are likely to be. So far there are very few data on the practical effects of the ELD. Hence, any analysis of those practical effects is largely speculative. However, so far it seems that (as with the Product Liability Directive) national legislation implementing the Directive is almost not used by victims in the Member States. That hence also raises important questions with respect to the usefulness of the entire exercise. One additional difficulty in assessing the practical importance of the ELD is that generally with respect to environmental damage, there is significant

3 This is made clear in preamble 29 preceding the Directive and in Art. 16 of the ELD.

4 Winter *et al.* 2008, p. 175.

5 Faure & De Smedt 2013. The ELD's effects in practice. In Bergkamp & Goldsmith 2013, p. 299.

6 Information provided by Hans Lopatta, Policy officer, Directorate-General for Environment, European Commission, 20 May 2014.

uncertainty relating to the probability of accidents and the size of their possible consequences, and significant incommensurability relating to the valuation of natural resources.

Accordingly, this chapter is structured as follows. Section 2 critically analyses the arguments for an environmental liability regime at European level from a law and economics perspective. Section 3 looks at the ELD transposition in Belgium, the Netherlands and Germany in order to assess whether the ELD establishes a common framework for the prevention and remedying of environmental damage in the EU. In section 4 the question is asked whether the ELD has in practice led to a harmonization of environmental liability rules. Section 5 examines the effects of the ELD in practice and reflects on the way forward, with the forthcoming Commission report in mind. Finally, we provide some conclusions, albeit tentative, given the paucity of available information on the ELD's implementation in practice.[7]

2. Environmental Liability at European Level: a Law and Economics Analysis

2.1. *Justification for the ELD*

It is well-known that the division of labour between the Member States and the European level has originally been laid down in the single European act as far as environmental policy is concerned in the so-called subsidiarity principle. The subsidiarity principle, which was enshrined in (then) Article 5 of the EC Treaty, stated that in areas which do not fall within the Community's exclusive competence, such as environmental policy, the Community shall take action, in accordance with the principle of subsidiarity, *only if and in so far the objectives of the proposed action cannot be sufficiently achieved by the Member States and can therefore, by reason of the scale or effects of the proposed action, be better achieved by the Community.*[8] In the area of shared competences (like environmental policy)[9] the subsidiarity principle still applies since the entry into force of the Treaty of Lisbon. It is now held that an important condition for action at the level of the European Union is that the Union can only act 'if and in so far as the objectives of the proposed action cannot be sufficiently achieved by the Member States'.[10] The subsidiarity principle is now further explained in Protocol No. 2 attached to the Treaty on European Union (TEU) and the Treaty on the Functioning of the European Union (TFEU).

The subsidiarity principle is connected with the principle of proportionality, which requires that *any action by the Community shall not go beyond what is necessary to*

7 See also Faure & De Smedt 2013. The ELD's effects in practice. In Bergkamp & Goldsmith 2013, p. 299-314.

8 At the time when the Environmental Liability Directive was drafted the subsidiarity principle was incorporated in Art. 5 of the (then) EC Treaty. See also Jans 2000, p. 11-12.

9 See Art. 4(2)(e) of the Treaty on the Functioning of the European Union (TFEU).

10 Art. 5(3) of the Treaty on the European Union (TEU).

achieve the objectives of this treaty.[11] The proportionality principle is now enshrined in Article 5(4) of the TEU.[12]

Yet, in view of the fierce debates during the adoption process of the ELD precisely on the Community's competence to harmonize environmental liability, it is striking that in the final text of the ELD, the Commission fails to explain why a harmonized liability regime is necessary or why its goals cannot be achieved by the Member States, as required by the subsidiarity principle. Indeed, although the subsequent documents in the ELD adoption process provide arguments for Community action, a clear overview of arguments and hence the estimated benefits for a harmonized liability regime cannot be found anymore in the final text of the ELD. Preamble 3 of the ELD states that subsidiarity is met because the ELD's objective, namely to establish a common framework for the prevention and remedying of environmental damage, cannot be sufficiently achieved by the Member States and can therefore be better achieved at Community level by reason of scale or effect.[13] The Commission does not explain why it is necessary to establish such a framework or why it cannot be achieved by the Member States. Moreover, the Commission's reasoning in Preamble 3 is, as Bergkamp and Faure indicate, merely a description of the subsidiarity principle itself and does not provide any justification. Therefore, legal doctrine has held that quite often, also as far as the ELD is concerned, the Commission merely states that 'by reason of the scale or effects of the proposed action' the proposed action cannot be sufficiently achieved by the Member States which would justify community action. This, however, is a mere repetition of the subsidiarity principle, but does not at all explain why this particular issue (like environmental liability) would necessarily need action at the European level. Scholarship therefore holds that in fact the Commission, the Parliament and the Council have not explained that the ELD would be justified from the perspective of the subsidiarity and the proportionality principle.[14]

It is, however, interesting to examine why the Commission felt it necessary to issue rules concerning environmental liability at the European level. In order to obtain some insight, the subsequent Commission documents in the ELD decision-making process should be examined.

Three subsequent documents in the ELD decision-making process can be referred to in order to examine the reasons for a shift of environmental liability rules from the Member States to the European level: the Commission Green Paper on Remedying Environmental Damage,[15] the White Paper on Environmental Liability,[16] and the Explanatory Memorandum to the Proposal for a Directive on Environ-

11 This was at the time laid down in Art. 5 §3 of the EC Treaty.

12 See for a discussion of the principles of subsidiarity and proportionality after Lisbon Jans & Vedder 2012, p. 13-20.

13 ELD, Preamble 3.

14 See Bergkamp 2005, p. 97; Fogleman 2004, p. 102; Faure 2005, p. 8.

15 Commission Communication of 14 May 1993, Green Paper on Remedying Environmental Damage, COM(93) 47.

16 Commission Communication of 9 February 2000, White Paper on Environmental Liability, COM(2000) 66.

mental Liability with regard to the Prevention and Restoration of Environmental Damage.[17]

A careful study of these documents allows us to summarize the main estimated benefits given by the EU Commission for European action in the field of environmental liability: (i) a solution for transboundary environmental damage, (ii) a solution against the race-to-the-bottom, (iii) equal marketing conditions in the EU, (iv) the realization of the precautionary, polluter-pays and preventive principles,[18] (v) decontamination and restoration of the environment, and (vi) guaranteeing a minimum level of protection.

2.2. *The Arguments of the Commission tested*

We will discuss the different arguments presented by the European Commission to justify action at the European level and analyse to what extent these arguments may also justify harmonization of environmental liability from an economic perspective. This will hence also give us an opportunity to discuss the economics of federalism with respect to environmental liability.

A first argument which is presented to justify the ELD is that a European environmental liability regime would provide a solution for transboundary damage. However, in principle, for transboundary damage a kind of transboundary regime could solve the problem. The argument by itself therefore is not sufficient to justify a harmonization of environmental liability rules in the EU.

A second argument for and preceived benefit of the ELD, was the prevention of a race-to-the-bottom.[19] Yet, the relation between environmental regulation, on the one hand, and regulatory competition and industry competitiveness, on the other hand, is heavily debated. In its preparatory documents, the Commission argued that, without a harmonized framework of liability for environmental damage, economic actors might exploit the differences in stringency of liability between Member States, which might lead to distortions of competition.[20] The 'race-to-the-bottom' argument may well be the most frequently advanced argument to justify EU environmental regulation.[21] If there is a risk that a destructive 'race-to-the-bottom' regulatory competition will arise, there may be an economic argument for

17 Communication of 23 January 2002, Proposal for a Directive of the European Parliament and of the Council on Environmental Liability with regard to the Prevention and Restoration of Environmental Damage, COM(2002) 17 final, OJ C 151 E/132.

18 At the time of drafting the ELD these principles were incorporated in Art. 174 § 2 of the EC Treaty; they can now be found in Art. 191(2) of the TFEU. For a more detailed analysis see Jans & Vedder 2012, p. 41-52.

19 For a summary of the economic literature with respect to the race-to-the-bottom in environmental law see Faure 2011, p. 385-416.

20 *Green Paper on remedying Environmental Damage, White Paper on Environmental Liability* and the Proposal for a Directive on Environmental Liability with regard to the Prevention and Restoration of Environmental Damage, Explanatory Memorandum.

21 The term 'race-to-the-bottom' refers to an ever increasing relaxation of state regulatory standards caused by interstate competition to attract industry. This relaxation of regulatory standards results in a reduction of social welfare below the level that would exist in absence of this race. Engel 1997, p. 274.

the centralization of regulation as a remedy for such welfare-reducing competition. The theoretical and empirical evidence for the existence of a 'race-to-the-bottom' in environmental regulations is, however, ambiguous.[22]

In theory, a Member State could try to attract industry by reducing the liability burdens imposed on industry. For example, a Member State might impose a higher burden of proof on claimants regarding environmental damage, it might set a high standard of proof of causation, or it might neglect the enforcement of its environmental laws.[23] This kind of behaviour would be difficult to detect and to prove. It has been claimed that the most important risk of regulatory competition would be a 'regulatory chill'.[24] This would mean that state officials, fearing industry relocation and under political pressure, would not adopt, not implement, or not enforce environmental standards instead of lowering standards. This kind of behaviour, however, is not likely to lead to a lenient environmental liability regime. This is so because such a regime would also limit a state's ability to seek compensation for environmental damage caused by non-domestic companies, and thus adversely affecting the state's interests.[25]

Turning to the specific situation of the ELD's introduction in the EU, the question is whether a 'race-to-the-bottom' indeed had to be feared.[26] In theory, more so than for environmental regulation in general, a 'race-to-the-bottom' in environmental liability law seemed to be unlikely, because Member States hardly gain an advantage from a lenient liability regime. On the other hand, Member State officials may erroneously believe (or be pressured to assume) that a stringent liability regime would scare away investors. This, in turn, could induce them to implement and apply the ELD as 'lenient' as possible, or put differently, to do the minimum and enforce leniently. A recent study seems to confirm this proposition,[27] but whether it is relevant to environmental liability is hard to confirm. At the time of the coming into being of the ELD, a 'race-to-the-bottom' was probably not a big problem. At that moment, the new 'Central and Eastern European' Member States were not part of the EU, however. It has been argued that EU enlargement may lead new Member States either to be lax in the implementation of environmental laws generally, or at least to be lax as far as the enforcement is concerned.[28] Empirical evidence has shown that the retrospective liability that, in some cases, was applied in Central and Eastern Europe on purchasers of contaminated land seriously limited the possibilities for privatization in those countries. Potential investors were scared away by the

22 See, for example, Jaffe *et al.* 1995, p. 157-158; Xing & Kolstad 1995, p. 1-22.

23 Ackerman 1996, p. 429.

24 Esty & Geradin 1998, p. 19. Cf. Gray 2002, p. 310-311.

25 Faure 2003, p. 49.

26 See also Oates 1998, p. 1-13.

27 Jans *et al.* 2009 showed that Member States only sparingly and accidentally use their power to enact or maintain more stringent environmental standards after a EU harmonization measure. Some Member States have adopted an explicit 'no gold-plating policy,' meaning that they do not go beyond the minimum requirements of a directive. The main reason for this policy is to protect the domestic industry. Jans *et al.* 2009, p. 434-435.

28 Faure & Johnston 2009, p. 205-274.

foresight of having to pay for the pollution of the past.[29] This may have created incentives for the new Member State governments to be lax in the ELD's implementation.[30]

On the other hand, in some markets affected by ELD regimes, a contrary movement may occur and the ELD may be a driver of competitive performance improvements.[31]

Likewise, it is unlikely that the ELD has exercised any significant effect on the EU industry's international competitiveness. In theory, an onerous liability program could adversely affect the EU industry's international competitiveness, if other jurisdictions do not have a similar onerous liability program in place. For instance, if the US had a very light or no environmental liability program in place, the costs imposed on the EU industry by the ELD could place it in a worse competitive position. Any such effect is highly unlikely, however, because the ELD does not impose substantial cost generally; it does so, only if an operator causes environmental damage for which it is liable. And the US does have an environmental liability regime that resembles the ELD; or, rather, the ELD was inspired by the US approach to assessing and restoring environmental damage.

Nevertheless, the way in which the ELD is implemented and especially enforced in the different Member States determines whether there is a risk of a race-to-the-bottom, or a regulatory chill. The question remains whether the ELD – considering the fact that important issues were left to the Member States – is really able to prevent a race-to-the-bottom.

A third benefit arising from the ELD perceived by the Commisison was the establishment of a level playing field and equal economic conditions throughout the EU. The Commission has argued repeatedly that the EU should legislate in the area of environmental liability to avoid a distortion of competition.[32] This argument is a species of the theory that justifies harmonization of environmental regulation to ease the tensions created by the differences in the stringency of environmental regulations of various countries. These differences would result in a distortion of competition and high administrative and transaction costs, since companies must learn and comply with the rules of each country. Under this theory, harmonization would result in even economic conditions and reduced administrative and transaction costs. In this respect, however, a distinction must be made between products, which cross borders, and manufacturing operations, which are stationary. Although trade could justify the harmonization of environmental product or process standards, it does not call for harmonization of environmental liability rules applying to stationary facilities.

29 Cliffton & Panayotou 2000, p. 335-337.

30 See on liability avoidance also Faure 2012, p. 304-305.

31 For an example for the European building and construction sector, see Testa, Iraldo & Frey 2011, p. 431-432.

32 *Green Paper on remedying Environmental Damage, White Paper on Environmental Liability* and the Proposal for a Directive on Environmental Liability with regard to the Prevention and Restoration of Environmental Damage, Explanatory Memorandum.

Hardly surprisingly, the 'level playing field' argument has been rebutted since the Commisison first presented it.[33] Equal economic conditions would not be achieved through the harmonization of environmental liability rules, since there are many other, far more important factors that determine the conditions of competition.[34] Further, Member States cannot use environmental liability rules to engage in disguised protectionism, because a causal link between the environmental harm and the product concerned must be proven.[35] Thus, environmental liability rules are unlikely to act as trade barriers or to cause competitiveness concerns.[36]

Moreover, due to the fact that crucial elements of the liability regime were passed on to the Member States, it was doubtful that the ELD would realize a level playing field.

With respect to arguments 4 and 5, the realization of the polluter pays, precautionary and preventive principles and the decontamination and restoration of the environment do not explain or justify, at least from an economic perspective, why environmental liability regulation should be issued at the European level and why this cannot be achieved by the Member States themselves. Finally, although the minimum level of protection argument (6) might in some circumstances justify the harmonization of regulation, it is doubtful whether it is really necessary to harmonize environmental liability rules.[37]

2.3. *Centralization to Satisfy Demand of Interest Groups?*

In sum, it is doubtful that the arguments which one could find in documents preceding the ELD justified European action in the field of environmental liability and hence, the necessity of the Directive can be seriously questioned.[38]

Moreover, as we stated above, also the content of the Directive itself lead to heated debates during the development of the Directive. Various provisions were heavily debated at political level as well as at academic level. From a law and economics point of view, it could be argued that, as far as the choice of liability regime is concerned, the ELD complies with the economic analysis of tort law.[39] The economic analysis of tort law predicts that a strict liability rule is more efficient in case of hazardous activities since in those situations it is more important to control the injurer's activity. For other situations, a fault regime can suffice,[40] which is precisely what the ELD proposes. However, some provisions in the ELD might seriously undermine the ability of the Directive to exert a preventive effect and to ensure restoration of damage. Indeed, in theory, strict liability could provide a

33 Faure 2003.

34 Faure 2003, p. 55.

35 Bergkamp 2001, p. 381-382.

36 Faure 2003, p. 61.

37 De Smedt 2007. See also De Smedt 2008, p. 106-117.

38 For a critical analysis in this respect see Faure & De Smedt 2001, p. 217-237; Bergkamp 2002, p. 294-314 and p. 327-340.

39 Arcuri 2001, p. 37.

40 For the choice between strict liability and negligence from an economic perspective, see the literature review by Schäfer & Müller-Langer 2009, p. 3-45.

strong incentive for operators to take all possible risk-minimizing measures and it could be a way of implementing the precautionary principle. However, the restricted scope of the Directive,[41] the fact that the burden of proof lays with the authorities,[42] the (possible) availability of the permit and the state-of-the-art defence[43] and the absence of mandatory insurance[44] might cause that the ELD does not set a strong incentive for the potential liable operators to invest in risk-minimizing measures.

Therefore, additional explanations can be sought for the existence of the ELD and for certain provisions in the ELD by means of a private interest approach. Indeed, in order to understand why the decision making level of environmental liability rules was shifted from the Member States to the European level, how the ELD got to its final form, and why certain provisions are as they are, rent seeking behaviour and lobbying of different interest groups in the decision making process of the ELD should not be ignored.[45] The use of private interest theories might help to unveil reasons for the harmonization of environmental liability rules in the European Union, that cannot be explained by the economic theory of federalism.

Initially, industry lobby groups opposed a European environmental liability regime. Yet, commentary papers of industry lobby groups showed that industry in the end did not oppose the public law regime as proposed by the ELD,[46] maybe to obtain a consistent approach throughout the Community. Moreover, during the decision-making process industry fiercely lobbied for the insertion of defences and the absence of compulsory insurance. Indeed, the final text of the ELD shows that important concessions were made to industry groups by inserting broad defences against liability in terms of regulatory compliance and state-of-the-art knowledge at the time of the damage. With respect to the insurance issue, Member States are merely encouraged to develop financial security mechanisms.[47]

Environmental NGOs from their side believed in all stages of the decision-making procedure that 'a strong EU-wide regime on Environmental Liability is vital to improve the protection of Europe's most vulnerable wildlife and further the process of sustainable development. The adoption of the Directive is a necessary

41 ELD, Art. 3(1).
42 Wagner 2005, p. 90-91.
43 ELD, Art. 8(4).
44 ELD, Art. 14(2).
45 Oates & Portney 2001, p. 5.
46 CEFIC, EUROPIA, OGP and UNICE, Commission Proposal for a Directive on Environmental Liability, Common proposals from CEFIC, EUROPIA, OGP and UNICE: 'Recognising the difficulties of dealing with damage to the environment in all Member States, and bearing in mind the studies and consideration in general by academics, NGOs and European and national authorities to progress this matter, we recognize that the Commission proposal of 23 January 2002 makes a significant contribution in this regard.'
47 Clarke 2003, p. 261.

step in the right direction'.[48] As far as the final text of the ELD was concerned, environmental NGOs, however, were

> 'disappointed that the final Directive was not nearly as ambitious as the previous proposals and that it allows Member States to introduce serious derogations from the 'polluter pays' principle, in particular the 'permit' and 'state-of-the-art' provisions, as well as the restricted scope and limited requirements for financial security'.[49]

The Commission on its side might have welcomed a European environmental liability regime for other reasons than only public welfare and protection of the environment as for example enlarging its own competences in fields for which it did not have any direct competence yet, as soil protection policies.[50]

Clearly, the Union would have been unable to adopt the ELD without the approval of the Member States. Yet, Member States' opinions on the ELD were diverse and large disagreement between Member States on key issues such as financial security, subsidiary state liability and permit and state-of-the-art defences existed.

Nevertheless, the Directive being adopted, the proof of the pudding is in the eating. In the remaining of this article we will examine the implementation of the ELD in the Member States and its practical effects, based on the available information to date.

3. Implementation of the ELD in the Netherlands, Belgium and Germany

The objective of the ELD is to establish a common framework for the prevention and remedying of environmental damage in the EU. One way to consider whether the ELD's objective is met is to review the ELD's implementation in three Member States. For this purpose, we review the transposition of the ELD in Belgium, the Netherlands, and Germany.[51]

48 Birdlife International, Greenpeace, WWF, Friends of the Earth, EEB (joint declaration), The Directive on Environmental Liability, The European Parliament's Third Reading Vote, 31 March 2004.

49 Birdlife International, Greenpeace, WWF, Friends of the Earth, EEB (joint declaration), The Directive on Environmental Liability, The European Parliament's Third Reading Vote, 31 March 2004, See also Birdlife International and WWF, The European Directive on Environmental Liability – 'Polluter Pays': from principle to practice? An Environmental NGO commentary on the Environmental Liability Directive: its adoption at EU level and what it means for the future, July 2004.

50 See Van Calster 2004, p. 3-17.

51 See also Faure & De Smedt 2013. The ELD's effects in practice. In Bergkamp & Goldsmith 2013, p. 300-307.

3.1. *Relevant Aspects of the ELD's Transposition in Belgium*

Belgium has a federal structure. Legislative and, to a large extent, enforcement powers in environmental matters have been delegated to the regions, i.e. the Brussels capital, the Walloon, and Flemish regions. The federal government, however, retained legislative and enforcement powers over nuclear energy, marketing and transport of hazardous substances (including genetically modified organisms), waste transfer, and the marine environment. Accordingly, the ELD had to be implemented not only by the three regions (Flanders,[52] Wallonia,[53] and Brussels[54]), but also by the federal government.[55]

In the Flemish region, the ELD has been implemented by means of a new chapter on environmental damage in the Decree containing General Provisions on Environmental Policy. The remediation of land damage, however, is regulated separately in the Decree on Soil Sanitation of 22 December 1995, which has been amended to transpose the ELD. In the Walloon region, the ELD has been implemented via a new chapter inserted in the Environmental Code (Part I, General provisions), and a few small amendments of the Decree on Nature Conservation. In the Brussels region, the ELD is implemented by an Ordinance. In all three regions, the main transposing laws have a non-sectorial, horizontal dimension.[56]

To promote a consistent implementation of the ELD, inter-regional consultations were conducted. The regions made the same political choice in relation to the permit defence and state-of-the-art defences. In general, the Flemish and Walloon regions' ELD-transposing legislation is the minimum required by the ELD; the Flemish Environment Minister's policy is to transpose European legislation correctly and timely, but to avoid 'gold-plating'.[57] In some respects, however, the Brussels region went further than what was strictly required by the ELD.

52 Decreet tot aanvulling van het decreet van 5 april 1995 houdende algemene bepalingen inzake milieubeleid met een titel XV Milieuschade, tot omzetting van de Richtlijn 2004/35/EG van het Europees Parlement en de Raad van 21 april 2004 betreffende de milieuaansprakelijkheid met betrekking tot het voorkomen en herstellen van milieuschade (*Belgisch Staatsblad*, 12.02.2008, p. 9139).

53 Décret modifiant le Livre Ier du Code de l'Environnement en ce qui concerne la prévention et la réparation des dommages environnementaux (1), 22 novembre 2007, (*Belgisch Staatsblad*, 19.12.2007).

54 Ordonnantie betreffende milieuaansprakelijkheid met betrekking tot het voorkomen en herstellen van milieuschade, 13 November 2008. (*Belgisch Staatsblad*, 14.11.2008 - Ed. 3).

55 Wet houdende diverse bepalingen April 2007, N. 2007 - 1848 [2007/201376] and Koninklijk besluit betreffende de preventie en het herstel van milieuschade bij het in de handel brengen van genetisch gemodificeerde organismen of van producten die er bevatten, 3 August 2007.N. 2007 - 3873 [C - 2007/23299] (see <www.emis.vito.be>).

56 <www.avosetta.org>, Avosetta Meeting Ghent 1-2 June 2007, Environmental liability Directive in different countries, L. Lavrysen, D. Misonne, R. Slabbinck, P. De Smedt, Belgian Report, p. 5.

57 Beleidsnota Leefmilieu en Natuur 2004-2009, Flemish Government, December 2004, policy document by the Flemish Minister for the Environment, 81 p., available on: <www.vlaanderen.be>.

As far as the scope is concerned, the Flemish and Walloon Regions did not broaden the regime's scope on the basis of Article 2(3) of the ELD, but the Brussels Region added additional habitats under the scope of its transposing law.[58] With regard to the activities covered by the ELD Annex III, the Brussels Region has gone beyond the ELD by adding the deliberate release of exotic species.[59]

All regions have made the permit and state-of-the-art defences available. These defences work as follows: the operator is required to take the necessary remedial measures, but if he can prove that his emissions were authorized under a permit, or that given the state-of-the-art he could not know that the emissions would cause damage, he has a right to recover the costs from the authorities. In Flanders, for example, the operator can recover the costs from the so-called 'Mina-fund'.[60]

All regions opted for joint and several liability. None of them require financial guarantees; rather, they merely encourage the development of financial instruments, as stipulated in the ELD.

3.2. *Relevant Aspects of the ELD's Transposition in the Netherlands*

In the Netherlands, after lengthy debates, the Dutch legislation transposed the ELD by adding a completely new section to the Environmental Management Act (*Wet milieubeheer*). This new law entered into force only 1st of June 2008.[61] The main argument for transposing the ELD in the Environmental Management Act, rather than in the Dutch Civil Code, was that the ELD was found to have more of a public character, rather than a private law character.[62]

Moreover, the main reasons why in the Netherlands an implementation in one general law (in this case the Environmental Management Act) was preferred rather than an implementation via several sectoral laws (such as the Surface Waters Act and the Flora and Fauna Act) were related to arguments of transparency, consistency, uniformity, and legal clarity.[63]

The current approach of The Netherlands towards the transposition of EU environmental directives is that the transposing law should be limited to the directive's minimum requirements. This policy is also reflected in the ELD transposition.

58 Ordonnantie betreffende milieuaansprakelijkheid met betrekking tot het voorkomen en herstellen van milieuschade, 13 November 2008. (*Belgisch Staatsblad*, 14.11.2008 - Ed. 3), [see definitions].

59 Ordonnantie betreffende milieuaansprakelijkheid met betrekking tot het voorkomen en herstellen van milieuschade, 13 November 2008. (*Belgisch Staatsblad*, 14.11.2008 - Ed. 3), Annex III, No. 13.

60 Decreet tot aanvulling van het decreet van 5 april 1995 houdende algemene bepalingen inzake milieubeleid met een titel XV Milieuschade, tot omzetting van de Richtlijn 2004/35/EG van het Europees Parlement en de Raad van 21 april 2004 betreffende de milieuaansprakelijkheid met betrekking tot het voorkomen en herstellen van milieuschade (*Belgisch Staatsblad*, 12.02.2008), Chapter V: defences, p. 9143.

61 *Staatsblad*, Nos. 166 and 178.

62 Kamerstukken 30 920. Brans 2007.

63 Explanatory Memorandum, Tweede Kamer, vergaderjaar 2006–2007, 30 920, No. 3, p. 3. Winter *et al.* 2008, p. 178.

There even is an explicit statement in the Explanatory Memorandum that the Netherlands will not make use of their power to extend the ELD's scope of application to other activities.[64] Consistent with minimum transposition, the Dutch government did opt to transpose all of the exclusions set forth in Article 4 of the ELD. Furthermore, with respect to the ELD's definitions (e.g. 'environmental damage'), there is either a direct reference to the corresponding definition in the ELD, or the text of the relevant ELD provision is copied into the implementing legislation. The Dutch legislature uses distinct terminology to avoid inconsistency with other legislation (for instance, with other sections of the Environmental Management Act or with the Dutch General Administrative Law Act, *Algemene wet bestuursrecht*).[65]

In the legislative debate in the Dutch Parliament, it was argued that the scope of the implementing law should cover all activities that might cause environmental damage, not only Annex III activities. An amendment was adopted to the effect that in the future the scope of the law can be broadened by means of secondary legislation (*Algemene Maatregel van Bestuur*, AMvB).[66] Consequently, it is possible that more and other types of activities will be brought under the scope of the law. The ELD itself did not require this, so in this respect the Dutch transposition goes further than what was required, although the adoption of new legislation would be necessary to effectively broaden the scope.

With respect to the implementation of Article 8(4) of the ELD (permit defence and state-of-the-art defence), the Dutch legislation also appears to go beyond the ELD's minimum requirements. The defences were transposed in the Dutch legislation but in a restricted manner. Article 17.16 Environmental Management Act provides that the competent public authority may decide not to recover the costs in cases in which the permit or state-of-the-art defence can be invoked, if a decision to do so would be unreasonable. This leaves discretion to the authorities, but it is not yet clear under which circumstances a full recovery would lead to unreasonableness. The Explanatory Memorandum refers to 'exceptional circumstances'; other, non-exceptional circumstances, such as economic consequences and bankruptcy, are not taken into account,[67] and the burden of proof lies with the operator.[68] Note that the concept of unreasonableness applies only to the permit and the state-of-the-art defences.

3.3. *Relevant Aspects of the ELD's Transposition in Germany*

Germany implemented the ELD by means of the federal 'Act on Environmental Damage' (*Umweltschadensgesetz*, USchadG) that entered into force on 14 November

64 Explanatory Memorandum, Tweede Kamer, vergaderjaar 2006–2007, 30 920, No. 3, p. 4.

65 Winter *et al.* 2008, p. 178.

66 Art. 17.7 Environmental Management Act (Wm).

67 Winter *et al.* 2008, p. 179.

68 Tweede Kamer der Staten-Generaal, proposal to change the Dutch Environmental Management Act with respect to the Implementation of the Directive (Voorstel van wet tot wijziging van de Wet Milieubeheer in verband met de implementatie van richtlijn No. 2004/35EG (milieuaansprakelijkheid)), memorie van toelichting, Tweede Kamer, vergaderjaar 2006-2007, 30 920, No. 3, p. 15.

2007. Germany already had comprehensive legislation in place for the prevention and remediation of environmental damage.[69] Administrative agencies had pre-existing powers to order polluters to prevent and remediate environmental damage on a non-fault basis under laws such as the Protection of Nature Act, Water Act, and Federal Soil Protection Act.[70]

In some respects, the ELD did not go so far as the pre-existing German law. This is so, for instance, for the definition of damage to land, which was not defined to include the condition of a threat to human health. The German legislature did not lower its standard when transposing the ELD: if damage to soil is imminent or has occurred, the polluter is responsible for preventing or remediating this damage even if there is no danger to human health.[71]

On the other hand, the German legislature has not extended the scope of the ELD regime as permitted by Article 2(3), ELD. The definition of damage to natural resources is limited to Natura 2000 sites and species, and does not include areas, biotopes or species protected only under German law.[72]

In other areas, however, German law was improved. In relation to nature and water protection (less so in relation to soil protection), the basic obligations of operators to investigate, notify, prevent and remediate damage were rather fragmented. The new Environmental Damage Act provides a structured system of both basic obligations and administrative powers. According to Winter *et al.*, this has three consequences. First, in cases of imminent or existing damage, operators are now under a comprehensive duty to inform the competent authority of all relevant aspects of the situation. Second, the ELD-based system obliges administrative authorities to force polluters to act in the first instance. Until then, authorities often took remedial action themselves and rarely sought compensation of the costs from the operator, although they had the power to do so. Third, as a related matter, administrative agencies now not only have powers but affirmative obligations to order operators to take action. Thus, under the new law, they are required to make use of their powers.[73]

Further, the German federal government did not allow the permit and state-of-the-art defences on the basis of Article 8(4) of the ELD. The German Environmental Damage Act imposes obligations on the operator to prevent, notify, and manage environmental damage, and requires that operators take measures even if the Article 8(3) and (4) exceptions would apply, thus, even if the activity was authorized or corresponded to the-state-of-the-art and the law.[74] If the law explicitly so provides, operators may recover their costs from the state or other responsible persons, which might have significant consequences. Winter *et al.* explain that the reason for this choice is that German police power law imposes responsibility on causers of damage, irrespective of whether the activity was authorized. Police

69 Rehbinder 2007, p. 201.
70 Winter *et al.* 2008, p. 175.
71 Brinktrine 2007, p. 345-346.
72 Winter *et al.* 2008, p. 175-176.
73 Winter *et al.* 2008, p. 175-176.
74 Sections 5 and 6, USchadG.

power law is, by and large, restricted to cases of accidental and serious damage, and Winter *et al.* argue that the new law extends this to any significant damage.[75]

German federal law leaves the *Länder* (i.e., the states that make up the federal republic of Germany) free to allow operators to invoke the permit and/or state-of-the-art defences. The rationale for this policy is that the wealth of the States varies, and therefore the *Länder* should decide whether they can afford to exempt operators from the cost burden of remediation, and remediate at public expense.[76] Additional state legislation therefore may be enacted in the future. As the defences are exceptions from rules set by the federal law, the default rule is that operators are liable in all cases, unless state law provides otherwise.[77]

Having sketched the relevant provisions of the laws of Belgium, Germany and the Netherlands, we can start to explore what the ELD transposition in these three Member States suggests with respect to the realization of the ELD's objectives, notably, ensuring the prevention and restoration of environmental damage, as well as risk spreading and insurance for environmental damage. In some instances, we refer also to the ELD transposing legislation of other Member States.

4. Harmonization via the ELD?

From the above brief look at the implementation in three Member States (Belgium, the Netherlands and Germany) it already becomes clear that there is a lot of heterogeneity and that existing differences at least between those three Member States will remain into existence. That is not only the case for Belgium, Germany and the Netherlands, but for many other Member States as well. Indeed, crucial elements that determine the effectiveness of a liability regime are the scope of the regime, the decision on compulsory financial guarantees and the insertion of a permit or a state-of-the-art defence, issues that – in the case of the ELD – have been passed on to the Member States.

With respect to the scope of the Directive, environmental damage includes damage to protected species and habitats, water damage and land damage.[78] Yet, damage to protected species and habitats is limited to species of birds listed in the Wild Birds Directive[79] and their habitats and those listed in the Habitats Directive[80] and any other habitat or species so determined by a Member State.[81] Water damage only falls within the Directive's scope if the water course is covered by the Water

75 Winter *et al.* 2008, p. 175-176.
76 Rehbinder 2007, p. 201.
77 Winter *et al.* 2008, p. 175.
78 ELD, Art. 2.
79 Council Directive 79/409/EEC of 2 April 1979 on the conservation of wild birds, OJ L 103 of 25 April 1979.
80 Council Directive 92/43/EEC of 21 May 1992 on the conservation of natural habitats and the protection of natural habitats and of wild flora and fauna, OJ L 206 of 22 July 1992.
81 ELD, Art. 2(3) (c).

Framework Directive (Directive 2000/60/EC)[82] and the Directive is only applicable to land contamination if there is a significant risk that human health is adversely affected.[83]

The Member States do have the possibility to enlarge the scope of the Directive, on the basis of Article 2(3), and of Article 16 of the ELD. Moreover, Member States may, on the basis of Article 2(3) (c) of the Directive, designate any habitat or species, not listed in the Wild Birds Directive or Habitats Directive. It is required though, that these habitats or species are protected by national law.[84] If Member States do not use the possibility to enlarge the scope of the Directive, the scope of the Directive will hence be rather limited.

It appears that the optional extension of the scope of 'damage to protected species and natural habitats' pursuant to the Wild Birds[85] and Habitats[86] Directives (Art. 2(3) ELD) has been used by fourteen Member States. These Member States included species and habitats protected under national or regional protection schemes in all or part of their jurisdiction (Austria, Belgium, Cyprus, Czech Republic, Estonia, Greece, Hungary, Latvia, Lithuania, Poland, Portugal, Spain, Sweden and UK). On the other hand, with respect to the scope of activities covered by strict liability, several Member States exempted the spreading of sewage sludge from waste management operations (Bulgaria, France, Latvia, Malta, Portugal, Romania, Slovakia, Slovenia and UK). Yet a number of Member States included further activities not mentioned in Annex III in the scope of strict liability (Belgium, Denmark, Finland, Greece, Hungary, Latvia, Lithuania, Netherlands and Sweden). Finally, another key definition, that of 'operator', was extended by all but one of the Member States, with some opting to give this definition a particularly broad scope (Estonia, Finland, Hungary, Lithuania, Poland and Sweden).[87]

With respect to the three Member States discussed above, the Netherlands goes further than the ELD by enabling a possible scope expansion through secondary legislation, as noted above.[88] The Brussels region enlarged the scope of its ELD regime by adding additional activities and by broadening the scope to more habitats. Flanders, Wallonia, and Germany did not enlarge the ELD's scope, but in Flanders additional protected species and natural habitats can be designated by the Flemish government.

82 Directive of the European Parliament and of the Council 2000/60/EC of 23 October 2000, establishing a Framework for Community Action in the Field of Water Policy, commonly known as the 'Water Framework Directive', OJ L 327 of 22 December 2000.

83 ELD, Art. 2(1) (c).

84 Brans 2007, p. 538.

85 Directive 2009/147/EC of the European Parliament and of the Council of 30 November 2009 on the conservation of wild birds, OJ L 20 of 26 January 2010, p. 7.

86 Council Directive 92/43/EEC on the conservation of natural habitats and of wild fauna and flora, OJ L 206 of 22 July 1992, p. 7.

87 Report from the Commission to the Council, the European Parliament, the European Economic and Social Committee and the Committee of the Regions under Art. 14(2) of Directive 2004/35/CE on the environmental liability with regard to the prevention and remedying of environmental damage, COM/2010/0581 final of 12 October 2010, p. 3.

88 Art. 17.7 Wet Milieubeheer (Environmental Management Act).

Most Member States opted for a system of joint and several liability, whilst a minority chose proportionate liability (Denmark, Finland France, Slovakia and Slovenia).[89] The Belgian regions and Germany opted for joint and several liability. Joint and several liability places increased burdens on operators. Member States may have made this choice to guarantee that the polluter pays principle will be implemented effectively. Only the Netherlands Environmental Management Act (*Wet Milieubeheer*), which transposes the ELD, does not deal with multiple causation situations; this is to be addressed elsewhere in the law.

In the debates regarding the proposed ELD, a large majority of countries was against mandatory insurance, including the UK, Italy, France and Ireland, plus the European Commission itself, which originally proposed to leave this issue to the Member States. Germany and Belgium argued for mandatory insurance, although they indicated that clear guidelines were needed before the obligation could enter into force. Denmark initially opposed mandatory insurance, but accepted it later.[90]

Belgium, Germany and the Netherlands do not require financial guarantees, but merely encourage the development of financial instruments. This could potentially create a risk of under-deterrence, if the operator takes less than optimal care.[91] In environmental damage cases, the insolvency risk is real, because restoration costs can be substantial.[92] On these grounds, it has been argued that strict liability should be combined with measures to remedy the insolvency risk, such as financial guarantees.[93] Financial security, notably, insurance, on the other hand, may diminish the operator's incentives to take optimal care and thus increase environmental damage. This would be the case when the moral hazard risk cannot be adequately remedied. But viewed only from the perspective of risk spreading, the absence of mandatory financial security creates a risk that no funding will be available for some relatively large environmental damage cases.[94]

It appears that only a minority of the Member States did include a provision on compulsory financial guarantees in their national law. Eight Member States have introduced mandatory financial security entering into force at different dates up to 2014: Bulgaria, Portugal, Spain, Greece, Hungary, Slovakia, Czech Republic and Romania. These systems are subject to risk assessment of relevant sectors and operators, and dependent on various national implementing provisions providing for issues such as ceilings, exemptions, etc. However, mandatory financial security is delayed in all three countries where it was supposed to come into effect in 2010

89 Report from the Commission to the Council, the European Parliament, the European Economic and Social Committee and the Committee of the Regions under Art. 14(2) of Directive 2004/35/CE on the environmental liability with regard to the prevention and remedying of environmental damage, COM/2010/0581 final of 12 October 2010, p. 3-4.

90 ENDS Europe Daily, <www.endseuropedaily.com>, 10 June 2003.

91 Landes & Posner 1994, p. 417.

92 Corporate limited liability contributes to the insolvency risk too. Hansmann & Kraakman 1999, p. 1879.

93 See Shavell 1986, p. 43-58.

94 Faure 2001, p. 191.

(Portugal, Spain, Greece) because essential provisions were not yet in place. The remaining Member States rely on voluntary financial security.[95]

The possibility to adopt a permit/state-of-the-art defence also caused lot of controversy. In theory, the combination of the permit/state-of-the-art defence and the absence of subsidiary state liability may result in environmental damage not always being restored. None of the three countries under consideration has used the possibility to introduce subsidiary state liability. In practice, however, in the countries discussed above, this does not appear to create a significant risk: the Netherlands allow the defences only if the outcome would otherwise be unreasonable, and the Belgian regions require that the operator take remedial measures, and allow the operator to recover the costs. In Germany, thus far, the states have not provided for the permit and state-of-the-art defences.

Overall, fewer than half of the Member States decided to allow both defences: Belgium (at regional level, but with the requirement to take remedial measures and to recover the costs), Cyprus, Czech Republic, Estonia (except GMOs), Greece, Italy, Latvia (except GMOs), Malta, Portugal, Slovakia, Spain, UK (except GMOs in Scotland, Wales). Equally, fewer than half decided not to make use of them: Austria, Belgium (at federal level), Bulgaria, Germany, Hungary, Ireland, Netherlands (applicable only after check of reason), Poland, Romania and Slovenia. Denmark, Finland and Lithuania decided to allow the 'permit defence' but not the 'state-of-the-art defence', while France allowed the 'state-of-the-art defence' but not the 'permit defence'. Sweden took a middle position, admitting permit and state-of-the-art defences as mitigating factors in the decision process.[96]

In sum, the ELD's implementation data reveal that most Member States did not opt to go beyond the ELD's minimum provisions. Moreover, as the ELD provided a flexible framework, it has resulted in less harmonization than some initially thought. The transposition of the ELD into the national law of the Member States has not resulted in a level playing field but, rather, in a patchwork of liability systems for preventing and remedying environmental damage across the EU. There are significant variations in implementation and enforcement between the Member States, and the burden for industry in various Member States might well differ significantly.[97]

The question that obviously arises is what does this mean with respect to the practical effects of the Directive and the way forward?

95 Report from the Commission to the Council, the European Parliament, the European Economic and Social Committee and the Committee of the Regions under Art. 14(2) of Directive 2004/35/CE on the environmental liability with regard to the prevention and remedying of environmental damage, COM/2010/0581 final of 12 October 2010, p. 4.

96 Report from the Commission to the Council, the European Parliament, the European Economic and Social Committee and the Committee of the Regions under Art. 14(2) of Directive 2004/35/CE on the environmental liability with regard to the prevention and remedying of environmental damage, COM/2010/0581 final of 12 October 2010, p. 3-4. Of course this report only takes into account the Member States that had joined the EU at the moment of reporting (2010). Croatia joined later and was therefore not included in the report.

97 Bio Intelligence Service 2013, p. 7-8.

5. The ELD's Effects in Practice and Way Forward

Based on the Member States' reports and the Commission's own evaluation studies, it appears that the ELD's application in practice varies significantly among the Member States, but overall it's application is limited. The number of cases falling under the ELD, as reported by the authorities, is small, with some exceptions, such as Poland, where there is a significant number of cases brought under the ELD transposing law. On the other hand, there are several Member States with no ELD cases at all.[98]

Does this mean that Member States are circumventing the ELD, or that Member States want their industry not to be scared away by a strict application of the ELD?

The Commissions's report of 2010 speculates

> 'that the reasons for the relatively low number of ELD cases could include limited knowledge by operators. Another reason for the limited experience may be that some Member States maintained their existing laws for soil or water remediation which included more stringent measures than the ELD. Indeed, in several cases, pre-existing national legislative frameworks were used instead of the ELD regime. Moreover, the exceptions and defences of the ELD, including insolvency and non-identification of the responsible operators may have led to fewer ELD cases'.[99]

Furthermore, the limited number of cases reflects also the high threshold for environmental damage ('significant') to fall under the ELD regime. On the other hand, the small number of cases may also suggest that the ELD does have a significant preventive effect. To determine how strong this effect might be, the number of incidents resulting in significant environmental damage before and after the effective implementation of the ELD could be compared. This, however, is methodologically quite difficult since incidents of significant environmental damage are obviously not only dependent upon the influence of environmental liability legislation; it is hence quite difficult to test the real effects of an instrument like the ELD.[100]

Thus, the Commisison does not believe that the Member States are intentionally not implementing and enforcing their ELD regimes. Accordingly, so far, there is no indication that Member States are circumventing the ELD. Further experience with the ELD will provide additional information in the future.

Companies, too, could try to avoid or circumvent the ELD regimes, or reduce their bite. However, we have previously seen the reasons why companies do not relocate in response to the ELD. Although groups of companies do use the corporate form for tax, liability, and other reasons, they are not likely to use it for the sole purpose of avoiding ELD exposure, because doing so would have a lot of

98 Bio Intelligence Service 2013, p. 13.

99 Report from the Commission to the Council, the European Parliament, the European Economic and Social Committee and the Committee of the Regions under Art. 14(2) of Directive 2004/35/CE on the environmental liability with regard to the prevention and remedying of environmental damage, COM/2010/0581 final of 12 October 2010, p. 5-6.

100 Faure & De Smedt 2013, p. 311-312.

other consequences (eg, in the tax area). Further, financial security requirements and other demands placed on groups of companies do not support such a possible strategy. For all practical purposes, companies do not appear to have incentives to restructure and use the corporate shield to address potential ELD-related liability.[101]

As a general conclusion with respect to the ELD's effects in practice it could be argued that, although there is no doubt that the ELD could have gone much further in many respects and that it leaves some issues open, it has certain strengths and innovative features, at least in relation to the laws of some Member States.

Stakeholders considered that the ELD is realizing one of its main objectives, notably the prevention of environmental damage. The ELD encourages operators to implement precautionary measures or to engage in voluntary remediation and hence, in this respect, the ELD can be regarded as effective and preventive function works. Moreover, the ELD is also considered to contribute usefully to the remediation of environmental damage. Indeed, in some Member States, the ELD provides for higher remediation standards that did not always exist previously.[102]

Furthermore, the ELD prompted some Member States to re-evaluate and improve their national laws relevant to environmental damage. In the Netherlands, for example, the ELD was transposed by introducing Title 17.2 to the *Wet Milieubeheer*. This new law entered into force on 1st June 2008.[103] During the Parliamentary discussion of the proposal for the ELD's implementation, the motion Spies[104] was adopted. This motion concerned a request to provide to full overview of regulation in the Netherlands that contained liability provisions for damage to the environment. Moreover, it asked to examine whether the current Dutch provisions were sufficiently clear, simple, and comprehensive and to provide – if necessary – proposals to improve the Dutch environmental regulation, whereby the protection of the environment and business interests should balance.

The research institute Metro of Maastricht University conducted this research.[105] In its report, Metro concluded that, although the current system to prevent and remedy environmental damage appeared to be comprehensive, it could be further improved. Metro devised proposals to reduce complexity and to minimize the use of different rules for different types of environmental damage. Hence, the transposition of the ELD caused the Dutch government to critically review its environmental regulations. This should have a potential positive effect on the coherence and consistency of the environmental regulatory framework.

Hence, the ELD arguably contributed to the realization of the polluter pays and preventive principles (Art. 191(2) TFEU), and to ensuring the decontamination and restoration of the environment, including across Member States' borders.[106]

101 Faure & De Smedt 2013, p. 311-312.
102 Bio Intelligence Service 2013, p. 15.
103 *Staatsblad*, Nos. 166 and 178.
104 *Kamerstukken* II, 2006-2007, 30 920, No. 15.
105 Faure *et al.* 2010.
106 Art. 15 of the ELD provides that Member States shall cooperate when environmental damage affects or is likely to affect several Member States.

On the other hand, there are certain challenges to the ELD. Experience with the ELD so far revealed that the combination of a list of activities subject to strict liability together with the significance thresholds is too limiting for the ELD to be efficient or to achieve its goals in halting the loss of biodiversity and preventing environmental damage. The combination also results in a complex regime that is not harmonized with the environmental liability regimes of Member States that apply to damage to the environment to which the ELD does not apply, that is, damage that does not exceed the ELD thresholds. The major differences between this national legislation and the legislation transposing the ELD makes the legislation that transposed the ELD difficult to implement and enforce.[107]

Furthermore, it is doubtful that the ELD did much to solve the 'race-to-the-bottom,' which, to the extent it existed, was not a significant problem. Moreover, as noted above, the ELD did very little to create equal competitive conditions or a level playing field. In these respects, the ELD has not delivered any significant benefits.[108]

Therefore, amendments to the ELD in respect to the scope of strict liability and the significance thresholds might improve the application and effectiveness of the ELD. Moreover, the deletion of the defences from the ELD would help to create a level playing field. This approach would also promote the polluter pays principle and be effective from a law and economics approach as shown above.[109] It has to be awaited, however, which amendments will be proposed in the first quarter of 2015. Moreover, there is obviously always an important difference between on the one hand changes that would be desirable from an academic perspective and on the other hand political reality at the policy level. Many interest groups (both from industry as well as from NGOs) obviously have an interest in the contents of an environmental liability regime and may therefore lobby in favour or against particular changes. It is hard to predict what the effects of this lobbying process and therefore the final contents of eventual amendments would be.

6. Conclusion

Based on information available to date, we draw the following tentative conclusions about the ELD's effectiveness in achieving its objectives and its practical effects. These tentative conclusions will need to be corroborated in the future by further analysis and studies, including the report that the Commission will produce in 2015 pursuant to the ELD.

For now, we suggest five preliminary conclusions, and a more general point about how an effective ELD implementation can be advanced. First, it can be concluded that there is divergence among the Member States on crucial elements of the ELD regime, such as the precise scope of the regime (in relation to protected habitats and species) and the permit and state of the art defences. The ELD thus does not realize a 'level playing field' among the Member states. This, however,

107 Bio Intelligence Service 2013, p. 15-17.
108 Faure & De Smedt 2013, p. 308.
109 See also BIO Intelligence Service 2014, p. 11-17.

should not be a major problem, and the lack of a level playing field allows the Member States to implement their own preferences.

Second, the transposition data demonstrate too that most Member States did not opt to go beyond the ELD's basic provisions. They limited the scope of application of their ELD regimes by decisions such as not to add protected natural resources, and not to provide for subsidiary state liability. According to the reports so far there are only very few cases where the ELD is applied in practice. One could optimistically hold that there would be fewer cases causing environmental damage with a significant effect and that, hence, the ELD has had a preventive effect. However, there is no indication that there are today in the EU less of those incidents than before the implementation of the ELD. Moreover, in Member States there still are environmental liability cases; there are just few cases where the ELD applies. Hence, one has the impression that the ELD simply has limited effect in practice; whenever environmental liability cases in Member States arise, very often existing national legislation is applied.

Third, as the ELD's scope is limited to significant environmental damage, the national ELD regimes are triggered only in large, relatively exceptional cases. This, in turn, means that the ELD regimes are not intended to be invoked regularly, and that it will take time to have sufficient case experience to draw generally applicable conclusions.

Fourth, conflicting, speculative arguments can be made for and against the ELD's favourable effects on national legal systems and on the realization of its objectives, including the protection of the environment. In this contribution, we sketched some of the ELD's effects in practice. Further research should provide a basis for more definitive conclusions.

Fifth, in the Member States we examined in this chapter, the ELD did not result in a single environmental liability instrument, since some issues are regulated in the ELD-implementing legislation, while other issues (like causation, multiple parties, etc.) are still regulated in other statutes (or in the Civil Code), As a result, in some cases, the ELD's transposition may have consolidated or even increased the fragmentation of the environmental liability legislation. How this may affect the coherence and consistency of the Member States' environmental and general liability systems, however, is an open question.

To conclude, we should note that the ELD has fundamentally changed the European environmental liability landscape by introducing liability for damage to protected habitats and species and rules for the assessment and remediation of such damage. But it also left some important issues, as well as the actual application and implementation, to the Member States. Thus, the Member States' policies and practices relating to environmental liability are critical for the ELD's effects and, ultimately, its failure or success. Likewise, industry's response to the challenges posed by the ELD will be an important factor. This, in turn, suggests that further rules or guidance by Member States and otherwise will be greatly helpful. Such guidance can go a long way to achieving the ELD's objectives of preventing and restoring environmental damage.

Bibliography

Ackerman 1996
Ackerman, R.M., 'Tort Law and Federalism: Whatever happened to Devolution?', *Yale Law and Policy Review* (Symposium Issue) 1996, p. 429-463.

Arcuri 2001
Arcuri, A., 'Controlling Environmental Risk in Europe: the Complementary Role of an EC Environmental Liability Regime', *Tijdschrift voor Milieuaansprakelijkheid,* 2001, p. 37-45.

Bergkamp 2001
Bergkamp,L., *Liability and Environment. Private and Public Aspects of Civil Liability for Environmental Harm in an International Context,* The Hague: Kluwer Law International 2001.

Bergkamp 2002
Bergkamp, L., 'The Proposed Environmental Liability Directive', *European Environmental Law Review,* 2002, p. 294-314.

Bergkamp 2005
Bergkamp, L., The European Environmental Liability Directive and its Effects on Industry and Economy, in R. Mellenbergh & R. Uylenburg (eds.), *Aansprakelijkheid voor schade aan de natuur,* Groningen: Europa Law Publishing 2005, p. 95-132.

Bergkamp & Goldsmith 2013
Bergkamp, L. & Goldsmith, B.J. (eds.), *The EU Environmental Liability Directive. A Commentary,* Oxford: Oxford University Press 2013.

Bio Intelligence Service 2013
Bio Intelligence Service (in collaboration with Stevens and Bolton LLP), *Implementation challenges and obstacles of the Environmental Liability Directive,* Final Report for the European Commission, DG Environment, Brussels: European Commission 2013.

Bio Intelligence Service 2014
Bio Intelligence Service, *ELD Effectiveness: Scope and Exceptions,* Final Report for the European Commission, DG Environment, Brussels: European Commission 2014.

Bluffstone & Panayotou 2000
Bluffstone, R.A. & Panayotou, T.H., 'Environmental Liability and Privatization in Central and Eastern Europe: Toward an Optimal Policy', 17 *Environmental and Resource Economics,* 2000, p. 335-352.

Brans 2007
Brans, E.H.P. 'Het wetsvoorstel tot implementatie van de EU richtlijn Milieuaansprakelijkheid (2004/35/EG)', 27(9) *Tijdschrift voor Milieu en Recht,* 2007, p. 536-545.

Brinktrine 2007
Brinktrine, R., 'Der Bodenschutz im Umweltschadensgesetz', *Zeitschrift für Umweltrecht*, 2007, p. 337-346.

Clarke 2003
Clarke, C., 'The Proposed EC Liability Directive: Half-Way through Co-Decision', 12(3) *Review of European Community and International Environmental Law*, 2003, p. 254-268.

De Smedt 2007
De Smedt, K., *Environmental Liability in a Federal System. A Law and Economics Analysis* (dissertation Maastricht University), Antwerp: Intersentia 2007.

De Smedt 2008
De Smedt, K., 'Environmental Liability in a Federal System: a Law and Economics Analysis', 17(2) *European Environmental and Energy Law Review*, 2008, p. 106-117.

Engel 1997
Engel, K.H., 'State Environmental Standard Setting: Is There a "Race" and Is it "to the Bottom"?', 48 *Hasting Law Journal*, 1997, p. 271-398.

Esty & Geradin 1998
Esty, D.C. & Geradin, D., 'Environmental Protection and International Competitiveness. A Conceptual Framework, 32 *Journal of World Trade*, 1998, p. 5-46.

Faure 2001
Faure, M., 'The White Paper on Environmental Liability: Efficiency and Insurability Analysis', *Environmental Liability*, 2001, p. 188-201.

Faure 2003
Faure, M., 'How Law and Economics may contribute to the Harmonisation of Tort Law in Europe', in: R. Zimmermann (ed.), *Grundstructuren des Europäischen Deliktsrechts*, Baden-Baden: Nomos Verlagsgesellschaft 2003, p. 31-82.

Faure 2005
Faure, M., 'De Europese Richtlijn Milieuaansprakelijkheid: kritische inleidende bedenkingen', in: R. Mellenbergh & R. Uylenburg (eds.), *Aansprakelijkheid voor schade aan de natuur*, Groningen: Europa Law Publishing 2005, p. 3-20.

Faure 2011
Faure, M., 'Does Environmental Law Matter?', in: M. Faure & J. Smits (eds.), *Does Law Matter? On Law and Economic Growth*, Antwerp: Intersentia 2011, p. 385-416.

Faure 2012
Faure, M., 'Effectiveness of Environmental Law: What does the Evidence tell Us?", 36 *William & Mary Environmental Law and Policy Review*, 2012, p. 293-336.

Faure & De Smedt 2001
Faure, M. & De Smedt, K., 'Should Europe Harmonize Environmental Liability Legislation?', *Environmental Liability*, 2001, p. 217-237.

Faure & De Smedt 2013
Faure, M. & De Smedt, K., 'The ELD's Effects in Practice', in: L. Bergkamp & B.J. Goldsmith (eds.), *The EU Environmental Liability Directive. A Commentary*, Oxford: Oxford University Press 2013, p. 299-314.

Faure & Johnston 2009
Faure, M. & Johnston, J.S., 'The Law and Economics of Environmental Federalism: Europe and United States compared', *Virginia Environmental Law Journal*, 2009, p. 205-274.

Faure et al. 2010
Faure, M., Peeters, M., Philipsen, N.J. & De Smedt, K., *Milieuaansprakelijkheid goed geregeld?*, Den Haag: Boom Juridische uitgevers 2010.

Fogleman 2004
Fogleman, V., 'The Environmental Liability Directive, 3 *Environmental Liability*, 2004, p. 101-115.

Gray 2002
Gray K.R., 'Foreign Direct Investment and Environmental Impacts - is the Debate Over?', 11(3) *Review of European Community and International Environmental Law*, 2002, p. 306-313.

Hansmann & Kraakman 1999
Hansmann, H. & Kraakman, R.H., 'Toward Unlimited Shareholder Liability for Corporate Torts', *Yale Law Journal*, 1999, p. 1879-1934.

Jaffe et al. 1995
Jaffe, A., Peterson, S., Portney, P. & Stavins, R., 'Environmental Regulation and the Competitiveness of US Manufacturing: What does the Evidence tell Us?', XXXIII *Journal of Economic Literature*, 1995, p. 132-163.

Jans 2000
Jans, J.H., *European Environmental Law*, Groningen: Europa Law Publishing 2000.

Jans & Vedder 2012
Jans, J.H. & Vedder, H.B., *European Environmental Law after Lisbon* (4th edition), Groningen: Europa Law Publishing 2012.

Jans et al. 2009
Jans, J.H. & Squintani L. (with Aragao, A., Macrory, R. & Wegener, B.W.). 'Gold Plating of European Environmental Measures', 6(4) *Journal of European Environmental and Planning Law*, 2009, p. 417-435.

Landes & Posner 1994
Landes, W. & Posner, R., 'Tort Law as a Regulatory Regime for Catastrophic Personal Injuries', *Journal of Legal Studies*, 1994, p. 417-434.

Oates 1998
Oates, W.E., 'Environmental Policy in the European Community: Harmonisation or National Standards', 25 *Empirica*, 1998, p. 1-13.

Oates & Portney 2001
Oates, W.E. & Portney, P.R., *The Political Economy of Environmental Policy*, Resources for the future, Discussion Paper 01-55, 2001.

Rehbinder 2007
Rehbinder, E., 'Implementation of the Environmental Liability Directive in Germany', 5 *Environmental Liability*, 2007, p. 199-204.

Schäfer & Müller-Langer 2009
Schäfer, H.-B. & Müller-Langer, F., 'Strict Liability versus Negligence', in: M. Faure (ed.), *Tort Law and Economics*, Cheltenham: Edward Elgar 2009, p. 3-45.

Shavell 1986
Shavell, S., 'The Judgment Proof Problem', *International Review of Law and Economics*, 1986, p. 43-58.

Testa, Iraldo & Frey 2011
Testa, F., Iraldo, F. & Frey, M., 'Environmental Regulation and Competitive Performance: New Evidence from a Sectoral Industry', 18(5) *International Journal of Sustainable Development and World Ecology*, October 2011, p. 424-433.

Van Calster 2004
Van Calster, G., 'Will the EC get a Finger in Each Pie? EC Law and Policy Developments in Soil Protection and Brownfields Redevelopment', 16(1) *Journal of Environmental Law*, 2004, p. 3-17.

Wagner 2005.
Wagner, G., 'Die gemeinschaftsrechtliche Umwelthaftung aus der Sicht des Zivilrechts', in: R. Hendler *et al.* (eds.), *Umwelt- und Technikrecht, sonderndruck aus Umwelthaftung nach neuem EG-Recht. 20. Trierer Kolloquium zum Umwelt- und Technikrecht, 5-7 September 2004*, Berlin: Erich Schmidt Verlag 2005, p. 177-189.

Winter et al. 2008
Winter, G., Jans, J.H., Macrory, R. & Krämer, L., 'Weighing up the EC Environmental Liability Directive', 20 *Journal of Environmental Law*, 2008, p. 163-191.

Xing & Kolstad 1995
Xing, Y. & Kolstad, C., 'Do Lax Environmental Regulations Attract Foreign Investment?', *Environmental and Resource Economics*, 1995, p. 1-22.

IUS COMMUNE EUROPAEUM

A peer-reviewed book series in which the common foundations of the legal systems of the Member States of the European Union are the central focus.

The *Ius Commune Europaeum* series includes horizontal comparative legal studies as well as studies on the effect of treaties within the national legal systems. All the classic fields of law are covered. The books are published in various European languages under the auspices of METRO, the Institute for Transnational Legal Research at the Maastricht University.

Recently published:

Volume 123: *The Treaty on European Union 1993-2013. Reflections from Maastricht*, M. DE VISSER and A.P. VAN DER MEI (eds.)
Volume 124: *Inside Police Custody. Training Framework on the Provisions of Suspects' Rights*, T. SPRONKEN, J. BLACKSTOCK, E. LLOYD-CAPE, J. HODGSON, A. OGORODOVA and M. VANDERHALLEN
Volume 125: *Coordinating Ombudsmen and the Judiciary. A Comparative View on the Relations between Ombudsmen and the Judiciary in the Netherlands, England and the European Union*, M. REMAC
Volume 126: *Legal Evolution and Hybridisation. The Law of Shares Transfer in England*, M. SOLINAS
Volume 127: *The Role of EU State Aid Law in Promoting a Pro-innovation Policy. A Review from the Perspective of University-Industry R&D Cooperation*, M. CISNEROS
Volume 128: *Tradition, Codification and Unification. Comparative-Historical Essays on Developments in Civil Law*, M. MILO, J. LOKIN and J. SMITS (eds.)
Volume 129: *Nobody's Perfect. Comparative Essays on Appeals and other Means of Recourse against Judicial Decisions in Civil Matters*, A. UZELAC and C.H. VAN RHEE (eds.)
Volume 130: *Legal Aid in the Low Countries*, B. HUBEAU and A. TERLOUW (eds.)
Volume 131: *State Aid and Public Procurement in the European Union*, S. SCHOENMAEKERS, W. DEVROE and N. PHILIPSEN (eds.)
Volume 132: *Property Law Perspectives III*, A. APERS, S. BOULY, E. DEWITTE and D. GRUYAERT (eds.)
Volume 133: *Multi-Party Redress Mechanisms in Europe: Squeaking Mice?*, V. HARSÁGI and C.H. VAN RHEE (eds.)
Volume 134: *Europe at the Edge of Pluralism*, D. GOZDECKA and M. KMAK
Volume 135: *Cooperative Agreements between Public Authorities. The Influence of CJEU Case Law on National Legal Systems*, K. WAUTERS

www.ingramcontent.com/pod-product-compliance
Ingram Content Group UK Ltd.
Pitfield, Milton Keynes, MK11 3LW, UK
UKHW051926100926
8556IPUK00022B/1391

9 781780 683256